GLOSSOLALIA

Behavioral Science Perspectives
on Speaking in Tongues

H. NEWTON MALONY
A. ADAMS LOVEKIN

New York · Oxford
OXFORD UNIVERSITY PRESS
1985

Oxford University Press

Oxford New York Toronto
Delhi Bombay Calcutta Madras Karachi
Petaling Jaya Singapore Hong Kong Tokyo
Nairobi Dar es Salaam Cape Town
Melbourne Auckland

and associated companies in
Beirut Berlin Ibadan Nicosia

Published by Oxford University Press, Inc.
200 Madison Avenue, New York, New York 10016

Z 204 30
Library of Congress Cataloging in Publication Data

Malony, H. Newton.
Glossolalia: behavioral science perspectives on
speaking in tongues.
  Bibliography: p.
  Includes index.
  1. Glossolalia—Psychological aspects. I. Lovekin,
A. Adams. II. Title.
BT122.5.M35 1985   248.2′9   84-20606
ISBN 0-19-503569-0

Printing (last digit): 9 8 7 6 5 4 3 2 1

Printed in the United States of America

Preface

One of the authors is glossolalic—the other is not. H. Newton Malony has never spoken in tongues, but he has come to have deep appreciation for those who do; speaking in tongues has been a part of A. Adams Lovekin's experience for many years.

This book is the result of a collaboration. On the one hand, the endeavor is an effort to understand a strange phenomenon; on the other hand, it is an attempt to deepen a treasured dimension of faith.

Little did Lovekin know when he began a graduate program in clinical psychology in the early 1970s that he would be able to continue a serious investigation of glossolalia, which had begun with a master's thesis at the University of the South in the early 1960s.

A providential meeting of two former seminary classmates explains the willingness of Malony to enter into such a study. As he states it:

> Yale Divinity School in the 1950s was not a place known for its religious expressiveness. So it is not surprising that, when I heard from a good friend and classmate that he, a Presbyterian minister, had received the "gift of the Holy Spirit" and was glossolalic, I should advise him to see a psychiatrist. I was sincerely worried about the mental state of my friend and thought he had had a nervous breakdown.

> We had lost touch with each other for several years. However, in 1970, when he walked into a classroom at Fuller Seminary in California where I was then teaching, I recognized my friend. He was taking courses at the seminary and had entered the classroom by mistake.

> We renewed our friendship. Much to my surprise I found my friend soundly normal. He was a successful associate pastor at a nearby church, had a fine family, and paid his bills each month—yet he still spoke in tongues!

> This astounding discovery prompted me to investigate the phenomenon of glossolalia. I truly desired to understand fully this unique expression of religious fervor that had transformed the life of my friend but had left him as normal as anyone else. This began a twelve-year programmatic study of speaking in tongues from the viewpoint of the social/behavioral sciences.

Fuller Seminary's research program into glossolalia has resulted in numerous master's theses and five doctoral dissertations. Many of these investigations are noted in this volume. Credit should be given to Robert Pavelsky, James Ramsey, John Rarick, Aune Strom, and Nelson Zwaanstra, all of whom participated in these efforts.

Into this program of research, Lovekin came as a new graduate student. As he states:

> I had been and still am, an Episcopal priest. While I was at St. Luke's Church in Monrovia, California, my senior priest, Morton Kelsey, had become inspired by my master's thesis and was prompted to write one of the better-known books about glossolalia from a Jungian perspective—a point of view that sees glossolalia as a positive and integrative experience.
>
> I have been charismatic for years and have led seminars for many who were seeking deeper spiritual lives. Most of these seminars have resulted in persons' becoming glossolalic.
>
> Out of a concern to assess whether persons changed as a result of these seminars, I undertook a doctoral-level project with Malony.
>
> The invitation to write this volume came as a result of the publication of that research in the *Journal for the Scientific Study of Religion* in the late 1970s.

We are indebted to Steve Wilburn and Cynthia Read, our editors at Oxford University Press, for their confidence in us and their conviction that these issues are important for the contemporary study of religion. Their patience during a project that extended far beyond original deadlines was commendable.

A sequence of secretaries who helped in this endeavor also deserve commendation. They are Joyce Callahan, Kathy Carder, Carey Haynes, Mary Isburgh, Ann Lovekin, Mindy Tallent, and Donna Viselli. We appreciate their skill and their interest.

Turi Hoversten translated French for us. The staff of Zimmerman Library at the University of New Mexico assisted us in many ways. Ellen Robertson of the reference department completed several important searches. Nina Chambers of the technical services section and Anna Broussard of the reference department procured several interlibrary loans for us.

We hope that these state-of-the-art discussions will provoke dialogue, controversy, and excitement about our conclusions, as well as offering future possibilities for research.

Although it is impossible to bracket out biases entirely, we have attempted to do so—with only a modicum of success, we freely admit. As will be seen, our evaluation is more positive than negative. However, we have made an effort not to be judgmental or selective.

This is a treatise on the social/behavioral sciences—not theology. However, we have tried to respect the self-reports and testimonies of those who have witnessed these events. We have also tried to incorporate glossolalia into balanced teaching about the work of the Holy Spirit.

As psychologists, we have written for other social/behavioral scientists like ourselves. Yet our hope is that historians, religious scholars, cultural analysts, ministers, graduate students, and interested Christians generally will find these ideas presented clearly and provocatively.

Epiphany Season, 1984   H.N.M.
Pasadena, California   A.A.L.

Contents

GLOSSOLALIA

Introduction: Speaking in Tongues—
A Contemporary Enigma

Glossolalia is a term that appears in few dictionaries of the English language. Although it stems from the Greek words *glosso,* meaning tongue, and *lalein,* meaning to speak, the combined word "glossolalia" has come to have a much more esoteric and specific meaning than its roots would imply and, thus, its use is relatively unfamiliar to most persons. It has been defined as "fabricated speech in a strange tongue, occurring chiefly in states of religious ecstasy, but found also in psychopathic cases" (English & English, 1958, p. 226). Although this definition lists religion and psychopathology as two different settings in which glossolalia has occurred, many of those who have studied the phenomenon have made the two synonymous. They have inferred that those who expressed themselves in this manner were, in fact, abnormal or mentally deranged.

This suspicion that glossolalia and mental illness are synonymous has prompted much of the research into this phenomenon by the social/behavioral sciences during this century. Lombard (1907) illustrated this tendency, in its most benign form, when he suggested speaking in tongues was a speech automatism induced by hypnosis and, thus, outside conscious control. Mackie (1921) exemplified a more serious suggestion. Glossolalia was, for him, a pathological ecstatic utterance in which language fragments were released from the subconscious mind.

Without question, glossolalia has been unusual enough to evoke much speculation as to its causes and its meaning. The parameters of this phenomenon have been of interest even when there was no overt suggestion that such behavior was pathological. Flournoy (1900/1963), for example, examined the spiritistic glossolalia of the medium Hélène Smith who claimed to speak in a Martian language. He concluded that it was no language at all, but a series of random sounds. Further, the Swiss psychiatrist, Carl Jung, studied tongue speaking in an adolescent girl as a part of his doctoral dissertation. In addition to her ability as a medium, she also had visions, made prophecies, and could do automatic writing. He noted the apparent ease with which she exhibited the behavior:

> She spoke fluently, rapidly and with charm. It was possible to make out a few words, but not to memorize them, because the language was so strange . . . the absolute naturalness of the performance was amazing. (1902/1970, p. 28)

Seemingly, the "words" in which glossolalics speak are just as different from the word salads and the neologisms of many psychotics and of those suffering from organic brain disorders as they are from any recognizable language.

The study of the glossolalic phenomenon has followed the path of other scientific endeavors, in that it has largely been fragmented and exploratory. Although Pattison (1968), Hine (1969), and Samarin (1972c) have all undertaken careful evaluations of glossolalia, their surveys do not include the research of the past decade. C. G. Williams (1981) wrote a more recent survey. This volume extends his work and fills the need for an exhaustive and up-to-date interpretation of these endeavors in the social/ behavioral sciences.

Initially, an understanding of the tradition of glossolalia in religion is necessary. Although it has been characteristic of certain forms of Judaism and Islam, it has been most noteworthy in the Christian tradition where it has been a significant aspect of religious practice since the first century A.D.

In the New Testament, there are two primary references to glossolalia. According to Acts 2, speaking in tongues occurred on the day of Pentecost. On this occasion, the early Christians were praying together in Jerusalem when

> suddenly a sound came from heaven like the rush of a mighty wind and it filled all the house where they were sitting. And there appeared to them tongues as of fire, distributed and resting on each one of them. And they were all filled with the Holy Spirit and began to speak in other tongues as the Spirit gave them utterance. (Acts 2:2–5, RSV*)

Subsequently, persons who spoke different languages heard these Christians talk to each of them in their own native language. The implication is that this incident included intelligible speech, a phenomenon not characteristic of most glossolalia since that time.

The second major reference to glossolalia in the New Testament is in 1 Cor. 12–14 where "spiritual gifts" are discussed. Here, speaking in tongues is included in a list of ways in which God acts in people's lives. There was a controversy in Corinth about which gift was best. Instead of quarreling about whether healing, prophecy, wisdom, speaking in tongues, and so on, is to be preferred, Paul encourages the Christians in Corinth to seek the higher gift of "love." He says, "If I speak with the tongues of men and of angels, but have not love, I am a noisy gong or a clanging cymbal" (1 Cor. 13:1).

There are two important differences between these two New Testa-

---

* Revised Standard Version.

ment references to glossolalia. In Acts 2, intelligible languages were heard by persons from other countries with other languages, in spite of the fact that none of the speakers knew these languages beforehand; in 1 Cor., this is not the case. Ecstatic utterances rather than recognized languages were the norm in Corinth. Corinthian glossolalia required an interpreter for its meaning to be understood.

Thus, the first difference was between intelligible and unintelligible glossolalia. As will be seen, this has been an important concern for subsequent study. Although tongue speakers often claim that their new language is French or Italian or Spanish, and so on—languages they never knew before—scientific studies to date have not confirmed their claims. The research about this issue is ongoing, however, and some glossolalics still affirm that this ability has been demonstrated.

The second difference in the New Testament accounts lies in the implication in the Corinthian report that glossolalia was a sign of God's presence in certain persons but not in others. The account in Acts 2 carries no such implication. All the persons who were there began to speak in tongues—not just a select few. The issue is one that has been debated through the years and has been studied by religionists and scientists alike.

Is glossolalia an indication of growth in religious devotion, a second blessing (as some have termed it)? Or is glossolalia an indication of a special temperamental quality or even an abnormality? Here, again, the research is inconclusive, although at this moment the results seem to suggest that there are no differences in the personalities of glossolalics and nonglossolalics.

Although glossolalia was reported by the church fathers and by the saints, historically it has not been the norm for most Christian worship, but it has been more characteristic of sect-type groups, such as the Jansenists, the Mormons, the Shakers, and the members of the Catholic Apostolic Church.

The theological tradition of Jacobus Arminius has been the basis for much of this emphasis among Wesleyan and Holiness groups over the last three hundred years of Christian history. Arminius emphasized the reality of the changes that occur in peoples' lives as a result of receiving God's grace in conversion. This point of view was in marked contrast to the Lutheran and Calvinist position that persons remain sinners and are only transformed when they die and are recreated in heaven, not before. The Wesleyan revival of the eighteenth century popularized this Arminian tradition through its concern for "growth in grace" and "scriptural holiness." Holiness was expressed again and again through glossolalia, wherein believers reported themselves to be blessed by the Holy Spirit "as on the day of Pentecost."

In the nineteenth century, many felt that the Methodist Church, which supposedly embodied this concern for continued spiritual growth, had become secularized and had lost its passion for holiness. Numerous groups broke off and started what came to be known as the Holiness movement (Synan, 1971). Speaking in tongues became a sign of the second blessing and public expressions of being taken over by the Holy Spirit became the norm.

This movement was given a new emphasis by the Pentecostal revival, which stems from an evangelistic meeting that took place on Azuza Street in Los Angeles in 1906 (J. R. Williams, 1974). Although the ferment for such an outbreak of spirituality had been present for some time in the Holiness movement, this event seemed to provide the spark for a veritable explosion of interest in such phenomena as spiritual healing and glosso-lalia in this century.

Classical Pentecostalism, a combination of nineteenth-century Holiness movements and twentieth-century independent groups, has been a small but significant part of American religious life up to the present (Knox, 1950). Increasingly over the last twenty years, representatives of these groups, such as Du Plessis (1961/1970), have made contact with those in larger religious bodies. During these same years, a remarkable revival of interest in the "gifts of the Spirit," including glossolalia, has occurred in traditional Protestant and Roman Catholic churches (Quebedeux, 1976). Although such interest seemed to peak in the 1970s, there remains a stable, significant, and growing group of neo-Pentecostals and Catholic charismatics, as they have come to be called, who exist alongside the classical Pentecostals whose roots go back to the turn of the century.

Various terms have been used by these groups to describe this unique expression of religious fervor. These range from "speaking in tongues" to "spiritual gift," "second blessing," "prayer language," "singing in the Spirit," "being annointed," "being on fire," "claiming the blood," and "God talk." All these labels refer to the aforementioned sense in the minds of persons that they have been infused with the power of God and that the words they are speaking are entirely under divine control. It is, as Riggs (1949, p. 94) states: ". . . Gods' method whereby the Holy Spirit may possess men [sic] completely and be able to control them." Several examples illustrate this conviction.

C. G. Williams (1981) quotes a report of a woman who heard a group "singing in the Spirit" in Rochester, New York, in 1907:

> One of our group who had no knowledge of music and no natural voice for song, was given a like gift so that she sang as clear as a bird and sweet as an angel with a range and compass past belief. At times several sang together in perfect harmony. A dozen voices would be swelling into a grand oratorio, then sinking into the softest whisper with all the thrills and variations of a practised choir, not one of them knowing the melody until it burst from their lips. (pp. 78–79)

Sherrill (1964) recounts the experience of Agnes N. Ozman on New Year's Eve, 1900, in Topeka, Kansas, when Charles Parham laid his hands on her and she began to speak in tongues, an event Pentecostals depict as the beginning of the movement in this century:

. . . It was late at night. "I wonder what would happen," he [Parham] said, "if tomorrow we were all of us together to pray to receive the Baptism in the same way it is described in the Bible: with speaking in tongues?"

The next morning, everyone, in Stone's Folly joined in prayer. They prayed throughout the morning and into the afternoon. The atmosphere around the mansion was charged with expectancy. But the sun went down and still nothing unusual had occurred.

Then at about seven o'clock that night . . . a young student named Agnes N. Ozman remembered something. Wasn't it true that many of the Baptisms described in Acts were accompanied by an action, as well as prayer: didn't the person offering the prayer often put his hands on the one who wished to receive the Baptism? . . .

Miss Ozman went to find Charles Parham. She told him about her new thought.

"Would you pray for me in this way?" she asked.

Parham hesitated just long enough to utter a short prayer about the rightness of what they were doing. Then gently he placed his two hands on Miss Ozman's head. Immediately, quietly, there came from her lips a flow of syllables which neither of them could understand (pp. 37–38). [May (1956) reported that these syllables were identified as Chinese.]

Through our research (Malony, Zwaanstra, & Ramsay, 1972), we became acquainted with a woman in her mid-30s who began to speak in tongues as she was praying at her kitchen table after her husband had recovered from a serious operation. The day before, her brother had shared with her that he had been greatly blessed by having become glossolalic at a service at his church. As she prayed, her prayer of thanks for her husband's health she reported thinking "Why don't I let God pray through me—perhaps He will bless me as He did my brother." When she opened her mouth and began to pray the nonsense syllables that came forth felt awkward but she allowed them to flow without resisting. She has been glossolalic for several years now and her "tongue" sounds like French, although she has never studied the language. Many have told her they understood what she was saying and have been given messages from God through her words. Her praying was recorded and analyzed by a French native. Many French words and phrases were there, but, taken as a whole, it was not French. Nevertheless, she continues to pray in this fashion and to feel that God is using her as a blessing for others.

Boisen (1955) recounted the experience of

an ignorant colored woman (as the world counts wisdom) who addressed the meeting and under the power of the Holy Ghost she broke forth with the marvel of an unknown tongue, a tongue that the intelligent observer could easily perceive was classic. . . . When the demonstration ceased, the sister said, "Now you all know that wasn't me. I can't speak my own language right, much less a foreign one. That wasn't me. That was the Holy Ghost." The leader called for an interpreter. A sister rose and said, "I'm not an interpreter but I can speak the Spanish language and the sister spoke in that tongue. I didn't get it all, but the last phrase was Glory to the precious name of Jesus." (p. 80)

Although a definitive understanding of glossolalia is not yet available, the results of the studies to date do shed important light on many of the recurring questions about these experiences. Some of the questions are:

1. Are the people who speak in tongues temperamentally different from those who do not? Are they more suggestible? More hysteric? More anxious? Do they have weaker egos? Are they more conforming to authority influence? Are they more religious?
2. When persons speak in tongues are they experiencing an altered state of consciousness? Do they go into a trance state? Are they fully aware of their surroundings? Can they control themselves? Are they dissociative? Neurotic? Psychotic? Abnormal? Is glossolalia an automatism?
3. Under what conditions do persons become glossolalic? Is it learned? Does it change over time? Are certain socioeconomic classes more likely to speak in tongues? Is it a phenomenon of cultural conformity? Does it function to give one status? Can it be a habit without meaning?
4. What kind of language is glossolalia? Do people speak in real languages that they have never studied? Is the tongue speaker communicating with anyone? Are there different kinds of glossolalia? When a person interprets another's speech, is real understanding going on?

The chapters that follow will present the current state of knowledge pertaining to these and other related questions.

Preparatory to considering these issues, it will be helpful to consider the paradigms that have guided the research in this century. Hutch (1980) suggests that there have been three major approaches. Some have thought glossolalia to be *anomalous* behavior; some have considered it to be *aberrant* behavior; others have concluded it was *extraordinary* behavior.

The first label under which the study of glossolalia has been undertaken is anomalous behavior. Anomalous is understood to mean that which is distinct or different from something not only in degree but in kind. Xenoglossy, speaking in a language one has never learned, has been claimed by tongue speakers on many occasions. This has been thought to be proof of the similarity of modern tongue speaking to that which was reported in Acts 2 on the day of Pentecost (cf. Bach, 1969). Numerous psycholinguists and anthropologists (notably, Lombard, 1910; Pfister, 1912; Nida, 1964; & Samarin, 1972c), have investigated these phenomena and concluded that there is no scientific evidence that glossolalia includes known languages, although elements of other languages do appear. In fact, Samarin (1972c, p. 227) has stated, "glossolalia is fundamentally *not* language," meaning *any* language. If it is not language, then what is it? This has been the question.

Much of the research has focused on the meaning and function of the behavior both for the group with whom the individual identifies and for the individual himself/herself. Virginia Hine (1969) concluded that the experience could best be understood as learned behavior that indicated commitment to a religious group through which one was seeking to achieve personality reorganization. Others, such as Hutch (1980), have interpreted the experience symbolically in terms of its meaning to the believer as a sign of the presence of God. Thus, it functions as both a private and a public ritual in which human existence is lifted above the mundane. It includes taking a role in a divine/human drama through which life is given purpose and meaning (Sunden, 1974).

Glossolalia as *aberrant* behavior is a second model used by a number of scholars since the turn of the century (e.g., Lombard, 1910; Mosiman, 1911). To them, aberrant is understood to mean abnormal; those who speak in tongues are thought to be emotionally disturbed before, during, or after the experience. Alexander Mackie even entitled his 1921 book *The Gift of Tongues:—A Study in Pathological Aspects of Christianity.* Cutten (1927) was convinced that glossolalics were schizophrenics at worst or hysteric neurotics at best. The experience was labeled "regression" by both Le Baron (1896–1897) and Pattison (1968). However, they differ as to whether this process reflects ego disruption or integration. Further, glossolalics have been considered to be the culturally deprived who achieve their status through unusual behavior but who, after the act, still remain on the fringe of society—just as maladjusted as they were before (Boisen, 1939; Holt, 1940). We consider these issues in greater detail later.

The third paradigm for understanding glossolalia has been that it is *extraordinary* behavior. Extraordinary is understood to mean that which is atypical or unusual for either the individual or for the society at large. Numerous studies, for example, have been concerned with whether glossolalics remained fully conscious of their behavior or whether they go into some altered state of consciousness (e.g., Alland, 1961; Pavelsky, Hart, & Malony, 1975). Beckman (1974), on the one hand, suggested that speaking in tongues was a stylized form of trance; Jaquith (1967), on the other hand, maintained that there was no evidence of an altered state of consciousness because of the element of voluntary control. The question of whether the speaker is possessed, under hypnosis, cognitively disorganized, dissociated, or amnesic after the event have all been addressed both with, and without, the presumption that the answers to these questions implied psychopathology.

The perception of glossolalia as extraordinary behavior has led researchers to study the atmosphere in which the event occurs; in other words, its culture and its organization. Illustrative of this line of research has been the investigation of what distinguishes the several types of glossolalics (Bradfield, 1979; Rarick & Malony, 1981), wherein it has been noted that what the larger society considers deviant has been normative for certain groups for well over one hundred years. Moreover, as Morentz

(1966) noted, the meaning of glossolalia in groups where such behavior is unexpected (as in mainline Protestantism) is quite different from the same behavior in groups where it is the norm. Pattison (1968) concluded that the psychodynamics of the behavior is a function of the setting in which it occurs. These dynamics are related to the type of deprivation that several researchers have presumed to be present as a precursor for speaking in tongues (Aberle, 1965; Glock, 1973).

Thus, these three, the anomalous, the aberrant, and the extraordinary, provide an overview for the investigations into glossolalia undertaken by social/behavioral scientists in this century. Although they could be said to pertain to the psychological, the sociocultural, and the linguistic aspects of the experience, their purview is somewhat broader and more interdisciplinary. Under the heading of glossolalia as anomalous behavior, there are discussions of the differences among various forms of tongues, the question of whether tongues are languages, and the changes that these experiences evoke in persons. Under the paradigm of glossolalia as aberrant behavior, there are discussions of the emotional stability, the personality types, and the multifaceted effects of speaking in tongues. Under the paradigm of glossolalia as extraordinary behavior, there are discussions of the impact of being disadvantaged and the circumstances under which speaking in tongues occurs. Also discussed here is the research on mental states and cognitive control.

We also note the difference between classical Pentecostalism within and outside the Holiness tradition, neo-Pentecostalism in the mainline Protestant churches, charismatic expressions of glossolalia in contemporary Catholicism, as well as the distinctions among tongues as ecstatic experience, public testimony, ritualistic practice, and private devotion.

Glossolalia as
Anomalous Behavior

1

Spiritistic Language

Many disciplines have had strange if not esoteric beginnings. For example, chemistry had its beginnings in alchemy—the quest to change common elements into more valuable ones, like gold. Similarly, the first attempts of social/behavioral scientists to understand glossolalia began in spiritualism. Many studies were reported in the *Proceedings of the Society for Psychical Research* (e.g., Jung, 1902/1970; Le Baron, 1896–1897; Richet, 1905), in which the researchers examined the linguistic characteristics of glossolalia. It is important to note that not one of these studies pertained to religious glossolalia. Nevertheless, it was from this somewhat unrelated field of study that the first investigations of the phenomenon were undertaken, and it was from these studies of spiritualism that the early linguistic understandings of religious glossolalia were developed.

Thus, early studies of glossolalia were of spirit messages, reported apparitions by persons at the point of death, automatic writing, and clairvoyance. Several of these investigations are noteworthy. They provide many of the important themes for understanding glossolalia as anomalous behavior.

William James, the pioneer American psychologist at Harvard, published in the *Proceedings of the Society for Psychical Research* (Le Baron, 1896–1897) an account of glossolalia that was attributed by the speaker to a spirit talking through him. Le Baron (a pseudonym) reported:

> When it (the spirit) ceased giving me prose, it gave poetry in "unknown tongues." As the foreign verbiage came *viva voce,* I pencilled it down, mostly in an archaic mono-phonetic form, and the subsequent blending into di-phonetic and other forms was governed by the principle of conjectural euphony. (p. 293)

James and Le Baron sought in vain for an English translation to what had been written down. In the introduction to the article, James refers to another case of a woman he had known:

> When she gave herself permission, her vocal organs would articulate nonsense-syllables with the greatest volubility and animation of expression and with no apparent fatigue, and then stop at the behest of her will. (p. 277)

This woman and her friends believed she was speaking with tongues comparable to the Pauline experience in I Cor. 14. James commented that, even though experts were consulted, the words had not been recognized as any *bona fide* foreign language, but rather that "all its phonetic elements were palpably English" (p. 277).

The most important work studying spiritistic glossolalia was Flournoy's classic, *From India to the Planet Mars* (1900/1963). Flournoy describes in great detail the seances in which he participated with Hélène Smith (a pseudonym for a woman later identified as Catherine Elise Muller). Even though she had been born and raised in Geneva, she was convinced that she had had a prior incarnation in India as a Hindu princess and that she traveled in her seances to Mars where she held conversations with the inhabitants there. Flournoy (1900/1963) describes the experience:

> Presently Hélène begins to recite with increasing volubility and incomprehensible jargon, the beginning of which is as follows (according to notes taken by M. Lemaître at the time, as accurately as possible): "Mitchma mitchmon mimini tchouainem mimatchineg masichinof mézavi patelki abrésinad navette naven navette mitchichénid naken chinoutoufiche." . . . From this point the rapidity prevented the recognition of anything else, except such scraps as "téké . . . katéchivist . . . méguetch," or "méketch . . . kété. . . . chiméké." After a few minutes, Hélène interrupts herself, crying out, "Oh, I have had enough of it; you say such words to me I will never be able to repeat them." (pp. 154–155)

Besides these fragments noted, there were four "Martian" words repeated several times by Hélène which had some meaning for her: *metiche* (monsieur), *médache* (madame), *métaganische* (mademoiselle) and *kin't'-che* (four). Flournoy comments:

> the Martian language is only a puerile counterfeit of French, of which she preserves in each word a number of syllables and certain conspicuous letters. (p. 158)

> We are constrained to believe that these first outbreaks of Martian characterized by a volubility which we have rarely met with since then, was only a pseudo-Martian, a continuation of sounds uttered at random and without any real meaning, analogous to the gibberish which children use sometimes in their games of "pretending" to speak Chinese or Indian. (p. 159)

After the hypnotic seance, being pressed for the meaning of the four words, Hélène Smith gave a meaning that "was only created by an unskilful(sic) distortion of French" (p. 159).

Eighteen months later, during these trances, Hélène Smith began writing the "Martian" language in a mysterious hieroglyphics. These characters were analyzed by Flournoy as resembling French letter equivalents (1900/1963, p. 208). For three years, Flournoy recorded the spirit messages from forty seances. In analyzing the written language, Flournoy stated that the "Martian" phonetics, grammatical rules, construction, and syntax were the same as French. Only the vocabulary bore no resemblance to French. He concluded, "This fantastic idiom is evidently the naive and somewhat puerile work of an infantile imagination, to which occurred the idea of creating a new language." (p. 253)

It should be noted that there were two stages in the development of this "Martian" language: the early stage during which the speech was very difficult to transcribe and the second stage when meaning was attributed to certain spoken "words."

The third case study of spiritist glossolalia was C. G. Jung's study of Miss S.W., a 15.5-year-old German girl, whose case was the subject of his doctoral dissertation. Jung observed glossolalia only one time in a seance in his case study. He reports:

> She went on speaking in the same conversational tone but in a strange idiom that sounded like French and Italian mixed, recalling now one and now another. She spoke fluently, rapidly, and with charm. It was possible to make out a few words, but not to memorize them, because the language was so strange. From time to time certain words recurred like *wena, wenes, wenai, wene,* etc. (1902/1970, p. 28)

When she came out of her trance, Jung reports:

> She was told she had been talking in her sleep, whereupon she became wildly annoyed, and her anger increased still more when she learned that she was talking in a foreign language. "But I told the spirits I didn't want to. I can't do it, it tires me too much." (p. 28)

In interpreting this phenomenon, Jung commented that the only intelligible words were variations on *wena* and that the remaining words and sentences were derived from the patient's slight knowledge of French. He was unable to get any exact translation of the sentences, because Miss S.W. refused to give them to him.

He compared his patient to Hélène Smith and her use of the "Martian" language:

> A more probable explanation is that our patient simply strung a lot of meaningless foreign-sounding words together, and instead of forming any true words, borrowed certain characteristic sounds from French and Italian and combined them into a sort of language, just as Hélène Smith filled in the gaps between the real Sanscrit words with pseudo-linguistic products of her own. (p. 85)

The fourth and last important case study of spiritist glossolalia is the study of a French medium, Madam X, reported by Richet (1905). In a state of partial dissociation, she wrote long sentences in modern Greek, a language that she had never studied. Therefore, Richet coined the word xenoglossia (*xénoglossie*) for the use of an actual foreign language by a person who had no conscious knowledge of that language (p. 162). Although Richet coined the word from the Greek (*xenos* = foreign, *glossa* = tongue) a more accurate term (as Stevenson has pointed out)

[1974, p. 8] would be xenographia (*graphia* = write) because Madam X was writing a language, not speaking it. Richet discovered that many of the Greek sentences came from a particular Greek-French dictionary. It was as if Madam X were reproducing from a photograph. It must be remembered that this instance of xenographia was the case of a medium engaging in automatic writing and not that of spoken glossolalia.

In summary, then, these four early studies in the field of parapsychology or psychic research contributed to the early understanding of glossolalia. These are examples of spiritistic rather than religious glossolalia. Linguistically the speech resembles known languages, but it is not one. The second stage of Hélène Smith's "Martian" language was evidently a subconscious fabrication owing to the suggestive pressure of her hearers, and Madam X may be a case of cryptomnesia—the repetition of forgotten memories.

The first person to call for a system of classification for glossolalia was Flournoy (1900/1963) in his careful study of the "Martian" language of Hélène Smith: "A good description and rational classification of all these categories and varieties of glossolalia would be of very great interest" (p. 196). A threefold classification was proposed:

1. *Simple, incoherent utterances* sometimes found in religious ecstasy (i.e., religious glossolalia).
2. *Neologisms* created in other mental states, such as in spiritist automatic speech and writing, psychotic speech, or in the speech of children.
3. *Foreign idioms* unknown to the speaker, at least consciously.

Flournoy (1900/1963) acknowledged the difficulty in establishing any classification system because of the many cases in which the characteristics were mixed, for example, French and Greek phrases.

Almost prophetically, Flournoy enumerated some of the questions that continued to plague the field of study and made any system of classification difficult to establish:

> In each of these cases, it is necessary to examine further whether, and in what measure, the individual attributes a fixed meaning to the sounds which he utters, whether he understands (or has, at least, the impression of understanding) his own words, or whether it is only a question of a mechanical and meaningless derangement of the phonetic apparatus, or, again, whether this jargon, unintelligible to the ordinary personality, expresses the ideas of some secondary personality. (p. 196)

Responding to Flournoy's challenge, Lombard (1907) extended this model and proposed a system of classification with three major categories and several subtypes of these linguistic phenomena. Because Lombard wrote in French and because none of his writing has been translated into English, we go into some detail about his classification systems.

Concerning his first major category, "inarticulate vocalizations and related phenomena," Lombard states:

The first stage of glossolalia is represented by vocalizations very distant from the articulated and organized word, confused vocal emissions, whether sometimes loud noises, cries, sighs, murmurs, or stutterings. (1907, p. 6)

He cites inarticulate cries observed in shamans and in Hélène Smith's "Hindu chant":

The utterances consisted of the Sanscrit word *gaya* "chant," repeated to satiety, with here and there some other terms, badly articulated and offering discouraging variations in the notes taken by the different hearers. (Flournoy, 1900/1963, p. 326)

Lombard's second category is "glossolalia." He describes it as

. . . an assembly of articulated sounds, simulating a discourse, but where the regular correspondence of some sounds or group of sounds is lacking to some determined ideas; this does not say necessarily that these pretended words, at the moment when they are spoken, are not associated with certain mental representations which give them a semblance of meaning. (1907, p. 19)

As examples of "pseudolanguage" (the first of three subtypes of glossolalia), Lombard cites several historical and contemporary examples. His contemporary examples included several texts from Le Baron (1896–1897) and from the first stage of Hélène Smith's "Martian" language (Flournoy, 1900/1963, p. 159). He points out that this pseudo-language has the illusion of being understandable but is not. He suggests, "therefore, the step is quickly established between the apparition of a pseudo-word and the acquisition of a neologism or a name, which keeps its representative value and which is able to become the center of crystallization of a complete subliminal vocabulary" (p. 29).

The second and third subtypes of glossolalia, namely, "occasional" and "systematized neological structures" respectively Lombard borrowed from Flournoy. In commenting on Hélène Smith's second phase of the "Martian" language, Flournoy (1900/1963) writes:

This somnambulistic language does not consist, as we have already discovered, either in speaking ecstatically or in religious enthusiasm, nor yet in the use of a foreign language which really exists; it represents rather neologism carried to its highest expression and practiced in a systematic fashion, with a very precise signification, by a secondary personality unknown to the normal self. It is a typical case of "glosso-poesy" of complete fabrication of all the parts of a new language by a subconscious activity. (pp. 196–197)

Anticipating later theorizing, Lombard (1907) noted that religious ecstasy was similar to somnambulistic experiences. He explained that the divine presence took the place of the self (ego) and became the center for all motor and sensory activities, so that the development of this glossolalic phenomenon was an action of the spirit. This seems simplistic and lacks the careful distinction that Flournoy had made. Lombard cited only automatic speech and writing given through a medium as examples of *glossopoièse*.

Lombard's third major category is "xenoglossia" (the term used by Richet, 1905); that is, the use of a foreign language not previously known to the speaker. Here, also, Lombard differentiates three subtypes.

The first of these subtypes is isolated cases (irruptions) of "foreign words." Lombard states, "it frequently happens that foreign words pass as such, or with distortions too subtle to make them unrecognizable, in the pseudo-language or the neological combinations" (1907, p. 36). He cites Le Baron (1896–1897) who had heard both a medium speak in a language purported to be Egyptian and Hélène Smith's use of some "Hindu" words in her seances.

The second subtype is "linguistic counterfeits" (pseudoxenoglossia). Lombard describes it thus:

> Instead of coming out in an isolated fashion or to appear in the middle of a talk without a definable linguistic character foreign expressions may be said in a series of sounds which don't mean anything but which by their context and their tonality surprisingly make one think of the language to which foreign expressions belong. Therefore one has an imitated idiom, a pseudo-language, with an authentic and consistent substrata which serve as a model for everything else. (1907, p. 39)

The third subtype is "xenoglossia" proper, which Lombard calls "the gift of languages." After citing several ancient Christian and pre-Christian literary sources, he discusses three current examples: a medium by the name of Lauri Edmonds, a woman in a state of ecstasy speaking Hebrew, and, finally, Madam X (reported by Richet, 1905). After discussing the theories of cyptomnesia (i.e., forgotten memories) and mental telepathy, Lombard concludes that there are some things that cannot be explained.

When Lombard (1910) later wrote on the subject of glossolalia in his doctoral dissertation (also written in French), he simplified his classification system by reducing his major categories from three to two (glossolalia and xenoglossia) and by abandoning the subtypes of xenoglossia.

In introducing glossolalia in his dissertation, Lombard (1910) said:

> If we leave aside provisionally, for the ease of this exposition, that which should arrange itself under the rubric of xenoglossia, we find ourselves still in the presence of three glossolalic types, perfectly distinct, in spite of the multiplicity of the combinations to which they lend themselves. These are the three degrees of progression which go from the most separated forms to those the most closely associated of that which we call organized language or word. (p. 25)

He subsumed his earlier first category under the category of glossolalia; his inarticulate vocalizations he now labeled *phonations frustes* ("rough sounds").

It was Lombard's simplified system that Cutten (1927) recapitulated for the English-speaking world in his often-quoted study *Speaking with Tongues* (pp. 169–181). The only enrichments in Cutten's discussion of Lombard's classification system were citations from Mosiman's dissertation (1911), which had been written in German. Mosiman did not suggest any typology or classification system for glossolalia. He had worked independently of Lombard, and the two evidently were not acquainted with each other's work.

The next development in a system of classification took an interesting but confusing turn in May's (1956) article, "A Survey of Glossolalia and Related Phenomena in Non-Christian Religions." May reviewed Lombard's (1910) simplified classification system and proposed a more elaborate one of his own. He also surveyed ecstatic vocalizations that occur cross-culturally in different shamanistic ceremonies. In his review of the literature, May candidly admitted

> that ecstatic vocalization is infrequently described. . . . It is difficult to determine from the laconic description "muttered unintelligible sounds," the exact nature of the vocalization. Were the sounds unintelligible to members of the shaman's own tribe or only to the ethnographer present? Were the sounds rapidly spoken words of the shaman's native dialect or were they nothing but meaningless gibberish? To avoid being overcautious and thereby discarding as unreliable and unusable fifty percent or more of the descriptive data, it will be assumed that the reporter-ethnographer's accounts of shamanistic utterances are more accurate than inaccurate, and that they coincide for the most part with the native's interpretation, conveyed to the investigator in a great many cases by an informant or interpreter." (1956, p. 78)

He also acknowledged that he was expanding the usual use of the term "glossolalia" as "ecstatic vocalization in the form of incoherent sounds and foreign words" (1956, p. 75) to cover *similar* phenomena in non-Christian religions.

May proposed a sixfold typology of glossolalic behavior in shamanistic utterances:

1. the language of spirits
2. sacerdotal language
3. the language of animals
4. *phonations frustes* (rough sounds)
5. xenoglossia
6. interpretations of tongues (*ermeneglossia*)

May concluded that the language of spirits is "an esoteric 'dialect' known only to the spirits and to the shaman who speaks it, [and it] is difficult to define in terms of sound quality" (p. 79). Although May did not mention it, this type of glossolalic behavior is closest to spiritistic glossolalia of mediums studied by Flournoy (1900/1963), Jung (1902/1970), and others. However, May (1956) did not supply any linguistic data or first-hand experiences to substantiate this type.

"Sacerdotal language" refers to the special language of priests. It is differentiated from spirit language because it does not presume to be of supernatural origin. May (1956) admitted that this was different from the usual definition of glossolalia. Rather, he stated that "the words have become sacred through many years of use . . . they are more in the nature of prayers and formulas than glossolalia" (p. 81).

The "language of animals," used by shamans, is depicted as an imitation of the cries and sounds of animals, birds, and natural phenomena. May quotes from a study about a person who "barks like a dog, sniffs at the audience, lows like an ox, bellows, cries, bleats like a lamb, grunts like a pig, whinnies, coos, imitating with remarkable accuracy the cries of animals, the songs of birds, the sound of their flight" (Eliade, 1951/1964, p. 97). As May admitted, this is hardly glossolalia in the usual sense of the word.

Although Lombard (1910) used *phonations frustes* (rough sounds) to specify preglossolalic sounds, May cited a miscellany of examples describing mutterings that varied from gurgling to meaningless syllables as used by shamans. May states: "Because the mysterious dialects and strange words of [these] cases are not described in detail, it is difficult to determine exactly what forms of speech-phenomena they represent" (1956, p. 83). It is rather doubtful that these shamanistic mutterings are comparable to the pseudo-language or preglossolalic sounds that Lombard was describing.

May (1956) cited numerous examples of xenoglossia (speaking recognizable languages) uttered in a trance by shamans who had no conscious knowledge of the languages they spoke. The difference between these citations and those in the language of spirits is that these citations are examples of recognizable languages that were unknown consciously to the shaman. May repeatedly called them examples of glossolalia. The question can legitimately be raised as to whether these were not cases of cryptomnesia, as in the case of Madam X, rather than comparable to religious glossolalia as it is known in the Christian tradition.

Finally, May cited examples of ecstatic vocalizations translated by either the shaman or an attendant to the shaman. Rather confusingly, he also called this glossolalic behavior "interpretation of tongues" (*ermeneglossia*). He states, "It is apparent that *ermeneglossia* and ecstatic vocalization are closely related and that functionally the former depends to a large extent upon the latter" (1956, p. 88). But it seems confusing to categorize ermeneglossia as a type of glossolalia, because it is rather complementary to glossolalia in function and has a linguistic form that is altogether different. Ermeneglossia is the use of a known language that is intelligible both to the speaker and the listener.

Rather than clarifying the types of glossolalia, May's article and classification system only confused the issue. Ignoring Lombard's (1910) proposals, May proposed an altogether new classification. As Samarin (1972c) has commented, "All that May has documented, therefore, is that some kind of anomalous vocalizations occur in some religious behavior in different parts of the world" (p. 131).

With the exception of Jennings (1968), who used May's classification system in another ethnological study of glossolalia, May's (1956) system has not proved useful in further research by other investigators. In essence, May's system is an empty one because it is too inclusive.

In summary, there was an interesting attempt at the turn of the century with Flournoy's (1910/1963) challenge to develop a linguistic system of classification for glossolalia. This challenge was accepted by Lombard (1907) who at first had a rather elaborate system of three categories with subtypes and then simplified his system (1910) to two categories with fewer types. Next, May (1956) tried to expand and generalize Lombard's 1910 system in an ethnological study of shaman's verbalizations.

The whole attempt to provide a classification system of glossolalia depended on definitions of terms used. However, these classification systems have not been particularly helpful in subsequent work in the linguistic analysis of glossolalia, but they are of historical interest as the behavioral sciences tried to understand glossolalia initially. Thus, these first attempts to study glossolalia were efforts to define parameters of its linguistic characteristics. Because the early studies were limited in their methodology to recording glossolalic speech by hand or with a phonograph, the real breakthrough for getting raw data was in the rather esoteric field of psychic research where the utterances or writings of persons in trance were studied. Later researchers would have the advantage of tape recorders to study the linguistic properties of religious glossolalia, but these earlier researchers did not. Considering the handicap under which they worked, it is remarkable what they were able to achieve.

2

Religious Language

In the last chapter, it was noted that most of the early research was conducted on nonreligious spiritistic phenomena. In this chapter, we consider the linguistic aspects of religious glossolalia.

On the occasion of the first appearance in Christian history of speaking in tongues, the assertion was made that although the words were strange to the speaker they, nevertheless, were familiar to others who heard them. The account in Acts reports: (1) ". . . they . . . began to speak in other tongues," (2) "Are not all those who are speaking Galileans?" (Acts 2:4, 7b, and (3) ". . . each one heard them speaking in his own language. . . . And how is it that we hear, each of us in his own native language?" (Acts 2:6b, 8).

It is not clear whether the early Christians thought that they were hearing a language foreign to themselves but used somewhere else or that they were hearing a "heavenly" language whose meaning was known only to God (note 1 Cor. 13:1 ". . . tongues of men and of angels"). In either case, the audience was ignorant of the meaning of the utterance and needed someone to interpret.

Paul (1 Cor. 14:13) implied that the speaker could also be the interpreter, but this was not typically the case. A person other than the speaker usually was inspired to interpret, and Paul admonished tongue speakers to be sure someone could interpret *before* they spoke. It is not clear just how one was to check this out beforehand because she/he theoretically did not know whether the event was to occur or which language was going to be used!

Suffice it to say that speakers and hearers from that day to this have assumed that what they heard was a connected sequence of sound from some language—natural or supernatural. Even St. Paul never doubted this, although he insisted that the event had no meaning and even was disruptive when there was no one present to interpret its meaning. The intent of this chapter is to examine the scientific evidence for these assumptions about the linguistic nature of religious glossolalia.

TYPOLOGIES OF RELIGIOUS GLOSSOLALIA

In 1910 Emile Lombard proposed a threefold typology of glossolalia. These were: *phonations frustres* (rough sounds), pseudo-language, and verbal fabrication. His classification was based on the idea that speech develops progressively from inarticulate sounds to sounds which resemble language.

The most recent classification is that of May (1956). He incorporated Lombard's classification into a sixfold categorization. These six were: the language of spirits, sacerdotal language, the language of animals, rough sounds, xenoglossia, and ermeneglossia.

The language of spirits (supernatural beings) is that type of tongue speaking in which the person claims to be speaking the language spoken by the gods themselves. Shamans in primitive tribes utilize this format in their divinations (Jennings, 1968). Usually no attempt is made to translate or interpret the meaning of these verbalizations. They are simply recognized. Some Bible commentators have suggested that this is the type referred to in 1 Cor. 13:1 "If I speak with the tongues of men *and of angels*" (emphasis added). One understanding of this Corinthian passage was that these "celestial languages" were sometimes spoken in the early Church as a testimony that the Holy Spirit had possessed the speaker but without any compulsion to have the words make meaning. However, Paul objected to this practice and suggested that Christian glossolalia should be utilized for the edification of others, not just for testimony.

Sacerdotal language is that special type of language used by priests and other religious leaders in ritual. Instead of the claim that this is the language of the gods, the assertion is often made that this is a special kind of language that only the gods understand. Not even the priest claims to know what the words mean, but he/she trusts that the gods do and that this form of mediation between people and the divine is necessary. Jennings (1968) reports a number of examples of this sort of special language in various African religions. Although not considered to be glossolalia, the use of Latin in the Roman Catholic mass for centuries is a similar instance.

The language of animals, is unfamiliar in the Christian religion but is common in religious folk medicine in many parts of the world. May (1956) suggested that the dynamic involved was the supposition that by speaking the language of certain animals, such as birds and lions, the secrets of those animals would be mastered and, thus, made available for the healer to use. The assumption is that human beings have become alienated from themselves, and by means of animal language, they become reunited with their essence and are able to communicate with the secrets of nature. Because most of these sounds are learned by imitation, it is questionable whether this is religious glossolalia as the term is usually used.

Rough sounds (*phonations frustes*) were discussed earlier. These ecstatic utterances are clearly evidence that one is in touch with the power of the divine in both Christian and non-Christian religions. They are indications to all who hear them that a state of possession is occurring. As May (1956) envisioned this type, it included much of what Lombard (1910) would call pseudo-languages, in which monotonous repetition of words in a melodious cadence and interspersed with meaningless chatter is heard. Jennings (1968) noted that this is often accompanied with states of frenzy and bodily manifestations. The jerks and whirls seen in classical Pentecostalism suggest this type of glossolalia.

The fifth type mentioned by May (1956) is xenoglossia—the miraculous ability to speak in a foreign language without ever studying it. Jennings (1968) suggests that this has been widespread and is by no means confined to Christian manifestations. He reports anthropological accounts of American Indians in the Pacific Northwest speaking languages they never learned and of Tibetan monks quoting Shakespeare in English. He further notes the case of the Winnebago Indians who sang a song in the fox language under the influence of peyote. However, it has been a specific claim of Christian glossolalia from the first century A.D. to the present. A clear example was that of Charles Parham's Topeka, Kansas, ministry where the Pentecostal movement in America was initiated. At a watch-night service on December 31, 1900, one of Parham's women students requested that he lay his hands on her and pray that she might be baptized with the Holy Spirit and receive the gift of tongues. What happened illustrated xenoglossia in a manner similar to that claimed by Acts 2. She began to speak in the Chinese language and was unable to communicate in any other language save Chinese (both verbal and written) for three days thereafter. Furthermore, as Synan (1971), a historian of the Pentecostal movement, writes:

> A remarkable claim made during these meetings was that the students, American all, spoke in twenty-one known languages, including French, German, Swedish, Bohemian, Chinese, Japanese, Hungarian, Bulgarian, Russian, Italian, Spanish, and Norwegian. In a conversation with a *Kansas City Times* correspondent, Parham claimed that his students had never studied these languages and that natives of the countries involved had heard them spoken and had verified their authenticity. (p. 102)

This claim that a foreign language has been spoken and understood has not been unique to the twentieth century.

These abilities have always been affirmed as miraculous gifts from God, given for the purpose of edification or evangelization. For example, Charles Parham, the initiator of the Pentecostal revival in the United States, taught that no foreign missionary would need to study the language of the country to which one was going. Instead, one need only receive the baptism of the Holy Spirit and one would be given the ability to speak that foreign language.

The final form of glossolalia mentioned by May (1956) is termed "ermeneglossia" and refers to the interpretation of tongues. This category raises the issue of whether the miracle claimed by glossolalists is in the speaker or the hearer. For example, Poythress (1977) analyzes the various options present at Pentecost (Acts 2) in which ". . . they were all filled with the Holy Spirit and began to speak in other tongues" (v. 4). To what degree did the speaker understand what she/he was saying? Fully? Partially? Not at all? In what way did the hearers understand what was being said? Was it in a strange language whose meaning they understood nevertheless? Or was it in their own language spoken with a Judean or Nazarene accent that made logical sense in spite of the pronunciation? Or was it mere gibberish in which the message of the Gospel was communicated to them apart from the words being spoken? In short, was the miracle in the speaking or the hearing?

In the Pentecost account, the weight of the evidence seems to lie on the side of xenoglossia, but the teaching of Paul in other sections of the New Testament clearly implies that ermeneglossia (the miracle of interpretation) is a special gift in itself.

Certainly, the ability to interpret has been claimed by many charismatic Christians. Although there are still many who attest that they have spoken in foreign tongues, more common is the report that God has spoken a message through their "tongue" and that this was interpreted by someone present who heard what God was trying to say. In neither case did the "speaker" understand what she/he had said. The "word of God" that is interpreted in this manner is typically a "prophecy" and pertains to some warning or admonition to which persons should attend. The phenomenon seems less common among other religions, as Jennings (1968) notes.

Wolfram (1966) offered a further comparison among initiatory and habitual, uninterpreted and interpreted, and public and private glossolalia. Initiatory tongue speaking resembles the rough sounds (*phonations frustes*) type of Lombard (1910) and frequently occurs in response to invitations or coaching of Christian leaders among subjects who are encouraged to mimic the leader. These beginning efforts are termed "initiatory" in contrast with speaking in tongues that has become a habitual form of religious expression. In habitual tongue speaking, the practitioner uses glossolalia frequently and the verbalization may take on the form of pseudo-language, verbal fabrication, or xenoglossia. Of course, these various types are not mutually exclusive, as May (1956) pointed out. They may all occur in succession within one episode of speaking tongues. As noted earlier, they are based on a progressive model that assumes xenoglossia is the apex. Further, they may occur in the same person at different times. In research, however, glossolalia has often been limited to verbal fabrication. (E.g., in the Lovekin and Malony (1977) study, initial tongues was distinguished from full tongues. Only those persons who sustained their verbalizations over a several-minute period and who continued the practice over at least a week's time were considered to have full tongues.) This, at least, resembles Lombard's (1910) verbal fabrication. Tongue speaking may occur as part of public worship services or in personal prayer or while performing daily duties.

Furthermore, glossolalia can be spoken, chanted, or sung. Although some report praying in their "tongue" as an act of surrender to God, others say that they pray in this manner when they are uncertain what to ask of God. Tongue speaking may occur while driving a car to take up time or when in a stressful situation as a call for help or at a public meeting where many are praying/talking all at one time. Thus, habitual glossolalia may be interpretable or noninterpretable by intent as well as in practice. By this is meant that some tongue speaking may be intentionally focused on a clear interpretation (or answer to prayer) and that other such behavior may never be intended to be translated, even though both may occur in private. The same may be true of public glossolalia, although here there is far greater likelihood that interpretation will be sought. Nevertheless, in all such habitual glossolalia, it is assumed by the speakers that "meaning" is involved, whether clearly stated or not.

LINGUISTIC AUTHENTICITY

A major question asked by social scientists in the twentieth century has been: Can the claims of glossolalists about their language and its meaning be validated?

More specifically, two questions have been posed. They are: Is glossolalia a language? and Is glossolalia a known language? We consider these in reverse order, first dealing with the issue of whether there is evidence that glossolalists speak in recognizable foreign languages.

Is Glossolalia a Known Language?

Kildahl (1972, p. 7) asked the question of a tongue speaker:

> Is your tongue speaking in another language spoken somewhere in the world or does the speaking consist of words and sounds which are not part of any known language?

He reports this answer:

> . . . Although I am not absolutely sure, I think it is a definite language, perhaps a lost tongue or any other language such as Hebrew, Aramaic, etc. I know of cases where important messages have been expressed in scriptural Hebrew and Greek, often by persons with no theological training and only a grammar school education or less. (pp. 7–8)

This is a similar claim to those numerous contemporary reports that tell of a foreign visitor who chanced to be attending a glossolalic religious service where he/she heard his/her own language spoken by someone who had not been abroad and had never before had any contact with the language. The visitor then testifies that the tongue speaker was indeed speaking the visitor's language. For example, Cyril G. Williams (1981) notes a recent incident recounted by an Assemblies of God missionary:

> One of our missionaries, also of the Congo, was present when a young man of his black flock received the Baptism of the Holy Ghost. He was amazed to hear the man speaking in perfect English, repeating Old Testament instances of creation and history. He knew no word of English and nothing of the instances he was recording. The missionary was so astonished at this mighty miracle that he left the hut in search of his wife as witness. When he returned with his wife the man was still speaking in his English "unknown tongue" but he had changed over to New Testament revelation concerning the imminent coming again of the Lord. (p. 181)

In one of the more readable volumes about glossolalia, John L. Sherrill (1964, pp. 98–101) reports numerous incidents of xenoglossia, many of them from personal acquaintances. Dennis Bennett, a charismatic Episcopalian rector from Seattle, had written Sherrill to say that a truck driver in his parish had received the gift of tongues and that it had been interpreted by a Chinese as Mandarin Chinese. Harold Bredesen, a friend of Sherrill, had said he had spoken in both Polish and Coptic Egyptian according to listeners who had been present. And a Jew, Jacob Rabinowitz, told of attending a worship service in Pasadena, Texas, during which an Irishman had prayed in "beautiful" Hebrew and, in fact, mentioned the name of Jacob's father. Sherrill asked his wife:

> "Do you believe these stories?" . . . She thought for a moment. "I believe the people who tell these stories," she said. I knew what she meant. It was impossible to think of Harold, Jacob, and Dennis as deliberately lying to persuade me of something, since they so obviously believed what they said themselves. (p. 101)

This conversation points up a dilemma in many of these accounts, namely, they are told second or third hand and although one trusts those who report the events, there is little objective corroboration available.

A partial substitute for this lack can be seen, however, in accounts of glossolalia where more than one person heard the message in a foreign language unknown to the speaker. Sherrill writes of two such incidents:

> [Nine U.S. Marines] one Saturday night, entered a small Petecostal church in Seattle, Washington, drawn by the music . . . [they] listened in growing amazement as an American woman whom they knew arose and gave a message in tongues. All nine of the Marines were Filipinos, all nine recognized an obscure Filipino dialect and agreed on the sense of what they'd heard. The woman, they knew, could not naturally speak Filipino at all, much less this strange dialect from a region rarely visited by Westerners.
>
> A somewhat similar experience took place on Easter Sunday, 1950, in a small Pentecostal church in Gary, Indiana. A member of the congregation, Paul Goodwin, stood up and delivered an exhortation in tongues. As he spoke there was an agitated stirring among a group of Italians in the congregation, and when he finished a young man named Leo Pella got up and said:

"We know Paul Goodwin, and he does not speak our language. But he has just spoken in perfect Italian, as though he had graduated from a college in Italy." (p. 107)

These illustrations imply confirmation by more than one listener. Until recently, however, no objective studies by social scientists or linguists have been conducted in these matters.

Anderson (1979) reports that a group of government linguists listened to a tape recording of the glossolalia of Harold Bredesen, the neo-Pentecostal friend of Sherrill noted above, and found no resemblance to any language, even though he claimed to speak in Coptic Egyptian in addition to Polish. His tongue speech was also analyzed by a conference of linguists in Toronto who had studied over 150 languages. They concluded that it was "highly improbable" that his glossolalia resembled any human language.

A native French person reached the same conclusion after studying the tape recording of tongue speaking by a Southern California glossolalist who claimed to speak in French through her tongue, even though she had never studied the language. The French woman to whom we submitted the tape said that the speech did indeed contain some French words but that the syntax was confused and meaningless.

Sherrill (1964) played over forty recordings of glossolalia to six linguists from graduate institutions in New York City. No one of them professed to hear a language that could be identified. Interestingly enough, however, they easily spotted two recordings of "made-up gibberish" that Sherrill had slipped into the presentation and one linguist reported that a given recording had the structure of a poem, a structure that he understood, even though the actual meaning of the words eluded him.

Again, no validation of xenoglossia was found by the psychiatrist Paul Qualben (Kildahl and Qualben, 1971). In a study of the recorded speeches of over sixty persons, there was no evidence of words from any known language. Similar conclusions were reached by the anthropological linguist William Samarin (1972c). He found that not one of the many tapes of glossolalia he analyzed contained more than an occasional word or phrase from a foreign language.

Of course, apologists for xenoglossia can, and do, counter these conclusions by saying that there are over three thousand known languages, not all of which could possibly be known by a single gathering of linguists. Moreover, they insist that there would be no way for analysts to be acquainted with all the dead languages that could be spoken in tongue speech. However, it can with certainty be stated that there has been little or no confirmation of the claims that glossolalists have spoken in modern languages currently being spoken.

There has been one significant exception to this conclusion. It is the case of the Jensen communications investigated by Ian Stevenson (1974) of the University of Virginia. He studied the speech of a Jewish housewife who had been raised in Philadelphia by parents who had emigrated from Russia before she was born. Under hypnotic trance she began to speak in Swedish, using the name Jensen Jacoby, who supposedly was communicating through her. Stevenson classified her as an example of "responsive" xenoglossia, in that she supposedly conversed in Swedish with other persons while in trance, as contrasted with simply speaking in Swedish in monologue fashion—a type he termed "recitative" xenoglossia. One of those who spoke with her said:

> By and large she used the correct articles (attached to the noun in Scandinavian) and correct inflectional endings. Having taught Swedish, I know how difficult it is for an American even to repeat after the teacher the correct endings. She even made the proper elisions, such as "ja." (Stevenson, 1974, p. 37)

Others who interviewed her agreed that she knew many Swedish words and that these were intermixed with Danish and Norwegian phrases. Interestingly, when she was not manifesting the Jensen personality, she did not understand any Swedish words, even when she was deeply hypnotized. Furthermore, she had no previous contact with Swedish and evidenced no aptitude for learning foreign languages, scoring low on the Modern Language Aptitude Test.

Although this is not a case of religious glossolalia, it is an illustration of a well-researched example of xenoglossia that is difficult to explain.

Far more typical, is the kind of "glossolalic" experience reported by Samarin (1968): two Englishmen claimed to speak in Temne, an African language spoken in Sierra Leone, however, when they were brought face to face with a native Temne speaker, he categorically rejected their claim.

The several ways in which such xenoglossia has been explained will be considered later. The question of whether glossolalia is a language at all will be discussed next.

Is Glossolalia Language?

The question of whether glossolalia is a language is related to, but distinct from, the issue of xenoglossia, that is, whether glossolalia is a *known* language. In a most general sense, the term "language" refers to a group of signs or symbols (i.e., a vocabulary) that are used according to a set of rules (i.e., a grammar) in certain prescribed relationships (i.e., a syntax) (Wolcott, 1970).

Although many tongue speakers would not claim that they were speaking some foreign language they had never learned, all would probably insist that they were speaking a "language" (in the sense of the above definition), and they would point to incidents in which someone had "interpreted" their exclamations, implying that meaning was being communicated in some sense. They would claim that the "miracle" was not that the language they were speaking was some foreign tongue they had never studied, but that their voices were being used by God to speak a heavenly language and that He had given another person the gift to undertand it. The issue is, therefore, whether this speech, xenoglossia or not, shows the characteristics of language, such as vocabulary, grammar, or syntax. But it should be recognized that those who faithfully practice speaking in tongues may not be convinced by such an analysis and may insist that if glossolalia is God's language, there is no reason to suppose that it has to follow the rules of human language!

Nevertheless, a number of researchers have considered these issues important. One intriguing approach has been to compare glossolalia with schizophrenese, the bizarre language often heard from psychotic individuals. Wolcott (1970) has termed this type of speech "private language." He reasons that although some writers have concluded that schizophrenese is not a language because it does not convey meaningful information or functionally include others who share its meaning, this conclusion does not consider the expressive function of language. Everyday language includes this expressive dimension and, in fact, communication of meaning often occurs without any predetermined necessity that an event be verified by community observation. For example, these statements would be believed without question: "I have a headache"; "I feel restless"; "I am sad"; "I couldn't sleep last night because I had too many thoughts in my head." However, the next statements would provoke some concern: "There is a funny noise in my head"; "I felt a presence in the room"; "I smelled perfume last night"; "My dead grandmother spoke to me"; "There is danger here." Nonetheless, we would term both sets of statements language.

It is when such statements go beyond "simple" delusions or hallucinations that we start to question whether a language is being used. For example, Wolcott (1970, p. 128) quotes from an essay entitled "The Diary of a Schizophrenic Man" as follows: "Lust, remorse, hatred, revenge, sin, A dungeon A gambling house Music Lorance Welk We all have talent" (p. 128). Yet, complex as it is, this word-salad utterance has obvious expressive meaning. And this expression of confusion and distortion can be understood without too much intuition or sophistication when translated. In this sense, it is possible to call schizophrenese "language" and even to claim that it has intersubjectivity. Thus, Wolcott (1970) concludes: ". . . it is possible to describe the source's meanings (emotions, commands), the receiver's meanings (emotions, interpretation of commands), and the joint meanings shared by both" (p. 127).

Although Wolcott (1970) does not discuss glossolalia, it is possible to make some comparisons between it and the psychotic language he considers. In Wolcott's example of schizophrenese, the speech departs from ordinary language primarily with respect to grammar and syntax rather than vocabulary. The words are familiar, but they are strung together in a meaningless fashion. However, in glossolalia, not even the vocabulary is familiar. An example reported by Jaquith (1967) illustrates this:

ke la la iy ya na now. key la la iy yey na yey now. key la la yey iy now.
key la la iy ya na key la ya a now. key la key la ho ra ya na yey la la iy ye
la ya na key la ya a now. . . . (p. 3)

This, nevertheless, resembles schizophrenic language in which neologisms (newly coined words) are used. An example of this is also given
by Wolcott (1970, p. 128) in a quotation from the *Autobiography of a
Schizophrenic Girl:* ". . . icthiou, gao, itivare, gibastow, ovede. . . ."

Questions to be asked concerning these types of communication are:
Do they, like the schizophrenese discussed earlier, illustrate the expressive
function of language? Do they communicate emotion in such a manner
that those listening to them understand? Here, the answers given for
glossolalia seem to be more definite than those that can be given for
schizophrenese.

Public religious glossolalia typically occurs in an environment of
shared expectations. The presence of God is assumed, and the power of
the Holy Spirit to speak through individuals is taken for granted. Furthermore, the probability that the Holy Spirit will give an interpretation
of the glossolalia to someone is presumed. It would be difficult to con-
vince such a religious gathering that genuine communication and understanding did not occur. And, most often, the nature of the communication is expressive in the sense that God is said to be speaking words of
encouragement or exhortation or concern or disapproval or comfort
rather than giving facts or offering predictions. Seldom, if ever, does the
literature of glossolalia report the interpreted message to be a prediction.
Thus, it could be said that glossolalia is an expressive language that includes intersubjectivity and shared communication.

Whether glossolalia is a language in the sense that it has vocabulary,
grammar, and syntax is another matter. Schizophrenese has a number of
words whose meanings are the same as in ordinary language, whereas
glossolalia contains none. Glossolalia is completely neologistic. Most
studies on glossolalic utterances have been analyses of single, as opposed
to several, productions. However, the few longitudinal studies that have
been made, along with comparisons among individuals, do suggest there
is a consistency within each person's speech. Although there is a tendency
among English-speaking persons, for example, to speak in tongues that
sound like Romance language derivatives, there is a uniqueness to each
individual's tongue, which can be heard and identified by glossolalics
themselves. In other words, a vocabulary does seem to be operative.

Glossolalics seem to be as unable as psychotics to explain the meanings of their words. Of course, some tongue speakers report that others
have recognized foreign words in their tongues. Among those we have
interviewed, for example, is a woman who said that she had been told
her tongue included the French words for "praise" and for "Lord." However, as far as we know, only two cases of glossolalia included an attempt
by the speaker to determine the meaning of the words that were spoken.
These were the cases of Hélène Smith and Albert Le Baron (discussed in

chapter 1) and both of these were psychic, as opposed to traditionally religious, manifestations. In the case reported by the psychoanalyst Oskar Pfister (1912), the interpretations of glossolalic speech in the course of treatment were of emotions rather than of the meaning of *specific words*. His understanding of the speech of a 24-year-old male patient named Simon, for example, was that it represented "painful thoughts which revived analogous experiences—for the most part infantile—repressed by consciousness but now brought forth in disguised form" (Pattison, 1968, p. 78).

Thus, glossolalics have not tried to produce lexicons, nor do they feel a need to do so. They readily acknowledge that they do not know what their speeches mean, and they trust God to interpret the meaning through the insight He gives to another person.

Whether glossolalia is a language in respect to *vocabulary* is, thus, problematic. Although there does seem to be consistency within a given person's tongue, no effort is made by the tongue speaker to define the meaning of specific words. Yet the speaker is confident the words have meaning and she/he depends on an interpreter to give that meaning.

However, as Samarin (1968) points out, the interpretations are usually shorter than the speeches and word-by-word (or phrase-by-phrase) translation has not been done, nor is it claimed. For example, Wolfram (1966) gives a sample of a glossolalic utterance at a Full Gospel Businessmen's Fellowship International (FGBMFI) in the mid-1960s and its interpretation given by someone else. The speech follows:

> 'vasta 'loito//'rakiri' 'memto, stela'toro//, 'tantala, vasaito, la'porto//,
> mos'toro 'kantolo, be'loro// 'hordo, la'sai, do// 'marta, lebn'tentantala,
> bala'sato 'loito// 'hordo, la'sito ma'kito//, mes'to prosu, dula' no//, pro'sutula
> 'pa, tuno//zebele'ko tuz'rusutu//, la'pa, un'kea 'zivolo koto'na// 'ropele
> 'sitola// Ro'su 'tela 'raiz, soko'sitala'me// 'nufa'ro 'tuloe, pe'tinoba 'sito//,
> la, pora' su 'dolo// Residila'mo 'tinema, tovosi'ta// le'po, Ro'si// 'rotela,
> sotu'no//, Res'ti, pa'lapa//
>
> (// in the above indicated breath breaks interpreted to be sentences, complete pronunciation accent marks are not included). (p. 31)

Whereas the speech itself took up eight lines, the "translation" went on for forty-three lines. The first and last segments were as follows:

> The whole world; liveth in darkness, and yea, men in the darkness search for truth and light. But the light is come and shined in the hearts of men. And yea, ye are the light of the world. Go therefore into the world of darkness and shine ye as light. Speak ye the words of truth so shall ye see that ye beget truth in the hearts of those who sit in the darkness. . . . And in the days that are ahead ye shall see that no man shall stay the hand of the Lord, but that which He has proclaimed, and that which He has ordained shall surely be fulfilled for the Lord is at work among those who are His. (p. 33)

Here, there is obviously no correlation between words in the speech and words in the interpretation. Thus, it could not strictly be called a translation. Further, there is a distinct style to the interpretation that resembles that of the King James (English) Version of the Bible and many liturgical prayers. Once again, the issue of vocabulary is somewhat confusing.

The question of whether glossolalia is a language in terms of *grammar* and *syntax* is a different matter, however. As early as 1968, Samarin, perhaps the foremost student of these matters, stated, "if a glossa [his coined term for a speech in tongues] is meaningless, this does not mean it is gibberish" (p. 60). He concluded that the principal feature that distinguished glossolalia from gibberish was the number of phonological (linguistic) units at various levels. Glossolalics do not speak in a mixed up mishmash fashion. They organize their verbiage into productions that include macrosegments (comparable to sentences), microsegments (comparable to words), and phonemes (sound units).

Thus, tongue speakers are speaking what sounds like a language with grammar and syntax (Samarin, 1968). For example, in analyzing the glossolalic speech of one of Wolfram's (1966) subjects, Samarin reaches the following conclusion:

> Thus, even a cursory examination of the sample text reveals that *siyanáyasi* occurs only at the end of a macrosegment [a sentence?] and is very often preceded by *kita*. In other words, glossic syllables are not simply spewed out in a haphazard sort of way. . . . (1968, p. 60)

Among the answers Samarin (1972c) received when he asked, "Why do you think glossolalia is a language?" were the following: "It sounds too much like a language not to be." . . . "I don't feel I'm the type to just rattle on making sounds." . . . "Because I seem to learn it" (*passim* pp. 105–107).

More thoughtful answers included references to the same words appearing over and over, short words (like conjunctions or prepositions) connecting phrases, different endings and prefixes being used, the rise and fall of voice tone, pauses for breath, rhythm cadence, and the seeming grouping of phrases into groups (Samarin, 1972c, pp. 106–107).

However, the word structure of a given utterance is not all that apparent nor is the dissecting of the material into phrases and sentences an easy task. For example, a prayer by Rev. d'Esprit (Samarin's prime subject studied over several days) began like this: "kupóy shăndré fîlé sundrukumă. . . ." Yet, Samarin (1972c) concluded:

> [Rev. d'Esprit] was undoubtedly influenced by the rhythm of the utterance, making each "word" come out with a final accented syllable. But there was no good reason for not beginning as follows: "ku póyshăn dréfî lésundru." Other linguistically trained persons have looked at this text, and none of them arrives at exactly the same results that are presented here. (p. 81)

Even when Rev. d'Esprit listened to his own tape-recorded prayer, he could not repeat back to Samarin what he had just heard! Samarin surmized, therefore, that the sounds were grouped by listeners into words, phrases, and sentences somewhat arbitrarily on the basis of cues from the accents, rhythms, and melodies of the breath groups. Further, he suggested that this arbitrariness could only be avoided when persons knew the meanings behind the words—a connection that is missing in glossolalia.

Several suggestions as to the psycholinguistic processes that may be going on in the interpretation of glossolalia can be found in articles on factors that determine the meanings of foreign words (Brackbill & Little, 1957) and on the perception of speech without typical auditory cues (Remez, Rubin, Pisoni, & Carreil, 1981).

In the Brackbill and Little study comparing various combinations of word pairs from the English, Chinese, Japanese, and Hebrew languages, it was found that "similarity of word lengths, vowels, consonant types, spacing of compound words, and connotations" (Brackbill & Little, p. 318) significantly affected agreement as to the sameness of meaning in the word pairs. In another study using made-up words, agreement as to "meaning" could be systematically varied by manipulating these variables. This suggests that some of the same processes may be occurring in the interpretation of glossolalia—especially given the religious climate of expectation in which most tongue speaking happens. A controlled study, such as that conducted by Brackbill & Little, might confirm such a hypothesis.

Remez et al. (1981) investigated the effects of varying harmonic, time sequence, and amplitude qualities of the sentence, "Where were you a year ago?" All properties were changed so as to be dissimilar to those generated by the larynx in human speech perception. Without being told that the stimulus was a human voice, subjects were unable to identify it as such. However, when told that the sound was human speech, they showed an amazing ability to perceive words and, in some cases, to identify meanings. The authors concluded that these abilities could not be explained in terms of the acoustical cues typically held to underlie speech perception. The subjects were capable through priming to direct their attention to the phonetic qualities of the stimulus and correctly identify it as speech. It is possible that these same cues may be operating in interpretation of glossolalia, although this has yet to be validated.

Although neither of these studies proves glossolalia to be a language, they provide a framework for understanding how those who perceive it as such could do so.

Nevertheless, there is evidence that argues *for* the presence of linguistic patterns within the speech of normal individuals that are distinct from the linguistic patterns of tongue speakers. These patterns support the possibility that glossolalia is a language—albeit a private language at best. The three types of evidence are: (1) comparisons of consonants and vowels between individuals, (2) comparisons of speeches of the same individual on different occasions, and (3) comparison of the speeches of individuals who claim to speak in different tongues on different occasions.

As for comparisons between individuals, Goodman (1969b) compared glossolalia in four different cultural settings in English- and Spanish-speaking groups within and outside the United States. In addition to some striking similarities in a word or two (e.g., *kálomahala* and *pálomalalaya*), she noted that all utterances followed an intonation pattern with "an onset in the medium range, a peak, and a sloping gradient leading to an often precipitous decay" (p. 236). She further observed that all "pulse" (her term for the smallest sound) units began with consonants, that "bars" (her term for groups of pulses separated by pauses) were usually of equal duration, and that the accent was typically placed on the first pulse of each bar. These were commonalities quite distinct from the English or Spanish in which the glossolalics in her study normally spoke. Although her interpretation of these characteristics led her to the conclusion that glossolalia was an artifact of the trance state, these characteristics could also be seen as support for the viewpoint that the phenomenon has common linguistic features.

Further, Samarin (1972c) noted similarities in "sounds" that seem to characterize tongue speaking in various sections of the United States. He has coined the term "diaglossa" to depict this phenomenon: He states:

. . . we observe that many people throughout the United States and Canada used a "word" that consists of an initial /s/ or /sh/, then a vowel, followed by /nt/ or /nd/ and another vowel: in other words, /shanda/, /santi/, and so forth. What is remarkable is that it should appear in a tenth of the responses to my question: "Do you recall any words from your tongues or from the tongues of other people?" The recurrent segment is here written as it was given in the questionnaires:

(ka) shun di	Seattle, Washington
schone do (ka)	California
shunto-	?
shan-da	Michigan
shawn-dye	Connecticut
shandah	North Carolina
ah-shon-da	?
shanda	New York

This segment also occurs in the glossolalia of a neo-Pentecostal from Toronto . . . in samples obtained from Rev. d'Esprit, in the Episcopalian samples, and even from the snake-handlers of Scrabble Creek, West Virginia. . . . (p. 99)

Although the presence of one "word" or "word" derivative is by no means conclusive, it is, nevertheless, suggestive of some type of language.

Turning next to comparisons of speeches of the same individuals on different occasions, Wolfram (1966) concluded that there were distinct individual patterns that suggested that persons used some type of system in their glossolalia. He reported individual analyses of tongues spoken the same day, one week apart, and at a three-week interval. In comparing speaking in tongues twice on the same day, ten of fourteen phonemes (i.e., consonants, vowels, and diphthongs) appeared both times. In the one-week comparison, the second occasion was considerably longer and included over 20,000 phonemes. However, there were only six phonemes that appeared solely on the second occasion. The most support for consistency came in the three-week analysis. There were no diphthongs (a vowel consonant pairing) spoken either time; of the eighteen consonants occurring on the first and sixteen consonants on the second occasion, fifteen were identical. Thus, although on all occasions there was evidence of a selection deficiency in relation to English (i.e., common English evidences greater variety), there was, nevertheless, a unique set of basic phonemes observed for each speaker over time. This is not atypical, as Samarin (1972a) and others have observed. People often talk about "their" tongue and report recognizable differences among people.

The final evidence supporting the language character of glossolalia comes from comparison of *different* "tongues" within the same individual. Motley (1967) provides samples of a sixty-year-old Pentecostal man who during the course of his religious experience had developed three types of tongues: Spanish, Oriental, and Russian. Portions of two of these (reported by Samarin, 1972c, pp. 80–81) are:

> "Spanish": travioxóta xiá exítamakapasán denisisiantiáda. animóto iamemóte existakantráo exitakantraviande. livísta lavasiándo nemórta meporpampírán-dara sontinisisian tiáda kepáltala patrabas tinisisiantiádadevióxota.

> "Russian": brŏsh abríshĭn bărevésh alavorót dăravíshikaravát talbedirísh drovés drováishdi bráshadráividivish akapărevét arivishĭndara váslĕvĕriv. vedísh atraveda díshatrobodiásh atravedivéshni pĕrísh.

Motley's (1967) analyses of these speeches revealed results quite different from those of Nida (1964), Wolfram (1966), and Samarin (1972c). The latter three had concluded that the sound patterns of the glossolalia they studied most resembled English and probably derived from it. In fact, Wolfram (1966) noted that non-English phonemes, although present, were extremely rare. In contrast, Motley (1967) found that the ranks and relative frequencies of "phones" (his term for phonemes, taking no account of the arbitrary nature of glossolalic "words") for the Spanish and Slavic samples more resembled the patterns characteristic of extant Spanish and Russian languages than they resembled English. Further, he found that the pattern for the two tongues was dissimilar. His conclusions were based on correlational analysis and, thus, lend support to the contention that glossolalia may have language characteristics.

By far the most common opinion, however, is that glossolalia *lacks* the essentials of a language as understood by linguists. Against the contention by Jaquith (1967), Nida (1964), and Wolfram (1966) that glossolalia is an English derivative, probably learned, Samarin (1972c) suggests:

> When the full apparatus of linguistic science comes to bear on glossolalia, this turns out to be only a facade of language—although at times a very good one indeed. For when we comprehend what language is, we must conclude that no glossa, no matter how well constructed, is a specimen of human lan-

guage, because it is neither internally organized nor systematically related to the world man perceives. (p. 127–128)

As early as 1968, Samarin had come to this conclusion when he compared glossolalia to Hockett's (1963) "universals of language design." Among the sixteen universals that Hockett suggested, Samarin noted that glossolalia could not measure up to five of them: semanticity, arbitrariness, displacement, prevarication, and reflexiveness.

Semanticity is most akin to vocabulary—words that denote parts of common experience. In spite of occasional recognizable or definable words, overall glossolalia does not meet this criterion. Samarin (1972c, p. 96) reports a study he did with the psychologist Laffal in which he asked Rev. d'Esprit to respond in tongues to a variety of subjects: strength/weakness, emptiness/fullness, beginning/ending, leading/following, death, and anger. The pattern of consonants, vowels, and diphthongs was similar across all subjects, seeming to suggest that the content of the speech was not responsive to the topic being considered in the mind of the speaker. There seems to be no difference, furthermore, in the order of sentences in a glossolalic prayer, save for the fact that some tongue speakers appear to have systematic ways of beginning and ending a speech. So, for example, the statement "diyăn tekriyămo pandri talava shande" (the first sentence in a prayer) could just as easily be replaced by the fifth sentence "tekiyandĭ lăvosăndrama kayă shĕndĭ lăvăsiyă." As Samarin states, "We assume that this is true because of the way syllables freely conjoin to make 'words' and 'sentences' " (1972c, p. 124).

Nor does glossolalia meet the standard of *arbitrariness*, meaning that a word bears no physical or geometrical relationship to the thing being referred to. In true language, for example, neither the word "house" in English nor the word "casa" in Spanish bears any logical relation to the building it denotes. No such systematic set of definitions exists in glossolalia. To reiterate, there is no lexicon for speaking in tongues.

Further, glossolalia does not include *displacement* or *prevarication*—the ability to refer to things distant in time or space and the ability to be meaningless in a logical sense. One cannot contradict oneself in a tongue nor can one clearly depict what one is praying for, save in the sense of saying, "we are now praying for John's mother who is sick in New York City." The utterance would not clearly communicate that without a preannouncement.

Finally, glossolalia is not *reflective* in the sense that one cannot use it to communicate about communication. Glossolalia cannot be used to talk about glossolalia, in spite of the fact that some wit has suggested that there will someday be a translation of the Bible in tongues about which critics will write—in tongues. No one expects that to happen.

Nevertheless, Samarin's (1972c) critique is countered by his own report on the responses of a group of persons who listened to the aforementioned speeches of Rev. d'Esprit on such subjects as emptiness/fullness, death, anger, and so on. Although the speeches were not distinguishable phonologically, there was remarkable consistency among the listeners in their ability to discriminate among the topics that were being addressed. This seems to suggest that although nothing was being communicated in the traditional semantic sense, something that was meaningful was being transmitted. It may well be that Hockett's (1963) universals are not inclusive enough and that glossolalia is, indeed, a language in a different sense of the word! The meaningfulness of the event of speaking in tongues for speaker and for listener may be something different from the denotative meaning characteristic of language as we usually understand it. These issues will be addressed in chapter 8.

In summary, we have considered the language of glossolalia and the types of glossolalia in this chapter. Whether glossolalia is xenoglossia (untrained persons speaking an extant human language) was discussed. Finally, the question of whether glossolalia is any kind of language at all was examined. There is support for opinions on all sides of these questions. The weight of the evidence, however, suggests that although there is pattern and form, speaking in tongues is most likely not a known tongue nor a human language as that term is presently understood.

Glossolalia as Aberrant Behavior

3

Psychological Models

In this chapter, there is further consideration of the early investigations of those psychologists and psychiatrists who tried to understand glossolalia by studying individual psychological dynamics. This survey provides the background for more recent studies of these phenomena. The classical studies of James (1902/1958), Flournoy (1900/1963), Mosiman (1911), and Lombard (1910) are considered first. Next comes psychoanalytic, then Jungian, and finally ego-psychological investigations are described. The chapter ends with a comparison of these approaches.

The prime question underlying these studies has been, "Is glossolalia therapeutic or harmful?" In answering this question, we are not trying to determine whether speaking in tongues is pathological or not, which is considered in chapter 5. Nor are we attempting to delineate the personality characteristics that might make a person more likely to speak in tongues (questions to be considered in chapter 8). The central focus of this chapter is on understanding how various models of personality perceive the function of this behavior in the life of the individual. It should be remembered that these early researchers largely relied on case studies as opposed to the controlled experiments that are more typical of such studies today.

CLASSICAL STUDIES

The word "classical" is used here to refer to the earliest efforts by social/behavioral scientists to investigate glossolalia. These investigations begin with the seminal thought of William James who evidenced a genuine interest in the psychology of religion in his Gifford lectures in the early 1900s. James wrote an introduction to Le Baron's article and acknowledged some observations he had made at the time of an earlier encounter with such phenomena. Although he never explored glossolalia per se in any depth, he did conclude that it represented an impulse coming from a "subliminal" part of the mind, in other words, from the unconscious:

The impulses may take the direction of automatic speech or writing, the meaning of which the subject himself may not understand even while he utters it; and generalizing this phenomenon, Mr. Myers has given the name of *automatism,* sensory or motor, emotional or intellectual, to this whole sphere of effects, due to "uprushes" into the ordinary consciousness of energies originating in the subliminal parts of the mind. (James 1902/1958, p. 189)

Automatisms, James concluded, "must be simply ascribed to the subject's having a large subliminal region, involving nervous instability" (p. 201).

Furthermore, he suggested that automatisms of one kind or another were very common among religious leaders:

You will in point of fact hardly find a religious leader of any kind in whose life there is no record of automatisms. I speak not merely of savage priests and prophets, whose followers regard automatic utterance and action as by itself tantamount to inspiration, I speak of leaders of thought and subjects of intellectualized experience. Saint Paul had his visions, his ecstasies, his gift of tongues, small as was the importance he attached to the latter. The whole array of Christian saints and heresiarchs, including the greatest, the Bernards, the Loyolas, the Luthers, the Foxes, the Wesleys, had their visions, voices, rapt conditions, guiding impressions, and "openings." (James, 1902/1958, p. 362)

James was the first scholar to identify glossolalia with automatic behavior and to say that it represented nervous instability coupled with extraordinary subliminal regions in the mind. He was likewise the first to state in such a bold manner that this was characteristic of religious leaders.

At roughly the same time as James was writing, Flournoy, a professor of psychology at the University of Geneva, undertook the first thorough case study of speaking in tongues (1900/1963). It is noteworthy not only for its linguistic analysis, but also for the psychological explanation it proposed. Flournoy knew of the Le Baron article and of James's explanations in his introduction. Flournoy either adopted James's point of view or came to the same conclusions on his own. He concluded that glossolalia represented automatisms that emerged from the subliminal mind (1900/1963).

It may be remembered that Flournoy's primary interest was in studying the mediumship of Hélène Smith who claimed to speak in a "Martian" tongue. He suggested that this language, which resembled glossolalia, was "the naïve and somewhat puerile work of an infantile imagination to which occurred the idea of creating a new language" (1900/1963, p. 253). Here we see for the first time the idea that grandiosity and infantile thinking might be the motivating forces underlying such behavior.

The proposal that such speech as glossolalia represented surrender to infantile or primitive impulses was new with Flournoy. He saw such speech productions as part of the regressive experiences through which mediums, like Hélène Smith, were able to engage in behaviors over which they had no conscious control.

The process by which this occurred was, for Flournoy, similar to hypnosis, and he concluded that mediums were usually susceptible to suggestion. This suggestibility was due to emotional shocks and traumas that these persons had experienced early in life. Their productions were seen by Flournoy as combinations of the current situation and forgotten memories.

Hélène Smith illustrated these processes. Flournoy felt that the several personalities she evidenced while in trance represented developmental stages in her own life adjustment with which she was in touch at a subliminal level:

> The secondary personalities are probably in their origin . . . phenomena of reversion of the ordinary actual personality, or of momentary returns of inferior phases, long since passed, and which normally should have been absorbed in the development of the individual instead of breaking forth again in strange proliferations. (1900/1963, p. 445)

In Flournoy's study of Hélène Smith, she evidenced three personalities, all of which spoke in "foreign" tongues. The "Martian" speech, Flournoy concluded, represented the most primitive and childish layer of her personality; the "Hindoo" [sic] voice represented a later, possibly adolescent, dimension; and the "French" was representative of a more recent emotional trauma in Hélène Smith's adult life.

In summary, Flournoy did a thorough psychological analysis based on an extensive case study of a medium. He proposed several dynamics that have been most instructive for later formulations. He understood glossolalia as part of the regressive experience of mediums and as manifesting an earlier developmental stage of life that had not been integrated into the personality. Because of the trauma of early stresses, these individuals retained many unsettled memories in the somewhat enlarged subliminal portions of their minds.

Turning next to Lombard (1910) and Mosiman (1911), it is interesting to note that both received theological training and combined theological perspectives with psychological understandings of glossolalia based on the theories of James and Flournoy. In fact, Flournoy wrote an introduction to Lombard's (1910) treatise.

Although they did not know each other's work, Mosiman writing in German and Lombard writing in French both approached the topic in terms of biblical criticism, church history, and cultural developments. They did not undertake case studies, as did Flournoy, or consider individual dynamics, as did James. They pioneered, however, a format that has been used by many theologically trained students of the field (Cutten, 1927, C. G. Williams, 1981).

Cutten (1927), writing in English, summarized the work of Mosiman and Lombard and combined his conclusions with theirs—thus giving their ideas much more publicity than their original writings ever received before.

Lombard (1910, pp. 110–157) perceived speaking in tongues to be an extremely contagious experience that could be provoked by group suggestion or by reading such accounts as those in the New Testament. Thus, it could occur when one was alone or when one was in a group. He made no distinction between those who did and those who did not become glossolalic as Flournoy and James had done. He did, however, emphasize the power of the experience and the overwhelming influence of leaders.

Lombard assumed that in the experience of speaking in tongues individuals went back to their childhood because their "tongues" sounded like childish speech. Furthermore, the reports of tongue speakers, that their feelings during and after the experience were more important to them than the content of their speech suggested to Lombard that child-like processes were going on. Adults would pay more attention to the substance than the emotion in their talk. It should be noted that this point of view is more descriptive than explanatory, as was Flournoy's.

Lombard sums up his position:

> . . . whether one can or cannot indicate by a precise date the stage of development in which the subject finds himself; theoretically reported this is not contestable: the glossolalic automatisms proceed from a rupture of mental stability which brings to the surface the states normally repressed and buried, states characterized by the psycho-verbal point of view and by the predominance of affective elements. (1910, p. 140)

The most interesting facet of Lombard's theorizing was his contention that glossolalia could have positive value in the lives of individuals. It represented the breakdown of an earlier structure and the beginning of a new personality. He suggested:

> For the religious individual or the religious crowd, automatism is born from a sort of hypnosis which disorganizes the ego to the benefit of emotional elements, which are ordinarily neutralized. This disorganization may be the beginning of a superior reorganization. (1910, p. 142)

Herein, Lombard introduces a theme that for the first time contends that glossolalia can be growth producing; he proposes a mechanism whereby this occurs, namely, the breaking apart of the old and the creation of the new. Glossolalia, for Lombard, was the indication both that such a process was occurring and that it had happened. As he wrote in the concluding paragraph of his book:

> From the point of view of the philosophy of religion, finally, the phenomena of glossolalia are interesting and significant through the accent which they place upon the role of feeling in the religious life. Do its affective origins do a grievance to religion? Shall we say that it brings human mentality back again to an inferior and an excessive state? It is necessary that we understand nothing is more grievous for a man than to fall back into infancy. But we

like well to hear it said: You are becoming younger. Certain mystical child-ishnesses are distressing due to ridiculousness and sterility. But how many times do we not see religious feelings reanimate the energies, tone up the affections, pour out in all mental thrift a new vigor which flourishes in high heroisms and in fruitful devotion? If this is regression, it indeed has its value. Thus, the infantilism which displays itself in glossolalia appears like the ransom price—all the more inevitable that psychology will have con-tributed to illuminating piety—of a process of rejuvenation that one can only salute with joy when it gives to life, for a motive power, this sublime passion: love of God and of men, imperishable charity. (1910, pp. 239–240)

These are themes that became central in the investigations of later re-searchers. It is noteworthy that Lombard would have attested to the pos-sible positive value of speaking in tongues at a date so early in this century.

Mosiman (1911) differed from Lombard in this regard. He did not per-ceive any rejuvenating or integrating aspects to the experience. He con-cluded that because speaking in tongues was not under the control of the conscious mind, it, therefore, could not be positive in its effect.

The term Mosiman used for speaking in tongues was ecstasy. All ecstatic experiences he equated with hypnotic states, which had two negative di-mensions. The first was the domination of the unconscious mind, as noted in the preceding paragraph. The second was the susceptibility to suggestion. Suggestion was the process by which entrance was gained into the unconscious. The implication was that such persons as became glosso-lalic were abnormally vulnerable to the stimulation of their unconscious. Thus, Mosiman discounted both the dimensions of the experience and those who succumbed to it. He even related it to a literal interpretation of the New Testament, as if to say that the tendency to naive acceptance of authority or concrete interpretation of the Bible were also character-istic of these persons. For him, regression to a childish state, which he considered typical for glossolalics, was anything but constructive. It sym-bolized an unhealthy departure from adult living.

One wonders what influence environment played in the theorizing of such as Lombard and Mosiman. Although both used the thinking of James and Flournoy, Mosiman proposed themes that have characterized American investigations much more than European, namely, the hypothe-sis that glossolalia represents pathological regression. Lombard evidenced quite the opposite conclusions. Why this difference? It could perhaps be due to the fact that Mosiman first wrote his treatise in English while studying at McCormick Seminary in Chicago and only rewrote it in Ger-man later. Thus, the American influence of early twentieth-century immi-grant Chicago and the Azuza revival of 1906 was part of his legacy. Many social/behavioral scientists thought despairingly of these events, so it is perhaps no surprise that Mosiman wrote the way he did. Lombard was much closer to the Jungian milieu in Geneva, which has continued to hold that such experiences can be integrating for the personality.

As an addendum to these classical studies, Shumway's unpublished dissertation (1919) should be mentioned. Although he knew of the work of Flournoy and James, he was unacquainted with the writings of Lombard or Mosiman. Cutten, writing almost a decade later in 1927, seemed to be unaware of Shumway's work, probably because it remained unpublished in the library of Boston University.

Shumway was an eyewitness to the Los Angeles revival of 1906 and based his conclusions on this experience. He utilized much of the earlier psychological theories in his writing. He noted six characteristics of the experience of speaking in tongues:

1. A complete loss of rational control—the speaker does not know what he/she does or says.
2. A dominance of emotion that leads to hysteria.
3. A feeling of prayer and praise coupled with the absence of thought or will.
4. An automatic functioning of the speech organs in the form of gibberish, which includes occasional foreign phrases.
5. An absence of memory as to what took place after the event has ended.
6. An occasional spasmodic physical manifestation alongside the tongue speaking (pp. 19–20).

Shumway's emphasis was on the fugue-state quality of the experience. Although his view was basically depreciative, his conclusions were presented as unbiased descriptions without any interpretations about how and in whom the experiences occur. However, Shumway set the stage for numerous later investigations into the question of whether glossolalics go into trance during the experience.

PSYCHOANALYTIC INVESTIGATIONS

Sigmund Freud never investigated glossolalia. However, his close friend and associate, Oskar Pfister, a Swiss pastor, undertook a prolonged case study (1912) of a 24-year-old-man, Simon. Freud was acquainted with this project and gave Pfister encouragement and constructive criticism about it in a letter dated September 27, 1910:

> From what you say I cannot yet form a very good idea of your gift-of-tongues effort, but I expect you will soon be in a good position to reveal all the so-called involuntary actions as the work of complexes. Certainly something can be done with it, first of all a stimulating paper in the *Zentralblott,* and then all sorts of other things.

> As you do me the honor of asking my advice about the writing of the book, let me say frankly that the way to which you feel less drawn seems to me the more appropriate and the more advantageous to the reader. In the present state of our knowledge all the fundamentals, consciousness, emotions, etc. are better left in the semi-darkness from which they stand out so well, while one occupies oneself with the outbuildings, approaches, etc. which are only

now becoming perceptible. For that the learner will be very grateful. (Freud, 1910/1963, p. 44)

Pfister did, indeed, conclude as Freud suggested, that glossolalia had dynamic meaning. In other words, it was the work of complexes. He intuited that glossolalia was an infantile regression directed toward auto-erotic satisfaction. Pfister was treating Simon in analysis. Simon had been raised and confirmed as a German Lutheran but began speaking in tongues when he was 20 years old at a meeting conducted by a Norwegian evangelist. Through the process of free association (in which Pfister had Simon report the thoughts that came to him as he spoke in tongues), Pfister concluded that Simon was confused about guilt feelings associated with masturbation. Simon wrote down two samples of glossolalia in addition to the two spoken samples that were recorded by Pfister.

Pfister concluded that in glossolalia, the painful thoughts that were rooted in infantile experiences were experienced over and over again through the experience of glossolalia. He compared the process of therapy to that in dream analysis wherein an organizing principle was sought beneath all the gibberish.

Pfister's case study is noteworthy, in that it concluded that speech in glossolalia had personal meaning to the speaker and that the words themselves could be utilized in therapy, just as in the treatment of any emotionally disturbed person. Although he did not state such, it could be assumed that Pfister would say that glossolalia was a symptom to be done away with in the process of healing.

Another psychoanalytic case study was undertaken by a psychiatrist in Oslo, Norway, Harold K. Schjelderup (1931). His patient, a 24-year-old neurotic woman, began to speak in tongues while undergoing analysis. There was no religious connection to the event. It was simply a neurotic reaction to the treatment according to Schjelderup. Although she was fully conscious while producing the speech, she could not enter the situation intentionally nor could she make the sounds voluntarily. She reported that she felt like a child while she was speaking in tongues. Schjelderup never heard her speak in tongues, although she brought written reproductions of a number of the sounds, and he had her free associate to them. She associated early childhood scenes to the words.

Schjelderup interpreted the words of her tongue to be "compression events," in other words, the bringing together of several words into one word. Furthermore, many of the words resembled those made by small children before they learn to talk. Schjelderup stated:

In my opinion there can be no doubt that traces of early remembrance play a part and that the activation of primarily infantile engrams are of basic importance to the phenomenon. (1931, p. 18)

The assumption that actual remembrance-traces of very early childhood experiences are of importance to the tongue-speech is based on the fact that other automatisms of the patient were also determined the same way and that it was possible to bring early childhood experiences to consciousness during analysis. (1931, p. 20)

Schjelderup reasoned that the narcissistic, self-affirming quality of these regressive acts should characterize religious speaking in tongues as well.

In reflecting on these two case studies, it is noteworthy that Pfister saw glossolalia as indicative of a conflict to be worked through, whereas Schjelderup conceived of it as representing self-preoccupation of a pleasureful kind. One theorist saw it as deprivation or conflict based; the other theorist conceived of it as based on fixation or indulgence. Although these clinical cases were somewhat divorced from more typical religious glossolalia, they did result in themes that, although similar to earlier conclusions, were yet provocative enough to stimulate later research.

A more recent psychoanalytic study was undertaken by Julius Laffal (Laffal, 1965, 1967; Laffal, Monahan, & Richman, 1974). While he was teaching at Yale, a neo-Pentecostal revival broke out on campus. He hypothesized:

> . . . speaking in tongues serves to provide verbal form to a conflicted wish while at the same time hiding the wish by stripping the verbalization of communal meaning. Some degree of conscious expression is allowed to the conflicted wish, but the wish itself escapes conscious recognition. (Laffal, 1965, p. 88)

This introduces another theme that has come to the fore since that time, namely, that glossolalia is a way of expressing that which the person wants to express but does not dare.

In 1974, Laffal et al. reported a study of samples of glossolalia from a pastor who spoke in tongues in response to specific themes suggested to him. These samples were played before listeners to see if they could identify the themes (e.g., love, forgiveness, etc.) to which the pastor was speaking. They did not agree with the pastor, although the audience did identify certain feelings to which they felt he was responding. This led Laffal to conclude that his earlier hypothesis was correct, namely, "that glossolalic speech has an expressive, cathartic function for the speaker" (Laffal et al. p. 289).

Laffal (1967) thus relates his conclusions about glossolalia to Freud's ideas that language, whether normal or glossolalic, is an energy discharge procedure whereby impulses are related in an acceptable manner to reality:

> Glossolalia, or "speaking in tongues," is perhaps the clearest example of the discharge function of language. This phenomenon sometimes appears in schizophrenic speech but is more often found in apparently normal individuals. A speaker, in a religious fervor, finds himself uttering "divinely given words" of a strange language which he does not understand. The fulfillment reported by individuals who speak in tongues is of inspirational proportions. We may assume that these utterances in which recognizability and specificity of reference have been lost serve the purpose of discharging the psychic

energy associated with wishes and conflicts. By the fact of verbalization, glossolalia brings close to consciousness what the individual cannot put into words. Since the specific social tokens are lacking, the shame, guilt, despair, or anxiety that might accompany the appropriate labeling are avoided while the person feels that he has expressed the ineffable. The idea of divine inspiration further propagates the feeling that he is not in the grip of the ordinary conflict and ungratified needs that characterize all of us and about which we have the most guilt and anxiety. (p. 63)

The most recent psychoanalytic comment comes from Pruyser (1978), who picked up Schjelderup's contention that glossolalia represents self-preoccupation. In an article on narcissism in contemporary religion, he states:

. . . we have to envisage the likelihood that some charismatics speak in tongues, jerk their limbs, writhe their bodies, break out in shouts, sing loudly to the Lord, and claim to receive the Spirit in notably pre-Oedipal ways, which may amount to an apotheosis of their selves. (p. 228)

Apotheosis is a strong word, but self-deification is exactly what Pruyser means. He is convinced that much of this behavior serves as self-indulgence and lacks the maturity that is seen in dignified worship and social action. It leads, furthermore, to spiritual pride rather than humble piety. This is psychopathology in a quite different form from that implied by those who used a conflict model, such as Pfister (1912) and Laffal (1965).

JUNGIAN INVESTIGATIONS

Carl Jung had much more interest in glossolalia than did Freud, perhaps reflecting his greater affinity for religion generally. According to Kelsey (1964), a Jungian scholar, there was an historical connection between Flournoy and Jung. In the German edition of his autobiography, Jung stated:

I read his book "Des Indes à la planète Mars: Etude sur un Cas de Somnambulisme avec glossolalie" which made a great impression on me. I wrote Flournoy that I would like to translate it into German. Only after half a year did I get an answer in which he excused himself for not writing sooner. To my regret he had already appointed another translator. (Cited in Kelsey, 1964, p. 196)

As previously noted, in his doctoral dissertation, Jung (1902/1970) undertook a case study of a 15.5-year-old girl, Miss S. W., who was a medium. In this investigation, he was greatly influenced by Flournoy's classic study of Hélène Smith, and he drew many parallels between the two. Miss S. W. also used glossolalia in her trance, but only on one occasion. The only recognizable words were variations on the Latin word *Wena,* which Jung identified as coming from an anatomical atlas the patient had read only a few days earlier.

Like Flournoy, Jung considered the medium's behavior while in trance to be indicative of a "heightened unconscious." Automatic writing, cryptomnesia, was another example of this atypical dimension of the mind seen in such persons according to Jung. The glossolalia of Miss S. W. was seen by Jung as an example of cryptomnesic images emerging out of the unconscious and expressing themselves verbally rather than through finger muscles. Kelsey (1964) commented that at this point in his career Jung had not yet developed his theory of the collective unconscious and, thus, did not have "the tools to do more than describe the experience of glossolalia which he encountered in his early years" (p. 198). As Kelsey noted, however, these ideas foreshadowed much of Jung's later work.

Another case study was undertaken by Maeder (1910) at the Zurich center of Bleuler and Jung. This was a study of a 41-year-old schizophrenic man who had been hospitalized for sixteen years. The patient, Mr. F. R., developed his own private language in order to communicate with himself in his fantasy world. Maeder considered this an instance of glossolalia. He examined the words of the patient both through free association and by having the patient define the terms. He concluded that Mr. F. R. created a myth from his own unconscious, one in which he was a giant and a hero. This compensated for his servile existence in the hospital. Analyzing this "superior" language (so-called by the patient), Maeder concluded that it was of an infantile, regressive character. This was similar to the conclusions reached by Flournoy and Lombard in their case studies.

There is a question as to whether schizophrenese should be considered glossolalia at all, as has often been claimed. Bobon (1947) reported case studies of the language of three psychotic patients at Liège. Each developed a private language, which was interpreted as a fanciful elaboration of ordinary French. The psychiatrist Spoerri (1967) differentiated clearly between the speech of schizophrenics and that of religious glossolalics. The linguist Samarin (1972c, p. 117) claimed that the "word salads" of schizophrenics were incontrovertibly different from religious glossolalia. Jung and his associates did not make any such distinction.

At a later stage, Jung developed his theory of the collective unconscious, according to which the unconscious of a given individual could contain more than personal memories. In addition, it could include memories of the race or from humankind in general. This would mean that glossolalia no longer had to be explained entirely in terms of the individual's own past experiences. It would allow for the possibility, as Lombard (1910) had suggested, that the unknown tongue of glossolalia could facilitate personality integration because it tapped the wisdom of the race, which was resident in the collective unconscious.

There are only two references to glossolalia in Jung's later writings. The first was in an article, "A Psychological Approach to the Trinity," written in 1948. He refers to glossolalia as an example of unconscious processes at work:

But the more the unconscious is split off [meaning not accepted], the more formidable the shape in which it appears to the conscious mind—if not in divine form, then in the more unfavorable form of obsessions and outbursts of affect. (1948/1958, p. 163)

In a footnote, he noted that the guidelines for ascertaining demon possession in the Roman Catholic Church included "speaking fluently in unknown tongues or understanding those who speak them" (p. 163*n*). Kelsey (1964) elaborated on this comment by suggesting that

. . . the more inhibited and out of touch with the unconscious, the more likely a person is to be a candidate for tongues, which is undoubtedly preferable to most neurotic forms of behaviors as a resolution of tension and inhibitions. (p. 199)

The second reference to glossolalia was a footnote to another article, "Transformation Symbolism in the Mass" (1940/1958). Here, Jung suggested that the cross was one of the prime symbols of order. In the article proper, Jung stated, "In the domain of psychological processes, it [the cross] functions as an organizing centre and in states of psychic disorder . . . it appears as a mandala divided into four. No doubt this was a frequent phenomenon in early Christian times and not only in Gnostic circles" (p. 284). In a footnote, Jung suggested that speaking in tongues was an example of the psychic disorder to which he referred as a frequent occurrence in the early church. Kelsey (1964) commented that Jung probably believed that glossolalia could be a positive preparation for personality integration. He quoted a letter from Jung dated 1955, in which Jung summarized his thinking about glossolalia:

Speaking with tongues (glossolalia) is observed in cases of ekstasis (= *abaissement du niveau mental,* predominance of the unconscious). It is probable that the strangeness of the unconscious contents not yet integrated in consciousness demands an equally strange language. As it does demand strange pictures of an unheard of character, it is also a traditional expectation that the spiritual demonic inspiration manifests itself either in hieratic or otherwise incomprehensible language. That is also the reason why primitives and civilized people still use archaic forms of language at ritual occasions (Sanskrit in India, old Coptic in the Coptic church, old Slavonic in the Greek-Orthodox church, Latin in the Catholic church and the mediaeval German or English in the Protestant church). There are case-reports about mediums that spoke foreign languages which were unknown to them in their waking state. Theodore Flournoy in Geneva has reported about such a case in which he showed that it was [a] matter of cryptomnestic Sanskrit the medium had picked up in a Sanskrit grammar whose existence nobody was aware of. It is exceedingly difficult to establish the authenticity of these cases on account of cryptomnesia. (Cited in Kelsey, 1964, p. 197)

It may well be that Kelsey has been more enthusiastic about the integrative function of glossolalia than Jung himself would have been. Never-

theless, there is some warrant in Jung's writings for making these infer-
ences, as subsequent writers have done.

Several scholars have utilized Jungian concepts in their study of glossolalia. Among them, the South African psychiatrist Vivier interpreted
glossolalia in terms of a religious dynamism and original religious experience—both Jungian ideas.

In his study of the archetypes (or basic components) of the collective
unconscious, Jung suggested that the religious function of humans was
just as important as the instincts of sexuality and aggression. This religious dynamism implied an awareness and even worship of dynamic
factors conceived as powers, spirits, demons, gods, laws, and ideals. Further, Jung proposed that there existed an original religious experience of
the unconscious that institutional forms of religion have channeled into
dogma, creed, and ritual.

Vivier concluded that glossolalia was related to these two ideas. He suggested that glossolalia was a healthy attempt to reunite persons with their
original religious experience and that there was great potential for it to
do good in the person. In summarizing his research, Vivier (1968) wrote:

> It would appear that glossolalia, as practised in its religious context, is
> manifested in normal, non-neurotic persons. It can serve a cathartic purpose.
> In a case which Jung would describe as an automatism arising from the
> subliminal or marginal consciousness, though not strong enough to change
> the well-knit ego complexes, we find that glossolalia, as described here, brings
> about a change in the person and a significant change in the ego complex.
>
> The change tends toward the more mature and tends, furthermore, to add
> quality and enrichment of feeling and depth of meaningfulness. (pp. 172–173)
>
> In other words, the practice of glossolalia in the religious context appears to
> relate to the impact of the religious dynamism or the original religious
> experience. Glossolalia appears to bridge the gulf of time and reinstate an
> original religious experience which has become lost with the curtailment of
> this type of worship in orthodox religious circles. (p. 174)

Thus, Vivier, using Jungian theory, gave a rationale (1) for asserting
the authenticity of speaking in tongues as well as (2) for explaining the
dynamics underlying the process whereby glossolalia could be a factor in
personality growth and development. Vivier found evidence for concluding that there was some change in the direction of personality integration among those who spoke in tongues.

Lovekin (1962) utilized Jungian concepts in his master's thesis. He
strongly affirmed the Jungian understanding that glossolalia was normal
and constructive:

> If the Jungian approach to the collective unconscious is followed, however,
> it can be accepted that a numinous, supra-personal quality does enter the life
> of one who speaks in tongues. This phenomenon is not, therefore, pathologi-
> cal nor infantile. Instead, it can relate the conscious mind to the ground of its
> existence in the collective unconscious. It can free the conscious mind from

its extreme rationalism. It can allow the emotional life of the psyche not only a means of expression but also a method of nurture. Speaking with tongues can be a most concrete means of expressing joy and praise to God. It is a genuine witness to the presence of the Holy Spirit in one's life. Speaking with tongues is one evidence of the Spirit of God working in the unconscious and bringing one to a new wholeness, a new integration of the total psyche, a process which the Church has traditionally called sanctification. (1962, p. 129)

Here we have a logical extension of Jung's ideas and an enthusiastic affirmation of the experience as being *not* pathological but probably normative and recommended for every person. It is to be noted in passing that although Lovekin (1962) thought that glossolalia was truly an unknown, but real, language that emerged out of the collective unconscious, it is not necessary to affirm this in order to assert the reality of this dimension of consciousness. Instead, one could propose that the content of glossolalic verbiage was inconsequential and but an indication that the depth of one's personality was being touched. Thus, the force, but not the substance, of the experience would be important.

Morton Kelsey has been the most prominent scholar to study glossolalia within a Jungian framework. Kelsey has been a pastor, a theologian, and a Jungian therapist. Although he did not speak in tongues, he understood the experience as a result of his study of Jungian theory. He interpreted the autobiographical accounts of seven of his parishioners in these terms (1964). In a balanced manner, he presented both the positive and negative aspects of the experience while affirming the reality of the religious dimension of the collective unconscious that broke through in glossolalia:

Speaking in tongues is a *rite d'entrée* to the deepest levels of the psyche. It is an initiation rite in the deepest and truest meaning of that word. But since it gives no more than entrance, its value lies not so much in what it is, as in what it brings and what results from it. (p. 231)

Here we see a new facet of interpretation. Kelsey is suggesting that the value of the experience lies not so much in the glossolalia itself but in the person's awareness of a new-found depth to the personality. Thus, the value is in what happens after the speaking in tongues.

It is interesting to note that Kelsey believed, along with Lovekin, that glossolalia was a real language:

If the Jungian idea of the collective unconscious is accepted, speaking in tongues makes real sense, as a breakthrough into consciousness of a deep level of the collective unconscious similar to the dream. Linguistic patterns belonging to the past, to some other part of the present, or to some other level of being take possession of the individual and are expressed by him. (p. 216–217)

It is difficult to know from this quote whether Kelsey is saying anything more than, "glossolalia has personal meaning." If so, he is saying no more than Pfister and some of the other psychoanalytic scholars said. However, if he is implying that there is a universal language imbedded in the collective unconscious that emerges at the times persons speak in tongues, then a further assertion is being made. Needless to say, the question of whether glossolalia is a language or not was an addendum to Jungian theory. It has been studied more thoroughly by linguistic scholars whose work was reported earlier in this volume.

In summary, Jungian theory has provided the basis for a positive understanding of glossolalia. Although some Jungian scholars have considered the experience regressive, none of them has portrayed it as infantile or pathological. The experience has been understood as signifying a breakthrough of the deep levels of personality into consciousness, which can have a positive effect on personality growth.

EGO PSYCHOLOGY AND GLOSSOLALIA

Two facets of ego psychology have been important for the study of glossolalia, namely, ego autonomy and ego regression. In regard to the former, Heinz Hartmann departed from the classical psychoanalytic understanding of the ego as a product of the conflict between the impulses of the id and the prohibitions of the superego. Hartmann (1939/1958, 1964) suggested that not all ego functions had to be the result of unconscious conflicts and wishes. The ego, he stated, relates or adapts to reality for its own sake in addition to using reality to resolve its conflicted wishes. Thus, there are spheres of the ego that are autonomous or "conflict free." This concept made it possible for behavior to be viewed either from a perspective of conflict reduction or from a perspective of adaptation without conflict. It, thus, became possible to think of glossolalia as not necessarily pathological or conflict laden.

The second construct by which the ego psychologists have reinterpreted clasical Freudianism is that of ego regression. Early precursors of this theory have already been noted in this chapter. Psychoanalysis had said that regression to earlier stages of adjustment occurred when the ego was overwhelmed by reality. Thus, there was ego loss in the sense that the ego became powerless. Ernest Kris, an analyst at the Yale University School of Medicine, concluded, however, that this was not always true. He suggested, "regression not only occurs during conditions of ego weakness—in sleep, in falling asleep, in fantasy, in intoxication and in psychotic processes—but also during many types of productive processes" (1950/1951, p. 487). Herein lies the possibility that such experiences as glossolalia, which appear to be childlike regressions, could be thought of as creative and constructive deviations from normal reality rather than pathological retreats in the face of problems.

Kris contended that the ego could voluntarily withdraw cathexis (interest and investment) from reality and could involve itself in creative pursuits for a time. Later, the ego could return to practical reality and be none the worse for the experience. In fact, the ego could profit from such experiences. Kris (1934/1953) coined the phrase "regression in the service of the ego" to denote this process and applied it to such endeavors as wit, poetry, and art.

However, as Kris and Kaplan (1948/1953) were quick to point out, there are some differences in these processes and the intellectual component should not be ignored. In other words, all regression may not be in the service of the ego:

> But the regression in the case of aesthetic creation . . . is purposive and controlled. The inspired creativity of the artist is as far from the automatic writing under hypnosis as from the machines recently marketed for "composing" popular songs. The process involves a continual interplay between creation and criticism, manifested in the painter's alternation of working on the canvas and stepping back to observe the effect. We may speak here of a *shift in the psychic level,* consisting in the fluctuation of functional regression and control. When regression goes too far, the symbols become private, perhaps unintelligible even to the reflective self; when at the other extreme, control is preponderant, the result is described as cold, mechanical and uninspired. Poetry is, to be sure, related to trance and dream, as aestheticians since Plato have never tired of observing. But it is also related to rigorous and controlled rationality. No account of the aesthetic process can be adequate without giving due weight to the "intellectual" component. (pp. 253–254)

This statement counters any wholesale affirmation of glossolalia as regression in the service of the ego without some consideration of the intellectual or rational component. Against this background, those scholars who have used ego psychology in their study of glossolalia will now be considered.

Alland, an anthropologist at Yale University, was the first investigator to use ego psychology to explain glossolalia. He studied possession (trance experiences) among black Pentecostals from the lower social class. On occasion, these persons would speak in tongues while they were in trance. He concluded that the trances (possession states) he observed were actually forms of hypnosis, which he defined as "a form of regression in the service of the ego in which the transference-dependency relationship is set up between the hypnotist and his subject." (Alland, 1962, p. 209) He postulated that glossolalics perceived themselves in a dependency relationship with the Holy Spirit. He took note of the environmental and cultural conditions that surrounded the event, yet he observed that some people entered into trance more easily than others and that once having occurred in an individual, the experience came again with less effort. Thus, he suggested that possession or trance was learned in a manner similar to many other ego functions.

Therefore, Alland confirmed that religious trance and the glossolalia that accompanied it were learned regressive abilities in the service of the ego. Although he did not specifically say so, it can be assumed that Alland felt that the experience had a positive effect on participants because "it seems reasonable, however, to regard the overall phenomenon of religious trance primarily as a sublimation of a range of frustrated drives which is patterned as a specific aspect of a given cultural vocabulary" (1962, p. 210). It is noteworthy, in this case, that Alland, although perceiving the experience to be in the service of the ego, did not see it as conflict free. "Sublimation of frustrated drives" is indicative of a constructive resolution of conflict.

In 1966, Ludwig, a psychiatrist, summarized the data on altered states of consciousness, among which he included religious trances and glossolalia. He concluded:

> In some instances the psychological regression found in ASCs [altered states of consciousness] will be proven to be atavistic and harmful to the individual or society, while in other instances the regression will be "in the service of the ego" and enable man (sic) to transcend the bounds of logic and formality or express repressed needs and desires in a socially sanctioned and constructive way. (p. 231)

Espousing the negative point of view, two pastoral theologians, Lapsley and Simpson (1964a, 1964b), applied ego psychological theory to their study of religious persons who began to speak in tongues while members in mainline or independent churches. These are referred to as neo-Pentecostals in contrast to classical Pentecostals, who are members of churches that have included glossolalia in their worship since the early part of this century. Although, in their reports of neo-Pentecostal worship, they did not note that they observed any cases of trance, such as Alland described among classical Pentecostals, they, nevertheless, interpreted glossolalia as a psychomotor automatism that "appears to be like trance states, somnabulism, mediumship, and automatic writing" (1964a, p. 50). They concluded that glossolalia was a dissociative phenomenon found in persons with a truncated personality development.

Their interpretation of speaking in tongues, although within the ego psychological perspective, perceived the ego as defending itself from onslaught rather than as adapting itself creatively to reality (cf. Alland, 1961). They stated:

> Glossolalia is understood to be regression "in the service of the ego," to use Hartmann's phrase. That is, a regression controlled by the ego and for the purpose of maintaining personality, rather than a disintegration of personality. It is a genuine escape from inner conflict, but . . . of itself it does not bring a further permanent integration of personality, which would usually require insight into the roots of the conflict. (Lapsley & Simpson, 1964a, p. 20)

Thus, for these authors, the main function of such regressive acts as glossolalia is conflict reduction. Although they perceived glossolalia to be helpful in personality integration, its effects were short-lived. True change in personality had to involve insight. Thus, the need for the intellect to be present was reaffirmed.

In regard to the conflicts they felt underlay speaking in tongues, Lapsley and Simpson (1964b) judged the glossolalic to have a special set of issues with which he/she was concerned. They hypothesized that since the glossolalic had "an unconscious attachment to parental figures characterized by strong feelings of both love and hate, neither of which can the individual express directly, thus producing tension, the glossolalia may be viewed as an indirect, though powerful, expression of primitive love toward the parent" (p. 19). This explained why some people spoke in tongues and others did not. It also presented a picture in which the glossolalic person could be construed as emotionally disturbed.

The reason the glossolalist experiences a feeling of great joy and release, Lapsley and Simpson (1946) hypothesized, was that the regression was to a level where the person could express his/her feelings without any ambivalence. In the act, there was a temporary undoing of the tangle of love and hate toward the parents. In an hysterical manner, negative feelings were projected onto the devil and positive feelings were expressed through speaking in tongues. Although this was not a resolution of the conflict, it did afford temporary relief, as many other neurotic symptoms might do.

Yet another theorist who utilized the concept of regression was E. Mansel Pattison, a psychiatrist who has studied glossolalia since the middle of the century. In a review of the literature written in 1968, Pattison interpreted the experience similarly to the ego psychologists, even though he concluded that sociocultural variables were more important than psychological ones. He compared glossolalia in possession states, as well as in more dramatic types of worship, with the glossolalia of middle-class persons. He concluded that there was little evidence of regression in middle-class persons who used glossolalia. He did not deny that regression occurred in some of the other types of glossolalia. He suggested, ". . . glossolalia may be a focal thought-speech regression that is highly restricted to specific ego functions" (1968, p. 84).

Pattison's understanding of the dynamic process included a distinction between inner and external speech. Inner speech was, to him, like thinking to oneself. Glossolalia was on the borderline between this thinking to oneself and outer expression of one's thoughts in words. Thus, he defined speaking in tongues as "a form of learned, organized vocal behavior . . . arising in internal cognition and then being externalized in audible speech" (1968, p. 81). Pattison further postulated, along with Freud, that all speech was a means of discharging affect or impulses. Thus, in glossolalia ". . . the 'feeling tone' part of inner speech is transposed onto the automatic, externalized phonemic sequences, thereby allowing an individual to express feeling and emotion without revealing their manifest content" (1969, p. 143). Thus, Pattison, like Lapsley and Simpson, saw the experience as assisting the ego in managing intrapsychic conflict. The position of all three is more like a classic psychoanalytic than an ego psychological position in this regard.

Another interesting facet of Pattison's thinking was the distinction he made between "playful" and "serious" glossolalia. In part, this depicted the contrast noted above between the classical Pentecostals and the neo-Pentecostals. Restating this distinction (noted as early as 1947 by Bobon), Pattison concluded, after a study of the speech productions of five subjects, that two of them demonstrated this "playful" quality, ". . . one giggling and laughing while speaking in her tongue, the other clowning with arms outstretched in a christ-like fashion. In both of these samples of glossolalia, the individuals seemed absorbed in their own utterances and seemed to be taking some delight from listening to themselves" (1968, p. 81).

Pattison suggested that in both "playful" and in "serious" glossolalia, there was tension reduction and emotional discharge. However, in "playful" glossolalia, the effect of the experience was simple diversion or distraction, whereas in "serious" glossolalia, the effect was defensive, in the sense that conflicted impulses were released and controlled thereby.

He found evidence for this distinction in a study of "meaningless" speech devised by Freida Goldman-Eisler (1958). Nonlinguistic aspects of speech, such as pauses, breathing rates, intonations, and so on, were related to the information content of words that followed. For example, planning and selection were associated with pausing, whereas continuous and rapid vocalization was the result of practice and occurred in sequences where the words were well learned. Furthermore, breath rate reflected variations in excitement, in the sense that a low rate indicated inhibition and control. Pattison concluded that "playful" glossolalia was "characterized by rapid, fluent speech devoid of hesitation pauses and with an increase of breath rate and an increased syllable output per breath," whereas "serious" glossolalia was "characterized by a slower rate of speech with numerous hesitation pauses, a lower breath rate and a reduced number of syllables per breath" (1968, p. 79).

More important for the question of differences among those who speak in tongues, Pattison concluded:

> The "playful" category of glossolalia is produced volitionally. It is characterized by rapid, fluent vocalizations of utterances, devoid of hesitation pauses and rendered in a monotonous or sing-song style. The breathing rate is regular and the individual usually appears relaxed and at ease.
>
> At the other end of the continuum is the "serious" category. . . . Here, the intonation pattern imposed on the automatic speech appears to reflect the strong emotional feelings of the subject. Often there are feelings toward others present . . . the vocalizations are not rapid, hesitation pauses are present and the intonation pattern is more variable and dramatic." (1968, p. 81)

This introduces yet another factor into the issues of regression, namely, conscious control. Pattison seems to suggest that all glossolalia involves regression and expression of pent-up thoughts or feelings but that in some glossolalia, the person consciously instigates and controls the process ("playful" glossolalia), whereas in others, it happens automatically and unintentionally ("serious" glossolalia). His contention is that the distinction can be verified by nonlanguage characteristics of the event. Studies attempting to demonstrate these differences have not conclusively verified this distinction but, as will be seen in research into trance states in chapter 6, there have been numerous methodological weaknesses that future research may avoid and, thus, validate Pattison's claims. Furthermore, it may be that his model is correct, even though such indices as pauses, breath rate, and intonational patterns may not reveal it.

Yet another pair of researchers, Kildahl and Qualben, have also incorporated ego psychology into their understanding of glossolalia. Their 1971 report of a project supported by the Behavioral Sciences Research Branch of the National Institute of Mental Health became the basis for a book written by Kildahl (1972). They compared two groups of glossolalics and nonglossolalics from mainline Protestant churches. These two groups of volunteers were matched for age, sex, marital status, education, and their participation in religious activities. Qualben, a psychiatrist, interviewed each of the volunteers; Kildahl, a psychologist, assessed the volunteers by means of psychological tests (i.e., the Rorschach inkblot test, the Draw-a-Person test, the Thematic Apperception Test [TAT], and the Minnesota Multiphasic Personality Inventory [MMPI]). Although the groups were originally equal in size, it was later discovered that six of the nonglossolalics had briefly spoken in tongues at an earlier time, and that one of them had actually practiced speaking in tongues regularly but had stopped. Thus, the two groups were finally made up of twenty-six glossolalics and only thirteen nonglossolalics.

Kildahl and Qualben (1971) had hypothesized that "regression in the service of the ego" ought to mean that the glossolalics would report gains in their mental health after the experience because the process would result in a release from tension and conflict. Some evidence supporting this hypothesis was found on the Depression scale of the MMPI, which was significantly lower for the glossolalic than for the nonglossolalic group. This difference was also observed on a one-year follow-up study. Interview data further supported their conclusion that the glossolalics had a greater overall sense of well-being than did the nonglossolalics. This suggested that the nonglossolalics did not possess the same channel for release that the glossolalics did and, therefore, remained tenser and more conflicted.

Second, Kildahl and Qualben suggested that there were innate differences among persons that predetermined who would and who would not become glossolalic. They proposed that these differences were similar to those observed in subjects for hypnosis. Because they found that almost all of the glossolalics initially spoke in tongues in a group situation, they hypothesized that these persons would be more submissive, suggestible, and dependent on authority figures than the nonglossolalics. In an analysis of autonomy—based on ratings of the TAT, utilizing the McKenzie Mental Health scale—Kildahl and Qualben found that the glossolalics were, indeed, less autonomous than the nonglossolalics. Combining these data with interview ratings, they concluded that the glossolalics tended toward dependency in relating to authority figures. Two statements by Kildahl summarize these findings:

> Our study has produced conclusive evidence that the benefits reported by tongue-speakers, which are subjectively real and continuous, are dependent upon acceptance by the leader and other members of the group rather than the actual experience of saying the sounds. (1972, p. 55)

> The deep subordination to an authority figure required for learning to speak in tongues involves a type of speech regression. The ego is partially abandoned; that is, the ego ceases its conscious direction of speech. Subordination also involves emotional regression; without it there cannot be the unconscious, automatic and fluent selection of audible syllables which constitutes glossolalia. (1972, p. 53)

Although Kildahl and Qualben's conclusions may be valid, there is serious question as to whether they are warranted by their data. The great weight of evidence from their tests and interviews seem to show no differences between the groups, and it is questionable whether such strong statements about the phenomenon are justified. They seemed to have approached their research with a negative bias toward glossolalics and to have found evidence to confirm their intuition that becoming glossolalic implied weak ego strength. Of course, this is not new and is supported by other theorists, such as Lapsley and Simpson (1964a, 1964b). However, it does reflect a lack of acquaintance with, or affinity for, conflict-free functions of the ego or for Pattison's (1968, 1969) theorizing, which was published just prior to Kildahl and Qualben's investigations.

The most recent and thorough treatment of glossolalia from an ego psychological perspective has been that of Brende and Rinsley (1979), two psychiatrists at the Menninger Foundation. They utilize ideas about the separation-individuation phase of ego development during which the infant begins to understand himself/herself as a distinct person separate from the mother. Although, in most cases, this process proceeds normally and the infant comes to understand the mother as an "object" apart from himself/herself, in some cases, there are problems. Through brain wave research and speech analysis Brende and Rinsley have concluded that these problems occur during the last half of the first year of life. This results, according to Kernberg (1975)—on whom Brende and Rinsley (1979) depend for their thinking—in an adult who has difficulty differentiating himself/herself clearly from others. These persons are known as borderline personalities and reflect "significant impairment of self-identity, of the capacity to develop and maintain meaningful object relations, of the sense of reality and of the ability realistically to cope and adapt, accompanied by undue degrees of overt and covert aggression (hostility) and depression" (Brende and Rinsley, 1979, p. 166). Glossolalics, they concluded, represent this type of person.

In an earlier study, Brende (1974) reported on four inpatient adolescents who spoke in tongues after exposure by peers to a Pentecostal movement known as "The Way." After treatment, all four ceased to be glossolalic. In their 1979 article, Brende and Rinsley recounted the experience of Lisa, a 16-year-old girl who was the most disturbed of the four:

> Her glossolalia served her as a form of regressive, affective and object-seeking communication representative of the "baby talk" which conveys emotion, expresses need, and serves to define and test the early self-object boundary in relation to the symbiotic, omnipotent parental (maternal) surrogate [i.e., the hospital]. Her glossolalia and the experiences related to it could also be viewed as examples of regression in the service of the ego . . . which served as a turning point, enabling her to begin, to some extent, to reinitiate emotional growth and the long-arrested process of separation-individuation within the context of a semistructured milieu [i.e., the hospital] which served Lisa as a sort of extended family and with the supportive assistance of a maternal staff member. (pp. 181–182)

Although they later comment that there are glossolalics who harbor no major psychopathology, Brende and Rinsley seem to imply that wherever glossolalia occurs it reflects weakness in the ego and is a constructive attempt to establish control. They contend that the experience of being under the control of God is, in and of itself, constructive because it allows the individual to experience the good part of themselves over against the bad part they at other times experience controlling them.

Brende and Rinsley bridge the ego psychological and the psychoanalytic points of view through their theorizing about the underlying infant-mother problems that provide the foundation for glossolalia, but it is questionable whether the phenomenon they observed in severely disturbed individuals can be compared to the more normal glossolalia of persons outside the hospital.

CONCLUSION

This chapter has considered psychological studies of glossolalia since the turn of the century. Initially, the classical studies of Flournoy (1900/1963) and James (1902/1958) were considered and their influence on the theological works of Lombard, Mosiman, and Shumway were discussed.

James understood the phenomenon to be psychopathological and, thus, set a tone that has persisted through to the most recent studies of Brende and Rinsley (1979). Flournoy, however, was more interested in the developmental stages represented by the regressions—another seminal idea that is still of concern.

Lombard (1910) considered the regressions to have rejuvenating effects, whereas Mosiman (1911) and Shumway (1919) found no positive value to the experience. This is another issue that is still being debated.

All of these early theorists suggested that glossolalia came from the subliminal parts of the mind—a theme that has persisted in spite of the fact that subliminal has given way to unconscious and subconscious designations. Further, Lombard's attempts to compare glossolalia to the language of children and Mosiman's and Shumway's relating the experience to hypnosis have continued to attract the attention of researchers.

After reviewing the early studies, this chapter considered subsequent psychological studies as they reflected the Freudian (psychoanalytic), the Jungian, and the ego psychological models of psychodynamics.

The psychoanalytic model understands glossolalia to be a regression to infantile levels of narcissism in which unconscious conflicts or complexes are allowed release through speech that evidences no conscious control or understanding. From this point of view, the experience of speaking in tongues is psychopathological.

The Jungian (sometimes called analytic) model understands glossolalia as a manifestation of the collective unconscious, which is the repository of the wisdom of the race. As such, speaking in tongues could mean that a universal language is being spoken or simply indicate that a deep part of the personality is being tapped. Glossolalia, from this point of view, can be preparatory to personal integration.

The ego psychology model understands glossolalia to be "regression in the service of the ego." Although, this idea was initially related to a conflict-free understanding, later theorists have allowed for both conflictual and nonconflictual regression. The distinction between "serious" and "playful" glossolalia noted by Pattison (1968) reflects this dual possibility. Nevertheless, from this point of view, speaking in tongues always suggests that the ego is doing something either to gain release from tension or to solve its problems. This allows for both a positive and a negative evaluation of the experience by these theorists.

As is seen in the chapters that follow, these theorists have posed the problems to which much attention has been paid by subsequent researchers who have considered the issues in somewhat greater detail.

4

Individual Differences

Distinct from the psychological dynamics involved in glossolalia, there is the question of what types of persons become tongue speakers.

There is a difference between *seeking* and *receiving* the gift of speaking in tongues. Not all who seek receive! This fact has often been overlooked. It has been presumed that if one prayed, sought, and waited for the experience, it would come. However, this has not always been the case as the Lovekin and Malony (1977) research clearly demonstrates. Some persons who attended every session of the "Life in the Spirit Seminars" (described in Chapter 5) never did receive the gift of tongues. This surprised the researchers because they presumed that it would be easier than it was for seekers to receive the experience.

This observation was similar to that made by Cutten (1927). He reported that Edward Irving, founder of the Catholic Apostolic Church, sought the gift but never received it. The great desire of his life was to have the church become more spiritual. He longed for an outpouring of the spirit of God and was stirred by the reports of tongue speaking in a Scottish invalid. Although he discouraged the use of tongues in public worship (he actually forbade it), it soon got out of hand and glossolalia became the mark of the new spirituality. Nevertheless, Irving himself never spoke in tongues, although he led worship services in which it became the norm and was surrounded by those he had encouraged to become glossolalic.

Cutten (1927, p. 128) also reported that Rev. A. E. Sweet prayed for twelve years before he had an experience in which he spoke in tongues. He frequently spent until five o'clock in the morning emptying his mind of thoughts and striving for humility, but the gift of tongues eluded him for over a dozen years.

These are but a few examples among many that could be noted. They illustrate the importance of individual differences among those who desire to become glossolalic. As we note later, there is evidence that there are personality traits that, in part, determine who becomes glossolalic and who does not, even when everyone in a group is desirous of the experience (Lovekin & Malony, 1977).

It should be said again that such a study of differences is a separate issue from that of whether glossolalia implies psychopathology, which will be considered in Chapter 5. The heterogeneity to be reported here belongs to individuality that is well within the normal range. Such individuality does not involve even a tendency toward abnormality.

The ascription to certain individuals of a predisposition to glossolalia does not entail an implicit bias against certain kinds of background or certain types of persons. Most deprivation theories of religion and the specific conclusion that classical Pentecostalism is the religion of the dispossessed (Niebuhr, 1929) do reflect such a bias, however, and the same unspoken bias has characterized research on the northern religion of southern immigrants and the general evaluation of the religion of the poor. Such social misfit hypotheses are not integral to the descriptions in this chapter of differences among people. These descriptions are offered without prejudgment in these matters.

Finally, these accounts of persons who do and who do not become glossolalic does not include a discussion of differences in environment. The environmental surroundings in which the experience occurs is discussed later. The issues to which this chapter attends are those of personality, that is, the traits, the structure, the makeup, and the background that accompany speaking tongues.

Five aspects of these personal differences are considered here. They are mental status, life situation, family background, development of the ability to speak in tongues, and personality traits that characterize tongue speakers.

MENTAL STATUS

Intellect, Education, Excitability

Cutten (1927) proposed an interesting fivefold model for the personal background of glossolalics: excitability, inferior intellect, illiteracy, suggestion, and expectancy. Although these conclusions were not based on empirical comparisons, Cutten reasoned that the first three were inherent qualities within individuals and that the last two depicted the social situation. The power of suggestion and group expectancy could be thought of as necessary environmental conditions that provide the setting but that are not sufficient to provoke glossolalia, except in persons whose nervous systems are hyperexcitable, whose intelligence is below average, and who are uneducated. These environmental variables are discussed later. The focus here is on those physiological and intellectual background variables that Cutten denotes in his first three factors.

Cutten's (1927) rationale was this: the process of evolution is one in which the brain becomes more convoluted and complex as one ascends the phylogenetic ladder. In human beings, thinking and rationality are comparatively late developments in cranial development. Many persons have not developed these capacities to the degree that they can consistently channel emotional excitement into thoughtful speech. Thus, because of immaturity in the growth of the nervous system as well as underdeveloped thinking capacity, these persons find it difficult to handle much excitement and, therefore, often speak in a confused manner. Their energy discharge is misdirected and undercontrolled. They are both nervous and excitable. Lower intelligence is the label often applied to those who cannot express themselves adequately in words. When lack of education or trained intellect is added to this, glossolalia becomes likely. "Persons of high ability, whose nervous energy would more easily flow into channels of thought, have sought the gift in vain" (Cutten, 1927, p. 6). Glossolalia thereby becomes an avenue for emotional discharge.

Laffal (1967) has suggested that such discharge presumes psychic conflict. He states that glossolalia is probably the clearest example of the "discharge function of language," but he adds that these utterances "serve the purpose of discharging the psychic energy associated with *wishes and conflicts*" (p. 88; emphasis added). Lapsley and Simpson (1964b) earlier had reached the same conclusion. More recently, C. G. Williams (1981) expressed this position thus: ". . . the speaker derives the benefit of discharge while avoiding the guilt of despair which could be generated by specific identification of his conflicts" (p. 155).

However, it is important to note that Cutten (1927) did *not* presuppose such a conflict base for his theory. He simply presumed cerebral immaturity without assuming psychodynamic disturbance. Samarin (1972c) was quite correct in criticizing Laffal (1967) for identifying religious glossolalia with schizophrenic speech because the overt motivation for the two is obviously quite different and the presumption of inevitable pathology among tongue speakers is erroneous (Malony, Zwaanstraa, & Ramsey, 1972). Cutten's hypothesis was concerned more with immature channels for energy discharge owing to emotional excitement than with either automatic or intentional regression of the ego to a more primitive problem-solving mode (note Deikman, 1966a, Lapsley & Simpson, 1946b). E. T. Clark (1937/1949) states the issue most specifically by arguing that tongue speakers are "nearly always the ignorant, in whom the lower brain centres and spinal ganglia are relatively strong and the rational and volitional powers residing in the higher centres of the cortex are relatively weak" (p. 97). The phenomenon is due to physiological rather than psychodynamic causes. Sargant (1949) concluded that the effect of the environmental suggestion in religious experience is determined by the type of nervous system and the constitutional stability of the individuals who are present.

Few studies have evaluated these contentions that glossolalics are less intelligent and less educated than nonglossolalics. Smith (1977) compared conventional and unconventional glossolalic and nonglossolalic

groups using the Shipley Institute of Living scale. Although he had predicted no differences among the groups, he found that nonglossolalics
were significantly more intelligent than glossolalics (112.3 compared to
107.3 IQs, respectively, which were determined by combining verbal and
abstract scores). Smith further concluded that nonglossolalics were more
educated and of higher socioeconomic status (SES) than glossolalics. It
should be noted, however, that although he asked the participants in his
study "How many years of school have you completed?", this data was
combined with occupational level in computing socioeconomic level and
was not reported separately. The inference about education was based on
the verbal IQ score of the Shipley scale, a vocabulary test presumed to
correlate highly with achieved knowledge. This method confuses achievement with ability to a moderate degree. Nevertheless, although the
methods used in this study are somewhat inexact, the results do lend
some support to Cutten's (1927) thesis about ability and literacy among
speakers in tongues. In contrast, Bradfield (1979) found neo-Pentecostals
(a contemporary group who typically speak in tongues) to be more highly
educated than the general population.

The issue of hyperexcitability has, also, not been investigated widely,
although such related issues as suggestibility have been studied (Kildahl,
1972). However, in spite of the fact that Kildahl called for controlled
research using such measures as the Harvard Group Scale of Hypnotic
Suggestibility, his own conclusion that glossolalics were "more suggestible,
submissive, and dependent" than nonglossolalics was based on content
analysis of Thematic Apperception Test (TAT) stories. This procedure
emphasized the relationship of tongue speakers to leaders and was only
an indirect measure of cerebral excitability, which was Cutten's (1927)
concern. In a somewhat related study among college students, it was
found that the experience of having been "saved" by means of transforming experience was associated with high suggestibility, as assessed
by the aforementioned Harvard scale, whereas low suggestibility was
not (Gibbons & De Jarnette, 1972). It is not known whether these students spoke in tongues or not. However, this conclusion may have implications for assuming that glossolalics, like those who have vital religious
experiences, have nervous systems that are more sensitive and excitable
than the average.

Smith's (1977) research included assessments of "energy discharge" and
"susceptibility to emotional upheaval" based on answers to the Minnesota Multiphasic Personality Inventory (MMPI). Again, although these
self-reports are only indirect measures of cerebral sensitivity, the findings
that glossolalics are higher than nonglossolalics on "energy discharge"
but not on "susceptibility to emotional upheaval" suggest that Cutten's
(1927) hypothesis is problematical. "Emotional discharge" (measured by
the Mania scale of the MMPI) may be no more than a behavioral tendency to be verbally expressive and expansive rather than an indication
that one person is more excitable than another. However, it is question-

able whether the participants' "susceptibility to emotional discharge" was truly measured because the method of computing it was to average all of the MMPI scale scores!

In sum, hyperexcitability is a postulate that sounds reasonable, but it has yet to be validated through direct measures. Nevertheless, as La Barre (1962) suggested, it may be one of those personal characteristics that is distributed normally in the general population and that quite possibly is associated with a tendency toward glossolalic experience.

LIFE SITUATION

Later, the study of Bradfield (1979) on neo-Pentecostalism is reviewed in detail. Among the five types of deprivation considered in that research are psychic (the lack of a purposeful system around which to live one's life), ethical (a sense that a conflict exists between one's values and those of the society at large, and organismic (the perception that one is at a mental or physical disadvantage). Bradfield concludes that although neo-Pentecostals did not feel deprived in the economic or social spheres, they tended to experience psychic, ethical and organismic deprivation prior to becoming glossolalic. It would seem that there is a tendency for those who become spirit filled and who join the Full Gospel Businessmen's Fellowship International (FGBMFI) (studied in Bradfield's, 1979, investigation) to be experiencing a loss of control over life, even in the midst of achievement and success. As Dr. Bob Jones, an educational psychologist and politician has said:

> I thought I had everything. I was in my third term in the legislature, had a lovely wife, four handsome sons, a good business, and prestige in the community. I was raised in a Christian home, had been active in the Church, and thought I possessed everything life had to offer.
>
> What a fool I was! I didn't realize what I'd been missing all of those years until June, 1971, when I received the baptism of the Holy Spirit. (cited in Bradfield, 1979, pp. 42–43)

About 90% of Bradfield's respondents reported that they had received a new sense of purpose and meaning in their lives. About 25% said they had sought the Holy Spirit as a result of some need for physical or emotional healing in themselves or others. This same conclusion had been reached earlier by Kildahl (1972) who reported that "more than 85% of the tongue speakers had experienced a clearly defined anxiety crisis preceding their speaking in tongues" (p. 57). Anxiety crisis was defined by Kildahl in a similar manner to Bradfield's deprivation, namely, problems in health, marriage, values, or finance.

Similar conclusions were also reached by Hofman (1975/1976) in a study of nineteen conversion experiences among Catholics who were members of a community that practiced, among other spiritual gifts, tongue speaking. Using Salzman's (1953) distinction between progressive and regressive types of conversion, Hofman found that although all adherents reported significant life changes and problem resolutions, those who had experienced progressive (maturational) types of conversion exhibited a higher level of social functioning than those categorized as having had mixed (both maturational and defensive) types of conversion. Both conversion types, however, had been seeking answers to life problems prior to becoming spirit filled. The experience, like that of persons in Bradfield's (1979) sample, was preceded by the sense of a perceived loss of control in life.

In support of this conclusion Vivier (1960) found that 50% of glossolalics in his sample had experienced problems of adjustment earlier in life. Thus, according to him, glossolalics brought to the experience a need for integration and healing. Further, Kildahl (1972, p. 58) reported that among the subjects in his study, 30% of those who did not speak in tongues and 85% of those who did speak in tongues had experienced a "clearly defined anxiety crisis." However, a later survey in Australia (Stanley, Bartlett, & Moyle, 1978) reported only 25% of glossolalics had gone through such emotional turmoil.

Although a distinction between classical and neo-Pentecostalism should be kept in mind when considering the conclusions that glossolalics have a predisposition toward loss of meaning, values, and health, this mental set is not unlike that reported by the historians of the Holiness movement (cf. Anderson, 1979; Synan, 1971; C. G. Williams, 1981). These glossolalics felt that the rapid social change going on about them and the growing liberalism of the mainline churches left them without a framework of meaning for their lives. These same conditions typified the lives of those involved in the Pentecostal revival at the turn of the century.

Thus, it might be said that the second background variable characterizing glossolalics is an inclination to be seeking, implicitly or explicitly, a resolution to life's problems, chiefly those related to meaning, health, and ethics.

FAMILY BACKGROUND

As might be expected, denominational and family background are definite predetermining factors in the likelihood that one will speak in tongues. The difference between classical and neo-Pentecostal glossolalia is based on the expectancy, or lack of it, that one will speak in tongues. As the historians of the movement have noted, tongues became not only the sign of the second blessing of the Spirit (sanctification), but a sign of conversion as well. Thus, it is not surprising that Zwaanstra and Malony (1970) found that over 65% of a sample of Assembly of God (classical Pentecostals) youth were glossolalic by age 16. The average age at which this group began to speak in tongues was 13.5 years, a typical time of conversion for young adolescents. The likelihood that they were glossolalic was highly related to their church participation, their having had a conversion experience, and the church attendance of their parents.

In neo-Pentecostal settings, the opposite would quite likely have been the case. Most mainline Protestant churches and families out of which these persons come are not glossolalic. Therefore, the expectancy inherent in the social situation would be less, and one might expect that *individual* determinants would predominate over the environmental precursors among those who did engage in this practice. It was on this basis that Pavelsky, Hart, and Malony (1975) defined a model that included group expectancy as the focal issue in predicting who would and who would not show evidence of psychopathology among glossolalics. It was predicted that those glossolalics who came out of church and family situations where speaking in tongues was not expected would be more likely to show psychophysiological changes (i.e., psychopathology) during the experience than those who were part of families and churches where it was the norm. Although the research did not support this hypothesis, the suggestion that environmental background predisposes many in traditional Pentecostal churches toward tongue speaking was validated.

Nevertheless, an interesting study by Ramsey and Malony (1971) found, among a sample of Assembly of God youth—where speaking in tongues would be expected—that although the *incidence* of glossolalia was highly correlated with membership in the church, *frequency* of the experience was more likely to be associated with personal religiosity than with either parental glossolalia or parental religiosity. This relationship between greater frequency and personal religiosity was further confirmed by a tendency toward a more intrinsic orientation to religion among this group. They tended to see religion as meeting individual rather than status needs more than did infrequent glossolalics. These religious dimensions will be discussed in more detail later in this chapter.

In a related study of the susceptibility of persons to trance and possession, Swanson (1978) found that firstborn children from larger families that emphasized collective (i.e., group or family) interests, as opposed to the special interests of family members, were most likely to report experience of "receptive trance." Receptive trance was understood as an inclination to become deeply involved in novels, music, movies, plays, and stories on television. This type of absorption, in which persons feel that they are part of what they are observing, is indicative of a tendency toward a passive receptivity to influence that could be related to becoming charismatic.

Swanson also concluded that children reared in larger families that emphasized collective interests were inclined to score higher on tests of hypnotic suggestibility—a finding that further confirmed a relationship between family decision-making patterns and a susceptibility to influence. Even more support for this hypothesis was seen in Swanson's finding that children from families that promoted more reflection (i.e., thinking before one acts) were less inclined to be susceptible to trance. Thus, the weight of Swanson's (1978) research suggests a possible connection between a family's rearing practices and size with the likelihood that one will become glossolalic. This hypothesis has yet to be evaluated on tongue speakers, but it is a very suggestive possibility.

In summary, the evidence that background preconditions for speaking in tongues has been considered. Cerebral excitability, level of intelligence, education, life situations, and family background were noted. Although it should be remembered that many of these studies confuse classical Pentecostalism and neo-Pentecostalism and also involve group comparisons in which persons have not been exposed to the same social situations, there is some evidence that many of these environmental factors play a part in predetermining who will and who will not become glossolalic.

THE ABILITY TO SPEAK IN TONGUES

Several types of development occur in the experience of speaking in tongues. Wolfram (1966), among others, has alluded to at least two distinct stages along a continuum of ability. There is an initiatory stage during which the persons haltingly speak words given to them in an imitative fashion and verbalize gibberish in a haphazard manner. At the other extreme is a habitual stage where the speech comes easily, often intentionally, and has assumed a stereotyped, unique quality that flows on and on. In the Lovekin and Malony (1977) study, for example, only those who developed into "full" tongues (flowing verbalizations that sound somewhat like sentences over a multiweek training program) were considered to be speaking in tongues. Just uttering a few words or phrases in one meeting was not judged to be glossolalia. Thus, the amount of practice in which one engaged since becoming glossolalic is a distinct development factor in assessing this behavior.

Another developmental dimension that influences glossolalia is chronological age. One can take into account both the age at which an individual initially began to speak in tongues and the present age of the tongue-speaking individual. Although no study has yet verified this, it stands to reason that glossolalia would typically be an adolescent experience in classical Pentecostalism and an adult experience in neo-Pentecostalism. In the Malony et al. (1970) study of Assembly of God youth, the average age at which they began to speak in tongues was 13.5 years, in the Bradfield (1979) research on the Full Gospel Businessmen's Fellowship International (FGBMFI) almost all of the participants had become glossolalic after age 25. This is understandable if one recalls that many classical Pentecostals have come to associate such a gift of the Spirit as tongues to be synonymous with conversion. Furthermore, there is some evidence to suggest (C. G. Williams, 1981) that, at least among classical Pentecostal groups, the practice of speaking in tongues follows a curve of acceleration and then a slow dissipation over time, so that older members are less frequently glossolalic than younger members. No comparable data on neo-Pentecostals is available, although the same conclusions might be expected, save that the practice would dissipate at a later age than among the Pentecostals.

Of interest are comments about age made by Bourguignon (1965) regarding Spirit possession in Haiti:

> Typically, first possessions occur among teenagers, although sometimes later. Old people are rarely possessed. It is said that the gods do not wish to tire them. Also, as people acquire more spiritual control over the gods . . . it is said they are more rarely possessed. (p. 49)

Similar processes may occur in glossolalia. Suffice it to say that age of onset and present age are both likely predeterminers of present practice among glossolalics.

A final developmental factor to be considered in tongue speaking is shift in social status after becoming glossolalic. Pattison (1974), for example, distinguished between two groups of classical Pentecostals, namely, those that had and those that had not moved into the middle class. In the first group, he noted little psychopathology, whereas in the latter group, he observed many real-life conflicts with their environment. These persons gained much emotional and psychic release from the practice.

As noted earlier, Pattison distinguished between "playful" and "serious" glossolalia, a difference that his later study seems to authenticate. Playful tongue speaking was compared to expressive speech, such as poets might use to convey light and enjoyable feelings. He states, "This playful quality was observed in several of our subjects—one giggling and laughing while speaking in her tongue, the other clowning with arms outstretched in a christ-like fashion" (1968, p. 81). In this type of glossolalia, persons seem to delight in hearing their own vocalizations. They enjoy words for their own sake. They seem to be relaxed and often engage in the activity of tongue speaking while driving, working, walking, and so on. They have it completely under control and can become glossolalic at will.

In contrast, "serious" glossolalia involves more strong emotional feeling, heavy breathing, less conscious control, more automatic expression, less awareness. For example, Pattison (1968) reports:

> One subject, whose glossolalic speech became pleading and quite serious, made it clear that she was simultaneously wishing to herself that the interviewer might accept glossolalia for himself. In another case the subject reported using her tongue while simultaneously thinking about a very personal and troubling problem. (p. 81)

It would appear that in his 1974 study, Pattison found that those who had not attained middle-class status among the glossolalics were using glossolalia more "seriously" than those who had attained such status.

In sum, there are certain developmental issues that function as predeterminants of glossolalia. These include the stage in the process, amount of practice, age of onset, age at time of observation, social class, religious background, and glossolalic frequency. These are all thought to be influential in determining the type and meaning of the event in an individual's life.

PERSONALITY TRAITS

The next issues to be considered are personality traits. Three types of comparisons are made: glossolalics with nonglossolalics, glossolalics with the general population, and certain glossolalics with other glossolalics.

One of the earliest studies comparing glossolalics to nonglossolalics was that of Vivier (1960) who investigated, in a South African setting, the personalities of those doctrinally opposed to glossolalia (1) with those who believed in glossolalia but did not practice it and (2) with those who engaged in speaking in tongues. Some have criticized Vivier because his samples were all originally from a nonglossolalic congregation, but, in fact, his design controls for environmental differences, which often confound studies in which two groups have not been exposed to the same situation. In this case, a group of persons within the congregation had become tongue speakers, whereas others became unalterably opposed to the practice. Further, another group was open to becoming glossolalic but had not done so up to that time. Yet they all had been given the opportunity to become glossolalic. Thus the differences that were observed could well have been due to different personality traits. Vivier's design strengthens his conclusions. Glossolalics scored higher on neuroticism, self-effacement, and impulsiveness but lower on suggestibility than did nonglossolalics. Although he did not test for it, Vivier further suggested that glossolalics certainly tended to develop intuitive or mystical thought patterns, even if these inclinations were not predispositions toward the experience.

Vivier's study was a doctoral project in South Africa. A similar investigation was conducted in the United States by Kildahl (1972) in collaboration with the psychiatrist Paul Qualben. They assessed twenty pairs of tongue speakers and nontongue speakers in mainline Protestant congregations in two midwestern states and matched for religiosity, sex, marital status, and education. Standardized psychological tests coupled with psychiatric interviews were used to reach the study's conclusions. Although the two groups did not differ in overall mental health and there was no predominant personality type characteristic of glossolalics in the two groups, those who spoke in tongues were found to be more dependent, submissive, and suggestible than those who did not. Further, tongue speakers were found to be less depressed and reported greater feelings of well-being than nontongue speakers. These characteristics persisted in a retest one year later.

It is difficult to know what cultural differences exist between the

Vivier (1960) and the Kildahl (1972) studies because they were conducted on different continents. It is not known whether those in the control groups in Vivier's (1960) study had ever been to a service where they were encouraged to speak in tongues, although one of the control groups believed in the practice but had not had the experience yet. However, among Kildahl's (1972) subjects, it was found that six persons had previously spoken at least a phrase or two in tongues and one person had been a regularly practicing glossolalic, even though at the time of the study none of these subjects was doing so.

If it can be assumed that the groups in the two studies were roughly equivalent, how can it be explained that they found different evidence for suggestibility? The answer, we believe, lies in the different means of assessment that were used. Although each researcher used the TAT, Vivier (1960) did not use this measure to assess suggestibility, instead, he used a self-report rating scale. Kildahl (1972), on the other hand, employed the McKenzie Mental scale for judging the TAT stories told by his subjects. This is probably a more trustworthy index of suggestibility than Vivier's rating scale. Interestingly enough, Vivier reported that his analysis of his participants' TAT stories revealed a tendency to "cling to objects in the environment for emotional support" (Vivier, 1960, p. 382)—a statement that is almost equivalent to what Kildahl (1972) had said.

In a study comparing glossolalics from classical Pentecostal churches (Foursquare and Assembly of God) and nonglossolalics from the Methodist church, Coulson and Johnson (1977) found that those who did not speak in tongues were more *external* in locus of control than those who did speak in tongues. This finding would seem contrary to the above conclusions about submissiveness and suggestibility. Although the constructs are by no means equivalent, the scale used to measure locus of control purports to assess the degree to which one believes that the events of life are the result of one's own behavior and thus under his/her control as opposed to thinking that events are unrelated to what one does and, thus, out of one's control. It would seem plausible that those who were more suggestible would be more likely to affirm the latter (external locus of control) than the former. But this was not the case. On the other hand, these results seem to confirm the findings that relate personal religiosity to internal locus of control (Strickland & Shaffer, 1971). Among glossolalics, for example, Malony et al. (1972) found that those who spoke in tongues more frequently were likely to be more intrinsic in their orientation to religion as measured by Allport's scale designed to measure this variable.

Two investigations have been concerned with Pentecostal college students. Rarick and Malony (1981), in a denomination–wide study of institutions related to the Church of God, Cleveland, Tennessee, found that well over 90 percent of the students spoke in tongues. Gilbert (1972) compared the 311 entering freshmen at one of these Church of God institutions, Lee College, to over 7,000 freshmen attending thirty-seven colleges in fourteen states on certain personality measures. In addition to finding that the Lee students were more orthodox in religious belief, he also noted that they were more altruistic, practical, feminine, and anxious but *less* scholarly and impulsive. This last is contrary to the higher impulsiveness found by Vivier (1960).

In a related study, Gonsalvez (1978/1979) compared Catholic charismatics (half of whom were glossolalic) with Catholic nonglossolalics on the MMPI Subtle Hysteria scale. The two groups differed significantly, with the glossolalics showing a greater tendency toward hysteric-type personality traits. It is important to remember that the use of this word does not imply psychopathology as such. However, characteristics associated with these scores: hyperexcitability, low frustration tolerance, emotional instability, suggestibility, and dependence do resemble several hysteric-type traits alluded to before.

Of less importance is the study of members of two Pentecostal churches in southern rural Creek County, North Carolina, and a non-Pentecostal sample by means of the Rorschach ink blot test by Wood (1961/1962). Although the exclusive use of this technique by itself is questionable, Wood's conclusion that glossolalia attracts persons with many conflicts who have an inclination to seek personality stability through religion is even more questionable. As C. G. Williams (1981) noted:

> No doubt, one can find the uncertain and the anxious among glossolalics, and no doubt, "tongues" tell us something about the speaker. But is it not equally true that such persons could be found in any religious group since in a religious person one finds an awareness of inadequacy, and, where there is an enlightened conscience as well, there will be a heightened sensitivity to the threats and strains presented by modern civilization. This is a far cry from classifying all glossolalics as psychopathological. Glossolalics belong to a variety of psychological types. (p. 128)

Although C. G. Williams's statement may be a bit strongly worded, he does reflect the state of the research, which seems to conclude that only on one or two variables, such as submissiveness or suggestibility, do glossolalics differ from nonglossolalics. And this conclusion seems to hold true for comparisons between Pentecostals and neo-Pentecostals.

Several efforts have been made to compare glossolalics with the general population through the use of standardized psychological tests. The group profile for a small group of glossolalics tested in a pilot study for his dissertation by Lovekin (1977) was found to describe to an extroverted type with feeling as the dominant function and sensing as the auxiliary function (Myers-Briggs Type Inventory [MBTI]). Lovekin (1977, p. 66) suggested this confirmed Kelsey's (1964) contention that "the extroverted person, the one most largely concerned with the outer world, in whom feeling or relating to differences in value is dominant, and who has been inhibited in the use of this function is the most likely to speak in tongues" (p. 220). It should be added, however, that these results, interpreted in terms of Jung's theory of personality, are based on a small sample and, thus, ought to be accepted with caution. They await a larger survey.

Simmonds, Richardson, & Harder (1972) utilized an adjective check list to assess members of a Jesus movement group living on a farm on the West Coast. One of the tenents of the group was that witnessing to the presence of the Holy Spirit through speaking in tongues was important. The participants proved to differ from the norm on a number of variables. Women tended to check few favorable and more unfavorable adjectives than was typical. Further, they scored lower on defensiveness, self-confidence, self-control, personal adjustment, dominance, endurance, and order than did the standardization group. Men showed a similar pattern. They, too, checked fewer favorable and more unfavorable adjectives than was typical. Moreover, they scored lower on defensiveness, self-confidence, self-control, personal adjustment, achievement, dominance, endurance, order, intraception, affiliation, and heterosexuality. Overall, these patterns could be thought to indicate maladaptivity, but the adjustment of these persons to the commune-type environment in which they were living was quite acceptable. Although this group was more similar to neo-Pentecostalism than to classical Pentecostalism, it is, nevertheless, quite distinct from the more typical tongue-speaking group, in that most glossolalics do not live in communes. Additional research utilizing this same adjective checklist would be needed to confirm whether these patterns typify other glossolalics. In a later essay, however, Richardson (1973) denied that there was any unique personality pattern among glossolalics.

Plog and Pitcher (1965), in an investigation of more conventional glossolalics, surveyed over eight hundred subjects in Los Angeles and Seattle. They reported that no consistent personality characteristics emerged from the administration of a number of standardized tests of personality.

The final types of investigations regarding personality traits include comparisons of various types of glossolalics with each other. Frequency with which persons speak in tongues has been one of the ways in which groups of glossolalics have been compared. Malony et al. (1972) reported two studies involving this distinction. Among Assembly of God youth surveyed in these studies, higher frequency of speaking in tongues was associated with a more intrinsic orientation to religion, a greater tendency to go to mission outreach work camps, and more frequent attendance at church. It was not related to extroversion, introversion, or internal/external locus of control. This is somewhat supportive of the Coulson and Johnson (1977) research.

In an effort to distinguish glossolalics on the basis of psychophysiological indices of alterations in states of consciousness, Pavelsky et al. (1975) used frequency as one of their variables. They concluded that there were act glossolalics and process glossolalics. Act glossolalics, those for whom glossolalia was similar to role playing, were characterized by insignificant alpha wave changes in brain activity during speaking in tongues; process glossolalics, those for whom the experience was related to deeper personal dynamics, were characterized by significant positive or negative alpha wave changes.

Process glossolalics were higher on exhibitionism (as measured by the Edwards Personal Preference Profile) than act glossolalics. This led Pavelsky et al. to conclude there were definitely two types of glossolalic experiences similar to Pattison's serious/playful distinction and that these types have certain personality traits associated with them, even if the comparisons cannot be made on the basis of frequency and social class.

In a novel approach, Gilmore (1968) studied members of three Pentecostal churches in the northwest and compared personality differences between high- and low-dogmatism believers. Her hypothesis was that the manner in which persons hold their beliefs should be related to unique personal traits as measured by the California Personality Inventory. The low-dogmatism group (who did not differ from the average in their ability to receive, evaluate, and act on relevant information from the outside) scored higher on sociability, social presence, tolerance, intellectual efficiency, psychological mindedness, and achievement through independence than did the high-dogmatism group, even though they were similar on religiosity.

A somewhat related finding was that of Lovekin and Malony (1977) who compared those who became glossolalic with those who did not become so after attending a seven-week course designed for those seeking the gift of the Holy Spirit. Those who never did become glossolalic were higher in anxiety and hostility, as measured by an adjective check list. It may be that the experience comes more easily to those who are less constricted and inwardly tense. Certain traits may make it difficult to attain glossolalia, even if one desires it.

Of course, the most typical comparison among glossolalics has been that made between Pentecostals and neo-Pentecostals. Protagonists for the charismatic movement, such as Dennis J. Bennett (1970) (Hamilton, 1975, pp. 15–32) have sought to make a clear distinction between the two groups on the basis of altered states of consciousness and the types of people involved. However, although Smith (1977) predicted a difference between conventional and unconventional tongue speakers, he found none. Moreover, such studies as Malony et al. (1972) have concluded that there are no socioeconomic differences and Pattison (1968), among others, does not feel that personality distinctions can be substantiated between Pentecostals and neo-Pentecostals. However, it should be added that conclusive comparisons of the two groups have yet to be undertaken. Nevertheless, overgeneralizations simply cannot be substantiated.

In summary, personality traits among glossolalics have been researched through comparisons of glossolalics with nonglossolalics, with the general population, and with other glossolalics. In general, it can be said that few specific traits have been identified, although a number of studies have been undertaken. However, it does seem that a tendency toward extroversion, intrinsic religious orientation, and suggestibility can be affirmed.

5

Psychopathology

From the beginning of tongue speaking in Christianity, the insinuation has been that those who expressed themselves in this way were deluded or beside themselves. These types of explanations were given on the day of Pentecost. Acts 2:12–13 reports that ". . . all were amazed and perplexed, saying to one another, 'What does this mean?' but others mocking said, 'They are filled with a new wine.' " Peter tried to correct this impression by saying, "Men of Judea and all who dwell in Jerusalem, let this be known to you and give ear to my words. For these men are not drunk, as you suppose, since it is only the third hour of the day" (Acts 2:14b–15). Nevertheless, one suspects that many remained unconvinced because this tongue speaking was strange behavior at best and abnormal behavior at worst.

A modern illustration of the behavior more clearly illustrates why those who have observed glossolalia have suspected pathology. Synan (1971) reports a description of the revival that hit the University of Georgia in 1800–1801:

> They swooned away and lay for hours in the straw prepared for those "smitten of the Lord," or they started suddenly to flee away and fell prostrate as if shot down by a sniper, or they took suddenly to jerking with apparently every muscle in their body until it seemed they would be torn to pieces or converted into marble, or they shouted and talked in unknown tongues. (p. 25)

Little wonder that from that day to this, glossolalia has been considered abnormal and those who practice have been thought to be mentally ill. This chapter will consider the evidence for these contentions.

William James (1902/1958) spoke for many academicians at the beginning of this century when he proposed that psychopathic temperament was often present in religious leaders. Although he did not mention glossolalia by name, he would doubtless have included it among those behaviors characteristic of fanaticism about which he wrote so despairingly. "Saintliness," James's term for those who take religion seriously, was characteristic of those seeking "spiritual holiness" in the last half of the nineteenth century. James suggests that these types of persons commit "error by excess" and take their religion to "convulsive extreme."

Certainly, this was the attitude of the 1894 General Conference of the Methodist Episcopal Church, South. So afraid were they of the growing power of the Holiness movement that they passed a motion disassociating themselves from it. At issue were the extremes to which Holiness followers, such as John P. Brooks and Benjamin Hardin Irwin, had gone. Brooks had been a loyal Methodist and had edited a Holiness newspaper from within the church for a number of years prior to leaving Methodism in 1885 because of his concern over the way in which unspiritual activities were tolerated in the church. He wrote what has come to be termed the "textbook of come-outism" entitled *The Divine Church* (1891, 1960), in which he called for all Christians who were attempting to live the spirit-filled life of perfection to "come-out" from the organized churches. Irwin—taking seriously John Wesley's colleague John Fletcher, who taught that there were several baptisms along the way to entire sanctification—taught not only a baptism by fire (the term often applied to the second blessing), but also a baptism of "dynamite," of "lyddite," and of "oxidite," that is a third, fourth, and fifth blessing!

The General Conference of 1894, in an effort to stem these excesses, passed the following resolution:

> But there has sprung up among us a party with holiness as the watchword; they have holiness associations, holiness preachers, holiness evangelists, and holiness property. Religious experience is represented as if it consists of only two steps, the first step out of condemnation into peace and the next step into Christian perfection. The effect is to disparage the new birth, and all stages of spiritual growth from the blade to the full corn in the ear. . . . We do not question the sincerity and zeal of these brethren; we desire the church to profit by their earnest preaching and godly example; but we deplore their teaching and methods in so far as they claim a monopoly of the experience, practice, and advocacy of holiness, and separate themselves from the body of ministers and disciples. (p. 25)

The disavowal and disassociation of Methodism from such fanaticism was clear from this point in time to the present.

It is understandable, therefore, that William James, writing less than ten years after this resolution, should declare that, "spiritual excitement" of the type seen in speaking in tongues "takes pathological forms whenever other interests are too few and the intellect too narrow" (1902/1958, p. 265). It was his opinion that such fanaticism occurred when there was an imbalance in psychic faculties (i.e., deficient intellect and will) and an impoverishment in the environment (i.e., too narrow interests).

As noted earlier, this theory that fanaticism was grounded in intellectual deficiency was directly linked to glossolalia by Cutten (1927) whose volume *Speaking with Tongues: Historically and Psychologically Considered* became the most widely quoted authority on glossolalia, in spite of the fact that it was based entirely on bibliographic sources and included little or no scientific research. Cutten was a Baptist minister and educator who depended heavily on written documents and casual observations. He conducted no research in the accepted sense of the term.

In writing of Isabeau Vincent, one of the seventeenth-century prophetesses of Cevennes, Cutten describes her as a young girl "who could neither read nor write" (1927, p. 52). Further, overtly retarded men and women in the Cevennes mountains were seized with ecstasy and began to speak in tongues during this same period. One shepherd was judged "incapable of instruction" and another person was considered "almost idiotic" (p. 58).

Cutten (1927, pp. 73–74) quoted a recorder of Mormon glossolalia as stating, "Those who speak in tongues are generally the most illiterate among the Saints, such as cannot command words as quick as they would wish, and instead of waiting for a suitable word to come to their memories, they break forth in the first sound their tongues can articulate no matter what it is."

Finally, Cutten noted that Edward Irving, the founder of the glossolalic Catholic Apostolic Church in the first quarter of the nineteenth century was an educated or "cultivated" man, as Cutten was wont to say. Tongue speaking first broke out in his congregation among the "uncultivated" (uneducated? illiterate?). According to Cutten, intelligence and glossolalia seemed to be inversely related and many intelligent persons such as Irving reputedly sought the gift in vain.

Cutten's explanation for this relationship between deficient intellect and a proclivity for glossolalia was as follows:

> Let us suppose, the conditions as already described: external and internal excitement, suggestion in some form, and an illiterate person about to speak. *Ex hypothesi*, the person has poor power of expression and a limited vocabulary. The excitement drives him to say something. Perhaps for a short time he speaks normally, then the pressure of nervous energy increases, so that with the inadequate power of expression he is unable to say what he desires; confusion reigns in the mind; the upper centers become clogged, rational control takes flight, the lower centers assume control, a trance condition may be present, the suggestion is for speech, and because there is no rational control or direction there breaks forth a lot of meaningless syllables. (1927, pp. 168–169)

Thus, from Cutten's point of view, lack of intellectual acumen implies reduced capacity to put thoughts into words. This results, under conditions of excitement and expectation, in a compulsion to say something. In turn, the pressure provokes confusion and verbal gibberish results. Those with higher intelligence are able to retain mastery of these impulses through rational control centered in the "upper" brain centers. In this description, Cutten not only legitimizes his contention about lower intelligence, but also hints at other processes, that is, excitement and suggestion, which is considered later in this chapter (trance is treated in chapter 6).

It should be restated that no researcher, much less Cutten, ever put the thesis of low intelligence to a test. It is merely inferred on the basis of social class observed in classical Pentecostalism. Hine (1969), reporting the research of a team of anthropologists at the University of Minnesota, said:

> [We] can only wish that Dr. Cutten had been able to join us in interviewing modern Pentecostals. A more verbal group of people it would be difficult to imagine. . . . As for "low mental ability" and "underdeveloped rational capacity," even those who began with very little formal education bring to their study of the scriptures an intensity of mentation that would stand any college student in good stead." (p. 213)

However, it should be noted that neo-Pentecostals at the middle of the twentieth century may well differ from the classical Pentecostals about whom Cutten wrote.

PSYCHIC CONTAGION

The process by which those of less intelligence become glossolalic was thought to be that of psychic contagion. This dynamic was thought to be operative through the impulses to imitate and to conform so prevalent in the theorizing about crowd psychology at the beginning of the twentieth century. Le Bon in his classic *The Crowd* (1896) detailed the phenomenon. He suggested that persons gave up part of their reason when they came together. Emotions became supreme and dictated action. Mob scenes were examples of this, in that they often led to group behavior, like lynchings, which were regretted later by participants when they calmly reflected on their behavior in the light of reason. Behaving on the basis of emotion and giving up rational control was the essence of psychopathology according to Le Bon and others who equated intelligence with reason. So strong was this conviction that group behavior implied abnormality, that one of the earliest journals of the American Psychological Association was entitled the *Journal of Abnormal and Social Psychology*. Suffice it to say, it was assumed that the ability to resist group pressure was a sign of greater intelligence. Thus, it was assumed that the process of psychic contagion, wherein people imitated each other and all began to speak in tongues, was abnormal behavior more likely to occur in those of lesser intellect.

Lombard (1910), using Le Bon's theory, termed this "psychologie des foules" or "mob" psychology and had concluded that those who spoke in tongues were "impressionable." By this, he meant that their egos were disorganized, an idea to which we shall return later. Nevertheless, he wanted to distinguish glossolalia from hysteria—a malady based on denial and repression—and at the same time to propose that revivalistic contagion presupposed a more serious condition than simple deficient intelligence.

An example of the process is the report of John Carlyle about a service conducted by Edward Irving in the early 1800s:

> . . . one of the prophetesses, a woman on the verge of derangement, started up and began to speak with tongues, and, as the thing was encouraged by Irving, three or four fresh hands started up in the evening. Whereupon the whole congregation went into a foul uproar, some groaning, some laughing, some shrieking, not a few falling into swoons—more like a Bedlam than a Christian church." (cited in Knox, 1950, p. 555)

A twentieth-century illustration was reported by Cutten:

> I attended the "Tongues" meeting at H—. Here I found men and women lying on the floor in all shapes, and the workers would put big blankets over them. These people on the floor would be jabbering all at once in what they called unknown tongues. While I was praying one of the workers got hold of me and said: "Holy Ghost, we command thee to go into this soul." The workers were jabbering and shaking their hands over me, and a hypnotic power (as I know now) took possession of me, and I fell among the people on the floor and knew nothing for ten hours. (1927, p. 131)

Although more recent glossolalia has sometimes been practiced in private, classical Pentecostalism was typically a group experience. Most persons came to the meetings with both an expectation that God would reveal Himself in a way similar to the experience of the biblical Pentecost and a desire to have the humdrum of their lives enlivened by a dramatic encounter with the supernatural.

As Mackie (1921), a polemicist against tongues, sarcastically noted:

> Men are "eager for the supernatural." . . . . The bringing in of the Kingdom of God through patient toil is not an undertaking which commends itself to many minds. Cataclysmic religion is far more interesting. (pp. 257–258)

This was very often true of Pentecostals. At best, this urge was a desire to restore vitality and enthusiasm to religious faith—ingredients that most charismatics have felt missing from the orthodox churches. Further, they anticipated that this renewal would take the form of the Holy Spirit's visitation to the apostles, which was reported in Acts. Thus, the stage was set for excitement and ecstasy even before the meetings began. Jennings (1968) infers yet an additional expectation, namely, that "some people with certain personality configurations are so constituted that they yearn to be vehicles of the supernatural" (p. 9). Lombard (1910) suggested that such anticipation occasionally provoked glossolalia even *before* persons got to the group meetings.

With this combination of expectation, group excitement, and a willingness to yield themselves, those who spoke in tongues were categorized as susceptible and suggestible (Cutten, 1927, p. 167). These were considered the components of hypnotism and theorists, such as Mosiman (1911), very early characterized glossolalia as representative of this type of phenomenon. It is interesting that research from that day to this has left unstudied the initial question of intelligence and has focused instead on whether glossolalics were more suggestible than nonglossolalics. However, without doubt, the inference is still present, namely: the more suggestible, the less intelligent one is. Suggestibility and giving over to emotion are, for practical purposes, one and the same.

Mosiman (1911) concluded that in ecstatic states, such as speaking in tongues, two hypnotic factors were operative. The first was a facility in following suggestions and the second was an active unconscious mind. He considered the extraordinary phenomena characteristic of the Pentecostals of his day to be evidence of conscious thought that had become "derailed" (dislodged) from conscious control by the power of suggestion. The place of the unconscious will be discussed in more detail later. However, it is interesting to note that Mosiman (1911) did not assume that expressions of the unconscious mind were necessarily psychopathological as others have done (note Lapsley & Simpson, 1964b; Mackie, 1921; Oman, 1963). In this regard, he aligns himself with William James (1902/1958), Carl Jung (1902/1970), and others who hypothesized that the unconscious is the repository of the essence of personhood and the channel for divine intervention into human life—a possibility often impeded by the hyperrationalism of modern culture.

HYPNOSIS

Suggestion in hypnosis is thought to be something more than the mass contagion or imitation of mob emotionalism. Suggestion is thought to be the process wherein one gives control of one's thoughts over to the direction of another person. Kildahl (1972) describes the similarity between glossolalia and this hypnotic procedure:

> When I hypnotize someone, I begin by saying to my subject, "lie back . . . shut your eyes . . . relax . . . breath [sic] deeply . . . and listen to the sounds of your breathing. As you relax, you can feel yourself getting tired and drowsy. . . ." In the dimly lit fireside of the First Presbyterian Church, a small circle of members quietly listened to their pastor say, "The Lord is in your presence . . . He is with you now . . . open yourself to him . . . let all your anxieties flow out of you. . . . The Lord wants to give you the gift of his Holy Spirit. . . . Open your mouth and he will give you utterance. (p. 37)

Although Kildahl (1972) is describing neo-Pentecostalism, he details the focusing of attention, the excluding of sensory awareness, and most important, the "special" kind of relationship that exists between the leader and follower both in hypnosis and in traditional glossolalia.

Alland (1961) described an incident more typical of classical Pentecostalism but one that illustrates these same processes. Elder B., an evangelist in Daddy Grace's House of Prayer for All Peoples was well-known for his ability to induce ecstasy in "seekers," those actively desiring to experience the Holy Ghost.

> First B. invited the band to come down off the podium. He asked them to join hands in a circle, that is, to form a star with their left hands, and to raise their right hands. He instructed all the men to close their eyes, to hold their lips tight and to think hard of Daddy. . . . After his success with the band, B. asked for young girls who were seeking. He said he did not want anyone to come up who had had the Holy Ghost. A group of young girls came up and formed a star. The band began to play but only one girl went into a trance. She went into violent trance and fell on the floor emitting cries of gibberish for over an hour.
>
> . . . B. told the congregation that they "were going to see something." He then asked the women to hold up their right hands and to look at the floor. They did so. B. told them that the Devil was down there and that no good came from that direction. Then he told them to look up at the ceiling. After they did this he told them that Jesus was up there and that He would come to them. He lowered his hand in a swift movement and three of the four women fell to the floor in a trance. This was the signal for several of the other women to go into trance and with this the band began to play. (pp. 207–208)

Trust and faith in a leader and a willingness to yield to that leader's direction appear essential to the instigation of glossolalic expression—just as in hypnosis. Alland (1962) noted that Elder B. could induce tongue speaking in those who had already received the Holy Ghost more easily than in new seekers. Apparently, glossolalia, like hypnosis, is a skill that can be cultivated with practice as one entrusts oneself more easily to the leader. Mosiman (1911) distinguished between initial and continuing tongues and suggested that the latter was more illustrative of self or autohypnosis. Thus, the phenomenon could be self-induced by recalling the leader and the situation in which tongues first occurred.

There have been several evaluations of the hypnosis theory of glossolalia. Cutten (1927) rejected this theory on the basis that Pentecostal meetings provided the conditions for mob action more than for the individual relationships necessary for hypnosis. He further concluded that the rapport observed between the hypnotist and the subject during trance was missing in tongue speaking: ". . . in hypnotism we have the *rapport* with others, or at least with one other who gives suggestions, while in ecstasy we find an introverted consciousness more difficult to enter or influence than the most extreme case or ego-centric type of dementia praecox" (1921, p. 166). He suggests that glossolalia is more like sleep than hypnosis. Empirical support for Cutten's (1927) hypothesis was found by Vivier (1960) who concluded on the basis of personality tests that glossolalics were lower, *not higher,* than nonglossolalics on suggestibility.

However, Kildahl (1972), writing some years after Cutten, reached the opposite conclusion on the basis of a study of neo-Pentecostals in a mainline denomination. He wrote:

It is our thesis that hypnotizability constitutes the *sine qua non* of the glossolalia experience. If one can be hypnotized, then one is able under proper conditions to learn to speak in tongues. While glossolalia is not the same as hypnosis, it is similar to it and has the same roots in the relationship of the subject to the authority figure." (pp. 54–55)

Although his research did not reveal any tendency for glossolalics to be of any specific personality type (e.g., hysteric, manic, compulsive, etc.), they were characterized by differences in certain personality variables that differentiated them from nontongue speakers. These variables constituted a hypnotic type of person who evidenced a strong need to be guided by some trusted authority and an inclination to experience euphoria when she/he was in a submissive relationship with a leader. The tongue speaker tended to transfer these feelings from leaders to God and to experience good feelings whenever she/he repeated the experience into which she/he was originally led by the leader whether alone or not. Kildahl's (1972) study revealed that those who no longer spoke in tongues tended to be those who had broken off their relationship with the leader or the group.

Kildahl (1972) called for an explicit study of suggestibility among glossolalics through such measures as the Harvard Group Scale of Hypnotic Suggestibility, but this has never been done. The nearest approach was an investigation by Vivier (1960) in which he found glossolalics to be no more suggestible than nonglossolalics—he used only two parts of the Harvard scale (body sway and levitation).

A somewhat related study was undertaken by Malony, Zwaanstra and Ramsey (1972) in which it was found that there was no tendency for frequent tongue speakers to be more externally controlled than less frequent tongue speakers. In regard to the psychopathology theory, it is interesting to note that Hilgard (1970) cites several studies that suggest that normals are more suggestible than schizophrenics or hysterics. This is a conclusion that accords with Kildahl's (1972, p. 48) overall conclusion that tongue speakers are as mentally healthy as nontongue speakers.

HYSTERIA

Le Baron (1896–1897), the tongue speaker whose experiences were reported by William James, concluded that one of the explanations for the experience was that glossolalia was "the loose jargon of a maniac" (p. 293). Others have been less equivocal in their judgments. Mackie (1921), for example, stated: "It ought to be a matter of common knowledge that such states of mind and action are the expressions of diseased minds and diseased bodies, that when we are dealing with an extraordinary religious experience we are very likely dealing with disease" (p. vii). Certainly, madness was one of the interpretations given to biblical glossolalics (1 Cor. 14:23).

Although linguists such as Samarin (1972c, p. 117) have suggested that the word salads of schizophrenics are incontrovertibly different from religious glossolalia, the two have often been compared. Maeder (1910), who worked under Jung, described the case of a paranoid schizophrenic man, age 41, hospitalized sixteen years. The patient created a new "superior" language to express the ideas that his abnormal state provided him. Getting the patient to free associate and describe in more detail the objects and images used in the stories, Maeder was able to analyze the vocabulary used. Bobon (1947) wrote three case studies of psychotic patients each of whom developed a private language based on fanciful elaboration of ordinary French.

Neurotic disorders have also been thought to underlie glossolalic expression. Schjelderup (1931) published a case study of a neurotic man, age 24, who began speaking in tongues during analysis. On the basis of the subject's written reproduction of some of the sounds and his free associations, Schjelderup concluded the "words" referred to different feelings related to the subject's painful childhood memories. This same conclusion was reached by Pfister (1912) in an earlier report of a subject in his 20s who free associated to each individual word in a glossolalic utterance. He considered glossolalia to be the expression of repressed thoughts in disguised form.

Lapsley and Simpson (1964b) have given a more recent formulation of these psychodynamic formulations. They suggested that although glossolalics would not be considered mentally ill in any clinical sense, they were, nevertheless, "uncommonly disturbed" in the sense that speaking in tongues functions like any neurotic symptom to reduce the anxiety brought on by traumatic experiences with parental figures. Thus, they concluded that glossolalia was indicative of developmental fixation and truncated personality development.

The most interesting account of glossolalia as a component of a neurotic conflict that later turned into psychosis is that of Finch (1964):

> A patient I saw expected God to give him professional skill as a pianist; then when that did not work, still as a vocalist. That did not work either. The subject seemed to progress from infantilism and extreme dependency feelings to an hysterical attempt to hold together his shattering ego by a frantic leap into glossolalia. . . . When the symptom could not carry the weight of the attempt, it splintered into schizophrenia. Eventually he had to be committed to a mental hospital. (p. 17)

Beginning with Janet (1907/1924), the most common psychiatric diagnosis ascribed to glossolalics has been hysteria. Hysteria is that form of mental illness that is associated with various forms of cognitive and emotional compartmentalizing, denial, and repression. Extreme forms of the malady include conversion symptoms in which psychic trauma is expressed in peculiar sensations, movements, hypersensitivities, or paralyses over which the person has no control as well as dissociative disturbances in which the individual displays amnesias or multiple personalities that have no cognizance of each other.

In regard to the former, classical Pentecostals have evidenced various forms of compulsive movements, such as jerking, whirling, and rolling, and they have appeared to go into trancelike states in which they seem oblivious to their surroundings. In regard to the latter, glossolalics have evidenced fuguelike states in which they speak with languages they have never learned and in which they seem possessed by knowledge or power from an outer source that controls their behavior.

Although Schwarz's (1960) report of mountain snake handlers in the southeastern United States is admittedly an extreme example, this vividly illustrates these two components of hysteria to which Cutten (1927) and others have referred in depicting tongue speaking. During the worship services the snake handlers went into frenetic states resembling mania as the "power of the Lord moved in on them":

> At these times they shout, scream, cry, sing, jerk, jump, twitch, whistle, hoot, gesture, sway, swoon, tremble, strut, goosestep, stamp, and incoherently "speak in new tongues." . . .

> When in deep dissociated trance the members appear as if they were intoxicated, and their faces are very similar to those seen with reactions induced by mescaline and LSD 25. They describe the depersonalization phenomena as: "I feel high in the spirits" . . . "happiness in the bones" . . . "I lose sight of the whole world" . . . "I can't tell if my head and face are all together" . . . "I can't stand under the power of God. (Schwarz, 1960, pp. 408–409)

These states are followed by an impulsive removal of snakes from wooden boxes, the application of flames from coal oil torches to parts of the body, and the drinking of strychnine dissolved in water by the most faithful of the saints. Amazingly Schwarz (1960) observed no person being harmed in any way from these activities on four field trips to these services of worship!

The snake handlers of Schwarz's (1960) study, although speakers in tongues, are a distinct type of sect differing not only from less extreme Holiness groups, but also from classical Pentecostals and from the neo-Pentecostals in the mainline churches. Gerrard (1970) concluded from a study of churches in rural Appalachia that most of the groups Schwarz studied and others like them were attended by the stationary as opposed to the upwardly mobile poor. Thus, they were resigned to spasmodic periods of employment, social deprivation, and dependency on welfare. Their religion was characterized by fatalism and the spontaneous drama described above. This is a far cry from the practice of Catholic neo-Pentecostals at the other extreme. These persons participate in highly stylized rituals (i.e., the Mass) and attend quiet, dignified prayer meetings where they sing or speak in tongues following gentle invitations.

Yet the research to date concludes that none of the tongue speaking groups is more psychopathological than any other or that glossolalics in general could be classed as clinically hysterical in comparison with either the normal or the mentally ill population. This can be said in spite of the acknowledgment of Pentecostal leaders that, when the movement began early in this century, it attracted a number of disturbed persons and in spite of the fact that charismatic expressions of any kind (be they serpent handling, laying on of hands for healing, or speaking in tongues) remain deviant behavior in terms of general societal norms.

Schwarz (1960) reported that psychiatric examination of six of the "saints" in the snake-handling sect revealed no "evidence of current neurotic, psychotic, or psychosomatic reactions, or of pathologic dissociative behavior" (p. 407). Further, Gerrard, Gerrard, and Tellegen (1966) compared Minnesota Multiphasic Personality Inventory (MMPI) profiles of members of Methodist and serpent-handling churches. An analysis of these tests by the Psychology Department of the University of Minnesota revealed:

> [Members of] the conventional denomination, compared to the serpent-handlers, are on the average more defensive, less inclined to admit undesirable traits, more ready to use mechanisms of denial and repression. The older [members of the] conventional denomination in addition, show indications of marked depressive symptomatology. The serpent-handlers appear less defensive and restrained. On the contrary, they seemed to be more exhibitionistic, excitable, and pleasure-oriented . . . and are less controlled by consideration of conformity to the general culture, particularly middle class culture. There is no evidence for systematic differences between the two groups on dimensions of thought disorder. (Gerrard, Gerrard, & Tellegen, 1966, p. 56)

An interesting side note of this research was the finding that four other psychologists were given the MMPI profiles and asked to sort them into snake handler and Methodist. They tended to assign the deviant profiles to the snake-handling group, in spite of the fact that the actual distribution showed the reverse to be true. This shows that there is a continuing bias among numerous behavioral scientists to ascribe psychopathology to those groups that are deviant in their religious expression.

More evidence for lack of psychopathology among glossolalics was reported by Alland (1962) who studied a black Pentecostal church in New Haven, Connecticut. Tongue speakers in this group were well-adjusted, functioning members of their community, except for their behavior at church. He did not feel that glossolalia was indicative of either schizophrenia or of hysteria. Schizophrenics would not be able to confine their problems to one form of expression as did the tongue speakers nor would hysterics be as much aware of the time when their symptoms would appear. Glossolalia is learned behavior, not a sign of personality disorder, according to Alland (1962).

This last conclusion is suggestive of a hypothesis we will discuss later in more detail, namely, that glossolalia occurs in a context of cultural expectation and functions as a rite of passage quite apart from the personal instability of the participant. As Alland (1962) observed, "our data show there is a wide range of susceptibility among members of the church . . . a limited but varied range of personality types can, under the proper conditions, ultimately achieve a possessive state" (p. 209).

In a similar study of ethnic Pentecostalism, Kiev (1963 and 1964a) compared ten West Indian schizophrenics in British mental hospitals to a group of West Indian Pentecostal immigrants to London. The differences between their behavior and psychotic symptoms was perfectly clear. As Kiev described it:

> . . . unlike non-psychotic individuals who participate in various religious cults and in the revivalist sects in which dissociative phenomena and possession are permitted and encouraged, the schizophrenic patients could not maintain sufficient control of autistic and regressive behavior to fit into the prescribed ritual patterns. (1964a, p. 18)

In fact, Hine (1969) suggested that many tongue speakers have developed pragmatic ways of evaluating those who desire to become glossolalic, and they discourage those whom they feel are unstable.

In the Vivier study (1960) three groups within the same traditional orthodox reformed church were compared. Although there were certain personality differences among the groups (the glossolalics evidencing more repressive tendencies and less cultural conformity), these were not associated with psychopathology.

Using the Rorschach inkblot test, Wood (1961/1962, 1965) compared Pentecostal and non-Pentecostal religionists in two southern rural communities. The subjects were matched for socioeconomic background. There was no indication that the tongue speakers were overtly abnormal on this measure, although Wood hypothesized that glossolalics had a strong need to feel close to others and that Pentecostalism attracted uncertain, inadequately organized persons.

Earlier, Boisen (1939) compared Holy Rollers to certain psychiatric patients in the hospital where he was chaplain. Although he noted that there was a similarity between the mentally ill patients' contention that they were controlled by an external power and the insistence by the Holy Rollers that they were possessed by the Holy Spirit, he nevertheless found no evidence for mental illness. In fact, he felt that glossolalia was therapeutic when it occurred within a social group who nurtured and supported it. Southard (1955) came to the same conclusion in his study of four hospitalized mental patients. Charles, a psychotic murderer, was befriended by a Pentecostal pastor and became relinked to society through charismatic faith. Fred, an impulsive reckless driver, was saved from delinquency through the continual ministrations of a sect-type group that stood by him throughout his ordeal. Doug, a returned veteran experiencing "nervousness," was nurtured by his church whose members were "praying for him." Finally, a young woman who had left her Baptist heritage to join a Holiness group returned to her former church after a psychotic episode in which her common-law husband agreed to help her seek a divorce from her estranged former husband. She had sought refuge in the sect-type fellowship to assuage her guilt for living out of wedlock. Southard (1955) concluded:

> (1) There is no evidence that membership in a sect, as such, indicated poor mental health, nor does entrance into a sect, by itself, signal a personality disturbance. (2) Rather, individuals who are socially isolated may find some redeeming fellowship in a sect, even when their loneliness has led them to the protection of a psychotic episode. . . . (3) However, sect preachers, through lack of sufficient understanding in certain fields, may sometimes precipitate a psychosis in persons who are already under severe emotional stress. (p. 590)

In an extensive survey, Plog and Pitcher (1965) studied tongue speakers in Los Angeles and Seattle and concluded on the basis of over eight hundred California Psychological Inventories and two hundred interviews that these persons were normal, responsible, well-controlled individuals. Gerlach and Hine (1968) likewise reached the conclusion that Pentecostals were effective and adjusted persons in their midwestern study.

The most recent comparison of tongue speakers with nontongue speakers was conducted by Kildahl (1972) and his associate Paul Qualben. They administered a number of psychological tests to members of mainline denominations who were glossolalic and to members who were nonglossolalic. Analysis of the MMPI profiles revealed lower scores on depression for the glossolalics but otherwise no significant difference between the two groups. On the Thematic Apperception Test (TAT), the glossolalics evidenced less autonomy and a tendency toward dependency. However, Kildahl (1972, p. 48) concluded overall ". . . the most significant finding of this research is that one group is *not any more mentally healthy* than the other" (emphasis added).

After a review of these studies, Richardson (1973) concluded that it was difficult to ascertain whether tongue speakers were, in fact, psychopathological before they became glossolalic because all of the research up to that time had been post hoc (done after that event). It could be, he hypothesized, that the experience healed them from their mental illness, because many apologists for the tongue speaking reported that such positive change occurred. Richardson (1973) called for longitudinal investigations that would assess persons prior to speaking in tongues and then follow them after the experience.

Acknowledging the importance of this suggestion, Lovekin and Malony (1977) assessed personality changes in 39 persons who attended "Life in the Spirit Seminars" in the Episcopal Church and in the Roman Catholic Church. This Life in the Spirit Seminar (S. B. Clark, 1972b) is a seven-week curriculum of study designed primarily for those seeking the gift of the Holy Spirit in the Roman Catholic Church. Participants were assessed prior to, during, and three months after the seminar on a number of personality variables measured by Zuckerman's and Lubin's Adjective Check List, Barron's Ego Strength scale, and the Mooney Problem Check List. On no measure did the participants evidence abnormality in comparison to standardized norms when assessed prior to beginning the seminar, although those who never spoke in tongues were higher in hostility than those who did so speak. Thus, although all persons (new, old, and no-tongue participants alike) showed evidence of changing in the direction of greater personality integration, there was no basis for saying that individuals who came seeking gifts of the Holy Spirit were psychopathological at the time that they entered the seminar. Thus, in answer to Richardson's (1973) concern about whether the lack of abnormality reported in previous studies was due to the effect of glossolalia, this research seems to suggest that even before they speak in tongues, glossolalics are not more disturbed than other persons. Of course, it should be remembered that this research was conducted on neo-Pentecostals rather than classical Pentecostals. Longitudinal research conducted in that setting might reach different conclusions.

The weight of the evidence seems to be that speaking in tongues does not occur, if it ever did, in persons who are mentally ill in any clinical sense of that term. Although there do seem to be certain ways in which glossolalia functions within the personality and although there do seem to be some identifiable personality needs and traits within those who speak in tongues, these seem to be within normal limits and, in fact, there is some evidence that glossolalics may be more healthy mentally than others. A discussion of who becomes glossolalic and when is discussed in chapter 8, and what changes glossolalia makes are discussed in chapter 9 through 13. To conclude, Hine (1969, p. 217) states, "Quite clearly, available evidence requires that an explanation of glossolalia as pathological must be discarded."

SOCIOCULTURAL DIMENSIONS

In place of a pathological explanation, a sociocultural one has been suggested by such writers as Pattison (1968). He proposes that glossolalia can be understood best by interpreting it in terms of the sociocultural context in which it occurs. Where glossolalia is practiced as part of expected ritual, then one does not expect to find psychopathology. The reverse is true for those situations in which it is not culturally expected. This is an intriguing hypothesis because it leads to the prediction that neo-Pentecostals in mainline denominations are more likely to evidence psychopathology than classical Pentecostals who tolerate, expect, and support glossolalia. This, however, is contradictory to the presumption of two psychiatrists in the Episcopal Study Commission of the Diocese of California who

. . . point out that there is a significant difference between the person who can "decide" to indulge in glossolalia and then withdraw from it at will, and the one whose conscious is overwhelmed by his unconscious until sufficient release has taken place. The latter hardly could be considered to be in emotional good health. (McDonnell, 1980, vol. 1, p. 86)

The commission returns to the issues of self-control and concludes that neo-Pentecostals who can speak in tongues at will in churches where it is considered deviant are thereby mentally healthy, whereas classical Pentecostals are not mentally healthy. Pattison (1968) assumes the opposite.

Paul Morentz (1966), a psychiatrist at the University of California at Berkeley, conducted research that Pattison (1968) quoted in support of his hypothesis. Morentz concluded that the meaning of tongue speaking was more pathological when it occurred in unexpected situations. In interviews with sixty glossolalics in mainline churches he found six dominant personality patterns: hostility to authority, the wish to compensate for feelings of inadequacy, the wish to rationalize feelings of isolation, the wish to dominate, strong feelings of suggestibility and dependency, and a wish for certainty.

In an attempt to test Pattison's (1968) hypothesis directly and to combine it with the deprivation hypothesis that had been used to explain the appeal of Pentecostalism in the early part of this century, Pavelsky, Hart, and Malony (1975) assessed psychophysiological changes during speaking in tongues among groups varying in socioeconomic class, glossolalic setting, and glossolalic frequency. It was predicted that those glossolalics from the lower social class who spoke in tongues frequently and in settings where it was not the expected norm would evidence more abnormality than those from the higher social class who spoke infrequently and in settings where it was typically expected. Abnormality was defined as a tendency for heart rate, brain wave patterns, and respiration rate to show greater changes when speaking in tongues than when in a resting state and praying in English. No support for the prediction was found.

The groups did not differ, thus lending even further support to the conclusion that glossolalia and psychopathology do not go together. It should be said, however, that all participants in this study could be considered neo-Pentecostals in the sense that they were willing to come into a psychophysiological laboratory and to speak in tongues on command of an experimenter. Nevertheless, the demands of the paradigm were met in terms of Pattison's (1968) hypothesis, and the conclusions can be taken as having at least moderate validity.

CONCLUSION

This chapter has considered the assumptions made by social/behavioral scientists in this century that speaking in tongues was evidence of low intelligence, hypnotic suggestibility, mass contagion, low ego controls, and outright psychopathology. Although these presumptions have been widespread, the evidence for them is weak or nonexistent. They would appear to be more the function of prejudgments and bias on the part of researchers or of attempts to discount deviant religious expressions. Nevertheless, there is some warrant for depicting such behavior as glossolalia in terms of psychodynamic processes that function in certain ways within personalities open to such experiences and for understanding glossolalia as normative in certain subcultures where it functions as a rite of passage. These issues are more fully discussed in subsequent chapters.

Glossolalia as
Extraordinary Behavior

6

States of Consciousness

Earlier it was noted that Hutch (1980) suggested that three paradigms had been used to study glossolalia, namely, aberrant, extraordinary, and anomalous behavior. Whereas the aberrant model considers the issue of whether glossolalia occurs in those who are emotionally or mentally disturbed, the extraordinary approach is concerned with the mental state of the individual at the time of speaking in tongues. Extraordinary does not imply, in and of itself, either normality or abnormality. Its prime interest is the question of whether speaking in tongues involves an altered state of consciousness.

Although numerous contemporary charismatics (for example, Basham, 1971; Bennett, 1970; M. Harper, 1965) have insisted that their glossolalia did not involve loss of consciousness and in spite of the fact that they attest to their ability to determine when and whether they express their "gift," the very essence of the experience has always been the presumption that one is taken over by the Holy Spirit and, thus, becomes *possessed* in a way that can be seen by anyone who is present. Indeed, "every Pentecostal and neo-Pentecostal tongue-speaker insists that he (sic) is speaking under the control, power or influence of the Holy Spirit" (Anderson, 1979, p. 12). Even though today's glossolalics have become acculturated and, thus, evidence fewer of the more obvious ecstatic characteristics, such as jerks, faints, or catatonic postures, nevertheless, they describe themselves as "Spirit possessed" and as able to distinguish those under divine control from those who are pretending to be so. In spite of their attempts to deny those aspects of the phenomenon they associate with the Holy Rollers or classical Pentecostalism, they, like the groups they discount, assume that the sine qua non of glossolalia is being in an other than ordinary, normal, day-to-day mental state. Speaking in tongues is, indeed, extraordinary. Anderson (1979) quotes several writers who attest to this fact:

> It is not ye that speak, but the Holy Ghost, and he will speak when He chooses.
>
> [It] is God's method whereby the Holy Spirit may possess men completely and be able to control them.

At a given point in this experience the seeker finds his tongue taken over and a new language being formed by a power other than his own. (p. 12)

With these statements, classical Pentecostals and neo-Pentecostals would both agree. Though they might disagree as to certain acts or certain labels, they all agree on the reality that glossolalia represents.

TRANCE AND POSSESSION

The two words that have been used to depict the altered state of consciousness to which glossolalics attest are "trance" and "possession." These are not synonymous, although they are often presumed to be. Trance is the phenomenon observed from the outside, whereas possession is the experience reported from the inside. Again and again, the labeling of an event as trance is used to confirm that possession has occurred. A vivid example of this connection of trance and possession is given by Bourguignon in a description of A.C., a Haitian peasant who claimed to be visited by a spirit, Papa Ogû.

> She put some water in a cup and placed it on the floor, the lighted candle and the cigar on the plate beside it. She called her neighbor to sing, tied a red kerchief (Ogû's color) about her head, sat on a chair, resting her arms on the table. Both A.C. and her neighbor began to sing . . . the singing was quite slow and rather sloppy. A.C. stared at the candle, but looked away again; breathed quickly, then heavily, then began to shake her head violently, then climbed down again, then raised her head with totally altered expression. This was Ogû who began to smoke the cigar, poured the water as a libation. Ogû greeted the two neighbors . . . and took three hops backward on each leg. . . . After a while he began to talk in a somewhat altered voice, etc., etc. (1965, p. 51)

The trance aspect was observed by anthropologist Erika Bourguignon. The peasant A.C. began to breathe more deeply, assumed a blank stare, changed the quality of her voice, began to shake violently, and acted out of character by smoking the cigar and speaking the words of another. The possession aspect was also observed by Bourguignon but, more important, possession was claimed by the peasant, although in this case, she reported amnesia for the content of the event—a common cultural component of such experiences.

Interestingly enough, in regard to possession, was the fact that A.C. *told* Bourguignon that she was going to invite Ogû to come because she wanted Ogû to meet her. Thus, possession was expected, foretold, and reported. In this case, trance and possession were synonymous.

More technical definitions of these two processes will, however, clarify their differences and reveal why it is possible for possession to be claimed with or without trance. English and English (1958, p. 561) defined trance as:

A sleeplike state marked by reduced sensitivity to stimuli, loss or alteration of knowledge of what is happening, substitution of automatic for voluntary activity.

Bourguignon (1965) adopted this definition. Pattison, Kahan, and Hurd (in press) define the trance state as "a mode of consciousness in which the person is conscious, but seemingly unaware or unresponsive to *usual* external and internal stimuli." These definitions are reminiscent of previous discussions of hysteria and hypnosis. However, the present discussion is undertaken without prejudgment as to whether such states reflect abnormality. There is no reason to presume that these mental states *necessarily* imply psychopathology. Pattison et al. (in press) conclude: "the trance state, in itself, is not pathological. Rather . . . it represents a particular mode of consciousness." Moreover, a neutral approach is appropriate when the focus of attention is less on predisposing personality traits and more on momentary states of mind occurring in a variety of cultures.

Although trance is, thus, defined observationally, possession is typically defined personally and culturally. In a wide variety of cultures, there is the belief that certain spirits or gods exist and that they can enter the bodies of human beings and take control of them. As noted before, when persons appear to go into trance in these cultures, it is often assumed that they are possessed by gods or spirits. However, it is important to note that possession is not absolutely dependent on trance. There are numerous reports in which possession is evidenced by a unique power to fight or to cure without any loss of self-consciousness (Harner, 1962). The incident of Jesus and the demoniacs at Gadara (Matthew 8:28 ff) also illustrates this phenomenon. They were clearly self-conscious, even though possessed.

Possession is defined culturally as observed behavior that the community perceives as deviating significantly from the expected. This can be benign, as in the case of glossolalia, or it can be threatening, as in amok behavior seen in certain primitive tribes.

Possession defined personally may include behavior not judged unusual by the culture, such as altruism, as well as that perceived as deviant, such as glossolalia. In both cases individuals might report that they were being controlled or guided by transcendent power, for example, God.

A helpful diagram of these relationships follows:

	Trance	
	Present	Absent
Present		
Possession		
Absent		

Using these definitions, glossolalia would seem to be an experience that always presumes possession but that may or may not include trance, depending on whether one is referring to classical Pentecostalism or neo-Pentecostalism. The culture of the experience is that of the Christian faith, which asserts that God has come to dwell with humankind in Jesus Christ and continues to be present and available through His Holy Spirit. Tongue speakers may chafe over the ascription of the term "culture" to their beliefs, but in the perspective of world religions and ethnic differences, it is exactly what the Christian faith is, that is, one of many extant cultural perspectives. It is the way a particular group of persons interpret their experience. Furthermore, the indwelling of the Holy Spirit is an experience that a group of people intentionally seek and covet. Just as A.C. purposefully sat in front of the lit candle to induce Ogû to visit her, so Christian charismatics today sing songs, pray, lift their hands, study Scripture, and open their mouths to let strange words come out—all in an effort "to get the Spirit" or "to let God come in and take over."

There is little spontaneous possession in Christian glossolalia. Most tongue speaking is sought after and desired. It is thought to be a sign that one's wish that God would come and dwell within has been fulfilled. The rituals of worship, prayer, meditation, etc., are agreed upon ways to put oneself in a position for God to come and possess him/her. This places "seeking the gifts of the Spirit" in the great tradition of Christian mystics, as one well-known apologist, O'Connor (1971), has noted.

The distinction between spontaneous and voluntary possession was made by Oesterreich (1921/1966) to denote those events over which the persons involved felt they had no control—a somewhat rare occurrence in Christian circles. However, this is by no means an absolute truth because it has been presumed that uninvited demons could possess a person. Furthermore, revival literature is replete with anecdotal cases in which uninterested bystanders were convicted of their sin and accepted Christ into their hearts quite apart from any intention of their own. Often, these spontaneous and unintended events evoked a sense of the presence of God and ecstatic expressions of joy. It is as if they, like Jacob in Genesis 32 had to wrestle with the visiting Spirit until they surrendered and gave way to the control of the divine. Thereafter, of course, spirit possession would probably be voluntary, in the sense that converts sought occasions to reaffirm God's presence in their lives.

IS TRANCE ALWAYS PRESENT?

The question of whether trance is always present in possession needs further elaboration. Felicitas Goodman (1969a) has taken the position that speaking in tongues (which all would agree implies that the speaker is possessed by the Spirit) always involves a change of mental state similar to trance. She reported cross-cultural research on the basis of which she concluded that, ". . . speaking in tongues, was not a linguistic, but rather a trance-produced phenomenon, with some linguistic and cultural overlay" (1971b, p. 92). She compared recorded tapes of glossolalia in four settings: a Streams of Power meeting, a tent revival, a mainline Protestant congregation, and a Mexican Pentecostal Church.

Three of the groups spoke English, the fourth spoke Spanish. The Streams of Power movement was a lower class group, located on the Caribbean island of St. Vincent, in whose lengthy services glossolalia was viewed as the words of Jesus Himself. The midwestern tent revival was typical of those week-long Pentecostal nightly meetings characteristic of summertime in mid-America. The mainline Protestant church was an unnamed congregation whose service was shown on National Educational Television in 1965. In the service, glossolalia was seen as evidence of being baptized in the Spirit. The first Apostolic Pentecostal Church was a congregation located in one of the poorer sections of Mexico City in which glossolalia occurred in response to altar calls and where all those kneeling prayed in their own tongues as evidence that the Holy Spirit was present. The four settings differed radically, and the characteristic traits of trance behavior were more evident in some locales than in others.

An analysis of intonation patterns across the several samples of glossolalia did reveal common characteristics, however, which Goodman (1969a) advanced as evidence that the experience was an artifact "of a dissociative state termed trance" (p. 128). These intonation characteristics were:

(a) On the phonetic level, every pulse begins with a consonant and there are no initial consonant clusters. Usually, the pulse is open, i.e., it does not end in a consonant.

(b) Bars are usually of equal duration, especially if the pauses are also considered, as would be so in music.

(c) The accentual system is one of stress, with a primary and secondary accent. The primary one falls on the first pulse of each bar, giving the impression of scanning, in a trochaic rhythm. The stress is always preceded by a pause.

(d) Phrases are of equal length. Within an utterance unit (i.e., with one peak), the intonation pattern regularly shows an onset in the medium range, a peak and a sloping gradient leading to an often precipitous decay.

(e) Glossolalia is not productive. Once an audiosignal has been internalized, it becomes stereotyped . . . Sometimes, within the same group, the low-energy utterances have a different pattern than the high-energy ones, and in these cases, the lower the energy level, the more varied the pattern.

(f) Glossolalia is noncommunicative. It does not transmit a specific message to the listener. All informants and observers agree that the glossolalist often does not hear himself, sometimes is not aware that he uttered an audible signal, and even if he did hear himself, he does not afterwards remember what he said, and thus cannot repeat it. (pp. 125–126)

These conclusions are printed in detail because they provide the basis for Goodman's conclusion that tongue speakers are in trance and that glossolalia is an *artifact* (i.e., the sign) of trance. Culture determines the typical behavior associated with the trance (e.g., the relative immobility of women but not men in the Mexican church during prayer) and the meaning attributed to the tongue (e.g., the assumption that the vocalizations are the words of Jesus in the Streams of Power meetings). But the deepest level of the experience and that which lies beneath glossolalia is trance defined as a dissociative (an altered) state of consciousness.

In a later study, Goodman (1971b) confirmed her earlier conclusions by comparing glossolalia and single-limb trance—that state associated with automatic writing. In both experiences, she suggested that the individual switched off cortical control in response to rhythmic activity (prayer or singing), hyperventilation, or relaxation. Initially, as the noncortical part of the brain becomes dominant, other functions, such as memory, fade and muscles tense, indicating a high level of energy. In neither graphic automatism nor glossolalia is anything produced in the conventional sense of the term. In the midrange of the experience, energy diminishes and tension reduces. The pattern of writing or speaking becomes less constricted and more varied. After this, stereotype sets in again and energy is discharged in pulsations until it subsides. Although in single-limb trance, the effect sometimes lingers for days, in glossolalia, the person usually returns to a normal state of mind quickly. Goodman's conviction, nevertheless, in analyzing the pattern in both this study and the earlier one comparing four cultural settings, is that the overall pattern of tension/release typifies a trance state.

This theory, that glossolalia involves an altered state of consciousness, is similar to that developed by Cutten early in this century (1927) and by Sargant (1949, 1957/1971), both of whom wrote about classical Pentecostals. Further, Lapsley and Simpson (1964a and 1964b), who included neo-Pentecostals in their hypotheses, stated that glossolalia "is thus a form of disassociation within the personality, in which a set of voluntary muscles respond to control centers *other than those* associated with consciousness" (1964b, p. 18; emphasis added). They suggested that the experience is one of regression in the service of the ego, in the sense that tongue speakers give up conscious control of their higher mental processes in the permissive atmosphere of a supportive group in order to resolve their hostility toward primary love objects. Lapsley and Simpson's psychoanalytic model suggests that classical as well as new glossolalics go into an altered mental state in an effort to integrate their personalities. The effect of this endeavor is discussed in chapter 10. However, at this juncture, it is noteworthy that Lapsley and Simpson support the position that a trancelike state is always involved.

Several attempts have been made to measure physiologically this presumed altered or trance state among glossolalics. Palmer (1966) studied skin conductance, breathing rate, heart rate, and brain wave patterns in an attempt to ascertain whether changes in these variables sometimes observed in hypnotized subjects and Yoga mystics would be found among glossolalics. His research is unpublished, but it is thoroughly summarized by C. G. Williams (1981). In his one study, Palmer (1966) used a galvanometer to measure changes in skin conductance among the members of two groups during meetings lasting up to an hour and a half. In one group, glossolalia was present but almost inaudible; in another group, the praying was easy to hear and, at times, included laughing and exclamations of joy. Galvanometer measures were taken of all participants during normal conversation, silent prayer, relaxation, and speaking in tongues. Hypothesizing that glossolalia would be more relaxed than other states (e.g., resembling changes observed in Zen meditators), Palmer predicted that this would be evident in greater electrical flow during speaking in tongues. In neither group were differences found.

In a second study, electroencephalographic recordings of brain wave activity were assessed by Palmer (1966) during periods of prayer in the Spirit (glossolalia), normal wakefulness, silent prayer, and conversation in experiments at the University of Minnesota medical school. The number and background of the participants were not reported. The results were inconclusive and evidenced no tendency for alpha brain wave activity to diminish during tongue speaking, as would have been predicted had there been an altered state of consciousness.

Heart rate changes were also measured in a third investigation comparing differences among the aforementioned conditions. On the basis of previous research, Palmer (1966) predicted that there would be cardiac acceleration under conditions of prayer and deceleration under conditions of wakefulness and conversation. As predicted, when participants were praying silently or in tongues, there was an increase in heart rate, thus confirming greater cortical activity when attention was directed to internal concerns, such as reception of the Holy Spirit. However, no differences between silent and glossolalic prayer were observed, suggesting that there was no greater likelihood of an altered state of consciousness when one prayed in tongues than in normal prayer.

There have been at least three other attempts to confirm the trance hypothesis. Pavelsky, Hart, and Malony (1975) attempted to refine Palmer's methodology by standardizing the length of time in which persons sat quietly, prayed in English, and prayed in their tongues while being assessed on breathing rate, heart rate, and brain wave pattern. The results confirmed Palmer's (1966) finding that heart rate increased under *both* prayer conditions but that there were no differences between prayer in English and prayer in tongues.

A subsequent study along these same lines was conducted by Strom and Malony (1979) utilizing the techniques of Kirlian (or negative) photography to assess possible changes in a subject's mental state during speaking in tongues. Earlier, Moss and Johnson (1972) found that changes occurred in photographs of the energy field surrounding the body when persons were in different states of emotion. Two groups of fifteen Presbyterian glossolalics and fifteen nonglossolalics matched for sex, marital status, years in their church, and so on, had their right index finger photographed during periods of rest, prayer in English, and prayer in tongues. The procedure was repeated three times after the method of Pavelsky et al. (1975) so that nine separate photographs of the energy field surrounding the finger were obtained for each person. No differences between groups or conditions were found on amount of white space, heighth or width of the energy field (auras), thus lending little support either to the prediction that glossolalics differ in mental state from nonglossolalics or that glossolalics go into some measurable change of consciousness when they speak in tongues.

In a direct test of Goodman's hypothesis that glossolalia could not occur without trance, Spanos and Hewitt (1979) assessed tongue speaker's amnesia during trance, disorientation immediately after trance, and memory loss for the experience of tongue speaking. These features along with closing the eyes and uncontrollable body activity, such as trembling or rocking, were the features of trance without which Goodman had predicted there would be no glossolalia. The alternative nontrance position suggested that amnesia during glossolalia was due to hyperconcentration during a complex event and memory loss could be explained in terms of poor recall for nonsense syllables, such as the "words" in tongues.

Experienced glossolalists were observed in repeated thirty-second intervals, periods during which they were instructed to speak in tongues with or without their eyes open. Spontaneous eye closure when they were instructed to keep their eyes open; twitching or trembling of limbs or face; shuddering, jerking, shaking, rocking or stiffening of the body; and interruptions of the flow of speech when instructions to open or close the eyes were all recorded.

The researchers concluded that there was no essential difference in the glossolalia they observed under these laboratory conditions and that they had observed many times in real life worship experiences:

> Our results run counter to all the predictions derived from the trance hypothesis of both Goodman (1972c, 1974a) and Kildahl (1972). Glossolalia was spoken easily with eyes open as well as closed and was neither accompanied by kinetic activity nor followed by disorientation. During glossolalia subjects' receptivity to external events and their ability to use information learned before glossolalia was demonstrated by their responsiveness to the "open/close eyes" signal taught before but administered during glossolalia. All of these findings are consistent with anecdotal reports (Kelsey, 1964; Samarin, 1972c)

indicating that individuals sometimes engage in glossolalia while carrying out activity that involves sustained visual attention to the external environment (e.g., driving a truck). In short, while glossolalia may be accompanied by kinetic activity, eye closure and disorientation in some social settings (Alland, 1962; Boisen, 1939), it can easily occur in the absence of these behaviors. (Spanos & Hewitt, 1979, pp. 432–433)

Of the twelve glossolalics observed in the above experiment, eleven said that their tongue speaking had improved over time. However, this did not seem related to a tendency to enter an altered state of consciousness, as evidenced by the fact that seven indicated they were fully conscious all of the time, and the remaining five reported being conscious part of the time.

In another part of their study, Spanos and Hewitt (1979) assessed the recall of words while speaking in tongues or while reading a short story aloud. Under neither of these conditions was memory as great as that for a control condition in which the participants listened to the list of words read without doing anything else. There was no difference in the number of words recalled while reading or while speaking in tongues, indicating that the presumed trance state of glossolalia did not interfere with thinking any more than when reading in English, an act that was not thought to involve an altered state of consciousness. Similar results were found for performance on a paper-and-pencil task immediately following these two conditions. Participants were able to match symbols and numbers equally well after they had spoken in tongues or read portions of a short story. Thus, once again, no evidence was found for the trance hypothesis.

To determine whether recall of the content of glossolalia was dependent on the trance state of participants or the meaningfulness of the words, a group of nonglossolalics were tested on their retention of words in a passage of English prose, random words on a list, and a transcribed portion of glossolalic speech. Results showed that more prose was remembered than random words and more random words were remembered than the nonsense syllables of glossolalia. Thus, the difficulty tongue speakers have in recalling their words can be explained in terms of word meaning without recourse to a trance hypothesis.

These conclusions accord with what McDonnell stated:

There would be almost universal rejection on the part of all Pentecostals and charismatics of the position that tongues is usually spoken in an ecstatic state or that it represents a product of trance. (1976, p. 82)

As a practicing glossolalic, Dennis Bennett stated:

. . . Christian speaking in tongues is done as objectively as any other speaking, while the person is in full possession and control of his wits and volition, and in no strange state of mind whatever. (cited in Hamilton, 1975, p. 32)

A more balanced statement is that of Samarin, the well-known anthropological linguist, who concluded:

. . . glossolalia is *sometimes* associated with *some* degree of altered state of consciousness, that this *occasionally* involves motor activity that is involuntary or, *rarely,* a complete loss of consciousness, and that in any case subsequent use of glossolalia (that is, after the initial experience) is *most often independent* of dissociative phenomena. (1972c, p. 33)

It is interesting that Samarin qualified his statement in the manner he did because his own first venture into glossolalia involved a state of dissociation. In a footnote to an earlier paper (1971a), he states:

I must confess that in spite of my claim that anyone can speak in tongues (except for psychological inhibitions), I put off experimenting with glossolalia for a long time. It was not until I found myself in a mild altered state of consciousness, induced by concentration on the reflection of light on leaves and water in a park, that I realized I was free enough to do something strange. I am satisfied that I spoke in tongues, and that I was fluent (more or less so) only so long as I did not think about what I was actually doing. (p. 67)

However, this is not inconsistent with his basic thesis that continued glossolalia, that is, the repeated speaking in tongues to which most practitioners attest, is grounded in rules for the development of a pseudolanguage rather than in some mental state. As he states in another footnote in the same article, "Any valid explanation must account for the behavior of one of my respondents: he talks to himself in tongues while testing new aircraft in the air!" (1971a, p. 67).

Samarin has disagreed sharply with Goodman over what he terms the "sociolinguistic vs. the neurophysiological explanations for glossolalia" (1972b, p. 293). At one point, he retorted: "Let us say it clearly: G's treatment is erroneous, speculative, contradictory, and incredible, because of her relentless hold on an idée fixe" (1974, p. 209). In this same review (of Goodman's (1972c) book, *Speaking in Tongues: A Cross-cultural Study of Glossolalia*), Samarin defends himself against her accusation that he was ignorant of the "diagnostic signals of the altered state" (Goodman, 1972c, p. 96) in a manner that may give a key to the vehemence of his reactions to Goodman's suggestions:

If I did not record my qualifications as an observer, it was because I felt there was no need. With St. Paul's diffidence, I am now forced to recite them. Born into a distinguished family in the pre-Pentecostal, tongue-speaking Russian sect of Molokan Spiritual Jumpers, I participated from childhood through adolescence in all types of major functions. Disassociation has always been a common feature of Molokan religious events, especially in the ever-rising "revivalistic" (in the ethnographer's sense) groups in the community. As an adolescent, I participated as a *critical observer* in a young people's movement where inspiration by the Spirit led to frequent, prolonged and intense dissociation. . . . And I know dissociation personally from two experiences, both of the "nature" variety, once unexpectedly and once self-induced for my research on glossolalia. (1974, p. 210; emphasis added)

One suspects that there may have been more than dispassionate analysis in Samarin's contention that glossolalia follows the linguistic rules for the development of a pseudolanguage anywhere and at anytime and is not just a product of an altered state of mind. His role as a "critical observer" in such a close-knit, charismatic group as he describes must have been, at one and the same time, status enhancing and painfully isolating.

Samarin's position comprises three points. First, he suggests that the examples used by Goodman are not *cross*-cultural, but *sub*cultural, in the sense that one would expect all Pentecostal worship to be similar. Goodman's Mexican, Caribbean, Brazilian, and American observations (1969a, 1969b, 1972c) as well as her later Mayan, and African observations (1971a, 1973, 1974b, 1980) were all of Pentecostal glossolalics. They should be similar, just as Anglican worship should show similarities, regardless of the country in which it was observed. According to Samarin (1974) Goodman was observing a subset of Christianity and not a cross-cultural sample.

Second, glossolalia should be understood as a linguistic anomaly similar to other speech phenomena that cannot be accounted for by the rules that apply to ordinary language. Thus, both the characteristics noted by Goodman and the development of a person's tongue resemble "a number of different kinds of speech behavior in natural language under conditions that all would take as normal" (Samarin, 1972b, p. 295). His contention is that given the motivation to produce a "heavenly language," the individual follows the steps for the development of a pseudolanguage.

He reports experiments in the production of such "languages" among graduate students. These illustrate that although there was a wide disparity in the facility with which the students accomplished the task, there were, nevertheless, features that were consistent and that resembled glossolalia (Samarin, 1971a). Defined as "an attempt to produce a stream of speech spontaneously with the fewest possible elements while at the same time avoiding the appearance of complete redundancy" (p. 60), the development of a pseudolanguage involved at least two processes: echoism and primitivization. Echoism is the tendency to repeat sounds in alternate forms in a stringing process. This is similar to what children do— Samarin infers that the procedure includes some form of regression to earlier forms of speech. Primitivization refers to the tendency to reduce the number of discrete phonological types to the proportions found in one's native language. He gives some analyses of comparative proportions of these elements in English and in glossolalia among English-speaking persons that show striking similarities (Samarin, 1973a, pp. 81–84).

A more detailed analysis of the linguistic features of glossolalia is presented earlier, but suffice it to say that in this regard, Samarin suggests speaking in tongues is an example of a speech anomaly rather than a product of a state of mind. As he concluded in comparing religious glossolalia with nonsense languages: ". . . it is, at least at this time, impossible to isolate the discriminating features in each kind of discourse—if there really are any" (1971a, pp. 56–57).

Samarin's third point is that glossolalia is learned behavior (1969b).

Here, he is talking about the motivation for, the meaning of, and the form of the experience:

> . . . there are some things that he [the glossolalic] does learn. First, that glossolalia (in some form) must be produced to be accepted as a member of the Pentecostal society. Second, that there are some phonological and paralinguistic features that are valued by the in-group and other features that are eschewed. He learns, also, that he can vary the features (hence the total discourse) according to what he would like to "say" (that is, through affect). Finally, he may learn to use (that is borrow) certain sequences of syllables that he hears from the lips of other glossolalists. . . . In other words, although every glossolalic discourse is potentially idiosyncratic, the glossas (that is, glossolalic "languages") of the members of a frequently-interacting group of individuals show similarities that are not purely random. (1973a, p. 87)

Thus, once again, the presumption is that a natural rather than an extraordinary mental state is involved.

In answer to Samarin's critique, Goodman (1972a) continues to insist that what is observed is more than a style of discourse characteristic of a Pentecostal subculture. She noted that Samarin has himself indicated that when certain syllables in glossolalia got extra stress and volume, it was probably "to be explained by intonational and emotional factors, not linguistic ones in the strictest sense" (Samarin, 1968, p. 74). Rather than discount these features of tongues, she suggests they should be emphasized. The intonational pattern within a given speech in tongues follows a systematic pattern cross-culturally and cross-linguistically according to Goodman (1972a):

> It is the *total "unit utterance"* that is characterized by an onset in the medium range, a rising to a peak, and then a drop which terminates at often very low levels. This kind of intonation curve is highly diagnostic of utterances spoken while in trance. (p. 298, emphasis in original)

Moreover, she continues to insist that her observations were, in fact, cross-cultural. In addition to the Caribbean, Ohio, Texas, and Mexican samples reported in her earlier research (1969a and 1969b), she found the same intonational pattern in glossolalia in a Mayan Indian Apostolic congregation in the Yucatan and in a church service on the island of Nias in Indonesia. According to Goodman (1972a), this variety composes a genuine *cross*-cultural rather than purely a *sub*cultural sample. Glossolalia in these settings does not follow the "native speech melody in all its variations, nor the intonation and accent patterns of the available prosody" (p. 298). Acknowledging that no human behavior, speech included, occurs in a cultural vacuum, she yet insists that the systematic universality she has depicted points to a common underlying subvocal mental state, which, incidentally, is overtly recognizable in most occasions of speaking in tongues.

How is one to judge between these two alternatives: the altered state of consciousness position of Goodman and the sociolinguistic viewpoint of Samarin? Although the research to date has not found glossolalia to be accompanied by clear indices of trance (brain wave, heart rate, breathing pattern changes), we are inclined for two reasons to agree with Goodman that the experience usually involves some change in mental status. First, the claims of glossolalics that they are not under their own control but that of the Holy Spirit is in and of itself an affirmation that some change in their normal status has occurred. Second, it is more appropriate to think of altered states of consciousness as existing along a continuum rather than in a strict dichotomy with a "normal" state. Thus, if one takes this point of view, states of trance are very common in the general population and are, in fact, the rule rather than the exception. Glossolalia might be an altered state of consciousness without those accompanying physical changes that would be more indicative of prolonged meditation or deep hypnotic trance. This is a position that theorists of hypnosis have long recognized, but which has only recently been applied to religious phenomena like glossolalia (Swanson, 1978).

Swanson, in an article entitled, "Trance and Possession: Studies of Charismatic Influence" (1978), suggests that religious experiences include characteristics of altered mental states that are common in secular experiences as well, "Trance and possession are often considered exotic, but they seem to me to be common experiences and also to be central to our lives as human persons" (p. 253). Although most religious charismatic experiences have been thought to occur spontaneously and are claimed to be valid apart from the approval of religious authorities, Swanson (1978) wants to regard those events that occur within established frameworks, such as rite and custom, as equally charismatic. Thus, similar processes are at work in daydreaming, freeway-driving, speaking in tongues, absorption in reading a book, tears of joy at a Mass, marching in an army band, shouting for one's team at a football game, or accepting the invitation of an evangelist to dedicate one's life to God.

Although classical hypnotic trance and classical Pentecostal ecstasy are examples of *deep* involvement in trance, many other events in daily life include, even *require,* trancelike processes. Swanson suggests that culture requires individuals to be committed to goals that are not their own but that they experience as compelling and desirable. It is similar to the process of identification that psychoanalysts have depicted as the means by which culture is passed down from parent to child. It is almost as if Swanson is saying that culture would not exist without some forms of trance whereby persons adopt a world view and perceive reality in terms of it.

This opinion becomes clearer when Swanson's definition of trance is considered:

To "be in trance" means to be absorbed with purposes that are not merely our own and it means to have a personal desire to fulfill those purposes. To be in trance means to act in the framework provided by such purposes: to

construe the world, and to relate to it, in the relevance which those purposes have given it. (1978, p. 254)

Thus, according to this definition, acting in a play would be a clear example of trance, particularly if one identified with the role one played
and—at least during the time of the run—saw the world through the
eyes of the character one was playing and became that person for the
time being. Knowing oneself as an Ohio State Buckeye because one chose
to attend that university and to identify with others who shout support
of the team at football games is another example of trance from this
point of view.

Swanson's (1978) definition of *possession* adds a further dimension to
his understanding of trance:

> [Possession] consists in a person's seeing himself as *not* having had a role in
> formulating the purposes he implements when in a trance *and* in his *not*
> having accepted those purposes before he implements them. He finds, in-
> stead, that he is pursuing purposes that originated apart from his desires or
> choices. (p. 255)

Although most American citizens would report that democracy is the
best way to live, they probably espouse this form of government quite
apart from any choice they made to support it. According to this definition, family, city, ethnic, and cultural identities are clear examples of
possession. In these and many other cases, persons become apologists for
positions they have had no part in choosing. They are possessed. Swanson's (1978) position is that society would not exist without both trance
and possession.

These distinctions between the two processes may be more apparent
than real, however. They are quite likely dimensions of the same process.
Although there seem to be situations where we choose and seek out those
authorities and groups to whom we will give allegiance and although
there appear to be other situations where we become aware that we did
not choose the viewpoint we are advocating, there is, nevertheless, a sense
in which this difference is meaningless. All our choices are determined by
the culture in which we are raised and even when we select one alternative over another we do so within the range of options available in our
society. Furthermore, when we self-consciously feel possessed by a power
outside us, as in glossolalia, this can be revealed to be only an extension
of inner forces that compel us in other circumstances (e.g., when we function within the limitations of a role, such as that of a bank teller or a
radiologist). In all such cases, we are driven by the rules of the situation.
In some cases, we are unaware of them. They have become habitual and,
thus, subconscious. In other cases, they have a radical feel to them, as in
speaking in tongues. Thus, overall, trance and possession, broadly defined, are dimensions of the same phenomenon, and they are at the very
center of what makes social life possible.

It is only a step beyond this discussion to assert that glossolalia is, indeed, an example of this essential and, therefore, normal, sociopsychological process. In many (if not most) cases, glossolalics are attracted to, and seek out, the experience. In fact, many Roman Catholic churches have "Life in the Spirit Seminars" to induce the experience through study and training (Lovekin & Malony, 1977). Many charismatics of both the classical and neo-Pentecostal types go to worship expecting to speak in tongues. In this sense, Swanson's (1978) definition of trance is sustained, namely, the desire to fulfill purposes that are not merely one's own coupled with the willingness to act in the way one is told to act to make this come to pass. Furthermore, both after and before the event, there is the self-chosen inclination to construe the world in terms of these purposes.

Speaking in tongues clearly meets Swanson's (1978) definition of possession because tongue speakers unanimously claim that God is speaking through them with words not of their own choosing—exemplifying Swanson's statement that those who are possessed see themselves as not having self-consciously chosen to be the mouthpiece of the power outside themselves.

There is a need for a more benign understanding of trance and possession in line with Swanson's (1978) delineation. Although glossolalia may involve an altered state of consciousness, it may not thereby involve an aberration so much as an extension of a normal and necessary psychological process inherent in the fabric of human development, speech production, and societal functioning. Although future research may show clear psychophysiological evidence that some glossolalics are in deep trance, it is not surprising that research to date has not found such evidence because the trance process can be assumed to exist along a continuum and is, thus, normative for all persons. The claims of many charismatics that they are not in trance is seen as a cultural protest based in a prejudgment that changes in mental state are psychopathological. However, the present discussion has demonstrated that such changes are not necessarily abnormal. Moreover, those who protest loudly that they are in full control and are completely conscious during the experience would do well to take a second look at the theology they espouse, for at the center of their claims is the assertion that God does, indeed, take control of them when they speak in tongues.

This point of view is supported by a neurological model for understanding glossolalia proposed by Shulka and Pattison (1983). These authors concluded that glossolalia—whether (1) as a religious practice engaged in by psychologically normal persons during states of full consciousness and religious trance; (2) evoked in normal persons during experimental hypnotic trance; (3) imitated by naive experimental observers; (4) replicated intentionally by experienced linguists; (5) spoken by borderline persons during states of regression; (6) expressed occasionally by regressed schizophrenics; or (7) classified as a new category (heretofore unreported), that is, as one element of temporal-lobe seizure patterns is a disruption of the psychobiological pathway of normal speech. Extending the brain mapping of speech centers, Penfield and Rasmussen (1950) postulated a model whereby: (1) thought is organized in Broca's motor speech area of the frontal lobe of the brain; (2) then it is linked to the ideational center of the temporal lobe; (3) next, it is transmitted to a lexical center and is organized into words and sentences; (4) the thought, now become words, is transmitted to the motor speech center at the back of the temporal lobe; (5) this center then sends messages to the motor cortex of the brain and subsequently to the larynx and the lips.

Glossolalia is seen as a disruption between steps 2 and 3. The lexical center of the temporal lobe is excited apart from any connection to ideas. Shulka and Pattison (1983) conclude that this disruption happens in *all* cases of glossolalia. They based their conclusions on an unusual case of glossolalia accompanying temporal-lobe seizures in a woman who had previously had surgery to remove an aneurysm of the left cerebral artery. At times, she would become "blank," close her eyes, evidence complex (but ritualized) arm movements, and utter strange sounds—like Indian chants. In her case, the attacks were ego dystonic and always resulted in severe headaches in the left temporal lobe. Shulka and Pattison diagnosed the cause as "paroxysmal excitation of the lexical center without connection to ideation or thought" (1983, p. 14).

They suggest that the process described is the same across all glossolalics. "Anyone can be glossolalic," they assent, and when they are the cerebral process of glossolalia is the same. Although their case study is of involuntary glossolalia, intentional glossolalia (be it religious or experimental) is provoked by this disruption of the normal speech process, too.

In conclusion, this study is one further evidence that glossolalia may involve an altered state of consciousness that is neither pathological nor exceptional, save in a few cases, as in the organic brain syndrome example, just cited.

7

Deprivation

Classical Pentecostalism was thought to be a lower class movement. Horace Bushnell, well-known early New England Christian educator, depicted the pietists of his day as from "the humbler stratum of life" (Hamilton, 1975, p. 89). An observer of a Chicago gathering of Holiness religion in the early 1900s described the group in this manner:

> The most of the people affected were foreigners, and, if I could judge correctly from their appearance and accent, they were Norwegians and Swedes. The most of them were quite intelligent and respectable in outward seeming, and would have sat in any ordinary religious congregation without attracting attention by any peculiarity of feature or dress. There were some, however, who seemed fit candidates for an insane asylum, evidently with small mentality and on the edge of nervous wreck. All seemed to belong to the working class, and there was an unusual proportion of middle-aged and elderly, fleshy women who appeared to be matrons and housekeepers from humble homes, and who probably found the only excitement in their humdrum existence in these services. (Hayes, 1913, p. 87)

A more recent assembly of over 3,000 members of the Church of God, Cleveland, Tennessee, impressed one reporter as noteworthy because they had come great distances at much expense to themselves in spite of being humble people with little material wealth or status. Furthermore, whereas the Holiness bodies had broken off from mainline Protestant groups, the origin of the Pentecostal revival can be traced to a group of black worshippers in a storefront church on Azuza Street in the slums of Los Angeles (Tinney, 1971). The black genesis of this movement was no sociological accident. As Anderson (1979) suggested, Pentecostalism has been the religion of the "disinherited."

Although few, if any, empirical surveys were conducted until recently (cf. Bradfield, 1979) to validate these impressions, social scientists have typically agreed that these movements were, indeed, largely confined in their appeal to persons in the lower socioeconomic classes. As will be seen, this assumption has not characterized neo-Pentecostalism since the 1960s nor does it typify contemporary classical Pentecostalism. However, the generalization does apply to the earlier expressions of these phenomena.

Of some importance has been the answer to the question, "Why should enthusiastic, tongue speaking, holiness-type of religion appeal primarily to the lower socioeconomic classes?" Several alternative, but complementary, explanations have been offered.

Some theorists have related the outgrowth of such pietistic movements to the increase in formalism and rationalism since the Renaissance (Knox, 1950, pp. 139 ff.). As persons felt increasingly distanced from the experience of faith through traditional ritualism, the meaning of which was appreciated only by intellectuals, they became restless for new vitality. The Enlightenment of the eighteenth and nineteenth centuries greatly affected traditional religion and left persons with average or below average intellect behind in its wake. Educated clergy became knowledgeable about Biblical criticism and contemporary philosophy, but these understandings were denied or misperceived by many church members (Knox, 1950).

When social upheaval is added to such an intellectual climate, much dissatisfaction can result, as may be seen in the emergence of Holiness groups within mainline Protestant groups after the Civil War in America (Synan, 1971, p. 13 ff.). It is no accident that the greatest response to these calls for deepening spiritual life and striving for purity and perfection should affect Methodism in the South, where the disruption of the economy was greatest. The appeal to return to Wesley's emphasis on spiritual perfection in this life was heard by those whose existence was most threatened.

Other theorists have suggested that the last quarter of the nineteenth century saw another major change that provoked much social unrest. This was the massive immigration of foreigners to America—a process that was encouraged by idealistic social values but that caused much stress in the competition for economic security (Anderson, 1979).

Another facet of this analysis has emphasized the migration to cities from rural environments—a move that typically caused much anxiety and strain. The churches of the city were often not as experienced, as familiar, or as equally supportive as those back home, even when they were part of the same denomination. Thus, independent Holiness-type gatherings were attractive. They offered an oasis and a vitality in the midst of the unfamiliarity and aridity of city life. In an early article, "Holiness Religion: Cultural Shock and Social Reorganization," John Holt (1940) observed that Pentecostal churches were most concentrated in counties of the southeast where there had been significant increases in population because of changes in residence by those seeking jobs.

All of this is to say that Western society was extremely anxiety producing during the years 1850–1925; this was especially true for blacks, immigrants, and rural poor people. During this period, revivalism reigned supreme among many religionists, the Holiness movement of the late 1800s became officially organized, and the Pentecostal emphasis on a transforming experience of the Holy Spirit evidenced through glossolalia came to the fore. The growth of these groups was extraordinary. To cite but one statistic, Anton Boisen, writing in 1939, noted that the Assemblies of God had grown from 11,000 in 1916 to 48,000 in 1926 to 175,000 in 1937 (p. 185). Holt (1940) reported that this number had increased to 200,000 by 1939 and that the Nazarene Church had grown from 6,600 to over 130,000 in the period 1906–1936.

In addition, Boisen (1939) suggested that this last surge of membership in Pentecostal groups coincided with the economic depression of the early 1930s, during which many more citizens than ever before were experiencing social displacement and survival anxiety. He observed that during the Great Depression there was no significant increase in mental illness. He suggested that sharing of things that matter most with others, suffering with them in the midst of travail, and joining them in attributing certain feelings and thoughts to the visitation of the divine satisfied the basic social needs of the Holy Rollers (as he called them). This kept them from becoming mentally ill, which he defined as social isolation in the midst of stress. To buttress his thesis, Boisen (1955, p. 88) reported a survey of admissions to a mental hospital over a period of six months in an area where these groups were especially active. Of 249 admissions during this time, only 15 were members of Pentecostal groups. Thus, this type of faith, appearing among the underprivileged, served a stabilizing function for those experiencing such situational stress.

The history of the Christian church provides many counterparts to these observations about the rise of Pentecostalism in America. Richard Niebuhr noted this phenomenon in his treatise *The Social Sources of Denominationalism* (1929). He called the underprivileged the "disinherited" and concluded that in numerous cases those who felt that the churches were not satisfying their needs in the midst of oppression would break away and start their own religious groups. Thus, their emergence is to be understood as a result not only of religious dissent, but of social unrest as well (Glock, 1973, p. 208).

The Methodists, the Shakers, the Lutherans, the Calvinists, and the Quakers were but a few of the examples noted by Niebuhr. Initially, all such groups espoused truths they felt were being ignored by the churches they rejected, placed confidence in lay persons as opposed to clergy, insisted on a radical conversion experience as a condition for membership, advocated a serious commitment to personal Christian living, and placed great stock on worshipping together.

Taking a cue from Max Weber (1904–1905/1976) and Ernst Troeltsch (1911/1931), Niebuhr labeled these types of groups "sects"—over against "churches" from which they had broken away. Churches were characterized by professional clergy, conservative social policies, compromises with culture, and formal ritual. Weber and Troeltsch offered this dichotomy as descriptive of social reality, whereas Niebuhr carried it a step further and suggested that churches start out as sects and, furthermore, that all sects become churches over time. Second-generation members of such groups tend to become less emotional, more rational, less dependent on lay leadership and more likely accommodate themselves to the culture.

Thus, Niebuhr saw sects as a stage in the development of religious organizations. This is essentially a Hegelian analysis of the social process, one in which the "disinherited" are seen as the opponents of the status quo. They are destined, however, to become the group against which others will later dissent. The process by which this occurred was the operation of the values of frugality, thrift, and industry, which came out of the discipline cultivated in Pentecostal groups. Thus, they remained poor for only one generation and became middle class or better in the next generation. This process is often said to be illustrated in the Assemblies of God where—according to some observers (Pattison, 1974)—glossolalia remains only a ritual or rite of passage in which many members make a "decision for Christ" as teenagers and speak in tongues once, but never practice this expression thereafter. Thus, the essence of the protest becomes muted in the face of societal conformity.

Returning to Niebuhr's developmental thesis, "deprivation theory" has been the way in which Glock (1973) and others (e.g., Aberle, 1965; Bradfield, 1979; Merton, 1957) have depicted the motivation that resulted in persons becoming part of such groups as Pentecostalism. The term, "deprivation" refers to "any and all of the ways that an individual or group may be, or feel disadvantaged in comparison either to other individuals or groups or to an internalized set of standards" (Glock, 1973, p. 210). This perception leads to efforts to compensate for or to correct the situation. The classic illustration according to Tinney (1971) was slave religion, with its emphasis on exuberance, dancing, and spirit possession. He states:

> . . . unlike the major expressions of Protestantism, [Pentecostalism] was not imported by the slave master to justify slavery and pacify those in chains. On the contrary, Pentecostalism developed on the black scene and became a contribution of the ghetto to the Christian nation at large. (p. 5)

Slavery was deprivation; spirit-filled religion was the answer. Blacks dissented from the dominant white religion of the day and hearkened back not only to Pentecost, but also to their African heritage, with its extensive use of drums and high emotion, including speaking in tongues. Tinney (1971) sees glossolalia as similar to the possession states of these tribal religions.

The delineation of the manner in which certain groups responded to deprivation has been the concern of both Charles Glock (1973) and Bryan R. Wilson (1959). They help to explain why persons experiencing certain types of deprivation gravitate to certain types of groups and how Pentecostalism differs from other sects. Bradfield (1979) used some of these insights to compare classical Pentecostals with neo-Pentecostalism.

Glock (1973) suggested deprivation could be of five kinds: economic, social, organismic, ethical, and psychic. Table 7.1 is illustrative of his contention that only one type of deprivation, economic, results in sect formation. This is a hypothesis that could be seriously questioned from a historical point of view.

Glock's explanation is that *felt* deprivation (not necessarily *real*, but by no means *unacknowledged*) is a necessary precondition for the emergence of any new social movement, religious or secular. It should be noted that, for Glock, secular solutions will be sought initially; where they are successful, there will be no need for seeking religious answers. This is especially true in regard to economic, social, and organismic deprivations, but it is less true where the deprivations are ethical and psychic. This is tantamount to saying, however, that secular resolution of deprivations deals with the elimination of causes, whereas religious resolutions only compensate for feelings. Although Glock would probably deny bias, this appears to be an unwarranted prejudgment.

Felt deprivation is only the efficient rather than the sufficient provocation for the rise of a new movement. The further conditions are that the felt deprivation be a shared perception, that no other organizations be perceived as being able to help, and that a leader emerge with enough charisma to attract followers into the new movement. When these sufficient conditions exist, a new movement, such as Pentecostalism, may emerge (Glock, 1973, p. 212). These conditions appeared to be present in the amazing and unexpected positive response to W. J. Seymour's glossolalic revival on Azuza Street in Los Angeles in 1906, which was a direct descendent of Charles Parham's ministry in the midwest.

Glock's contention that sect formation follows economic deprivation is grounded in his distinction among the five enumerated types above. Economic deprivation is the limited access of certain persons to the necessities and luxuries of life from a monetary and material point of view.

Table 7.1   Origins, forms, and development of religious groups

Type of deprivation	Forms of religious groups	Success expectations
1. Economic	Sect	Extinction or transformation
2. Social	Church	Retain original form
3. Organismic	Healing movement	Becomes cultlike or is destroyed by medical discoveries
4. Ethical	Reform movements	Early extinction due to success, opposition, or becoming irrelevant
5. Psychic	Cult	Total success, resulting in extinction through transformation, or failure due to extreme opposition

From Glock (1973), p. 220.

Social deprivation is the experience of low status, based on society's attributing more status to some than to others. Organismic deprivation is the disadvantaged person's experience as a function of being handicapped, disabled, or ill. Ethical deprivation refers to the experience of conflict over ideals and practice, pressures to conform to violations of conscience, and blocks to accomplishing goals. Psychic deprivation occurs when persons feel they have no meaningful system to give purpose to their lives.

Glock's contention is that different types of deprivation lead to different kinds of religious movements. As can be seen from Table 7.1, only economic deprivation results in sects, for example, the Pentecostals. Glock states, "sect members compensate for economic disadvantage by substituting religious privilege in its place" (1973, p. 213). For example, the gift of speaking in tongues takes the place of material wealth, which the members do not have.

Although he suggests that social deprivation results in church-type religious groups, Glock qualifies his statement somewhat by saying that it is most likely to be true where the lack of social status exists without a strong economic component accompanying it. In this situation, a complete transformation of society is not required as it is in most sect-type movements. Relief is sought, therefore, by changing a part of society, not its basic organization. These groups want to accommodate themselves to the larger society not transform it entirely or retreat from it.

Secular examples of this phenomenon are the National Association for the Advancement of Colored People (NAACP) and the National Organization for Women. Within mainline religion, the Good News movement in United Methodism and the English Synod within Missouri Synod Lutheranism are examples. However, Glock notes that very often social deprivation is a strong component along with economic deprivation and that in these cases, the religious solution resembles sects. This would seem to have been the case of whites in the post–Civil War South, immigrants at the turn of the century, and blacks even to the present day. These represent that combination of low status and relative poverty (the "disinherited" to use Niebuhr's term) that has been considered to be the breeding ground for Pentecostal religion.

Organismic deprivation more than likely results in an exclusive emphasis on healing and, thus, becomes cultlike in character as contrasted with both sects and churches. By this Glock means they tend to form groups off to the side of the culture and to have little interest other than their single preoccupation with health in its various forms. Christian Science is the prime example of a religious-type cult, whereas the American Association for Mental Retardation is a secular illustration. Glock does not mention the combination of a concern for healing in Pentecostal Holiness groups where healing is considered a spiritual gift alongside speaking in tongues. Here nonmedical healing for persons too poor to afford doctors is a central part of religious practice. These groups are not cults if one adopts the current distinctions made between cults and sects by such authors as Needlemen and Baker (1978). They depict a cult as the introduction of a hitherto unknown religion. Thus, the Hari Krishna movement is a cult, whereas the Brethren in Christ in America, a Pentecostal group, is not. In the latter, healing is a central component of worship.

Ethical deprivation leads to reform movements rather than sects or churches or cults. Here the sense of a neglected ideal or a disparity between standards and practices or of unequal dispensation of justice leads to special-interest movements with specific goals. Once these goals are met, reform movements usually pass out of existence or take up new objectives. Although Glock notes that both Lutheranism and Methodism were reform movements that resulted in long-lasting church-type groups, he does not seem to recognize that sect groups, such as the Pentecostals, had strong ethical concerns for moral purity which they felt the larger churches were neglecting in their efforts to accommodate to society. Nor does he acknowledge that they, too, may outlast their specific protests. Certainly, they seem to have done so if the continued growth of these groups is any indication.

Finally, Glock sees the religious resolution of psychic deprivation as cultlike in its form. It is here that the confusion of cult and sect in Glock's thinking is most apparent. He notes that psychic deprivation, the sense that there are no meaningful or stable values on which to ground one's life, evokes extreme measures and most often results in the rejection of the prevailing culture. He fails to note that this is as characteristic of sects as it is of cults. The Pentecostal movement is the classic example, with its rejection of education and wealth as conditions of membership or as helpful in acquiring the gifts of the Holy Spirit. For Glock, sects and cults are seemingly almost one and the same. In reporting on a study his group conducted, he stated:

> . . . members of a millenarian religious group showed that all had passed through a period of "church hopping," ultimately rejected all available religious perspectives, and passed through a period of religious despair before being converted to the new movement." (Glock, 1973, p. 216)

To be sure, this research (Lofland & Stark, 1965) was concerned with a group imported from Korea and, thus, qualified for the designation of cult (cf. Needleman & Baker, 1978). But sects, such as the Pentecostals, are often made up of individuals who also do much church hopping prior to becoming members of groups that have their origins within the culture's dominant religion, Christianity. For these persons, it was not that the truth of life's meaning could not be found in the Christian faith, but that mainline churches had lost it by accommodating themselves to the culture. Holt (1940), in his article relating culture shock and Holiness religion, noted that for many migrants from rural to urban areas, the mainline church was experienced as strange and nonsupportive. They fled from the church, even though it often had the same name as their church back home, and they joined independent, storefront groups that were more like what they had been used to in their rural environments.

Bryan R. Wilson (1970), British sociologist of religion, does not make this distinction between sect and cult, referring to them both as "minority religious movements" composed of persons engaged in a protest against the orthodox or institutionalized means of attaining salvation. He offers a typology of these groups and suggest that they all offer a unique claim to salvific truth, new identities for individuals, and opportunities for access to a new reality. Furthermore, they offer close-knit fellowships and evoke self-sacrifice and discipline. His typology (B. R. Wilson, 1970, pp. 37–40) encompasses the distinctions made by Glock (1973) and clarifies the unique kind of religious group to which Holiness and Pentecostal religionists belong.

The seven types of religious sects (B. R. Wilson's general term for all groups of religious protest) are: Conversionist, Introversionist, Revolutionist, Manipulationist, Thaumaturgical, Reformist, and Utopian. From a strict point of view, only the Conversionist type pertains to those groups where speaking in tongues is practiced because only in these groups is there both a distrust of ritual, of education, and of culture coupled with a sense that the world is evil as well as an emphasis on individual salvation in which persons have a subjective emotional experience to which they can attest. Introversionist sects, with their concern for community, come closest to this model. Here, however, there is little concern for converting others or for hyperemotional worship, such as glossolalia (e.g., the Hutterite Brethren).

Pentecostal groups have not typically been Revolutionists in the sense of being concerned with radically transforming culture, although they have often been millenarian in their outlook for the future. Thus, like the Jehovah's Witnesses (Revolutionists by B. R. Wilson's typology), Pentecostals have often expected the speedy return of Christ and the end of the world. As in slave religion, they have been concerned with remaining in the Spirit until the Lord comes. Yet Revolutionist groups, as such, are not characterized by ecstatic worship, as is typical of the Pentecostals.

Manipulationist sects, like Unity and Christian Science, are quite different from Pentecostals, in that God is impersonal, their philosophies are syncretistic, and their worship is hyperrational. Nor are they similar to Thaumaturgical, Reformist, or Utopian sects, in spite of the fact that the first of these emphasizes miracles and healing, as does Pentecostalism. Thaumaturgical groups emphasize magic and contact with the dead. Reformist groups emphasize the application of faith in works and efforts toward justice within society. Utopian sects remake society by reorganizing off to its side in perfect societies. No one of these concerns has been dominant in tongue speaking groups.

B. R. Wilson agrees with both Niebuhr and Glock that sects arise from deprivation. Conversionist sects, of which Pentecostalism is a prime example, often occur where there is social turmoil, economic disruption, a breakdown of traditional norms, and confusion over authority (B. R. Wilson, 1973, pp. 38, 498). Neither anomie nor existential disease nor spiritual discomfort are considered prime bases for explaining the emergence of sects. B. R. Wilson, like Aberle (1965) and other theorists, though not a rigid economic determinist, feels that social unrest is the essential condition for these phenomena.

Using the Marxist language of "compensation," B. R. Wilson (1961) concluded that sects provide a reinterpretation of the meaning of success, offer substitute status, make present circumstances more tolerable by promising hope of future "eschaton," and give emotional release and anxiety relief through their meetings. In particular, Conversionist sects, with such practices as glossolalia, counter the hyperrationalism of contemporary culture by appeals to the Spirit instead of to form and reason. They break through the heavily programmed superstructure through appeals to informal, immediate, emotion-laden experience.

In giving a psychological explanation of an exemplary Conversionist sect, the Elim Foursquare Gospel Church, B. R. Wilson (1961) concludes that those who are in mental anguish find in their experiences in the movement an escape from the dullness of their lives, deep emotional release, a sense of personal power in being able to speak in tongues, and reassurance that they are ultimately worthwhile.

Two recent studies of religion in southern Appalachia supplement the deprivation hypothesis of sect emergence in contemporary America. Gerrard (1970) studied the religion of what he termed the "stationary poor"; Bradfield (1979) investigated the neo-Pentecostal movement in the same region.

The distinction between the stationary and the upwardly mobile poor is that the latter group have hope that their children will not remain poor, whereas the former expect their children to remain poverty stricken. Although the upwardly mobile poor work at tedious laboring and farming jobs with little chance for advancement, they are regularly employed and feel humiliated when forced to accept welfare aid because of accidents or illness. The stationary poor are functionally illiterate, unskilled, seasonally employed, and receive public assistance. They do not foresee any change forthcoming and characteristically have a fatalistic outlook on life, which provokes them to be recklessly hedonistic, on the one hand, and consumed with a strong sense of religious predestination, on the other hand.

Although the upwardly mobile poor tend to follow the Niebuhrian (1929) prediction of moving toward churchlike affiliations, the stationary poor typically participate in independent, one-room, nondenominational fellowships, which meet in abandoned schoolhouses, tents, homes, or barns—rural equivalents of urban store front churches (Gerrard, 1970,

p. 103). Instead of sect or church names (e.g., Assembly of God, Church of Christ, Nazarene—all typical of the upwardly mobile poor), these churches bear either the name of the locale (e.g., Scrabble Creek [West Virginia]) or of the preacher/founder (e.g., Brother Homer's Church).

Although the upwardly mobile poor gravitate toward sects that have become churches, such as the Churches of God or the Free Will Baptists, it is questionable whether these religious groups of the stationary poor have the stability of either a church or a sect. Gerrard (1970, p. 113) suggests the term "religious band" to depict the somewhat spontaneous and impulsive quality of their organizational life. He further suggests that it is more appropriate to call them "Holiness" rather than "Pentecostal" because historically the latter were inclined to generate sect movements, whereas these groups seem to have no goals other than holding services on a given day.

In meeting the psychological needs of such persons as the stationary poor, these "churches" carry individualism to the extreme. The services last just as long as any participant desires to express himself/herself— through arguing doctrine (in a stream-of-consciousness and nonrational fashion) and through dancing, jerking, rolling on the floor, and speaking in tongues. Gerrard (1970) suggests that these activities alleviate feelings of status deprivation and social inadequacy and provide a sense of forgiveness for the sin that they associate with their poverty; opportunities for healing without going to physicians which they cannot afford; and, last but by no means least, recreational release from the boredom that otherwise characterizes their daily lives. In regard to this last Gerrard (1970, pp. 109–110) states:

> Holiness church services are spontaneous, exciting, rhythmical, dramatic, and frequently have elements of humor in sermons and testimonies. Unlike many participants in conventional churches, the participants in Holiness churches are seldom bored. The general atmosphere is one of joy and pleasure . . . "Jesus is fun" is a cry that is sometimes heard during services, or a preacher might say: 'Let's all have a good time in Jesus tonight.'

One wonders whether a sixth type of deprivation should not be added to Glock's list, namely, boredom. Numerous theorists have alluded to the sterility of poor people's lives. Their children stay at home because they do not have the money to go anywhere. Church becomes a significant social and entertainment outlet. This led Aberle (1965) to conclude that boredom was, indeed, a significant factor in deprived persons fleeing the stable predictability of mainline Protestantism and joining groups where one did not know from one week to the next what was going to happen to one or how long one would be there.

The second recent study was conducted by Cecil Bradfield (1979) on the Full Gospel Businessmen's Fellowship International (FGBMFI) a neo-Pentecostal group formed in the early 1950s by a successful Armenian immigrant, Demos Shakarian. Unlike classical Pentecostalism, this group has encouraged its members to remain in their own churches rather than form a new sect. The western Virginia FGBMFI groups Bradfield studied, for example, included only 3% who are members of Pentecostal churches. The rest were spread over Protestant and Catholic churches, with over 20% each in Presbyterian and United Methodist churches. About half the group had changed religious affiliation. Of this group, 60% had joined mainline churches. Thus, this group was quite unlike either the upwardly mobile or the stationary poor of Gerrard's (1970) study.

Furthermore, although the study was conducted in six rural counties where much poverty existed, family income among this sample of the FGBMFI revealed 75% of them with incomes over $10,000 and 18% with incomes over $25,000—significantly higher than the general population. These persons were upper middle class. They were not economically deprived. Yet they all spoke in tongues.

Bradfield (1979) surveyed these persons on all five of Glock's types of deprivation (i.e., economic, social, organismic, ethical, and psychic). His hypothesis was that some form of deprivation existed and that this felt need provoked their becoming part of the charismatic movement. As noted, no warrant was found for assuming economic deprivation nor was there any evidence of felt social or status deprivation. They were not overly young or old, were all male, had higher educational levels than those around them, were more likely to be in professional and managerial occupations than the general public, were upwardly mobile, and belonged to a variety of other organizations. As distinct from classical Pentecostals, they affirmed wealth as able to lead a person closer to God. These persons could be thought to be examples of the phenomenon observed among Pentecostals, namely, the values of thrift and temperance paid off in raising their economic standards. Yet individuals in this sample were not in the Assemblies of God, for instance, where such a dynamic has resulted in a middle- to upper-middle-class membership (Malony, Zwaanstra, & Ramsey, 1972). The FGBMFI studied by Bradfield were largely persons from mainline churches who had sought the gifts of the Spirit, having already attained middle-class status.

In regard to ethical deprivation, Bradfield's (1979) sample was decidedly conservative in a political sense. Their judgment of the ills of society was about equally divided between those that could be construed as social (e.g., inflation, crime) and those that could be considered spiritual (e.g., sin). Their recommendations for solutions were similar to classical Pentecostalism, namely, change had to come from within the heart and the best way to help society was to convert people to God. The FGBMFI in western Virginia did experience ethical deprivation in the sense that they felt strongly that Americans needed to return to God. Although they did not challenge society's basic structure, they did evidence a strong sense that things were not right and that what was needed was a return to basic religious values. They particularly felt a lack of such thinking among the mainline churches to which they belonged. They saw it as their mission to remain inside those churches and to work to change them. They felt that their witness to the work of the Spirit was the prime way they had of pursuing that goal.

Psychic and organismic deprivations were probably the most significant features of the motivation that led these men to participate in the FGBMFI. Nine-tenths of the groups reported that the baptism of the Holy Spirit gave them a new sense of purpose and meaning in life. Numerous participants reported that a new sense of identity resulted. One example reported by Bradfield was a controller for a manufacturing company who said: "Before the baptism of the Holy Spirit I was climbing a ladder of success, jealous of those ahead of me. Now I realize that my strength comes from God and He looks out for me" (1979, p. 45).

Others reported having a sense of failure and finding renewed confidence after receiving baptism. Again, several reported that their education got in their way of receiving the baptism and that now they had put their training in perspective. Of interest is the question whether these persons consciously felt these needs before the baptism of the Spirit or whether they perceived them only in retrospect. Numerous individuals reported that others coaxed them into coming to the meetings for the first time. They also admitted that they resisted. It was as if others perceived a need in them that they themselves did not acknowledge. The new sense of self they reported may be more of a self-fulfilling prophecy than the answer to felt deprivation. However, if one admits that deprivation can be experienced in retrospect by comparing the past to the present, then psychic deprivation could be inferred. Suffice it to say, the participants in this group of the FBGMFI attested to a quality of life that was transforming and vital in comparison to their former life experience.

Finally, organismic deprivation seemed to be a significant factor for about one fourth of the sample. They reported seeking help for themselves or someone else in time of illness as an aspect of their coming to the baptism of the Spirit. Neo-Pentecostals, like classical Pentecostals, acknowledge the importance of God in healing, yet although they pray for each other with the laying on of hands, they still retain a respect for physicians. It is important to note that the majority of these members of the FGBMFI did not report ill health to be a factor in their religious experience.

Bradfield's (1979) study on neo-Pentecostals suggests that traditional deprivation theory does not explain participation in the contemporary charismatic movement. Certainly, economic and social deprivation do not seem significant indicators, and ethical, psychic, and organismic deprivations, although noteworthy, are important only to a degree.

In sum, this chapter has dealt with the extent to which glossolalia could be considered extraordinary behavior, in that it occurs among deprived but not average persons. Although this may have been true in an economic sense of classical Pentecostals, it is not characteristic of neo-Pentecostals. This latter group are more characterized by ethical or psychic deprivation. The second generation of classical Pentecostals also deviate from their predecessors in this regard. On the whole, boredom may be the most influential type of deprivation in glossolalia.

8

Set and Setting Variables

In an undated study of neo-Pentecostals in a large urban center in Canada, Samarin stated:

> The study reported here was stimulated by a colleague who was asked to give a critical reading to the first draft of my TONGUES OF MEN AND ANGELS. He felt . . . that I should have said more about the culture in which speaking in tongues took place. . . .

> In faulting me for not describing Pentecostal culture, my colleague says that I gave the impression that glossolalia can happen in just about any kind of Christian groups in North America. This, he says, is simply not so. (1973, pp. 163–164)

With this Samarian would have no quarrel.

Glossolalia does, indeed, have its time and place. It would be a truism to say, "it occurs where it is expected to occur," but that is the truth in part. As Malony et al. (1972) reported well over half of the teenagers in a study of the Assembly of God were glossolalic by age 16. In this group, speaking in tongues was expected as a sign of spiritual growth. Similarly, in a study of youth attending the colleges and seminaries of the Church of God, Cleveland, Tennessee, a majority of the students reported that they, too, engaged in this practice (Rarick & Malony, 1981).

But conformity to a culture is not the whole story, even in conducive environments such as these, because a significant percentage in both groups was not actively glossolalic. For example, adolescents can react in several ways to their parents, as C. Stewart (1967) and others have reported. Therefore, "person" must be added to "time" and "place" in a discussion of the cultural setting in which this phenomenon occurs. It is to a discussion of these features that this chapter is devoted. How "extraordinary" are the situations in which this phenomenon occurs?

Before turning to a consideration of these matters, several distinctions must be made between this and earlier chapters. This chapter deals with circumstances and conditions that exist *at the time* that persons speak in tongues rather than such factors as social status and psychodynamic traits—both of which are assumed to be long-standing predispositions. Thus, this discussion is more concerned with the occasion than with the precursors of glossolalia. This approach has been termed "cross sectional" as opposed to "longitudinal," in the sense that it describes what *is* happening at a given time instead of what *was* happening in the past that led up to a given event. The question will be, What is the state or condition at the time? rather than, What are the traits or characteristics that predetermined the experience?

For example, John Sherrill reported the experiences of David du Plessis in South Africa and Dennis Bennett in Seattle. About du Plessis he wrote:

> In 1908—just two years after Azuza Street—two Americans who had witnessed that revival arrived in Johannesburg, rented a long-abandoned Presbyterian church, and began to preach. Their message of the Baptism of the Holy Spirit with speaking in tongues was new in South Africa and from the beginning large crowds gathered to listen.

> David's father was one of the people who dropped into the church out of curiosity. David was just nine years old at the time, but he can still remember the effect of that preaching on his father. "He acted like a man on fire," David recalls. "He wanted to leave his business right away and do something for the Lord." David's father was a carpenter by trade. Almost before the family knew it, they were out in the African bush, where his father built mission stations for Pentecostals who were carrying the message into native territories. (1964, pp. 54–55)

About Dennis Bennett he wrote:

> . . . one day in early 1960, Father Bennett received a call from a fellow priest who had noticed that something mysterious was happening in his church. Two of his parishioners were showing the most amazing change. . . . Investigating, Father Bennett's friend learned that the couple had received what they called the "Baptism of the Holy Spirit," and that along with this Baptism they had been given the gift of speaking in a language they did not understand. . . .

> Father Bennett was invited to come and see for himself. He attended a prayer meeting of the Spirit-filled parishioners and was so impressed he asked for prayers that he might receive the Baptism too.

> "There's only one thing," said Father Bennett. "I'd like the Baptism without the tongues."

> "Sorry, Father," he was told. "But tongues come with the package. . . ."

> Father Bennett was prayed for, he did receive the Baptism, with tongues, and nothing has been the same in his life since that moment. (1964, pp. 64–65)

In dealing with these illustrations, the method of the present chapter is to investigate the curiosity of David du Plessis's father and other attitudes the night he attended the Johannesburg revival as well as the various environmental conditions in the meeting itself that provoked his experience. Further, in regard to Father Bennett, the method is to examine the state of mind that led him to attend the meeting and the influence of the parishioners that resulted in his receiving the baptism of the Holy Spirit.

Such issues as the attitudes and perceptions of persons, the mood of society, the environmental conditions, and the associational contingencies (i.e., family, friends) at the time of glossolalia will be discussed. The issues will be grouped under two major headings: *The Set* and *The Setting*. By set is meant the tendency for persons to see situations in a certain way. It refers to an inner mood, disposition, or bias that determines the way in which persons perceive reality. By setting is meant the environment in which an event occurs. It refers to those physical, social, and programmatic conditions that surround glossolalia. Setting, as opposed to set, is an outside rather than an inside-the-person variable.

SET ISSUES IN GLOSSOLALIA

As was said earlier, glossolalia always occurs at a time and place. But it also occurs in *a person*. Persons bring attitudes, thoughts, feelings, and experiences to events. They do not come empty handed. Time and place never fully overwhelm individuals. The decision to enter into the experience of speaking tongues, whether made quickly—as in a person listening to a radio broadcast and spontaneously accepting the invitation to let God speak through him/her—or deliberately—as in those who attend workshop sessions designed for those seeking the gifts of the Spirit—always flows out of private and personal states of mind. One could even take a problem-solving point of view, as Lofland and Stark (1965) have done in their step-wise model for conversion, presuming speaking in tongues to be similar to (if not synonymous with) conversion. Thus, it could be assumed that glossolalia always met some felt need in the individual (Malony, 1978, p. 55–69). However, this has not always been the case, as the following illustrations from Stanley, Bartlett, and Moyle's (1978) survey of Australian charismatics will show. Less than a third of their sample reported a "crisis" experience in their lives prior to speaking in tongues. Examples of these respondents are:

> "I have been 'speaking in tongues' for 15 years. I was not a church-going person, nor was I in any emotional distress or physical handicap when I was told about speaking in tongues. . . . My life has changed from that time on. I had a peace and joy that came from within."

> "As a believer of the Bible, I find it (speaking in tongues) to be scriptural. . . . I was sitting and quietly listening to the radio when I received the gift." (p. 273)

Nevertheless, there were those whose sense of need at the time was very explicit and self-conscious. Examples of these respondents are:

> ". . . I could write a very interesting study on how I was delivered from dependence on drugs after over 20 years. . . . I had tried so many ways to get well and nothing helped."

"I was conscious and unhappy about a vacuum, an emptiness in my very being. . . . Several months passed . . . until I was led to receive this Charismatic experience. . . . It was as if dormant psychic faculties came alive." (p. 273)

These respondents represent the extreme of those who, on the one hand, are seeking answers to questions in their lives and those, on the other hand, for whom the glossolalic experience comes as a surprise. It is important to keep in mind, therefore, that no one of the identifiable sets to be discussed in the following pages is characteristic of all glossolalics nor can any one of the predispositions to be enumerated be said to typify classical, Catholic, or neo-Pentecostals exclusively. Thsee tendencies do reflect, however, identifiable dimensions of the phenomenon that have been detailed in the literature.

Perhaps the most common mental set among glossolalics has been a desire to deepen their spiritual life. As Greeley (1974) states in recounting the start of Roman Catholic neo-Pentecostalism:

> . . . four Catholic lay faculty members at Duquesne University in 1967, *seeking renewed spiritual vitality* for themselves and their students, sought out a group of Episcopal and Presbyterian neo-Pentecostals to learn how to receive baptism of the Spirit. Two of the laymen had the charismatic experience. From this tiny beginning the movement spread to other faculty members and students at Duquesne as well as to residents of the Pittsburgh area; and within a month, the experience had been recounted at Notre Dame University, where hope of *Pentecostalism as a means of individual and church renewal* was enthusiastically received. (p. 318; emphasis added)

This desire to become more serious and less superficial about faith has been characteristic of Holiness, classical Pentecostal, and Protestant neo-Pentecostal movements as well. There are numerous accounts from each of these sources that tell of desires to get beneath formality and convention and to experience God directly and more intensely. Without doubt these motivations stemmed from and closely resembled those of John Wesley who, in the eighteenth century, initiated Holiness religion by his earnest search for sanctification, that is, evidence that he was saved. More recently, "Life in the Spirit Seminars" (S. B. Clark, 1972b)—seven-session workshops offered in Roman Catholic churches—bespeak this motivation in their statement of goals:

> The Life in the Spirit Seminars, then, are concerned with what is most basic to the Christian life, *establishing a person in Christ*. To accomplish this goal, there are four things the Life in the Spirit Seminars try to do:
>
> 1. to help those who come to the seminars to establish or re-establish or deepen *a personal relationship with Christ;*
> 2. to help those who come to the seminars to yield to *the action of [the] Holy Spirit in their lives* so that they can begin to experience his presence and can begin to experience him working in them and through them;
> 3. to help those who come to the seminars to be joined to Christ more fully by

becoming part of *a community* or group of Christians with whom they can share their Christian life and from whom they can be supported in their Christian life;

4. to help them begin to make use of effective *means of growth* in their relationship with Christ. (pp. 9–10)

Very few, if any, charismatic Christians would disavow these objectives as representative of their motivations.

Thus, not all religious persons would be open to this experience of becoming Spirit filled. Only those who were seeking something more than a conventional faith would find glossolalia appealing. As Gerlach and Hine (1970) concluded:

> It is the serious Christian who feels he should read more of the Bible, who is vaguely aware of its "impossible ethic," and who has come to expect some sort of meaningful experience to occur within this religious institution, who can be touched by Pentecostal witnessing. (pp. 177–178)

Both Samarin (1973) and Oden (1972) agree that this places the search for the indwelling of the Holy Spirit in the last century within the pietistic stream of Christian history—that is, those periodic revivals of interest in immediate religious experience that attest to personal contact with the divine. As Samarin (1973c) states: "They . . . want to be, as they say, '100% Christian.' And the movement, through its positive personal interrelations (kinship and friendship networks), through its compelling symbols, and through its rituals, . . . provides them with the means for realizing their aspirations" (p. 174).

A descriptive term that has been suggested for this mind set is "transcendency deprivation" (Mawn, 1975), which is defined as a hunger for a personal-experience-based relationship to the divine. As might be expected, Mawn found that this need typified the quota sample of Catholic Pentecostals in the United States, which he surveyed in his doctoral dissertation. Most likely this finding could be generalized to all other charismatics as well. Thus, they may be representative of Havens's (1968) contention—in his book, *Psychology and Religion: A Contemporary Dialogue*—that the religious thrust of the last half of the twentieth century was a thirst for a religion of experience. Further, this need for depth religion may reflect a move toward recapturing the essence of religion as conceived by another contemporary psychologist of religion, Walter H. Clark (Clark, Malony, Daane, & Tippett, 1973). He perceived the mystical experience to be the essence of religion.

There have been two evaluations of this tendency to seek glossolalia out of yearning for heightened religious experience; one positive and one negative. Pruyser (1978) perceives the charismatic revival as a sign of the inappropriate self-interest of narcissism, whereas Haglof (1971) understands it as an appropriate indication that persons are trying to overcome their alienation from themselves.

Self-preoccupation is a trend that Pruyser (1978) sees as a dominant theme in society for the last quarter century. Self-actualization, sensitivity groups, self-assertion training, and so on, have emphasized this idea. Religious trends have paralleled this development, particularly in the rise of the charismatic movement, which emerged during the same period of time. Pruyser sees important similarities between persons letting themselves go, primal screams, getting in touch with feelings, and so on, and being possessed by the Spirit, speaking in tongues, instant conversions, and so on. He analyzes these dynamics by means of psychoanalytic ego psychology. He concludes that "instant mysticism" and "states of ecstasy" (as in glossolalia) allow certain persons with repressed aggression toward parents and God to regress temporarily and unite with them and, thus, experience momentary power over them. Pruyser further concludes that such experiences allow persons to set aside for the moment their sense of responsibility for themselves and to experience a unification with God in a manner that ignores His grandeur and judgment. He feels that much Spirit-filled activity is an example of projecting subjective feelings onto the notion of the Holy Spirit and that most of it is naive indulgence that needs to be redirected if one is to become religiously mature.

In contrast to Pruyser (1978), Haglof's (1971) evaluation is positive. He states:

> We take it for granted that such behavior—shrieking, convulsions, as well as less primitive manifestations of confrontation with the Spirit such as ecstasy, (apparent drunkenness), tongue-speaking, visions, hallucinations, etc.—are *the reactions of a human type on its way to perfection.* (1971, pp. 201–202; emphasis added)

Haglof sees the experience of being Spirit filled, with all its excessiveness, in a developmental perspective. He understands this development from the perspective of the theorizing of Carl Jung, who felt that maturity came from getting in touch with the *goodness* of the Unconscious—not by seeking to counter its evil domination, as Freud would have recommended. In fact, Jungian theory's concept of individualization (or ideal development) included a reunification with the depth of one's unconscious. Thus, Haglof suggests that glossolalia is but an example of the subliminal uprush of this depth part of the person, and people are to be commended on their willingness to let these experiences happen to them. He quotes both Jonathan Edwards and John Wesley as stating that although religion does not require these extraordinary evidences of the Holy Spirit, nevertheless, they both had such experiences in their own development. An observer of Wesley's preaching methods stated: "It is a well known fact that most of them [meaning persons who spoke in tongues, etc.] who have been so exercised . . . have peace and joy in believing and are more holy and happy than ever they were before. And if this is so, it matters not what remarks are made about their fits" (Haglof, 1971, p. 202).

From this point of view, the temporary abandonment of reason and the willing loosening of one's self-control is actually a healthy thing and puts one in contact with substrata of one's being wherein the possibility for wholeness lies. At these times, the person overcomes his/her alienation from his/her self and the potential for quieter, contemplative development becomes apparent. Without such experiences, one would remain bound by reason and environment.

Closely aligned with this need to deepen religious experience has been a disillusionment with the church. Usually this is experienced as a perceived trend toward modernism coupled with a sense that the vitality of old ways of worship have been lost. Certainly, this was the feeling of the Holiness revivalists in the nineteenth century after the Civil War. As Synan reported:

> Many churchmen lamented the loss of old Methodist institutions, such as the class meeting, the camp meeting, and the emphasis on plainness of dress. As young "progressive" ministers joined the ranks, older preachers looked sadly on such innovations as robed choirs, organs, and seminary-trained ministers. Some warned that if the camp meeting ceased, then the "heroic fires of Methodism" would die out. (1971, p. 35)

The emphasis on come outism—separating from mainline denominations—was characteristic of Holiness churches at the turn of the century and still typifies much of the ideology of classical Pentecostalism.

However, this concern for the church has also been a strong feature in neo-Pentecostal thinking. Although many persons have withdrawn their membership from mainline and joined Pentecostal churches, many more have retained their membership in spite of their concerns. This has been a radical difference between classical and neo-Pentecostalism, and it has been characteristic of both Protestant and Roman Catholic charismatics. They have chosen to reform their churches from within and to gain the spirituality they were missing through small ecumenical prayer or fellowship groups. Dennis Bennett's speech of resignation from St. Mark's Episcopal Church, Van Nuys, California, in 1960 typifies this pattern. His experience had met with strong disapproval.

> "I am sorry for the furor, and for the pain that has been caused. I ask every person in St. Marks whether they be for me or against me, *not to leave the parish or cancel their pledge.* . . . Any rumors that reach your ears that I am leaving the Episcopal church are false . . . no one needs to leave the Episcopal church to have the fullness of the Spirit." (Quoted in Quebedeaux 1976, p. 9)

Nevertheless, the feelings of charismatics remain strong about what the church is not providing, as evidenced by statements reported by Bradfield (1979) in his study of FGBMFI:

> "Mainline churches are becoming too Liberal, putting too much emphasis on social action and not enough on spiritual matters." . . . "People are becoming fed up with the game of playing church and listening to ministers who are trained by seminary professors who are personally unaquainted with Jesus

as Lord of their lives." . . . "I believe that most institutional churches have gotten away from the real Gospel of Jesus. They have a form of worship but deny the power." (pp. 15–16)

The same dissatisfactions have typified Roman Catholic glossolalics. Although some of their discontentment was present before Vatican II, this conclave was a catalyst for much unrest among these persons. Although they remained loyal to the Church, they experienced anxiety over the loss of structure that resulted from the recommendations of the council and were unnerved by the departures of many from the religious life. Roman Catholic charismatics at first found the liturgical reforms of Vatican II to be disruptive and called for a renewal of depth Christianity. As Harrison (1971/1972) noted, they emphasized personal religious experience over formalized ritual, and they were impatient with the lack of support they received from the hierarchy for a charismatic religious style. They also disapproved of the church's tendency to support social action over individual piety.

However, it should be noted that these concerns over ritual and social action have not been as strong as an interest in deepening the spiritual life. As mentioned earlier, neo-Pentecostals do not tend to withdraw as much nor, as Samarin (1973) found, do they tend, on the average, to be estranged from their churches. In a survey of tongue speakers in a main-line congregation in a Canadian city, Samarin (1973, p. 168) asked the question: "Before the Spirit Baptism, to what extent were you dissatisfied with the local church of which you were a member?" Answers were:

None at all	38.7%
A little	15.9%
Quite a bit	22.7%
Extremely so	13.6%

Thus, over 50% expressed little or no dissatisfaction. This is admittedly a small representation, nonetheless, it is probably more typical than one might suppose, and it indicates that the culture of contemporary glosso-lalia, although reflecting church disillusionment to some degree, is not overwhelmingly a culture of conflict and struggle.

A third set that some glossolalics bring to the experience is that of life crisis, such as poor health, vocational failure, family breakup. Although not as representative as the above issues of religious experience and atti-tudes toward the church, these sorts of predicaments have been reported by a significant proportion of persons. For example, Bradfield (1979) found that about one fourth of the members of the FGBMFI in western Virginia had sought the baptism of the Holy Spirit out of a need for mental or physical healing in themselves or their loved ones. A woman whom we interviewed in our studies illustrated the type of experience many people have reported. She said:

"I had been to see my husband every day for four weeks. He was hospitalized in the Veterans' Hospital and did not seem to be getting any better. In fact, the doctors did not seem to know exactly what was wrong with him even though they knew it was related in some way to that disease he contracted while he was in Viet Nam. I came home exhausted that Friday afternoon and sat down in the kitchen with my head in my hands. I prayed out loud, "God, I don't know what to do. Help me." I suddenly remembered talking earlier that week to Joe's cousin who had told me about receiving the gift of tongues at her church the Sunday night before. I thought to myself, 'Maybe something I'm doing is keeping Joe from getting well.' I prayed to God, 'Help me to surrender everything to you.' Suddenly strange sounds began to come from my lips. I didn't resist. I just let them flow. I remember thinking, 'Is this really happening?' Then I said to myself, 'Maybe this is the gift of the Spirit.' I began to cry. The words kept coming. I laughed and cried all at the same time. I said to myself, 'I'll pray for Joe this way.' I did. After it was over I called Joe in the hospital and told him what happened. He started getting better that very hour and was out of the hospital in a week. I know God answers my prayer when I pray with my tongue." (Malony, et. al. 1972, unpublished data)

It is no accident, therefore, that there is a distinct emphasis within Pentecostalism on all types of healing. Participants seem inclined to interpret life in terms of evil forces, that is, the devil, and to believe that miracles occur when persons surrender themselves to God's will.

A great percentage of Bradfield's (1979) sample reported they had been healed of one malady or another in spite of the fact that only 25% of them had originally sought the experience for that purpose. Although some of them felt that all healing was from God, others felt that God took over when medical science had exhausted its abilities. One person said, "Miracles seem to take place when medicine has done all it knows to do. . . ." (p. 53). Another said, "God does all the healing, whether by medical science or by laying on of hands. Neither is more acceptable. . . . God chooses the method. I walk in obedience" (p. 52).

As noted above, in many charismatic meetings there is laying on of the hands and intercessory prayer for healing of both mind and body. M. B. McGuire (1975) reported that exorcisms and rituals to resist evil were common in the Catholic charismatic prayer groups that she studied. Her subjects testified to God's help in a wide variety of problems, including finding lost articles, getting a job, granting good weather, and the cure of the common cold.

It is interesting to note, however, that Hine (1974) found that although there was a significant relationship between frequency of glossolalia and entrance into the movement because of a personal crisis, those who spoke in tongues most frequently were typically those whose initial entry did not occur as a result of such life predicaments. This ambiguity reinforces our earlier comment, namely, that personal problems of a mental and physical sort are predispositions for some but not for most.

Set can also be thought of as stance toward culture. Usually such attitudes are less well defined and more ambiguous than those we noted above, namely, a desire for deeper religious experience, criticism of the institutional church, and a need for healing of physical or emotional ills. For example, Greeley's (1974) finding that charismatic Catholics felt more culturally isolated than noncharismatic Catholics was a conclusion that would not be explicitly admitted to by those who attended Spirit-filled prayer meetings. They would not give this as a reason for seeking the baptism of the Holy Spirit. Nevertheless, her findings indicate that the mental set of such persons definitely suggested that they experienced themselves as estranged from society. It is one of those indirect but under-lying correlates of seeking an experience wherein one's faith in eternal verities can be renewed.

M. B. McGuire (1975) noted that many of the groups surveyed in such studies as Greeley's included a heavy preponderance of students and full-time religious professionals, such as priests and nuns. We would expect these persons to feel culturally isolated. In her research, McGuire asked, "Would the same be true of Catholic charismatic groups which were largely composed of lay persons?" She found the results to be quite simi-lar. Her respondents evidenced a "crisis mentality," namely, "they saw the church in a crisis of faith and society in a breakdown of law and order" (p. 97). Their uneasiness about the diminishing of rules in the aftermath of Vatican II and the blatant challenge to social structures in the 1960s provoked in them an intense need for security. They sought, through their participation in the charismatic experience, to find a new foundation of authority for themselves that was grounded in a personal assurance of their status before God.

This state of unrest in the face of social change has been termed "order deprivation" by Reidy and Richardson (1978). This is an extension of Glock's (1964) taxonomy of types of deprivation, which we discussed in chapter 7 and which was extended by Mawn's (1975) description of "transcendency deprivation." "Order," as used here, refers to the social world in which one lives. If this is seriously threatened, persons inevita-bly suffer anxiety and anguish. These authors suggest that neo-Pente-costal groups function to redefine the world and make it plausible again. Along with M. B. McGuire (1975) they refer to Berger's (1969) thesis that religion provides a "definition of reality" in an otherwise chaotic world. The experience of the baptism of the Holy Spirit and the confirmation of a close-knit group serve to assuage a sense of aimlessness and in-security.

Two comments about this attitude toward society and culture are of interest. The first has to do with the observation that this dissatisfaction with political and social reality has not led to active efforts to change the world. Quite the opposite: neo-Pentecostals have tended to be passive in attempts to quieten the unrest they see about them and to prefer to re-treat to a previous order of things. Spirit baptism is seen as a renewal of what always was the essence of religious living. M. B. McGuire (1974) terms this escapism. It is no accident that almost every study of Catholic neo-Pentecostals (e.g., Aita & Nye, 1977; Harrison, 1971/1972; McGuire,

1974) has found that these persons become more faithful Catholics after their experience. One study even referred to them as "over-conforming" deviants in reference to this fact. They retreat and escape back into the security of a structure that comforts their frustration about change, but they do not become socially active in confronting that change. Their new found security functions to further alienate them from the world and they predictably spend most of their time in church or group prayer activity. As Reidy and Richardson (1978) commented, "it does not appear to us that the neo-Pentecostal movement . . . will be responsible for effecting much social change" (p. 227).

The second comment regarding this restive state of mind regarding society is that it may be a *function* of *participation* in the movement rather than its cause, In an article on "The Deprivation and Disorganization Theories of Social Movements," Virginia Hine (1974) noted that in her study of Pentecostalism she found no reported dissatisfaction between the subjects' values and those of the world before the subjects became a part of the movement. According to McDonnell (1976) in this research:

> A sizeable number of the Pentecostals reported they were perfectly satisfied with dominant standards of society and with their own and others' behavior until a committed recruiter in a position to influence their thinking sensitized them to the biblical value system. (p.35)

This suggests that it was not so much a mental set of societal dissatisfaction that provoked the experience as the influence of a significant person who courted them into participation. After they became a part of the groups, they then appropriated the ideology of the movement, which included a judgment on the state of society. This conclusion would confirm Gerlach and Hine's (1968) analysis of the factors provoking the growth of a social movement, in which they emphasize the importance of social contact (i.e., friends and family) in recruiting members. We shall discuss this further in this chapter when we consider setting or environmental dimensions. Suffice it to say, the predisposition toward cultural anxiety may not be as pervasive as it might seem in inciting persons to seek the experience of speaking tongues.

In fact, there may be some warrant for suggesting that in classical Pentecostalism, dissatisfaction with society goes the other way. These persons may have little disagreement with the present social structure, instead, they may be strongly motivated to achieve within it. Javillonar (1971) reached this conclusion and used the construct of resentment to refer to the sour grapes phenomenon where sought-after but elusive goals are overtly rejected but secretly coveted. He found that men in the Pentecostal/Holiness sect had higher need-achievement scores than did members of mainline churches and other sects. These findings would accord with what is known of South American Pentecostalism, which is strongly identified with frugality, thrift, ambition, and hard work. However, it should be noted that the dynamics underlying participation in neo-Pentecostalism, as opposed to classical Pentecostalism, are likely to be quite different. It may well be that classical Pentecostals are striving to be upwardly mobile, whereas neo-Pentecostals are more socially critical and that these differences would not be reflected in comparisons of social class between the two groups. Both Bradfield (1979) and Malony et al. (1972) concluded that this was so.

Another group of set issues pertains to the immediate effect of the glossolalic experience. A number of theorists have conceived of the experience as a rite of passage (Hutch, 1980), a token of group acceptance (Lapsley & Simpson, 1964a), a rite of initiation (Ranaghan, 1974), a structured role enactment (Holm, 1978), and a bridge-burning act of commitment (Hine, 1970). These will be discussed separately as further illustrations of the mental states of persons at the time they speak in tongues.

Lapsley and Simpson (1964a) described in detail a small neo-Pentecostal prayer meeting, which they suggested was fairly typical of most such events. In the course of the meeting, the leader prayed in tongues and many of the members followed his lead during times of praise and singing. At another point, a person seeking to be baptized by the Spirit knelt while a number of the participants placed their hands on him and prayed that he might receive the gift. There was great approbation and many prayers of praise when the newcomer began to speak in tongues. It was as if the person was welcomed to the meeting and free to ask for the experience, but acceptance and approval came only after the individual became glossolalic. The authors construed the event as having a double meaning for participants. It pleased the group and, thus, brought group acceptance, but it also convinced persons that God approved of them and had visited them.

This dimension of glossolalia was even more clearly depicted by Ranaghan (1974) in his study of representative Pentecostal churches in the United States. Here speaking in tongues clearly functions as a rite of initiation. There is a clear distinction between water baptism, which symbolizes one's initiation into Christ, and tongues baptism, which symbolizes one's initiation into the Spirit. During much of Christian history since the Wesleyan revival of the eighteenth century, these two have been separated in time—the process of sanctification (or spirit baptism) coming some time after conversion. However, in many Pentecostal groups today, the two are synonymous and one experiences both at the same time or is not accepted as a member of the group. It is safe to say that speaking in tongues is still a requirement in many classical Pentecostal settings, whereas it is only a strong preference in numerous neo-Pentecostal groups. But, in both, it functions as an act of initiation after which one experiences a new identity in the group and is afforded membership privileges.

A somewhat different manner of describing the event is to term it a rite of passage as Hutch (1980) has done. In this context, however, the term is used to refer to an act in which one engages repeatedly, as opposed to a one-time event, like a ritual designed to transit a person from childhood to adulthood. The passage, in the case of glossolalia, is the periodic desire of the individual to pass out of a world determined entirely by pragmatic, rational, structured parameters and to pass into a new world of meaning where freedom, spontaneity, and feeling dominate. In this sense, glossolalia becomes a personal ritual (Hutch, 1980, pp. 262–264) and is intentionally used by the individual in an effort to control life. Thus, the person places himself/herself in a situation where the stylized act of speaking in tongues can be performed and in which one can suspend one reality in favor of another. Hutch (1980) utilizes the formulations of Van Gennep (1960) to indicate how such a ritual act as repeated glossolalia separates one from a situation and incorporates the person into a new social structure with a whole new set of expectations and roles to play. The important aspect of this understanding is that the person anticipates the need for such a transition and intentionally seeks out the opportunity to express the behavior; that is, speak in tongues.

Another way of expressing the set with which persons approach glossolalia is that the experience is a bridge-burning act of commitment (Hine, 1970). Although similar in some ways to the discussion of rites of initiation, this places more importance on glossolalia as an act that is entered into *after* a decision has been made and one's identity has been changed. Thus, glossolalia becomes something like baptism in many mainline Protestant churches, namely, a symbol of a conversion that has already taken place. Herein one goes through the act of immersion as a public testimony to the fact that one's life has been changed. Hine's (1970) view is somewhat similar, although she considers commitment to include the act of glossolalia as well as the subjective experience of identity change. This is to say that commitment is not complete until one has spoken in tongues. This resembles the bridge-burning acts of many missionary stories in which converted pagans publicly burned their idols. The act of speaking in tongues is just such a public event in which the person explicitly separates himself/herself from the general public and other friends who do not worship in this manner. The repeated practice of glossolalia was found to correlate highly with the ability to persist in the movement in the face of opposition from one's associates.

Finally, a less interactive model for understanding the experience is that of Nils Holm (1978) who has suggested that speaking in tongues could be conceived as structured role enactment. He utilizes the ideas of his colleague at the University of Uppsala, Sweden, Helmut Sunden, to depict this phenomenon. Sunden has conceived of all religious experience as typified by a perceptual process in which the individual adopts a role out of holy tradition (in this case Pentecost) and projects himself/herself into that role on the assumption that God will reciprocate in the manner that He did in times gone by. Thus, in the case of tongues, the models can be found in the biblical accounts of Pentecost. These accounts structure the situation for the believing person and the individual approaches the situation with the predisposition that the role enactment can be repeated—this time between the believer and God, just as it happened at Pentecost. Holm (1978) suggests that most glossolalics are prompted into this experience by the admonitions of a leader and the suggestion of a group. In the group, they are introduced to, and reminded of, the tradition after which they are invited to reinact the experience and are assured that God will be present to do His part. Thus, the individual takes over the role of one who is baptized by the Holy Spirit and every time thereafter that the experience is repeated, the individual clearly knows himself/herself to be participating in that interaction. The consequences of such an event are a sense of assurance and joy.

This section on the set dimensions of glossolalia has identified the several conscious perceptions that persons bring to the event. These have included perceptions of feelings that provoke persons to seek the experience as well as anticipated effects from participation. We turn next to setting variables, which will be a discussion of the various environmental dimensions that accompany these phenomena.

SETTING DIMENSIONS IN GLOSSOLALIA

Setting dimensions involve the environment in which speaking in tongues occurs. This is not limited, however, to the physical and interpersonal situation at the moment of glossolalia, that is, the worship service, for example, but it is also concerned with the recruitment environment that led the individual to seek the experience and the sustaining environment that provides the basis for the person to remain in the movement. These matters will, thus, be considered in three sections: setting issues prior to the event, setting issues during the event, and setting issues after the event of speaking in tongues.

Perhaps the most consistent determinant of participation in an experience whose goal is becoming filled with the Spirit prior to the event is that of acquaintance with someone already in the movement. As Harrison (1974b) stated in his survey of Catholic students at the University of Michigan, "mere exposure to a movement is insufficient to induce recruitment, even when the recipient of information is positively predisposed toward it" (p. 57). His research found that almost half of the participants had friends who were active in the charismatic movement prior to becoming involved, whereas only 9% of the noncharismatics had friends in the movement. As one young woman put it, "I was turned off at first, but through a roommate I had to ask questions of, I finally came around" (p. 58). Further confirmation of this factor can be seen in Hine's (1974) report countering the impression that Pentecostals were isolated, lonely people:

   . . . observations indicate that Pentecostalism in the United States and Latin America both, flourishes in small rural communities and villages where ties have not been disrupted, and among family groups whose very solidarity is one of the primary reasons for its contagion. Lack of intimate social relationships or personal ties and disrupted families were *not* characteristic of the Pentecostal pre-converts. (p. 648)

In an early volume (1970), Luther Gerlach, another anthropologist at the University of Minnesota, and Virginia Hine sought to clarify the importance of friends as compared to relatives in recruiting people into these groups. They compared four groups, ranging from an established classical Pentecostal Church to individuals who spoke in tongues in mainline denominations but who belonged to no group; that is, they were "hidden."

Relatives were responsible for recruiting seventy-one percent of the established Pentecostal sect members. This declines to fifty percent for the members of the large independent groups of fifteen or twenty years' duration. Relatives recruited forty-two percent of those in recently organized small independent groups, and only thirty-two percent of the "hiddens." (Gerlach & Hine, 1970, p. 81)

Spouses seemed to be more important toward the "hidden" end of the spectrum; parents were more influential at the sect end. Family appeared to be more important to those of the lower socioeconomic classes; friends seemed more significant at the upper levels.

These ties are so pervasive that they led Gerlach and Hine (1968) to conclude that "recruitment along lines of preexisting social relationships" (p. 30), such as friends and family, was one of the five factors determining the growth of such social movements as classical Pentecostalism and neo-Pentecostalism. Certainly, it could be said that the attraction to such a group does not occur in a social vacuum. This conclusion is no different from that reached by Lofland and Stark (1965) in a study of conversion to a nonglossolalic sect or that reached by Kelley (1972) in a study of the growth of conservative churches. The pertinence of the conclusion resides in the fact that participation in speaking in tongues, like most other religious activities, is heavily influenced by interpersonal relationships. However, a note of caution should be sounded, in that over 50% of the participants in all of the studies, save that of Gerlach and Hine's survey of the classical Pentecostal church (1970) did *not* report that family or friends influenced their decision to participate. Other setting determinants must have been operative.

In this regard, Samarin (1972c) reports further on their survey of the factors that 239 Pentecostals said influenced them to seek the baptism of the Holy Spirit. The factors included: being talked to privately about the baptism by another person, going to a service at a Pentecostal Church, attending the meeting of a small group, reading literature or tracts, the example of one's parents, attending a revival meeting, seeing somebody's life changed by the experience, and the mass media. Although contact with another individual outranked all others for every person, reading literature was second in importance to this for neo-Pentecostals in mainline denominations. Reading was relatively unimportant for the other groups. No other systematic patterns emerged from this research, but it does delineate other setting options for consideration.

Settings at the time of the occurrence of glossolalia vary widely. They range from classical Pentecostal worship services in which glossolalia has become routinized to some extent and occurs chiefly at preset times of prayer, testimony, or end-of-the-service dedication to small groups of one or two where there is laying on of hands and explicit prayer for the gift of tongues. The descriptions of the "Life in the Spirit Seminars" (S. B. Clark, 1973) and those given by Samarin (1972c) are thought to be fairly inclusive of the settings in which these events occur.

A "Life in the Spirit Seminar" is a seven-session workshop-type experience originally developed in 1969 by Ralph Martin of the Ann Arbor Catholic charismatic community out of a concern to systematize the way in which persons were being baptized into the life of the Spirit. A team manual—first published in 1971 and then revised in 1972 and 1973—provides for presentations and group discussions. The first three sessions are concerned with traditional Christian doctrines. In the fourth session, the gifts of the Holy Spirit are presented; at the end of the fifth session, experienced members lay their hands on persons seeking the Spirit and pray that they might receive the baptism.

Also in the fourth session, the possibility of being baptized in the Spirit is presented and obstacles to receiving God's gifts are discussed. The experience of the following week in which newcomers will be prayed for is outlined. Also during the fifth session, a note of expectancy is sounded and persons are instructed as to how to yield to God. Persons are urged to surrender their voices and to let God speak through them. They are cautioned to not be afraid and to not analyze what comes from their mouths. They are urged to relax and to allow the experienced glossolalics to put their hands on them. Obviously, there is a great deal of suggestion and explicit direction in these instructions.

Although the "Life in the Spirit Seminar" guidelines are the only available curriculum for inducing glossolalia, they are quite similar to the descriptions given by Samarin (1972c) of other charismatic meetings. Although he reported some cases of "spontaneous" glossolalia (i.e., speaking in tongues occurring apart from any social influence), he stated: ". . . these cases . . . are probably rare. More often than not the seeker receives a great deal of guidance and instruction" (pp. 51–52).

This guidance and instruction is often very specific. For example, seekers are commonly told to "speak whatever comes to you" and to make sounds as if they were talking to a baby in an effort to get started. On other occasions, they may be given some nonsense utterances to repeat. This imitation is thought to help people get over their self-consciousness and fear. Again, seekers are encouraged to think of a phrase and repeat it over and over to themselves. Sometimes this repetition assists persons in moving from brief to productive glossolalia. Meaningful words are also

suggested. For example, the Hebrew word for God, El Shaddai, is sometimes suggested. This is similar to the mantras often used in Buddhist
meditation, although the leaders of these groups would make a radical
distinction between themselves and such practices.

There are many other helps and conditions used on occasion, such as
lifting one's hands to heaven, breathing deeply, and opening one's mouth
up very widely. Singing is sometimes suggested, as is speaking to oneself
silently before attempting to speak audibly.

Although not all of these encouragements would be apparent at any
one event, they do include most of the means used to induce glossolalia.
The only single inducement that seems common to them all is the laying
on of hands by others as they seek the experience. This practice is based
on the teaching of Acts 8:17, "Then they laid their hands on them and
they received the Holy Spirit."

As Samarin (1972c) notes, these setting variables add up to a general air
of high expectancy, which is nurtured intentionally. He sums it up thus:

> In neo-Pentecostal groups, where glossolalia is acquired very often in small
> meetings, there may be a great use of silence and hushed speaking. But in
> other groups the denouement may be more flamboyantly announced. In some
> cases there is a parallel in the way a religious leader acts and the way a master
> of ceremonies introduces the next star at a variety show. In both cases the
> message is the same: "Great things are going to happen." (p. 56)

Two aspects of the experience are apparent. First, the event itself becomes stylized or ritualized so that the participants not only expect glossolalia to occur, but they know at what times and in what manner it will
happen. While many neo-Pentecostals make great effort to ensure that
their services do not include the excesses of emotion characteristic of
earlier Pentecostalism, they nevertheless adopt procedures that become
routinized to the point where the baptism of the Spirit is brought under
ordered control. Ritual always allows persons to place themselves in
roles in which their behavior is clearly prescribed and predictable. In this
respect, Clow (1976/1977) has hypothesized that the ritual of glossolalic
worship appeals to classical Pentecostals because it allows them to identify
with the middle class by affirming the work ethic and respectability and
at the same time distinguish themselves from that same middle class by
participating in that which emphasizes loss of control to the Holy Spirit.

The second aspect of the conducive, suggestive environment of glossolalic worship is the possibility that speaking in tongues is a learned phenomenon. All of the above descriptions would seem to point in that direction. Samarin (1972c) definitely agreed with this idea and noted that the
tongue of a given individual often resembled the tongue of his/her mentor. Kildahl (1972) emphasized strongly the place of suggestion in glossolalia and concluded that the Lutheran neo-Pentecostals he surveyed tended
to be very susceptible to the influence of a powerful leader. At the very
least becoming glossolalic could be depicted as a socialization process

(Holm, 1978) that included much support for conformity to group norms.

However, it should not be forgotten that such conformity is never total and as Samarin succinctly says, ". . . there are those who never succeed in getting the gift in spite of repeated and sincere attempt while following all the guidance that is given them" (1972c, p. 64). There are many individual differences. One of Samarin's samples sought the gift of glossolalia for over three years, and it will be remembered that Edward Irving, founder of a glossolalic sect, never did speak in tongues, but most of his followers did. Although the differences in acquisition of tongues may be simply a reflection of the normal curve of abilities one would expect for any skill (e.g., square dancing), the usual explanation given by the leaders of the movement has been that those who do not become glossolalic would not yield themselves to the Holy Spirit. Partial confirmation of this reluctance to yield was found by Lovekin and Malony (1977) in their study of "Life in the Spirit Seminar" participants. Although all participants were seeking the gift of the Holy Spirit, those who never became glossolalic tended to be higher on hostility, anxiety, and depression than those who did.

Nevertheless, among those who do speak, there is ample evidence for improvement in both the length of time they are able to sustain such verbalization and the fluency with which they are able to speak (Samarin, 1972c, p. 68). This would lend support to the hypothesis that a learning process is involved.

Turning, finally, to setting dimensions *after* the event of speaking in tongues, several things pertaining to the growth of the movement and people's continued participation in it should be noted. Here we are considering not so much the attraction to *enter* as the appeal to *remain* in the charismatic movement. That the movement has had wide appeal there can be no doubt. As early as the late 1960s, it was estimated that over 12 million persons in the world were a part of classical, neo-Pentecostal, or Catholic groups.

Gerlach and Hine (1968) attempted to delineate the factors that were crucial to the growth and development of this movement through a study of groups in Minneapolis/St. Paul, Minnesota; Haiti; Mexico; and Colombia. The five dimensions they identified were:

1. reticulate *organization*

2. fervent and convincing *recruitment* along pre-existing lines of social relationships

3. a *commitment act* or experience

4. a change-oriented and action-motivating *ideology* which offers (a) a simple master plan presented in symbolic and easily communicated terms, (b) a sense of sharing in the control and rewards of destiny, (c) a feeling of personal worth and power

5. the perception of real or imagined *opposition*. (pp. 23–24)

Because we have previously discussed the issues of recruitment, experience, and ideology, we shall emphasize points one and five, namely, organization and opposition.

What organizational features have characterized the Pentecostal movement and how have these features influenced persons to remain a part of these groups? Gerlach and Hine (1968) term these features "reticulate" or "intricate." Although there are numerous forms of organizations, ranging from organized Pentecostal churches to ecumenical and loosely structured prayer groups, they are similar in several ways that cut across formal lines.

First, the investigators were impressed with the broad personal networks of family and friends that seem to characterize individuals in the movement. There seems to be a great amount of cross fertilization—persons attend each other's meetings. In the second place, this interchange is cultivated by a great amount of leadership exchange and network of traveling evangelists. Gerlach and Hine (1968) note that no one leader evokes total support but that the mix of persons supporting a given leader includes persons from a wide variety of backgrounds. Third, the interchange of persons from all modes of Pentecostalism is encouraged by such large-scale membership organizations as the FGBMFI, which has conducted dinner meetings for all stripes of Pentecostals in hotel ballrooms in many nations. Fourth, there seems to be an informal grapevine of Spirit-filled Christians that operates to spread news in an almost uncanny manner. Gerlach and Hine (1968) mentioned the example of a young tongue speaker who was arrested for disturbing the peace in Minneapolis and how the news of his arrest was known throughout the Pentecostal community even before it got in the newspapers. Finally, the structure is fueled by a self-understanding along faith lines that equates all those who have had the baptism of the Spirit as brothers and that prizes individual contribution.

Thus, an organization with great vitality but without any central head is born. This type of movement is extremely difficult to suppress and, when spurred on by a sense of opposition, is very likely to grow. Although Gerlach and Hine (1968) see similarities between these features and those of other social movements, they do feel that this type of intricate, loosely organized structure facilitates the movement's appeal and tenacity.

Turning next to the perception that there is resistance and opposition to the movement, Gerlach and Hine (1968) conclude that this feature resembles the psychology of persecution typical of religious sects. It bespeaks the truth of the old adage: "the best way to strengthen a leader is to make him a martyr." Certainly, there is some truth to the perception that Pentecostalism, of whatever variety, has not met with unqualified support. The well-publicized criticism of the Episcopal Bishop James Pike is typical of the opposition of much mainline Christianity. Pike said that glossolalia (and other manifestations of the Spirit) were "heresy in embryo." His evaluation of neo-Pentecostalism was no different from that of church leaders to the Holiness movement at the turn of the century or to classical Pentecostalism prior to the 1950s.

Three examples are well known in the recent history of neo-Pentecostalism. First, there was the experience of the priest, Dennis Bennett, who after receiving the gift of the Spirit resigned as priest at St. Mark's Episcopal Church, Van Nuys, California, rather than provoke further the ire of his bishop who had forbidden further glossolalia in the parish. (Bennett subsequently relocated in a church in Seattle.) Second, there was the experience of the United Presbyterian minister, Robert Whitaker, who was asked to leave the Synod of Arizona in which he was a pastor because of the unrest he had caused after announcing that he had received the gift of the Spirit. Reverend Whitaker's experience later led to a General Assembly Committee report on the work of the Holy Spirit and to Whitaker's reinstatement in the denomination. Third, there was the experience reported by Gerlach and Hine (1968, pp. 37–38) of Lutheran Pastor Don Jones who after making his baptism of the Spirit known to his congregation had to promote alternate ways of financing the parish because of the opposition of the Synod.

The experience of Catholic neo-Pentecostals has been somewhat different. There are still very few charismatic parishes in this country, in spite of the fact that numerous requests to establish such have been made. Nevertheless, the Roman Catholic Church has not openly opposed the movement and has opened its parish halls for weekday prayer meetings as well as approved the curriculum and the offering of the "Life in the Spirit Seminars." There seems to be no doubt that the Catholic Church has learned from Pope Adrian's mistake (Gerlach 1974) in opposing Luther and the Reformation and has genuinely tried to incorporate dissident movements into itself since that time. The charismatic movement is no exception. Quite early in the movement, the work of the Spirit was presented as a conserving thrust designed to reclaim the orthodox faith, and it was supported by numerous religious professionals—priests, nuns, and brothers alike. Furthermore, participants very often became better Catholics (Aita & Nye, 1977) and became even more active in the traditional activities of parish life (McGuire, 1975). Thus, both the participants and the church hierarchy made an effort to keep the movement from being perceived as reactionary.

An interesting side note to this phenomenon has been the critique of Jane Massyngberde Ford (1976) who has differentiated between two types of Catholic Pentecostals: those interested in organizing a separate movement off to the side of Catholicism and those who are more flexible and less structured and who are concerned to remain integral participants in the life of the church. She sees the first type as represented by the University-of-Michigan-based Word of God group, which is male-dominated, authoritarian, and exclusivistic. Other groups composed of nonstudents and lay persons are representative of the second type, which is characterized by more openness, less central leadership, and less emphasis on the specific gift of tongues. Although her critics have accused Ford of being bitter because of the church's antifeminism, which she perceives as embodied in neo-Pentecostals of the first type, her observations are to some extent accurate and have been confirmed by at least one other researcher (McGuire, 1977).

Suffice it to say, an ideology of opposition has created a mentality in the Pentecostal movement which, according to Gerlach and Hine (1968) has added to its appeal to participants. It unifies them in a cause and provokes loyalty in an ongoing manner.

In summary, an intricate informal organization and an ideology of opposition are two of the setting dimensions that have influenced persons to remain participants in the Pentecostal movement and have, without question, functioned to maintain Spirit-filled activity, such as speaking in tongues.

CONCLUSION

This chapter has considered the issue of when and where persons become glossolalic. These factors were thought to be important for understanding the perceptions with which individuals initially came to the experience of speaking in tongues and the feelings and attitudes that facilitated their continuing to participate in these activities.

These dimensions were thought to be self-conscious attitudes that would determine behavior rather than psychological traits that would predispose persons to the experience. Two major types of determinants were considered: sets and setting. Sets were defined as inner attitudes and perceptions; settings were outer conditions and environments. Although no single feature or combination of features characterized any single glossolalic individual, these factors are thought to be operative in some manner in every case.

Effects of Glossolalia

9

Physical Changes

In this Part, we shall consider whether speaking in tongues has any effects on the glossolalic individual. Are there any changes in those who speak in tongues either physical, psychological, behavioral, cognitive, or attitudinal? This is a complicated question that presents two fundamental problems.

The first problem is the presence of the many different variables that confound the investigation of glossolalia. For example, the psychiatrist Paul Morentz (1966) first called attention to the importance of sample bias in investigating the meaning of glossolalia. "He noted that glossolalia tends to assume a different meaning in Pentecostal churches where it is part of the expected religious ritual, in comparison to its appearance among staid main-line churches where it is usually considered deviant behavior" (Pattison, 1968, p. 76). Morentz interviewed sixty glossolalics from mainline denominations and found six pathological personality traits dominant among them. He concluded that neo-Pentecostals who violated the group norm of expectancy of glossolalia in their mainline churches were more pathological than glossolalics in classical Pentecostal churches.

Paul Pruyser (1968), a clinical psychologist at the Menninger Foundation, also emphasized differences in motivation and degree of regression between glossolalics in mainline churches where the phenomenon was more of a protest, as opposed to glossolalics from classical Pentecostal churches where the phenomenon was socially expected. Later Pattison (1974) clarified Pruyser's position:

> The fundamentalist value system was a functional value system in an expanding agrarian culture of frontier America. . . . However, since the closing of the frontier, the industrialization and urbanization of America, this value system has become obsolescent. Rather than transform their value system, the fundamentalists have clung to their value system in face of increasing social and psychological dissonance. The price they have paid is measured in terms of personal and social dysfunction in participation in the society as a whole. (p. 444)

Stating his conclusions in terms of ego psychology and social psychology combined, Pattison (1974) wrote, "The evidence presented here argues for a sequence by which cultural dissonance leads to cognitive dissonance and then results in distortions in ego development and adaptive function" (p. 444).

One needs to be aware, therefore, that there are many different groups of persons who speak in tongues and that the findings in one sample do not necessarily apply in another. As psychologists O'Connell and Bryant (1972) at Saint Louis University have said, "It would serve the purposes of both science and religion alike to acknowledge that glossolalia may be manifested differently from culture to culture, in educated and uneducated, in classical, neo-, and Catholic pentecostals, in public and private prayer, and in leaders and congregations" (p. 976).

In addition to such variables as cultural and group expectancy, there is an even more important issue that must be considered when one asks, What changes occur from speaking in tongues? This is the problem of longitudinal versus cross-sectional studies. Longitudinal research with glossolalics, either before or after they become glossolalic, is scarce. Wood (1965, p. 100) was evidently the first researcher to suggest that longitudinal designs were to be preferred. Nevertheless, in his study of classical Pentecostals, he did not follow his own suggestion. He found the more "established" members (who had belonged "a number of years") to be more stabilized emotionally than newer converts, but his methodology was cross-sectional and inadequate because it did not assess changes over time.

A longitudinal study was conducted by Kildahl (1972) who compared neo-Pentecostal with nonglossolalic control subjects and who conducted a follow-up study a year later. However, their subjects were not assessed prior to their initial experience of glossolalia—a procedure that would have made the study even more valuable.

In his review of the literature dealing with psychological interpretations of glossolalia, Richardson (1973) commented on this problem of methodology:

> No research to date has assessed the personality characteristics of a set of potential converts to a tongue-speaking group, and then followed them up after conversion in order to assess (1) whether or not psychological changes had taken place, and (2) what types of changes had occurred. (p. 201)

He issued a clear call for longitudinal research, "We thus strongly recommend longitudinal research designs that allow some assessment of change over time" (p. 206). Administering tests over a time sequence "might allow researchers to 'catch' persons as they move from the 'pre-glossolalic' stage to the 'glossolalic,' and from the 'infrequent glossolalic' to the 'frequent glossolalic' " (p. 206).

Recognizing the need for longitudinal research even before Richardson's call, we initiated a longitudinal study in the summer of 1973 with subjects who were attending "Life in the Spirit Seminars" (S. B. Clark, 1972b) in Catholic and Episcopal churches (Lovekin, 1975/1977; Lovekin & Malony, 1977). Because the seminars were designed to initiate inquirers into the baptism of the Spirit with the resulting experience of speaking in tongues for the first time, we were able to get a genuine longitudinal design that utilized both a posttesting period at the end of the seminars and a three month follow-up testing period as well.

No other longitudinal research has been reported in the literature up to the present time. We would affirm Richardson's (1973) call for more long-term research to obtain sound findings for any and all types of changes that might result from glossolalia. Because of the difficulty of controlling the many important variables in longitudinal research, it may well be that any important breakthrough in understanding the changes produced by speaking in tongues will come in research with single individuals over time. Such a method would allow for an atheoretical, exploratory, and exhaustive study of the parameters of glossolalia in one person. This was the methodology used in the early classical studies of LeBaron (1896–1897), Flournoy (1900/1963), and James (1902/1958) who began the modern study of the phenomenon of glossolalia. However, even here most of the research was post hoc (after the fact).

Thus, the discussion of changes over time in this part should be considered suggestive and speculative rather than conclusive because of these fundamental problems. However, it is our hope that a review of the results to date will stimulate future research of a more valid nature. In the chapters to follow, we shall summarize the changes that occur in people from speaking tongues: physical health, personality, attitudes, behavior and values.

CHANGES IN PHYSICAL HEALTH

Cases of physical healings through prayer have been known within the history of Christianity from Apostolic times to the present. Kelsey (1973) has provided a most comprehensive history of these phenomena. However, no thorough treatment has been made of physical healings resulting from glossolalia. In this section, we shall cite some personal testimonials or self-reports of physical healings from leaders within the classical Pentecostal, neo-Pentecostal and Catholic charismatic movements. We shall also note how healing ministries are often combined with the Pentecostal experience and witness. Then we will review some research relating to these matters.

Self-Reports

Classical Pentecostalism

It is historically important to note that Charles F. Parham, who probably should be considered the founder of classical Pentecostalism, reported personal healings. His widow and biographer, Sarah E. Parham (1930) recorded his testimony about his own frail health:

> At six months of age I was taken with a fever that left me an invalid. For five years I suffered with dreadful spasms, and enlargement of the head, until my forehead became abnormally large. At nine years of age I was stricken with the first case of inflammatory rheumatism, virtually tied up in a knot; with other complications, I suffered much. Until, when the affliction left, I could count the bones in my hand by holding it up to the light. About this time I took medicines of various kinds to destroy a tape worm. One concoction was of such nature that it destroyed the lining of my stomach and dwarfed me so that I did not grow any for three years. Being very sick and weakly, my early days were spent at light-tasks, or when well enough, at herding the cattle. (p. 2)

As early as 9, Parham sensed his vocation to the ministry. At 13 years of age, he had an intense personal experience of conviction and conversion. He began to conduct public meetings by age 15. Continuing his religious work, Parham entered college at age 16. But he soon backslid in his faith and began to consider becoming a physician instead of a minister. In this state of rebellion against God and in his confusion over his vocation, Parham became critically ill with rheumatic fever again. Emaciated in body, semiconscious from narcotics, he heard a physician say he would die in a few days. His mind beclouded with drugs, he could not formulate his own thoughts or prayers, so he began to repeat the Lord's Prayer. In the middle of this prayer his mind cleared and he claimed God's healing for himself:

> With this and similar prayers upon my lips, every joint in my body loosened and every organ in my body was healed. And yet, after having the use of all my body my ankles remained helpless, the sinews and bindings had become so stretched by months of rheumatism that they were as useless as though tin cans were tied to my ankles. Doctors and scientists said I never would use them again. After some time through great necessity I learned to walk upon the sides of my feet, or rather upon my ankles with my feet thrown out to the side. (Parham, 1930, pp. 8–9)

Complete physical healing did not come to Parham until he made a total commitment to follow God's call to become a minister and an evangelist.

Soon, Parham not only had a public ministry of divine healing, but he also established a Divine Healing Home in Topeka, Kansas, the center from which the Pentecostal movement began. Sarah Parham quoted from her husband's autobiography written in 1901:

> Looking back over these years, I see how from the healing of a few individuals, I was lead [sic] to the establishing of a Healing Home in Topeka, Kansas; then followed the opening of the Bible School, where the presence of God was more wonderfully manifested than among any other people since the days of the Apostles. (S. Parham, 1930, p. 23; quoted from Charles Parham's autobiography, 1901)

The manifestation of God's presence of course was the baptism of the Spirit with glossolalia, which occurred on New Year's Eve 1900. However, it should be noted that in Parham's case, healing came prior to, rather than after, speaking in tongues.

In El Dorado Springs, Missouri, a dramatic change occurred in his ministry when Mrs. Mary A. Arthur received a healing in her eyesight through Parham's ministry. Mr. and Mrs. Arthur invited Parham to come to their home in Galena, Kansas, where a three-month revival of impressive proportions occurred. A correspondent from the *Cincinnati Enquirer* reported that Parham "has healed over a thousand people and converted more than 800" (cited in S. Parham, 1930, p. 96). This may be an overly credulous report, the point is, however, that Parham made his first impact on the public not so much from his teaching ministry about tongues as from his healing ministry. Parham's "full gospel" included not only tongues but faith healing as well. For Parham, his physical healings preceded his Pentecostal experience, and physical healings became an integral part of the Pentecostal tradition.

Later classical Pentecostals (in particular the Assemblies of God) went through a period of self-criticism with regard to their healers because of their "attacks upon local Pentecostal pastors, moral lapses, egotism, arrogant behavior and over-estimation of the value of bodily healing, and the false teaching that prosperity is an irrefutable sign of piety" (Hollenweger, 1972, p. 357). After this period of self-criticism, there was some revival of the healing ministry in classical Pentecostalism.

The account given by Malony (1979) is typical of this healing emphasis in classical Pentecostalism. He reports two cases of chronically ill children whose healings were communicated through glossolalia-type prayer. In both of these cases, the children died. However, the faith placed in the healings by the children's parents was against the background of many other healings they had witnessed in their churches. Although they had difficulty in interpreting the tragedies, the parents of both children remained firm in their faith in the power of the Holy Spirit to heal.

Neo-Pentecostalism

Physical healings have played an important part in the neo-Pentecostal movement as well as in classical Pentecostalism. For Agnes Sanford, an Episcopalian author and lecturer, it was only in the middle of a long and fruitful healing ministry that she experienced the baptism of the Spirit, which after six months came to include speaking in tongues. Feeling physically and emotionally drained from ministering to others, she and two friends prayed together for four days in the early 1950s:

> We prayed for strength, and no strength came. We prayed for the healing of various small ills that weariness had brought about in our bodies, and we were not healed. Finally at the end of three days we ceased praying the prayer of faith and prayed the prayer for guidance.

"Well, then Lord, what *do* you want us to pray for?" we demanded.

A voice spoke within all three of us saying, "Pray for the Holy Ghost." . . .

We prayed for each other with the laying on of hands, two for one, two for one, two for one. And the power of the Spirit fell upon us immediately. . . . We were healed immediately, every one of us, of all the small weaknesses that had troubled us. . . . I felt for the only time in my life . . . the radiation of a spiritual power all over me, from the top of the head to the soles of the feet. (1972, pp. 217–219)

On the other hand, the prominent neo-Pentecostal healer, Kathryn Kuhlman, who received her personal baptism in the Spirit in 1946, only subsequently found that people received healings in her services. She developed her own distinctive style of healing ministry. These services were described as follows:

There is often musical entertainment at the beginning, followed very frequently by a sermon. Charismatic activity is noticeably curtailed, though participants practiced the Pentecostal (and very ancient) *Orans* prayer posture (hands uplifted), and are almost always "slain in the Spirit" (falling backward into an usher's arms) when Kuhlman touches them *after* their testimonies to an alleged or verified healing. At the conclusion of her sermon (if there is one), the charismatic leader points to various places in the audience where she discerns healings have already occurred prior to that moment. She cites the ailment—everything from terminal cancer to allergies. . . . ——and asks those who feel they are healed to come forward to the platform to testify about what has happened. (Trained ushers try to screen cases and verify healings as much as possible beforehand). Quite often, there are physicians on the platform who themselves may be asked for confirmation; and everyone is urged to confirm an apparent cure with his or her own doctor. Some individuals, of course, testify, but are not healed; others seem to get better, but later regress; probably most in attendance are not cured at all. Nevertheless, the media and various respected authorities attest that a small number of people, at least, do receive an apparently miraculous cure. (Quebedeaux, 1976, pp. 85–86)

Kuhlman documented many of these miraculous cures (1962, 1969, 1974) in her three popular books. They included cases of people healed who were not even Christians.

Oral Roberts (1952) is another adventuresome pioneer who has moved from a healing ministry within classical Pentecostalism into an educational and mass media ministry of a neo-Pentecostal variety. At age 16, Roberts was struck with tuberculosis in both lungs, hemorrhaging on the basketball court. For five months he was ill, and then he was taken by his family to a classical Pentecostal healing service where he received a physical healing not only of his tuberculosis but also of stuttering and a fear of crowds. In two month's time, he was preaching, but it was twelve years later that he began his healing crusades, which lasted for two decades. In 1965, Roberts (1971) founded his University in Tulsa, Oklahoma. More recently he has built a medical complex of treatment, education, and research called City of Faith, which opened in 1981. Roberts has moved a long way from the antimedical stance of most classical Pentecostal faith healers to a thoroughly integrated approach of prayer and medicine, of spiritual and physical healing.

Catholic Charismatics

The Catholic charismatic renewal also has had a vital interest in physical healing. Francis MacNutt (1974), who was deeply influenced by Agnes Sanford's teaching and ministry, has been the primary proponent and practitioner of a healing ministry within the Catholic charismatic movement. He was a founder of the Association of Christian Therapists within that movement and remained active until his recent marriage, which put him at odds with the Catholic Church. MacNutt (1974) commented:

> On a typical Pentecostal retreat now when I ask for a show of hands of those who have seen the sick healed through their prayers, about half the hands go up. Similarly when I ask how many think, as far as they can judge, that any of their illnesses have been healed through prayer, about half the hands go up. (p. 10)

The French Roman Catholic theologian René Laurentin (1974/1977, pp. 100–131) has written a helpful history of healing within the Catholic charismatic renewal. Because he has done so much scholarly research at Lourdes, Laurentin's comparison of the criteria for verification of miracles at Lourdes and of charismatic healings are especially noteworthy. To develop meaningful criteria from a medical point of view, Laurentin suggests that it is appropriate to establish (1) the fact of the sickness (its organic character) and (2) the fact of the cure (complete, sudden, etc.). But he suggests that it is no longer appropriate to ask the question, Is this cure inexplicable? It is against the methodology of science in general and medicine in particular to admit that anything is inexplicable or an exception to the laws of nature. He suggests an alternative question, Is this cure ordinary or extraordinary? In other words, is there anything baffling, astonishing, or extraordinary in the cure. Then the religious question can be asked as to whether the cure is a beneficial religious sign that is accessible to faith. The important issue according to Laurentin, therefore, is not whether a healing violates our understanding of the natural order, but whether it is a sign that increases faith.

In summary, then, we can see that among the *leaders* of classical Pentecostalism, neo-Pentecostalism, and the Catholic charismatic renewal there has been *no* particular pattern of physical healings either before, concurrent, or subsequent to receiving a baptism in the Spirit with or without tongues. We do see a tendency for those who develop healing ministries to have had personal healing experiences in their own lives prior to their public ministry. But there seems to be no chronological or causal connection between the two gifts or charisms. On the other hand, whereas glossolalia occurs only concurrent with, or subsequent to, the experience of the baptism in the Spirit, physical healings reportedly occur prior to, or without, this experience. Thus, it may often occur that those who receive a physical healing or exercise a healing ministry are not at all related to the Pentecostal or charismatic movements.

Research

Most of the healings noted above are testimonies, often written long after their occurrence. Individual case studies, surveys, or research dealing with physical health and glossolalia have been few.

The anthropologists Luther Gerlach and Virginia Hine conducted seven field studies among glossolalics in North and South America, which included classical Pentecostals, neo-Pentecostals, and Catholic charismatics. As part of their fieldwork, they collected 239 self-administered questionnaires. They classified respondents into two groups according to their frequency in the use of glossolalia. Frequent tongue speakers were those who reported that they spoke in tongues more than once a week. The nonfrequent tongue speakers were those who reported that they spoke in tongues less than once a week. Hine (1969) reported their results with respect to physical health:

> Frequent tongue speakers perceived themselves as better off physically since the Baptism and the onset of glossolalic experience, as compared with nonfrequent tongue speakers (at the .003 level of significance). (p. 222)

They did not report in this article (1969) nor in their subsequent book (Gerlach & Hine, 1970), how physical health was quantified in the questionnaire, but the results are suggestive. Glossolalics who spoke in tongues at least once a week seem to have a greater sense of physical well-being than glossolalics who spoke in tongues less frequently.

The sociologist C. D. Bradfield (1979) also used self-administered questionnaires with neo-Pentecostals who participated in Full Gospel Businessman's Fellowship International (FGBMFI) chapters in western Virginia. He obtained 135 respondents. Unfortunately for our purpose, he combined physical and mental healing as one category. Bradfield reported:

> About eighty-five per cent of the respondents to the questionnaire said they or someone close to them had experienced physical or mental healing as a direct manifestation of the Holy Spirit. About one-fourth of the respondents indicated that they directly sought the baptism in the Holy Spirit as the result of the need, on their part [or] of someone close to them, for physical or mental healing. . . . Even though a majority of the respondents believed they experienced healing as a direct manifestation of the baptism of the Holy Spirit, only a minority said they had actually sought the experience on that basis. (1979, p. 51)

These results are tentative because of the confusion of categories, but again they are suggestive. Glossolalics do seem to have more of a sense of well-being, which includes the physical, after their baptism in the Spirit than they did before they received this baptism.

The psychiatrist E. M. Pattison and his collaborators (Pattison, 1974; Pattison, Lapins, Doerr, 1973) conducted a retrospective study utilizing individual case studies of forty-three fundamentalist-Pentecostal individuals, of whom thirty-nine were glossolalics (i.e., classical Pentecostals). They reported a total of seventy-one faith healings. "The mean interval between healing and interview was 15 years with a range of 2 weeks to 51 years" (Pattison et al., 1973, p. 399). This length of time between the healings and the study raises a question as to the degree of the validity of the data gathered. Nevertheless, the study is important because of the nature of research questions asked and because it used multiple measures to gather data. The four main research questions were (Pattison et al., 1973, p. 397):

1. Is there a typical personality among those claiming faith healing?
2. Why do people participate in faith-healing rituals?
3. Does faith healing result in alternate symptom formation?
4. Does faith healing result in significant changes in the person's life style?

The battery of tests used included the Spitzer Mental Status Schedule, a scaled self-report on different emotional traits, the Minnesota Multiphasic Personality Inventory (MMPI), and the Cornell Medical Index (CMI). They also used a structured interview to gather information in the four following areas (Pattison et al., 1973, p. 398):

1. The life pattern of the person in relationship to himself, his family, his work, and his social relations prior to the faith healing.
2. Life pattern in the same areas subsequent to faith healing.
3. Medical history prior to, and subsequent to, faith healing.
4. The perceived importance and function of the faith-healing experience in the person's life.

Pattison felt that the data gathered clearly substantiated the answers to the four research questions. First, there was a typical personality pattern that emerged:

These subjects present psychological characteristics of a strong need for social acceptance and social affiliation. This exaggerated need presents along with the extensive use of denial and repression as major coping mechanisms that are so pervasive that major disruptive events in their lives are ignored and interpreted as part of a normal, smooth, unruffled existence. (Pattison et al., 1973, p. 403)

Thus, the typical personality pattern that emerged included the use of denial, repression, projection, and disregard of reality.

Second, why do these people participate in faith-healing rituals? Pattison summarized his findings to this question:

> From the subjects' point of view, relief of symptoms is really a tangential issue. For them, faith healing reaffirms their belief system and their style of life. Faith healing serves to buttress their psychological style of life. From a scientific medical point of view, the question usually asked of faith healing is "does it cure the disease?" But that is not the question asked by the prospective applicant for faith healing. His question is, "Am I living in the right way?" Thus, faith healing is not an exercise in the treatment of organic pathology, but an exercise in the treatment of life style. (Pattison et al., 1973, p. 403)

According to Pattison this disregard of reality and the other personality traits noted above were not pathological or abnormal but rather were part of a coping system that provided ego integration for the individual and social integration for the subculture.

Third, with respect to the question of symptom substitution, Pattison reported, "We were unable to elicit any instances of suspected or manifest alternation of either organic or psychological symptoms" (Pattison et al., 1973, p. 400). In discussing this lack of symptom substitution, Pattison commented that the personality traits noted above meant that "these subjects do not perceive illness as a major disruptive event, nor do they perceive their faith healing as a major life-enhancing event" (Pattison et al., 1973, p. 403). He stated further:

> It is not surprising that no evidence for symptom alternation is found, for the subjects do not perceive their illnesses as conflictual events. Thus, in a sense their faith healing does not remove their symptoms. Remission of symptoms does not significantly affect their psychic balance of defenses, and therefore, emergence of alternate symptoms is not required to maintain psychic equilibrium. (Pattison et al., 1973, p. 403)

Fourth, in regard to significant changes in life-style, Pattison reported *"no change* was reported by our subjects using either indirect descriptive inquiry, or on direct questioning regarding change in life style" (Pattison et al., 1973, p. 400). They described their own emotional functioning, their work functioning, and their relationships with other people as always being serene and comfortable.

Expanding the original research questions to other changes, Pattison found no changes in religious behavior (i.e., church attendance, private devotions, Bible reading, or religious interest) subsequent to their faith healing. He did, however, find one major change that was reported by all respondents: "All reported that their *certainty* in their belief in God and in their religious convictions was *markedly increased* after their faith healing experience" (Pattison et al., 1973, p. 401).

Unfortunately for our present inquiry, Pattison et al. (1973) did not report when these subjects became glossolalic. However, they do report:

Most of the subjects had been Christians throughout their lives, although a number who had been reared in religious environment had not been "born again" (i.e., experienced religious conversion) until adulthood. However, only in two instances were the "rebirths" coincident with their faith healing, and here the healings were subsequent to their conversion, not preceding it. In all other cases of adult conversion, the conversion had preceded the healing by at least 1 year. (pp. 398–399)

As mentioned earlier, these findings, both the data and the conclusions, may be an artifact of the long period between the reported healings and the data gathering. The research would be most appropriate to replicate with subjects in a longitudinal research project that was specifically related to glossolalia per se.

A second study was completed recently by Ness and Wintrob (1980) among classical Pentecostals in a Newfoundland coastal community of four hundred people. This was a correlational investigation relating scores on the CMI to six distinctively different religious behaviors encouraged in the Pentecostal Church: glossolalia, testimonials, seeking possession by the Holy Spirit, requesting ritual healing, helping at the altar, and consistent attendance. These behaviors were assessed over a one-year period. Distinct sex-role differences in religious behavior between the twenty-three men and twenty-eight women in this church were noted. Over the one-year period, four men used glossolalia in public worship, whereas only two women used glossolalia. Nineteen men made testimonials in public worship, whereas only eleven women made testimonials. Ten men requested ritual healing as compared to only five women. This involved the laying on of hands by the elders and by the preacher within the context of intense group support. Four men and two women engaged in possession behavior, which was called "dancing in the Spirit" and involved gyrating around the church or rolling on the floor. Seven men helped at the altar and only two women did the same. Attendance was practically equal for both sexes.

The CMI was administered to all church members after this thirteen-month observation period. A physical complaints score was calculated from 144 CMI questions relating to physical health and a psychological complaints score was calculated from 50 CMI questions relating to emotional health. Six psychological complaints were also noted in particular: inadequacy, depression, anxiety, sensitivity, anger, and tension.

There was *no* significant relationship between their physical complaints score and any of the six types of behavior. Ness and Wintrob (1980) comment:

This finding is entirely congruent with the well established view that it is the subjective evaluation of specific symptoms, rather than the number of symptoms *per se,* that is crucial in the decision to seek ritual healing.

Observational data spanning 13 months indicate that many of the people delivering testimonials or seeking ritual healing are emotionally distressed individuals. (p. 310)

In other words, the men sought ritual healing or made testimonials for *emotional* rather than *physical* reasons.

As far as the physical complaints scores for women are concerned, there was a positive significant relationship to both glossolalia and possession behavior. Ness and Wintrob (1980) interpreted these correlations as suggesting that for women "as physical complaints increase, the likelihood of possession behavior and glossolalia increases" (p. 310).

The fact that there was *no* correlation between physical complaints and seeking ritual healing suggests that for both men and for women ritual healing is sought more for emotional than physical reasons.

In conclusion, although the two self-report surveys by social science investigators indicate that most glossolalics subjectively feel better physically after they speak in tongues, the two studies (Ness & Wintrob, 1980; Pattison, 1974) found no evidence for physical healing *resulting from* the experience.

Thus, although anecdoctal reports have been numerous, empirical evidence to date does not demonstrate that the use of glossolalia has any correlation with or makes any change on physical health. To date, behavioral science research has not substantiated the claims that have been reported. Obviously, more research is needed.

10

Personality Changes

Before examining changes in personality among glossolalics, it is important to raise the question of experimenter bias and the utility of psychological test data in assessing such a subcultural group. To illustrate the issue, we shall consider two of the most frequently used psychological tests: the Minnesota Multiphasic Personality Inventory (MMPI), an objective true-false questionnaire, and the Rorschach, a projective test.

Anthropologist Weston La Barre (1962) wrote an historical account of the serpent-handling cults in Southern Appalachia. He also presented a detailed case history of a cult leader using psychoanalytic concepts of intrapsychic conflict, which La Barre then generalized to other members of the sect. The Gerrards, a husband and wife team of sociologists, were dissatisfied with La Barre's work and undertook another study utilizing the MMPI. The MMPI was administered by means of a tape recording of the questions for those whose educational level precluded reading the written form. Although the administration was unusual, the motivation and cooperation of the subjects remained high. To compare this lower-working-class serpent-handling church in Gauley Bridge, West Virginia (population: 900), with middle-class society, the Gerrards also assessed an upper-working-class Methodist Church in a community (population: 2,000) twenty-five miles away whose members were upwardly mobile, rather than stationary, poor. In two group administrations, they were able to obtain ninety completed MMPI protocols, which were matched as closely as possible with respect to age, sex, and social class to the members of the serpent-handling church. The serpent-handling church was a sectarian cult split off from the Holiness-Pentecostal tradition.

Tellegen, Gerrard, Gerrard, and Butcher (1969) reported:

> Specifically using our data we wanted to determine how the knowledge that a person belongs to a snake-handling sect might affect an experienced diagnostician's impression of that person. . . . If it were found that clinical psychologists do have certain preconceptions in this area which affect their evaluation of the individual's adjustment, we would, of course, wonder about the

possible operation of similar biases in other subcultural studies. (Tellegen et al., 1969, p. 225)

In an effort to address this issue, they utilized four clinicians from the University of Minnesota who were well trained in personality assessment, but who had no special expertise in the study of religious subgroups. They were given group descriptions of both church groups, which detailed the socioeconomic conditions and occupational characteristics as well as the different religious practices of the two groups. They sorted the ninety-six profiles into two groups: one for the serpent-handling church and the other for the conventional denominational church. Then, they were asked to rate the psychological adjustment of each individual by classifying the profiles in one of four diagnostic categories: normal, neurotic, behavior disorder, and psychotic. Tellegen et al. (1969) reported that the results clearly demonstrated that

> the experienced judges tended to assign "normal" profiles to the conventional denomination (31 out of 35) and "abnormal" profiles to the serpent-handling groups (15 out of 23, including all 8 "psychotic" profiles and 3 out of the 4 profiles labeled "behavior disorder"). (p. 227)

Using only those profiles for which there was unanimous agreement by the four judges and sorting by church (twenty-five in the conventional denomination and eighteen in the serpent-handling sect), the researchers calculated the average profile for each church. This analysis produced an essentially normal profile for the conventional denomination and a clearly "abnormal" profile for the serpent-handling cult (i.e., five of the ten clinical are in the marked range).

The data was reanalyzed using only those profiles for which there was agreement of at least three out of the four judges in regard to the diagnostic category classification. They found that the "normal" profiles were distributed equally between the churches (twenty-two in each) and that there were more "abnormal" profiles among the Methodist than the serpent-handling sect (twenty-eight as compared to thirteen). The distribution of "psychotic" profiles was equal between the churches (two in each) as was that of "behavior disorders" (four in the conventional and five in the serpent handling). The researchers concluded that the experienced diagnosticians had a definite bias to link serpent-handling with psychopathology.

On the basis of this conclusion, Tellegen et al. (1969) recommended that partially blind interpretations be made. They suggested that, in the case of deviant subcultural groups, diagnosticians be provided with background information of a geographical, socioeconomic, and cultural nature that is *common* for any two groups being compared, but that no information be provided as to the differences between the groups in regard to their unusual religious practices.

These researchers also warned that psychometric data can only fulfill a supplementary function in assessment, especially when an assessment device like the MMPI is used with a deviant subcultural group that was not part of the sampling upon which the assessment device was validated.

As far as we are aware, only one research project investigating glossolalia has utilized blind ratings on psychometric instruments. This was the project of Kildahl (1972) and his collaborators who utilized blind ratings by two psychologists for the McKenzie Mental Health scale rating of autonomy on the Thematic Apperception Test (TAT).

The Rorschach ink blot test provides a second illustration of the problem of experimenter bias. Earlier we mentioned that Wood (1962, 1965) was one of the first researchers to attempt a quasi-longitudinal research among classical Pentecostals. He undertook a seven-month field study and used the Rorschach as a psychometric assessment instrument to supplement his field observations.

However, he tried to control for bias by not scoring any of the Rorschach protocols until he had finished all of the administrations. However, as noted in the previous section, the value system of a diagnostician can influence how psychometric data is interpreted. In a situation like this, where there is no accompanying psychometric data to suggest pathology, an interpreter of the Rorschach may feel compelled to choose between a positive and a negative mode of interpretation. Three criteria are often used to make that choice: the internal consistency within the Rorschach, the presence of any clearly pathognomic indicators, and non-test data, such as prior history or field observations that might indicate pathology. Because there are no clear indicators of pathology in Wood's research, the problem of interpreter bias or the diagnostician's value system influencing the choice of a positive or a negative mode of interpretation is made even more acute.

Table 10.1 gives the percentage of vista (V), color (C, CF, FC), and human movement (M) responses for the two groups according to Wood.

A vista response (V) is often seen as an indicator of anxiety. The much higher frequency of vista responses by Pentecostals could be interpreted by some as an indicator of excessive anxiety based on counterphobic qualities. Others could interpret the higher frequency of vista responses as an indicator of more openness to experiences of anxiety in the absence of anxiety-producing situations.

Color responses (C, CF, FC) are often seen as indicators of affectivity or of emotionality. The greater frequency of color responses by Pentecostals could be interpreted by some as indicators of an excessive emotional reactivity. Others could interpret the greater frequency of color responses as a greater ability to accept feelings with spontaneity. It should be noted that the affective experience of the Pentecostals is not intense and out of control because the pure color (C) response is four times lower than the response frequency of the non-Pentecostals.

Human movement response (M) is often seen as tendency to sift emotional and perceived experience through an ideational or intellectual framework. The relatively low frequency of human movement responses

Table 10.1 Frequencies of vista, color, and human movement responses in the purified samples of Wood (1965) on the Rorschach

Response category	Frequency of Pentecostal responses	Frequency of non-Pentecostal responses
Vista (V)	13.8%	5.0%
Color responses (sum of C, CF, & FC)	15.2	12.8
Pure color (C)	0.5	2.1
Human movement (M)	3.2	5.0

by Pentecostals might be interpreted by some as a reduced ability to modulate feelings or a lesser capacity to place ideas between feelings and their expression. This could be labeled as noncritical, impressionistic, or naive. Others could interpret the relatively low frequency of human movement responses as an ability to be more open to affective experience without the use of labels and without ideational content. Indeed, Wood (1965) interprets the greater frequency of human movement responses by the "established" Pentecostal members as a positive change from the lower frequency given by the "others," that is, the newer members.

Whether the anxiety is excessive or the emotionality is too great or whether there is not enough intellectual filtering of impressions should not be decided arbitrarily. In this case, all the indications are that the Pentecostals were capable of functioning adequately and had the capacity to work and to love, and by all measures they were psychologically healthy.

The Rorschach material can be used to inform us about the quality of a person's perceiving and experiencing the world. However, to use the Rorschach scores in the absence of any signs of pathology as an indicator of pathology is biased and pejorative. It is presumptuous to move from that perception to a judgment that one way to perceive the world is correct and another is incorrect. It is clear that most Pentecostals experience the world in ways that are different from most people who do engage in psychometric research. However, this is not indicative necessarily of disturbance.

This tendency by clinicians to make a negative interpretation of a greater affective experience accompanied by anxiety and minimal intellectual content may account for the fact that Pentecostals have been repeatedly labeled as hysterics. A more positive interpretation of the same data would see Pentecostals as having an acceptance of feelings generally and of anxiety in particular. This could mean a greater capacity to experience life spontaneously without ideational elaboration. Either interpretation from the data still leaves open the question of whether such personality characteristics are a precondition or a result of a Pentecostal experience.

Much greater care than has been used in the past needs to be taken in controlling for experimenter bias or for the imposition of a particular value system on the data of psychological tests and measurements in research dealing with a deviant subcultural group, such as those who speak in tongues. Such experimenter bias raises the probability that much research in the area of glossolalia, whether utilizing psychometric data or not, may not meet the necessary level of scientific objectivity.

Acknowledging these sources of possible bias, what can be said about any changes in personality for classical glossolalics? Theoretically there are three possibilities of change over time: A change for the worse, no permanent change, and a change for the better. Cases have been described where the use of glossolalia seems to increase a person's pathology. Other research suggests that there is no permanent change or that whatever change there may be is only temporary. Finally, other research suggests that there is a more permanent change in personality for glossolalics that seems to better their mental health.

Anton T. Boisen (1939, 1955) was one of the earliest investigators of classical Pentecostalism not only from a socioeconomic point of view, but also from a mental health perspective. A clergyman who himself had had psychotic episodes requiring psychiatric hospitalization, Boisen was one of the founding fathers of clinical pastoral education for clergy. Much to the puzzlement, if not chagrin, of his peers in the mental health field, he maintained a long-standing interest in classical Pentecostals, or Holy Rollers as they were labeled in his day. In 1939, he wrote, "For the psychological data I have relied upon studies made over a period of sixteen years" (p. 185). Although Boisen found more positive than negative features in the Pentecostal experiences, nevertheless, he did observe that the experiences could have negative results for some people:

> Among those who belong to holy roller cults and pass through such experiences there are, as we might suppose, some who become mentally disordered. I have dealt with a number of these. (1939, p. 190)

In this category of Pentecostal experiences, Boisen (1939, 1955) included the full range of unusual and abnormal behaviors of the Holy Rollers of his time.

> The Pentecostals have the peculiar belief that the presence of the Holy Spirit is manifested by the phenomenon of "speaking with tongues." This accompanied by other abnormal manifestations such as dancing, jumping, jerking, thrusting up the hands, falling on the floor, and even passing into a state of unconsciousness. (1955, p. 78).

Reflecting on the frequency and intensity of the negative results that these classical Pentecostal experiences produced for people, Boisen (1955) reported:

> However, the amount of actual disturbance which is attributed to them [the pentecostal experiences] is much exaggerated. In my recent study of the Holy

Rollers, I took the occasion to examine the new admissions in the mental hospital which was serving in a region in which these groups were especially active. I was surprised at the relatively small number of cases in which the influence of these sects had been clearly a causal factor. Out of 249 new admissions in a six months' period there were only 15 which could be considered at all. Closer study indicated that in these cases the disturbance was due to an accumulation of unsolved personal problems, and the influence of these sects, where it did appear, was never more than an upsetting factor. (p. 88)

Thus, according to Boisen, there are only a few people, for whom Pentecostal experiences generally, and speaking in tongues particularly, does cause some psychological disturbance. The question then becomes: What types are those for whom the experience is destructive rather than constructive?

The British psychiatrist William Sargant (1949) did fieldwork among Pentecostal snake handlers in North Carolina and among other subcultural groups. Sargant recognized that "some persons can be altered profoundly in both their behavior and outlook" (p. 372) by techniques of group abreaction (or catharsis) in different cultural settings. By the term "abreaction," Sargant meant the release of emotional tension through recall of the original situations that caused the conflict and subsequent tension. However, for some people, these group cathartic methods were damaging, not helpful.

I was able to study several persons who had become mentally deranged by these methods. Attacks of schizophrenia, depression, and severe anxiety hysteria were all seen at the Psychiatric Clinic at Duke Hospital [Durham, North Carolina], which dated from attendance at various revival services [of snake-handlers]. Some patients had also experienced hysterical hallucinations of a vividness that I had not encountered previously in psychiatry, except in some of the acute cases of battle exhaustion in the war. (Sargant, 1949, p. 372)

In considering the question as to who would be helped and who would be harmed by these group cathartic methods, Sargant (1949) compared these revival services of snake handlers to his experiences with drug cathartic techniques with World War II soldiers.

Our experience with drug abreactive techniques should give us some general guidance as to the psychiatric types likely to be helped or harmed by such methods. Excitatory abreactive treatments are found most valuable in persons who, though normally fairly stable, have become reactively depressed, or anxious, or have developed hysterical symptoms after severe environmental stresses and mental conflicts. In such people they may break up "dynamic stereotypy" of thought and behavior and help towards the solution of outstanding conflicts. Chronic constitutional hysterics can be made worse, however, especially by repeated abreaction; severe obsessives are sometimes flared up in their symptomatology without being helped in any way; endogenous depressive patients are too retarded to abreact at all in most instances. I felt that results were roughly the same at these meetings though the severity of the group emotional pressure, and psychological shock methods applied, got at some who, I feel, would be quite untouched by our own methods. (p. 372)

In other words, Sargant was suggesting, by his analogy to drug cathartic treatments, that the more severely disturbed worshiper with long standing psychiatric problems, as a general rule, would find intense pentecostal experiences of no help. Such experiences could even exacerbate the pathology of the more seriously disturbed person.

He cited two clinical cases of severe depression for whom participation in the cathartic Pentecostal experiences only made their pathology worse and for whom only electric shock treatment was able to bring them out of their severe depressions. On the other hand, mild depression, he observed, could be helped by group cathartic Pentecostal experiences.

Agreeing with Sargant, Episcopalian author and lecturer Agnes Sanford (1966) also cautioned about praying too quickly with a person for the baptism of the Spirit:

> This can be good, but it is strong medicine, and strong medicine should not be given without a knowledge and understanding of the particular weaknesses and tendencies of the one to whom it is given. (p. 14)

Commenting further about the possible negative effects of praying for the baptism of the Spirit without proper preparation, Sanford (1966) explained in more detail:

> Those who in their enthusiasm lay hands on anyone with a minimum of preparation probably do not know that while some are blessed by this, others are thrown into confusion and depression. I do know, for I often pick up the wreckage. And after they have been burnt over by such a premature experience it is much more difficult for them to receive the real, deep, life-giving power of the Holy Spirit. They were induced into a spiritual experience that they were not prepared to assimilate. This increases the cleavage between the spirit and the subconscious. It widens the cleavage in the personality. (p. 177)

The anthropologist Virginia Hine (1969) made this observation on the basis of observations of the Pentecostal movement in the United States, Mexico, and Haiti:

> Our interview data support this observation. Pentecostals of a wide range of socioeconomic and educational backgrounds are aware of the different results of glossolalic experience for normal as compared with emotionally unstable individuals. Many Pentecostal leaders have pragmatically developed ways of evaluating potential converts, and do not encourage the glossolalic experience in persons they consider to be in questionable mental or emotional health. (p. 214)

Pastoral theologian Morton Kelsey (1964), who had neo-Pentecostals in his parish, stated that, "I have observed no case in which the individual was more neurotic after the experience of tongues, nor have I had any medical or psychological reports suggesting this" (pp. 209–210).

However, he enumerated a number of negative consequences that can happen to those who speak in tongues:

1. Tongue speakers may become "over-inflated" in the Jungian sense, meaning that they become so identified with the "God" complex that they feel they speak for God to other people. "They become inflated by the experience, proceeding to judge everyone else who has not spoken in tongues as religiously inferior and trying to force other people into the experience" (p. 223). This obviously leads to conflict and division.
2. For a person "who has a weak ego" (p. 224) being forced into the experience of speaking in tongues by emotional, social, and personal pressure, "may become a contribution to psychological illness" (p. 224).
3. Tongue speakers may so overemphasize this gift in their lives "that tongues becomes a way to suppress inner problems rather than resolving them" (p. 224). This suppression can lead to the eruption of uncharacteristic emotional behavior.
4. "For the person who is already uninhibited and needs to keep a tight rein on what inhibitions he has, tongue speaking may allow too much freedom and too much breakdown of control. This accounts, at least in part, for the moral excesses of the early days of the [classical] Pentecostal movement so lamented by their more perceptive writers; some people were undoubtedly involved who were not suited for the experience and not prepared for it" (pp. 224–225).
5. Tongue speaking may result in excessive emotionalism. "The experience may result in a starry-eyed burst of emotion which weakens the individual and makes him more unstable than before" (p. 225).
6. Finally, tongue speakers may develop a moral rigidity and perfectionism that is not internalized. For example, such a tongue speaker may appear religious to others, whereas at home, he tyrannizes his wife and children.

Although psychologist John Kildahl (1972) and his associates did not find any significant differences in mental health between glossolalics and nonglossolalics, they reported:

> As with many other experiences, the use to which glossolalia is put is often a reflection of emotional maturity. In our study persons with a low level of emotional stability tended to be extreme in their affirmation of the benefits of glossolalia. A well-integrated tongue-speaker generally made no wildly exaggerated claims for its powers, used it in a way that was not sensational, and did not allow it to dominate his life or use it as an instrument by which to manipulate others. (p. 59)

Thus, in their sample, there was a difference in how persons used glossolalia, depending on their previous levels of psychological maturity.

In considering whether there is change for the worse, Pruyser (1968, 1979) differentiates between the dynamics that may occur for classical

Pentecostals and neo-Pentecostals; nevertheless, he emphasizes the basic point that the use of glossolalia, a dissolution of articulate speech, is in all cases a regressive phenomenon psychologically as well as linguistically. Thus, for both psychologically strong as well as psychologically weak individuals, the use of glossolalia is essentially a change for the worse.

As noted earlier, others in the psychoanalytic or ego psychological tradition have interpreted glossolalia as linguistic and psychological regression, that is, in part, under the control of the ego. Even though there is a temporary regression, the long term result is of benefit to the ego and is positive rather than negative for personality growth. However, some psychological conditions of weak ego strength, such as borderline personalities, do not have the normal capacity to reverse such a regression, if, indeed, there is the capacity at all. As the Blanks (1974) point out, "borderline structures have potential for irreversible, or, at best, difficult-to-reverse regression, and often this is in itself a diagnostic sign" (p. 131). It may well have been such a case of a borderline personality that decompensated into a full-blown psychosis, described here by Finch (1964):

> A patient I saw expected God to give him professional skill as a pianist; then, when that did not work, skill as a vocalist. That did not work either. The subject seemed to progress from infantilism and extreme dependency feelings to an hysterical attempt to hold together his shattering ego by a frantic leap to glossolalia (in this case a hysterical symptom). When the symptom could not carry the weight of the attempt, it splintered into schizophrenia. Eventually he had to be committed to a mental hospital. (p. 17)

Thus, although these investigators do not claim that the experience of glossolalia *causes* psychopathic tendencies, nevertheless, glossolalia and other Pentecostal phenomena can be the occasion for the *expression* of psychopathological tendencies. Lapsley and Simpson (1964b) described such tendencies:

> For persons whose conflicts have been partly intellectualized and who are, as a consequence, prone to have grandiose ideas concerning themselves and their place in the scheme of things, the experience of the glossolalia group may be so stimulating and exciting that they either seek to impose themselves on the group as leaders or have great difficulty in functioning outside the group, or both. Such persons present severe problems for glossolalia groups, as they are frequently attracted to such groups, and are likely to be divisive in the effect they have on the group. (p. 23)

A classic study illustrating this possibility was the study by the anthropologist Weston La Barre (1962) of Beauregard Barefoot, a minister of an Appalachian snake-handling cult that practiced both the handling of snakes in worship as well as glossolalia. La Barre labeled Barefoot as a "psychopathic character." The essential concept of a psychopathic *personality* is that of a person who does not have the usual conscience of the average person and, therefore, commits antisocial acts without a feeling of guilt. In psychoanalytic terminology such a person is deficient, if perhaps not totally lacking, in superego development. La Barre felt that Barefoot was not a pure psychopath, in the sense of lacking any superego development. In fact, Barefoot was socialized into his deviant subcultural group and did experience some neurotic conflicts. Therefore, La Barre classified him as having a "psychopathic character" rather than considering him a "psychopathic personality."

If we accept that concept, the Pentecostal snake-handling cult may have been the occasion for Barefoot to manifest his psychopathic tendencies, but it certainly could not be considered to be the cause for his psychopathic behavior.

The practice of snake handling became illegal in many states because of the accidental deaths from snake bites in worship services. With the practice outlawed, the cultists took up a kind of cat-and-mouse game with the police. Outside of the snake-handling cults, however, Pentecostal worship in the United States has never resulted in antisocial deviation from the law of the land. Psychopathic behavior, such as stealing, lying, and cheating, is much less tolerated or accepted in religious deviant groups than it is in other subcultural groups who violate the law of the land and the generally accepted moral codes.

To summarize this section, investigators who have studied both classical Pentecostals and neo-Pentecostals agree that those who start from a point of psychological weakness, a lack of psychological maturity, or a lack of personality integration may not benefit from a glossolalic experience. In fact, for them, the experience may cause a change for the worse. There is some indication also (e.g., Sargant, 1949) that the greater the severity of the deficit before a glossolalic experience, the greater the probability that there will be a harmful outcome. There does not seem to be agreement among these investigators about changes among those who enter the experience from a point of psychological strength, maturity, or integration. The next section considers the literature that suggests that no changes occur.

In his study of classical Pentecostals, Sargant (1949) stated, "those helped do not seem to change their basic personalities" (p. 372).

In their study, which was primarily with neo-Pentecostals, Lapsley and Simpson (1964b), pastoral theologians at Princeton Theological Seminary, concluded that glossolalia is "a dissociative expression of truncated personality development" (p. 16).

> Glossolalia is understood to be a regression "in the service of the ego" to use Hartmann's phrase. That is, a regression controlled by the ego and for the purpose of maintaining personality, rather than a disintegration of personality. It is a genuine escape from inner conflict, but . . . of itself it *does not* bring a further permanent integration of personality, which would usually require insight into the roots of conflict. (p. 20; emphasis added)

Thus, the experience of glossolalia produces neither a simple regression to infantilism nor a permanent integration of personality. According to these authors, glossolalia primarily serves a maintenance function without any permanent change in personality.

In our longitudinal study, primarily with Catholic charismatics (Lovekin, 1975/1977; Lovekin & Malony, 1977), we were attempting to see if there were any personality changes for people who became glossolalic while attending "Life in the Spirit Seminars" (S. B. Clark, 1972b). Ten measures for assessing personality change were used in a battery of pencil-and-paper self-report questionnaires in this longitudinal study. Five measures were found to be highly interdependent: three measures of the affective state from the Multiple Affect Adjective Check List (i.e., State Anxiety, Depression, and Hostility); Trait Anxiety (as measured by the IPAT* Anxiety Scale Questionnaire); and Guilt (as measured by the Perceived Guilt Index). The five other measures were found to be independent of each other: two measures of the Salience of Religion (i.e., rated importance and hours per week of church activities), Ego Strength (as measured by a revised form of Barron's Ego Strength scale), Extrinsic Religiousness (as measured by Feagin's Intrinsic/Extrinsic scale), and problems (as measured by the Mooney Problem Check List). A series of analyses of variance were conducted for the interrelated measures as well as for each separate variable across groups and over time.

All three groups (i.e., New Tongues, Old Tongues, and No Tongues) who attended the seminars showed a significant change over time on three of the measures. They became less anxious on Trait Anxiety; they reported less problems; and they increased in Ego Strength. But for those who became glossolalic during the seminar (i.e., the New Tongues group) there was only one measure on which they changed when the others did not, namely, the State Anxiety. There was a significant lessening of State Anxiety from pretest to posttest, but this difference did not hold up at the time of follow-up.

Thus, new glossolalics improved on only one measure of personality integration, and that improvement was not maintained statistically over time. Also of interest was the fact that the new glossolalics were within the normal range on those measures where normative criteria were available. In other words, the new glossolalics showed no pathology or maladjustment prior to their initial experience of glossolalia. However, the study did not find that there was any pervasive resolution of neurotic conflicts nor any long term reestablishment of the ego as a result of becoming glossolalic. All groups participated together in changes for the better on the other measures. We, therefore, interpreted the other positive changes over time as being the result of group support or effect rather than of becoming glossolalic.

The clinical work of Boisen (1939) and Sargant (1949) with classical Pentecostals, the more theoretical study of Lapsley and Simpson (1964b) with neo-Pentecostals, and our own longitudinal study (Lovekin & Malony, 1977) with Catholic charismatics indicate that for many people who

* IPAT = Institute for Personality and Ability Testing.

become glossolalic, there is no permanent change of personality either for the worse or for the better. It is important to note that people studied here were all normal individuals without any significant pathology. The populations studied did not start from a place of poor mental health or from a lack of psychological maturity or personality integration. The clinical study of Kiev (1963) with psychotic classical Pentecostals also showed no change in personality structure.

Finally, consider the question of whether there is evidence that glossolalia actually does cause basic personality changes for the better or not. Pentecostals repeatedly testify to basic personality changes for the better.

As noted above, Boisen (1939) was an early participant observer of classical Pentecostals, or Holy Rollers. Although he recognized that Pentecostal experiences could be harmful for some, nevertheless, Boisen judged them to be positive overall:

> For the most part however their experiences may be regarded as constructive. With all the excesses that characterize the holy roller groups, we must give them credit for helping many individuals to re-organize lives that had been quite unsatisfactory and to make a better job of living. (p. 190)

> With all their regressive features, these sects are none the less manifestations of nature's power to heal. They are the spontaneous attempts of the common people to deal constructively with the stresses and trials which fall with particular severity upon them. (p. 194)

The situational stress to which Boisen was referring was of course the socioeconomic stress that these lower-class people were experiencing during the economic depression of the 1930s. When Boisen specified the constructive elements of which he wrote, he referred to cognitive restructuring, to changes in value systems, and to changes in attitudes—all of which we will discuss later. However, these were not measures of basic personality structure.

Psychiatrist L. M. van Eetveldt Vivier (1960, 1968) conducted an exploratory study in South Africa with classical Pentecostals. His study is often cited as substantiation that glossolalics experience personality integration.

It is worth noting that the type of classical Pentecostals Vivier studied were not stereotypic enthusiastic, emotional worshipers, but rather highly disciplined persons who allowed glossolalia to be used in public worship no more than three times, strictly following Paul's injunction in I Cor. 14:27. They used their glossolalia most frequently in private devotions rather than in public worship. Vivier utilized two control groups: twenty nonglossolalic Pentecostals (Control Group A) and twenty nonglossolalic, non-Pentecostals (Control Group B) of an orthodox reformed traditional church that did not approve of glossolalia in doctrine or in practice. Vivier attempted to match the three groups for sex, occupation, and religious conviction.

However, he did *not* match the groups for age because he had difficulty finding enough nonglossolalic Pentecostal subjects from the church he was sampling. He explained that more recent converts had to be used, that is, younger members. The nonglossolalic Pentecostal group had an age range of 29 to 32, whereas the age ranges of the other two groups was between 37 and 40 (see Table 10.2). This lack of overlap for one of the control groups raises the question of validity regarding comparison use of this group (because of the possible length of time involved in their religious life). Vivier also made some comparisons within the experimental group between the infrequent glossolalics ($N = 7$) and the frequent glossolalics ($N = 17$), evidently without any attempt to match the subgroups on any such variable as age or sex. Therefore these groups were of unequal size. Other problems in Vivier's study included the large number of tests he used and his use of statistical procedures that ignored chance variations.

Nevertheless, Vivier's research concluded that normal persons made significant changes toward personality integration because of their glossolalic experience.

A subsequent study that concluded that the use of glossolalia produces positive changes in personality was Kiev's (1964b) research with West Indian Pentecostal immigrants in England. Kiev did not find any basic personality changes among the West Indian psychotic inpatients who became glossolalic, but he did conclude that for normal West Indian Pentecostals with some neurotic problems, their religious beliefs and practices were therapeutic.

Table 10.2 Frequency of subjects by age range in Vivier's (1960) research

Age range	Experimental group	Control group A	Control group B
16–20 (18.0)[a]	0 (0)[b]	5 (90.0)[b]	0 (0)[b]
21–24 (22.5)	0 (0)	1 (22.5)	1 (22.5)
25–28 (26.5)	1 (26.5)	1 (26.5)	1 (26.5)
29–32 (20.5)[c]	4 (122.0)	1 (30.5)	1 (30.5)
33–36 (34.5)	6 (207.0)	6 (207.0)	7 (241.5)
37–40 (38.5)[d]	5 (192.5)	4 (154.0)	5 (192.5)
41–44 (42.5)	4 (170.0)	0 (0)	0 (0)
45–48 (46.5)	1 (46.5)	2 (93.0)	2 (93.0)
49–52 (50.5)	1 (50.5)	0 (0)	2 (101.0)
53–56 (54.5)	1 (54.5)	0 (0)	0 (0)
57–60 (58.5)	1 (58.5)	0 (0)	1 (58.5)
Sum of subjects[1]	24	20	20
Sum of products[2]	(927.5)	(623.5)	(766.0)
Division of 2 by 1	39	31	38

[a] Numbers in parentheses indicate the average age within the age range.
[b] Numbers in parentheses indicate the product of multiplying frequency by the average age within the age range.
[c] Median age range for Control Group A.
[d] Median age range for the Experimental Group and for Control Group B.

Although there is no evidence that emotional instability is a necessary in-
gredient for participation in the services, behavioral [*sic*] patterns institutionalized in the meetings are sufficiently broad as to provide suitable channels for the expression of a variety of needs and personality traits. For the
depressed and guilt-ridden the sin-cathartic basis of the ideology and services
provides a useful guilt-reducing device; for the hysteric a socially acceptable
model for acting out; and for the obsessional the encouragement of a reduction of inhibitions and increased emotionality. For such accompaniments of
neurotic and real suffering as feelings of inferiority, self-consciousness, suspi-
ciousness and anxiety, the social aspects of the movement would seem of
value. (p. 135)

Unfortunately, these conclusions were not related to clinical data that
would substantiate them. These generalizations may be true, but Kiev
did not show how he arrived at such conclusions from his clinical material. The value of these broad conclusions becomes even more questionable when we observe that Kiev (1966, p. 147) stated exactly the same
conclusions almost verbatim in a subsequent study of voodoo, the Haitian
folk religion, where those possessed by the *loa* were said to "speak in
tongues."

Wood (1965), in a later study, reported positive personality integration
for classical Pentecostals. He was not acquainted with the work either of
Vivier or Kiev, but he did build on the work of Boisen (1955):

The study closest to mine in its objective is that of Boisen. It demonstrates
a relationship between emotional religious experience and personality crisis
originating in social and economic disorganization. My study is complementary to Boisen's. (p. 2)

After summarizing his field observations of the enthusiastic and emotional Pentecostal services, which at times included motor automatisms
(like jerking and dancing), Wood concluded that for unidentified, deprived, or disorganized individuals, the close, positive interpersonal relationships were therapeutic or at least rewarding.

Although the sociological analysis was thorough, the psychological part
of Wood's research is much less informative. Wood compared Rorschach
responses between two groups: a Pentecostal sample ($N = 25$) and a non-
Pentecostal sample ($N = 24$). He stated that these original samples were
fairly well matched for socioeconomic class, educational level, sex, and
age, that is, "the two samples contain about the same proportion of old
and young individuals" (Wood, 1965, p. 82), but no ages were given.

He then proceeded to qualify his samples. Because few responses on a
Rorschach protocol make any interpretation tentative, Wood eliminated
from both samples those protocols that had fewer than ten responses.
Further, he eliminated three Methodist protocols from the non-Pentecostal sample, which gave him a pure Baptist sample ($N = 18$). He also
eliminated from his other sample seven Pentecostals who had not become
official members of any Pentecostal church, which gave him a pure Pentecostal church sample ($N = 12$). At this stage, Wood provided no informa-

tion as to whether the matching on any of the other variables was sustained by these adjustments.

There is an even more important problem from our point of view. Wood provides no evidence as to whether the members of the Pentecostal group were glossolalic or not. Wood had very carefully described the three distinct stages of spiritual progress to which Pentecostal Holiness members subscribe. Stage 1 is salvation or regeneration, in which a believer is forgiven, accepted, and given a spiritual nature by the Holy Spirit. Stage 2 is sanctification, in which a person is cleansed by the Holy Spirit of his unspiritual nature. Stage 3 is the Baptism of the Holy Spirit, in which a person is given the desire and the ability to maintain his holiness. The initial evidence of this Baptism of the Holy Spirit is speaking with other tongues. Thus, official members in good standing of Pentecostal Holiness churches may be at either Stage 2 or Stage 3 in their spiritual progress. In other words, members in good standing could be either nonglossolalic or glossolalic. It cannot be assumed that all the members of the Pentecostal sample were glossolalic because when Wood later divided his original Pentecostal sample into two categories of "established" ($N = 13$) and "others" ($N = 12$), he wrote, "those persons who have been active members for a number of years and who at the same time have experienced *at least* salvation and sanctification are grouped into the category 'established'; the remaining persons are grouped in the category, 'others' " (p. 100; italics added).

Therefore, some subjects in the "established" group were not glossolalic and we may infer that some subjects in the "others" group were probably not glossolalic either. Wood did not provide enough data for us to reconstruct a pure glossolalic sample. The net result is that we cannot with any degree of confidence use the comparison between the Pentecostal and the non-Pentecostal samples as findings about glossolalia per se. Neither can we use the comparisons between the "established" group and the "other" or newer groups as findings about glossolalia per se. In all fairness, it should be said that Wood's (1965) study was about the Pentecostal Holiness religion, *not* about glossolalia per se *nor* about the Baptism of the Spirit per se.

However, one of the hypotheses Wood advanced on the basis of his research was that participation in this Pentecostal Holiness religion leads to personality integration or stabilization. He made two assumptions about Rorschach interpretation: "I assume that vista occurs during periods of strong motivation to reorganize and that human movement occurs when adequate reorganization has resulted" (1965, p. 95). Therefore, he hypothesized that for the "established" members, there would be a significant reduction in vista and a significant increase in human movement when compared with the "others." He found, however, that there was no significant reduction in vista but that there was a significant increase in human movement. He interpreted these findings as an "interesting confirmation for a part of my hypothesis" (p. 101). However,

Wood's assumptions about vista and human movement presume much more than most Rorschach interpreters would grant. Thus, we cannot say that Wood has strongly demonstrated that participation in Pentecostal Holiness religion produces personality integration.

Somewhat later, Gerrard, Gerrard, and Tellegen (1966) reported positive personality growth as a function of speaking in tongues. In their study, as in that of Wood (1965), it cannot be assumed that all the Pentecostal subjects were glossolalic just because these members of a snake-handling cult also came from a Pentecostal Holiness background.

[Members of] the conventional denomination, compared to the serpent-handlers, are on the average more defensive, less inclined to admit undesirable traits, more ready to use mechanisms of denial and repression. The older [age group in the] conventional denomination, in addition, show indications of marked depressive symptomatology. The serpent-handlers appear less defensive and restrained. On the contrary, they seem to be more exhibitionistic, excitable and pleasure-oriented. It seems they are more bound on enjoying the immediate and the present and are less controlled by considerations of conformity to the general culture, particularly middle class structure.

Comparison of the two age groups indicates that the older subjects are more "strict" and moralistic in outlook, show more social introversion, somatic preoccupation, lack of vitality and—particularly in the conventional group—depression. As a group, the older subjects present a more dysphoric, defeated picture. A high incidence of health problems would fit into this picture.

Finally, males as a group appear more sociable, outgoing and self-assertive than females. (Gerrard, et al., 1966, pp. 56–57)

Further confirmation for these conclusions was obtained when a quantitative analysis was made by four additional clinicians who rated the prominent qualitative statements from the group profiles. These raters used a scale from 0 to 8, and they rated the individual MMPI profiles on eight dimensions, which were again averaged and three-way analyses of variance were conducted for each of the eight dimensions (Tellegen et al., 1969). These ratings confirmed the earlier conclusions of Tellegen.

Unfortunately, there may be a serious confounding of variables in this unique study. Certainly one of the most striking findings was the difference between the older members of the conventional denomination (Methodist) and the older members of the serpent-handling cult (Holiness-Pentecostal background). The sociologist Nathan Gerrard commented on that difference:

The old member of the conventional denomination may yearn for the highly emotional prayer meeting of his youth, but he is unwilling to pay the price for such experiences in the present. The price is status degradation for someone who identifies with the middle class and its norms of respectable behavior. But the member of the stationary lower class is not afraid of losing that which he does not possess and to which he does not aspire. (Gerrard, et al., 1966, p. 73)

In other words, the variable of social class was not really controlled. The personality differences that were discovered may be more the result of different social classes than religious practices.

The most recent research project on classical Pentecostals that reports positive personality gains was published by Ness and Wintrob in 1980; however, their fieldwork was done in the early 1970s. We have reviewed this study earlier with respect to changes in physical health. Of interest to us in this study of Pentecostals are the findings about glossolalia in particular rather than all six of the religious behaviors studied. For glossolalia, as for the other behaviors, there was a distinct difference in sex roles according to the cultural expectations of a small isolated coastal Newfoundland community:

> Glossolalia was found to be primarily a male activity, functionally similar to the leadership role men assume in other contexts, such as representing the household and serving on committees within the community. (Ness & Wintrob, 1980, p. 306)

Glossolalia for both men and women was the lowest of the six religious behaviors over the thirteen-month period of the study. Only four men and two women were observed to use glossolalia twice a month or more. The rest never did use glossolalia.

For these classical Pentecostals evidently the precondition or method of seeking the gift of tongues was to dance in the Spirit first. The researchers classified this as possession behavior because it involved gyrating around the church or rolling on the floor.

The statistically significant findings for men for both possession behavior and glossolalia are of interest:

> The more frequently men engage in possession behavior, the *less* likely they are to report complaints of depression, sensitivity, and anger. Furthermore, the frequency of glossolalia is negatively correlated with feelings of anger, which suggests that as the practice of glossolalia increases, feelings of anger decrease. (Ness & Wintrob, 1980, p. 310; emphasis added)

The statistically significant findings for women, however, were quite different:

> Among Pentecostal women, the positive correlation between glossolalia, possession behavior, and physical complaints suggest that as physical complaints increase, the likelihood of possession behavior and glossolalia *increases*. However, in contrast to men, Pentecostal women who experience glossolalia do not appear to derive relief, measured in terms of reduced reporting of symptoms of emotional distress. That is, no statistically significant correlations between glossolalia and total psychological complaints for women were found. This finding is congruent with observational data on the social context of religious behavior indicating that: 1) few Pentecostal women consistently engage in glossolalia, and 2) those women who do engage in glossolalia do so with much less fervor and for a substantially shorter period of time than men. (Ness & Wintrob, 1980, p. 310; emphasis added)

It should also be noted that the two women who spoke in tongues were elderly widows. It may well be that we have a confounding variable of age and possible concomitant poor health, which might account for the relief of physical complaints for the women rather than relief of psychological complaints. Ness and Wintrob acknowledged that further research is needed to determine the impact of both age and sex. They also emphasized that their sample population consisted of normal people who were functioning adequately without any psychiatric illnesses among them.

To summarize, these six studies claim positive personality changes for classical Pentecostals who speak in tongues. We will comment on the setting, the methodology of the research, the quality of the research, the conclusions that can be substantiated, and some hypotheses that can be raised for further experimental testing.

The setting for glossolalia among classical Pentecostals is not homogeneous, either in belief or in practice, rather it varies greatly. Pentecostals of the Holiness tradition believe in a three-stage theory of Christian experience, that is, conversion, sanctification, and then the baptism of the Holy Spirit. Other classical Pentecostals believe in a two-stage theory, that is, conversion and the baptism of the Holy Spirit. Much more care needs to be taken in future research to identify to which stage of experience a classical Pentecostal belongs, especially if the focus of the study is to be glossolalia per se. Only Wood (1965) attended to this issue, although even he did so inadequately.

Further, the worship setting of classical Pentecostals in these studies varies greatly from restrained, orderly, highly structured worship, such as in the Apostolic Faith Movement (Vivier, 1960); to enthusiastic, spontaneous worship (Gerrard et al., 1966; Kiev, 1964b); to worship that includes motor automatisms, like jerking, dancing, falling on the floor (Ness & Wintrob, 1980; Wood, 1965) and even, in some rare instances, the handling of poisonous snakes (Gerrard et al., 1966). These differences need to be controlled or analyzed.

The methodologies employed in these studies were theoretical discussion coupled with a modicum of empirical data (i.e., Boisen, 1939; Kiev, 1964b) and a number of empirical studies with control groups (i.e., Gerrard et al., 1966; Ness & Wintrob, 1980; Vivier, 1960; Wood, 1965). No longitudinal designs were attempted. The quality of this later research, for the most part, left much to be desired because of the confounding of variables, such as age, sex, and social class, and because of the possible existence of experimenter bias. Thus, we do not have definitive findings. In most studies, the conclusions were not carefully tied to the research findings and, therefore, were poorly substantiated.

Two fairly well-substantiated conclusions were that glossolalia reduced depression (Gerrard et al., 1966) and that glossolalia reduced anger (Ness & Wintrob, 1980). Some hypotheses can be raised from these studies, which need further experimental testing and research. The psychometric data from Wood's (1965) research in particular raise the possibility that the use of glossolalia may increase affectivity, may increase the capacity to cope with anxiety, and may increase the ability to be spontaneous without ideational elaboration for classical Pentecostals.

Turning next to neo-Pentecostals, there are several studies that claim glossolalia causes personality integration. Although Agnes Sanford (1966) has cautioned about praying too quickly for the baptism of the Spirit, nevertheless, she herself prayed with many for them to receive this baptism in her Schools of Pastoral Care. She did not believe that glossolalia was the initial evidence of this baptism but that it could be a subsequent gift. She wrote that in her own experience, the baptism of the Holy Spirit gave her a subjective experience of power. She also commented on the emotional results of the baptism: "This entering in of the Holy Spirit, with or without the gift of tongues, can grant to us spiritual blessings of joy and peace" (1966, p. 177). Of course, her statements are subjective reports, not empirical findings.

Although Kelsey (1964) had enumerated a number of negative consequences that can occur as a result of speaking in tongues, nevertheless, he put much more emphasis on the positive results: "Tongue speaking is a religious experience which, from the evidence we have, seems to lead to a greater ability to function in the world" (p. 209). In fact, Kelsey went so far as to speculate that, "tongue speaking may well be an unconscious resolution to neurosis" (pp. 207–208). As we noted earlier, Kelsey interpreted Jung's writings as indicating "that Jung believed that tongues could be a positive preparation for integration of personality" (p. 199). In his own evaluation of tongues, Kelsey (1964) wrote:

Speaking in tongues is a *rite d'entrée* to the deeper levels of the psyche. It is an initiation rite in the deepest and truest meaning of that word. But since it gives no more than entrance, its values lie not so much in what it is, as in what it brings and what results follow it. Tongues can be a beginning of spiritual life, not the end, and for some people it may be the best, or even the only way of opening them to a religious experience. (p. 231)

We have commented above that Kelsey (1964) had hypothesized that:

The extroverted person, the one most largely concerned with the outer world . . . in whom feeling or relating to differences in value is dominant, and who has been inhibited in the use of this function, is most likely to speak in tongues. The experience is also of great benefit to such a person, liberating him to use far more of this unconscious power. Tongues can be a breaking down of obsolete barriers and an entrance into a new life for such a person. (pp. 220–221)

Although Lovekin (1975/1977) conducted a pilot study testing this hypothesis with Catholic charismatics, to date we know of no reported study that has tested Kelsey's (1964) hypothesis with neo-Pentecostals. In this theoretical work, Kelsey has suggested that not only will the extroverted person with a dominant feeling function be more *able* to speak in tongues, but also that he will *benefit* more than other personality types. Both hypotheses need to be verified by empirical research.

We reviewed earlier the work of Kildahl (1972) and his associates in some detail. Even though Kildahl used the concept of regression in the service of the ego, he emphasized the negative aspects of this regression. Interesting, however, is the fact that the longitudinal part of the research with the MMPI revealed positive findings and conclusions. One of his experimental hypotheses was "that the emotional benefits of tongue-speaking did not last for a long period of time" (Kildahl, 1972, p. 38). This hypothesis was *not* confirmed because the lower level of depression remained the same after a year's period of time:

> When tested a year later, the glossolalists continued to experience the same feelings of well-being; they were no more—nor less—depressed than a year previously. They continued to say that they were "changed persons" and continued to feel a definite assurance that God loved them. Furthermore, they described themselves as more sensitive and loving towards others. Many felt they had better marital, including sexual, relationships. Most reported higher moral and ethical responsiveness, which they attributed to the glossolalic experience. (pp. 45–46)

Thus, these neo-Pentecostals not only maintained for a full year their lack of depression as measured by the MMPI, but they also sustained their sense of well-being.

Earlier the theoretical and clinical work of Brende (1974) and Brende and Rinsley (1979) at the Menninger Foundation was discussed. In his 1974 article, Brende presented four case studies that included material from his psychiatric interviews with four adolescent inpatients:

> Psychiatric interviews held with four adolescents who were being treated on an inpatient basis and who had all engaged in glossolalia will further clarify the above noted psychological picture [i.e., a regression "in the service of the ego"]. None of them had a Pentecostal family background. (p. 341)

> In summary, the four young adults who engaged in glossolalia were told by others in advance that this was a gift of God and a sign of being in a special relationship to Him. The sense of joy was linked with being a special person, a child loved by God. The previous feeling of worthlessness was replaced by a sense of specialness. There was now awareness of being filled with something new, vital, and powerful. This seemed to become the basis for a feeling of identity. The new identity was achieved without any attempt at gaining control over internal impulses or the threatening outside world. . . . The unifying parent-child experience seemed to be the basis for the feeling of wholeness. . . . This allowed each of the four the opportunity to experience his positive regressive experience whenever necessary to regain a sense of wholeness with his self. In all four cases, the new ability to trust in someone seemed to provide a basis for receptivity to therapeutic intervention and personality growth. (pp. 348–349)

Thus, Brende's presentation of clinical material, based on an ego psychological viewpoint, is cautiously positive. It is the only empirical study that we know of to evaluate religious glossolalia as having a positive personality outcome for those who begin with poor mental health. But we also note that these adolescents with borderline personality disorders were also undergoing intensive psychiatric treatment in a hospital—an unusual and an abnormal setting for the initiation and maintenance of religious glossolalia.

In sum, these six studies claim positive personality changes for neo-Pentecostals who speak in tongues. There is less variability in the setting for neo-Pentecostals than for classical Pentecostals. The belief system does not include a three-stage theory of Christian experience, but beliefs do vary as to whether glossolalia is a necessary concomitant of being baptized with the Holy Spirit or not.

The methodology of these studies with neo-Pentecostals is predominantly theoretical (Brende & Rinsley, 1979; Kelsey, 1964). These theoretical presentations are only supported, however, by case studies and not by more stringent research designs. Only one study (Kildahl, 1972) used a control group and included a longitudinal dimension.

The only well-substantiated conclusion about the use of glossolalia for neo-Pentecostals is that it reduces depression or, to put it in positive terms, that it increases a sense of well-being. Kildahl's research substantiated this much better than the Gerrards (1966) did with classical Pentecostals because he used a bona fide longitudinal research design, whereas they only used a comparison study of different groups and different age subgroups.

The hypotheses raised by these studies that need further experimental testing and research are much more closely related to a particular theoretical orientation than were the hypotheses raised by the classical Pentecostal studies and perhaps will be more difficult to substantiate. Brende and Rinsley (1979) proposed that glossolalia involves a positive regression that allows trust and that, therefore, provides the basis for personality growth. Kelsey (1964) proposed that glossolalia initiates a person to the deeper levels of the unconscious psyche and again may be the beginning of personality integration. More easily tested, perhaps, is Kelsey's hypothesis that an extroverted person with a dominant feeling function will not only benefit the most from becoming glossolalic, but will also have his/her feeling function strengthened.

Finally, we come to the empirical studies that have been conducted with Catholic charismatics. This renewal movement, which began in American Catholicism in 1967, grew quickly in the United States as well as elsewhere. There quickly developed within this renewal movement a catechetical preparation (i.e., Life in the Spirit Seminars, S. B. Clark, 1972a) for candidates who wanted to receive this baptism of the Holy Spirit.

Lovekin (1975/1977) undertook a pilot study with a "Life in the Spirit Seminar," which utilized the Myers-Briggs Type Inventory (MBTI) for personality types and the California Psychological Inventory (CPI) for personality changes. Only six subjects, two men and four women, were pretested and posttested. The group profile on the pretest (as well as on the posttest) was that of an extroverted attitude with the feeling function dominant (i.e., an extroverted feeling type). This seemed to support Kelsey's (1964) hypothesis that this extroverted feeling type is the most likely to speak in tongues. Another part of his hypothesis was that potential candidates were inhibited in the use of the feeling function. In this pilot study, one man had his personality type change from the time of the pretest to that of the posttest—from an extroverted thinking type to an extroverted feeling type; and the group profiles showed an increase of 12 points from pretest to posttest for the feeling function. Although these changes were not statistically significant, an analysis did reveal a statistically significant lessening of the judging attitude from pretest to posttest on the judgment-perception (JP) preference. According to Myers (1980) the qualities of a person preferring a judging attitude include having a system in doing things, maintaining order with possessions, having a planned life, keeping up a sustained effort, being decisive, exercising authority, and having settled opinions. On the other hand, the qualities of a person preferring a perception attitude include being spontaneous, being open-minded, trying to understand, being tolerant, having curiosity, having a zest for experience, and being adaptable. Thus, the experience of becoming glossolalic at the time of receiving the baptism of the Spirit for these six subjects in the pilot study decreased the former set of qualities and increased the later set of qualities.

In a subsequent study of Catholic charismatics, Lovekin and Malony (1977) found interesting but only suggestive findings. They compared an Old Tongues to a New Tongues group. These groups were not matched in any respect but were comparison groups that emerged during the research itself. When those who were already glossolalic prior to the study (the Old Tongues group) were compared to those who became glossolalic during the study (the New Tongues group), the Old Tongues group was found to be significantly higher in Ego Strength as measured by a revised form of Barron's Ego Strength scale. They were also higher than the New Tongues group on two measures of the Salience of Religion: one defined as a self-report rating regarding the importance of religion and the other defined as a self-report of the number of hours per week spent in religious activities. Even though these were statistically significant differences, they are only suggestive rather than conclusive findings because they are based on post hoc analysis.

Lovekin and Malony (1977) also compared the Old Tongues and New Tongues groups with those who never became glossolalic (the No Tongues group) after the research ended and several months later. They found that at all times the Old Tongues group was higher on Ego Strength and the rated importance of religion than the other two groups. In addition, they were less Extrinsic in their orientation to religion and spent more hours per week in religious activities than the other two groups.

Again, it should be emphasized that these findings only *suggest* that engaging in glossolalia over a period of time produces these differences. The fact that an analysis of changes in the New Tongues group found only one significant change, that is, toward less State Anxiety, from pre- to post- to follow-up time, highlights the problems in cross-sectional as opposed to longitudinal research designs. Apparent differences can be an artifact of studying persons at a given moment and presuming that the differences resulted from the influence of a given variable over a period of time. However, the fact that the Old Tongues group had practiced glossolalia for an average of three years prior to the study and that the New Tongues group was assessed only for a five-month period, allowed Lovekin and Malony (1977) to propose the hypothesis that there may be personality growth as a function of glossolalia.

Nancy L. Niesz (1977), who has worked primarily with Roman Catholic charismatics, compared the Rorschach inkblot profiles of neo-Pentecostals and Catholic charismatics with the norms from Beck's scoring system (Beck, Beck, Levitt, & Melish, 1961) and the results of Wood's study (1965). Her five subjects averaged more than four years in the use of glossolalia and were referred to her by prayer-group leaders as "good examples of Pentecostals." They were characterized as in "good mental health." Her findings were consistent with Woods, in that her subjects also had higher than average scores in nonpathognomic affective experiences. Her findings (1977) were different, in that her subjects were not only more productive in their responses than those of Wood (1965) but they were also well above the average as reported by Beck et al. (1961). They also evidenced more Movement responses. Niesz (1977) did not offer an explanation for these findings, and it is possible that the observed differences in ideational activity and productivity may be due to sociocultural differences because her subjects had more years of education and were from a higher socioeconomic class than those of Wood. However, the findings that were consistent with those observed by Wood do suggest that glossolalics, whether classical Pentecostals, neo-Pentecostals, or Catholic Pentecostals, are more open to anxiety and affectivity than the average person. Although Niesz did not offer judgments regarding negative or positive personality characteristics as evidenced on the protocols, she did suggest: ". . . Rorschachs of non-Pentecostals and even non-glossolalic Pentecostals often seem duller and flatter than those of the glossolalic neo-Pentecostals, like soda drinks without carbonation" (p. 9). Again, this research is only suggestive of personality changes occurring over time as a function of glossolalia. We do not know whether these differences were characteristic of these persons before they became glossolalic or afterwards.

In a second study, Niesz (Niesz & Kronenberger, 1978), followed Richardson's (1973) suggestion that a study needed to be made of subjects from the same religious background who were in various stages of involvement with Pentecostalism. She evaluated Roman Catholics who were nonglossolalic and non-Pentecostal and compared them to those who were nonglossolalic, *neo*-Pentecostal, and those who were glossolalic and neo-Pentecostal. She studied only lifelong Catholics (i.e., no converts) who were single and Caucasian. They were all college students who were judged to be in good mental health on the basis of their MMPI short-form profiles. The twenty subjects in each group were matched as closely as possible on sex, age, grade-point average, year in school, and socio-economic status (SES).

In an analysis of measures of Time Competence and Inner-Directness, she concluded that there was a gradual increase in self-actualization from nonglossolalic non-Pentecostals to nonglossolalic neo-Pentecostal to glossolalic neo-Pentecostals. However, only one of the eight comparisons was significant. She acknowledged that these results may have been the result of a group effect, but she noted that there was some indication that glossolalia by itself may have contributed to the increase in self-actualization.

Even more dramatic results were obtained by Niesz and Kronenberger (1978) when they included those subjects who had been excluded on the basis of their MMPI profiles. Six of nine comparisons were significant in the expected direction. These results clearly indicate that when pathology is not ruled out, there is a significant increase in self-actualization among Catholics who become Pentecostal with or without glossolalia. The further acquisition of glossolalia does not significantly increase their development. As in the Lovekin and Malony (1977) study, it would seem as if the predominant variable influencing the change is that of the group experience rather than the individual experience of speaking in tongues.

In evaluating this Niesz and Kronenberger study (1978), it should be noted that, even here, the requirements for a longitudinal study are not fully met. Different rather than the same persons were used, in spite of the fact that they were at different points in their religious development.

To summarize these four studies, which claim positive personality change for glossolalic Catholic charismatics, it should be noted that there is even less variability in the setting for Catholics than for the neo- or classical Pentecostals. Their belief system does not include a three-stage theory of Christian experience, nor is it presumed that glossolalia is necessary for the baptism of the Holy Spirit. In fact, the reverse is true. Glossolalia is proposed as *not* necessary for spirit baptism, although it is certainly encouraged. Their worship setting is restrained and orderly and they are introduced to the idea of glossolalia in a catechetical, as opposed to an experiential, manner. Their procedures, such as "Life in the Spirit Seminars," afford unique opportunities for longitudinal research, as exemplified by Lovekin and Malony (1977).

Perhaps because Catholics are the most recent group to become glossolalic, there are no studies in our survey that are theoretical in nature. Of interest is the fact that both the Lovekin and Malony (1977) and Niesz and Kronenberger (1978) studies suggested that the changes they observed were attributable to the effect of the group experience rather than to glossolalia. J. Massyngale Ford (1976), a biblical scholar at Notre Dame University, suggested this might be true in a descriptive interpretation of contemporary Catholic charismatics. This group effect needs to be controlled for in future studies in order to establish the specific effect of speaking in tongues.

At this point the suggestion that becoming glossolalic among Catholic charismatics causes personality changes is probable but uncertain. It is interesting to note that more recent research (Brende & Rinsley, 1979; Niesz & Kronenberger, 1978), both with neo-Pentecostals and Catholic charismatics, suggests that those who begin with poor mental health as well as those who begin with good mental health *do* make changes for the better rather than changes for the worse. This is in contrast to early research that concluded that those who began with poor mental health became worse, whereas those who began with good mental health changed for the better. Table 10.3 summarizes these studies.

To conclude, the research that has investigated the positive aspects of becoming glossolalic for all three subcultures of classical, neo-, and Catholic charismatic Pentecostals is summarized in Table 10.4.

What emerges from this survey is the conclusion that depression among most glossolalics is reduced and remains low over time. Further, glossolalics become more open to feeling and to the affective dimension of their experience. They become more spontaneous and better able to cope with anxiety. There is a need for investigations to determine whether this affectivity is a precondition for becoming glossolalic or whether it results *from* the experience. Finally, no apology needs to be made regarding the difficulties in this research or the tentativeness of these conclusions. It has also been difficult to demonstrate the effectiveness of psychotherapy. It simply means that there must be more sophisticated, longitudinal investigations conducted in the future.

Table 10.3 Personality changes in three subcultural groups for subjects with good and poor mental health according to the researcher's own conclusions

Subcultures	Change for the worse	No permanent change	Change for the better
Classical Pentecostals:			
Boisen (1939)	Good and poor mental health		Good mental health
Sargant (1949)	Poor mental health	Good mental health	Good mental health
Vivier (1960)	Poor mental health		Good mental health
La Barre (1962)		Poor mental health	Good mental health
Kiev (1963)	Poor mental health		Good mental health
Finch (1964)			Good mental health
Wood (1965)			Good mental health
Gerrard, Gerrard, & Tellegen (1966)	Good and poor mental health		
Pruyser (1968)			Good mental health
Ness & Wintrob (1980)			Good mental health
Neo-Pentecostals:			
Kelsey (1964)	Poor mental health		Good mental health
Lapsley & Simpson (1964b)	Poor mental health	Good mental health	
Sanford (1966)	Poor mental health		Good mental health
Hine (1969)	Poor mental health		Good mental health
Kildahl (1972)	Poor mental health		Good mental health
Pruyser (1968)			Poor mental health
Brende & Rinsley (1979)	Good and poor mental health		
Catholic charismatics:			
Lovekin (1977)			Good mental health
Lovekin & Malony (1975/1977)		Good mental health	
Niesz (1977)			Good mental health
Niesz & Kronenberger (1978)			Good and poor mental health

Table 10.4 Summary of research on glossolalics showing personality changes for the better in three different subcultures

Aspects of the research	Classical Pentecostals	Neo-Pentecostals	Catholic charismatics
Setting:			
Beliefs	Two and three stage theories of Christian experience	Tongues necessary and unnecessary in baptism	Tongues unnecessary in baptism
Worship	Range from highly emotional to restrained	Usually restrained and orderly	Only restrained and orderly
Methodology:			
Mostly theoretical	Boisen (1939), Kiev (1964b)	Kelsey (1964), Sanford (1966), Hine (1969), Brende (1974)	—
Pilot studies	—	—	Lovekin (1975/1977), Niesz (1977)
Control group studies	Vivier (1960), Wood (1965), Gerrard, Gerrard, & Tellegen (1966); Ness & Wintrob (1980)	Kildahl (1972)	Lovekin (1975/1977), Lovekin & Malony (1977), Niesz & Kronenberger (1978)
Longitudinal	—	Kildahl (1972)	Lovekin (1975/1977), Lovekin & Malony (1977)
Quality	Most control groups poorly matched, most conclusions poorly substantiated	Two very good theoretical studies, more attention to extraneous variables	Extraneous variable of group effect confounds the findings
Conclusions	Depression and anger reduced	Depression reduced	—
Hypotheses	Increase in: affectivity capacity to cope with anxiety spontaneity	Deeper levels of the psyche revealed Extroverted feeling person benefits the most Positive regression allows trust, which provides basis for personality growth	Increase in: affectivity capacity to cope with anxiety spontaneity ego strength salience of religion intrinsic religious orientation self-actualization

11

Cognitive and Attitudinal Changes

In the preceding chapter we were concerned with changes in basic personality structure among those who speak in tongues. Personality structure involves *how* a person perceives and understands the world, and how she/he uses thinking and feeling rather than the specific *content* of either her/his thoughts or feelings. There was no major consensus regarding these changes. However, in this chapter, there is a general consensus. All the studies acknowledge that there is a real, even a radical, change in attitudes for those who become glossolalic. This is the change to which glossolalics testify and about which they make their self-reports.

In his pioneering study of classical Pentecostals, Boisen (1955) described the cognitive set (or the cognitive interpretation) of the experience that classical Pentecostals made in their new-found religion.

> Most important is the sense of reality which pervades the religion of these newer groups. They share the conviction that they have found God. They feel themselves able to bear witness to His presence in their own lives, as evidenced by their sense of release from the burden of guilt and by certain unusual experiences. . . . They find themselves doing things they cannot account for, or uttering words that do not seem to come from themselves. These experiences they interpret as possession by a power beyond themselves. We may question the correctness of their interpretation, but that does not alter the fact that to many of them it gives a power to reorganize their lives and kindles in them a faith that is contagious. (p. 85)

This cognitive restructuring, has been repeatedly noted by subsequent investigators.

Sargant, who studied snake handlers in the United States (1949), compared their revivalist conversions to brainwashing and psychoanalysis. He proposed that physiological mechanisms are the basis for cognitive changes in radical conversions. In an introductory chapter called, "The Physiology of Faith"—which Sargant later added to his book, *Battle for the Mind* (1957/1971)—he summarized his twenty-year research into

> what seemed to be similar neurophysiological phenomena occurring during states of supposed "possession" by a whole variety of different gods and

spirits in many parts of the world. These phenomena seem also to have helped in the creation of states of absolute and certain faith in the existence and powers of all sorts of gods, demons and spirits by those so possessed. (Sargant, 1957/1971, p. 2)

He applied some principles of animal physiology, which Pavlov had discovered in his work with dogs, to human beings, correlating stages of brain mechanisms in animals with stages of obtaining sudden unsubstantiated faith that is held with absolute certainty. Sargant emphasized five stages of brain mechanisms that Pavlov had discovered with animals. When a nervous system—whether of an animal or a man—is put under increasingly severe degrees of psychological and physical stress, the brain retreats in various stages of protective inhibition or dysfunction.

The first stage of such protective brain inhibition is what Pavlov called the "equivalent" phase of brain activity. Here all varieties and strengths of outside stimuli produce the same brain responses so that the individual now gets the same amount of emotional feeling whether he is given a thousand pounds or sixpence. The next phase of induced brain inhibition is the "paradoxical" phase. Here the patient receives a greater emotional stimulus and experiences far greater emotional feelings from a small stimulus than from a much larger one. In this state people may get intense emotional satisfaction from quite minor happenings while remaining indifferent to normally overwhelming blows of fortune. (Sargant, 1957/1971, p. 10)

The third stage is

The "ultraparadoxical" phase of brain activity, in which many of our positive conditioned responses suddenly become negative, and all our previous negative conditioned responses suddenly switch to positive. Both dog and man then start to hate the persons and mode of life they previously loved, and start to become attached to ideals, faiths, and persons they previously despised. This inevitably results in the break-up and often dramatic alteration in many of the ideas, faiths and interpersonal relationships of the individual concerned. (pp. 10–11)

It is in this third stage of "ultraparadoxical" brain activity that individuals start to have "feelings of possession which serve to create so much faith. For instance, a person thinking about God suddenly feels instead that he has suddenly become possessed by Him, or has become part of Him" (p. 11).

The fourth stage of dysfunction or "protective" inhibition

is what Pavlov described as the "hypnoidal" state of inhibiting brain activity. A state similar to the hypnotic state in man supervenes. And it is mostly in this particular state of abnormal brain activity that the brain stops computing critically the impressions being received. New impressions, new commands, new ideas become suddenly imperative in their need of acceptance, and ring absolutely true. (p. 11)

The fifth and final stage, which extreme stress can produce, Pavlov called "transmarginal" collapse:

There was a final stress which could disrupt all the animal's previous conditioning, break up implanted patterns of behavior, and so allow new ones more easily to be put in their place. This was a state of great excitement and fear, carried even beyond the point of ultraparadoxical brain activity, which finally resulted in the total "transmarginal" collapse and temporary total inhibition of much brain activity. (p. 13)

Having delineated these different stages of brain dysfunctioning when an organism is under stress, Sargant then proposed that these different stages of brain physiology can be found in sudden religious conversions, brainwashing, shock treatments, drug treatments, lobotomies, and psychoanalysis.

Sargant (1957/1971) primarily used literary/historical examples rather than clinical or experimental findings to illustrate his thesis in the area of sudden religious conversions. He quoted frequently from the journal of John Wesley, the English Methodist evangelist of the eighteenth century, and from Jonathan Edwards's own account of the revival he began in Massachusetts in the eighteenth century. Sargant also cited Acts 9— which tells of Paul's radical conversion—as an example of "transmarginal" collapse. Sargant also noted that new faiths, new beliefs, and totally new outlooks could be suddenly acquired not only by overexciting the nervous system, but also by the opposite extreme of "sensory deprivation."

As interesting as Sargant's thesis of physiological dysfunction may be, it is not necessarily applicable to the average case of glossolalia. Snake handling is practiced by only a very small sample of those who speak in tongues, and the kind of emotional stress that Sargant described simply does not exist for most samples of glossolalia. Reporting on her case histories of glossolalics, Hine (1969) did not find verification for Sargant's thesis of physiological dysfunction:

It is difficult to find evidence for this degree of physiological breakdown in most of the Baptism or glossolalic experience we have observed, even though cognitive changes were reported by participants. However, it is not impossible that this process involves a greater or lesser degree of interruption of normal functioning, and that there are physiological correlates of lesser intensity. (p. 223)

No researcher has evaluated Sargant's thesis of physiological dysfunction for glossolalics in experimental studies. If there are such cases of physiological dysfunction, they must be quite rare.

Although American psychiatrist Jerome D. Frank (1961) did not study either glossolalia nor Pentecostals, he did continue Sargant's discussion about religious conversions. Again his interest was "confined to sudden conversions characterized by drastic and far-reaching psychic upheavals, usually accompanied by strong emotion and leading to permanent changes in attitude and behavior" (p. 76). Commenting on the changes produced by such sudden religious conversions, Frank wrote:

This experience is intensely emotional and may be followed by a sense of inner joy and peace. The change in the convert's perception of himself in relation to the deity implies certain changes in his picture of social participation. The invocation of supernatural forces to support certain attitudes may resolve certain intrapersonal conflicts and so promote personality integration. It also enhances the convert's sense of self-worth at the same time that he paradoxically feels a new sense of humility. (pp. 76–77)

Frank did not use Sargant's thesis that there was *physiological* dysfunction in religious conversion, brainwashing, and psychoanalysis, but he did explore common *psychological* features in these experiences. However, the intense emotional stress that both Frank and Sargant assume for sudden religious conversions is infrequent for glossolalics. McDonnell (1976) has commented about the infrequency of the intense emotional stress assumed by those researchers.

The sampling of Wood, Sargant, and Frank would still be typical of some groups of classical Pentecostals in the United States, Africa, South America, and Indonesia. However, their sampling would not be typical of large areas of the classical Pentecostal world, in Europe, and places like South Africa, and in most parts of the United States. The intensely emotional atmosphere of the groups they studied would be highly untypical of almost all Protestant neo-Pentecostal groups, and would bear no resemblance to Catholic charismatic groups. For this reason their studies have little general significance for vast areas of the Pentecostal-charismatic movement. (pp. 97–98)

Although we would not include Wood's (1965) research in the same category here, nevertheless, we would agree with McDonnell about both Sargant and Frank. Although Sargant's thesis about physiological dysfunction has been clinically verified for war-induced neuroses, for brainwashing of political prisoners and hostages, and other extreme situations, it has not been verified among glossolalics.

For example, there was nothing sudden about Agnes Sanford's experience of the baptism of the Holy Spirit and her subsequent experience of speaking in tongues more than six months later. Although her experiences touched the emotions, they would not be described as highly emotional or occurring under the type of stress both Sargant and Frank assume in sudden religious conversions. Sanford (1966) has written about the changes that occurred for her at the time of her baptism in the Holy Spirit:

The gifts we became aware of at that time were: first, the joy of the Lord (John 15:11), which brought with it such a tingling of joy all over the body that we were instantly healed of our physical ills [tiredness and weakness]; second, the gift of the peace that passes understanding (John 14:27) because it does not depend on earthly circumstances, not the peace of inactivity but the peace of intense activity proceeding with smoothness and harmony; and third, the gift of truth (John 14:17), an inner power to guide one into right decisions and toward an understanding of things beyond the sight of man. (p. 159)

Later at the time when she received the gift of speaking in tongues, Sanford (1972) wrote:

> Within me there was a great melting, even unto tears of joy and of comfort. I felt as though the love of Christ, already in me, now moved down, down to a deeper level, and I am sure it did! (p. 221)

This testimony, or self-report, about the new feelings of joy, inner peace, comfort, and a cognitive restructuring are recurring themes of Pentecostals and glossolalics.

From the larger sampling of glossolalics discussed earlier, Virginia Hine (1969) and her collaborators (in the Department of Anthropology, University of Minnesota) confirm Sanford's individual self-report:

> Case histories invariably include a "before and after" statement describing changes in attitudes, behavior, and often social situations. These changes were traced by our informants not to glossolalia per se, but to the experiential complex of which the linguistic behavior is one component. The perception of themselves as being different after the glossolalic experience was characteristic. Attitudinal changes were generally described in terms of greater *capacity for love toward others, a sense of tranquility and joy, and more confidence in their beliefs.* (p. 222, emphasis added)

Jeanrenaud (1972) conducted an interesting pilot study with high school and college-age neo-Pentecostal students. He investigated the amount of joy these students experienced subjectively when they were baptized in the Holy Spirit. After they had received their baptism, he administered a quesionnaire to determine which students spoke in tongues at the time of the baptism and which students did not speak in tongues at all. He also asked all the students to note the amount of joy they experienced at the time of their baptism on a scale from one to ten. Those who spoke in tongues at the time of their baptism felt a statistically significantly ($p < .05$) greater amount of joy than those who were baptized in the Spirit without the experience of speaking in tongues. His groups were small ($N = 10$ and $N = 12$) and were not matched for age, sex, or years of education. Nevertheless, his survey indicates that people may feel more joy being baptized in the Spirit when they speak in tongues than when they do not.

There is no doubt that the experience of being baptized in the Spirit with or without glossolalia produced an intense feeling of joy. This has been verified by self-reports, by interviews, and by questionnaires. It may well be that this experience of joy is responsible for the decrease of depression and the sense of well-being noted above as a personality change for glossolalics.

In their four-year research of movements of social transformation, anthropologists Gerlach and Hine (1970) studied both the Pentecostal and Black Power movements. They concluded that both the psychological maladjustment model and the social deprivation model were inadequate bases on which to predict where a movement would spread or who would become involved. Instead, they identified five key factors they felt had to exist for any group of people to be considered a movement dedicated to either personal or social change:

1. *A segmented, usually polycephalous, cellular organization* composed of units reticulated by various personal, structural, and ideological ties.
2. *Face-to-face recruitment* by committed individuals using their own pre-existing, significant social relationships.
3. *Personal commitment* generated by an act or an experience which separates a convert in some significant way from the established order (or his previous place in it), identifies him with a new set of values, and commits him to changed patterns of behavior.
4. *An ideology* which codifies values and goals, provides a conceptual framework by which all experiences or events relative to these goals may be interpreted, motivates and provides rationale for envisioned changes, defines the opposition, and forms the basis for conceptual unification of a segmented network of groups.
5. *Real or perceived opposition* from the society at large or from that segment of the established order within which the movement has risen. (p. xvii)

Of particular interest are the cognitive changes or restructuring that Gerlach and Hine (1970) termed the ideology factor in their analysis. They identified eight qualities of the cognitive set that characterize a movement such as Pentecostalism.

1. *Dogmatism or certitude:* outsiders would call this quality of the cognitive set dogmatism; insiders would call it certitude. It is what Milton Rokeach (1960) has called "a closed cognitive organization of beliefs." Gerlach and Hine (1970) felt that this dogmatism or authoritarianism had little to do with a personality type or rigidity of thinking. Rather, they concluded that the certitude resulted from the commitment process, that is, the Pentecostal baptism of the spirit and speaking in tongues. The quality of certitude came from the "cognitive closure" that climaxed the cognitive restructuring process. It brought a sense of finality. Cognitively, everything fell into place so that the process was often described as a revelation. "The belief system of the individual may be expanded, developed, elaborated, even changed to some degree subsequently, but there remains the certainty that on basic points, there will never again be any question." (p. 161)
2. *Codification:* the revelatory nature of the commitment experience, that is, the Pentecostal baptism of the Spirit and the speaking in tongues, requires the use of a conceptual framework—intellectual building blocks out of which cognitive restructuring can take place. After the Pentecostal experience, converts find that biblical verses suddenly take on a new and profound significance. The new ideology

is codified into a common rhetoric or what might be called a party line. This party line has a twofold function. First, it provides quick and easy answers to opponents. Second, it helps transmit the ideology to new converts and inquirers.

3. *A split-level ideology:* on one level of Pentecostal ideology, there are those few basic concepts on which all participants agree. These are reduced to creedal statements or slogans. On another level of the ideology, there are an infinite variety of emphases, interpretations, adaptations, and exegetical detours that promote both ideological and organizational diversity.

4. *Personal power and personal worth:* a sense of personal power comes to the Pentecostal because of the personal experience with a power perceived as external to himself/herself. This experience confers power on the convert. It also frees the convert to be more of a risk taker. Converts feel they have more control over their own destiny and even the destiny of the world. This sense of control is combined with what appears to be a fatalistic or passive attitude because God is considered to be omnipotent. Actually, the attitude is not a passive-dependent one but rather an actively striving one where God remains in control.

The increased sense of personal worth or self-worth also comes from the profound experience of the baptism of the Holy Spirit. Using biblical language, Pentecostals consider themselves to be "new creatures in Christ." They have a new relationship with God. They are no longer "servants" but "sons and daughters." They perceive themselves as having a new stature or a new relationship to other persons both inside and outside the Body of Christ.

5. *Rejection of the ideal-real gap:* in established social orders where social change is slow and institutions are relatively unchanging, there is a general acceptance of the gap between ideal creedal values and actual practices. As children become socialized, they learn not only the ideals of their society, but also the inconsistencies or the exceptions that are considered to be practical or functional in their society. Characteristic of movement ideologies like Pentecostalism is the strong and verbalized rejection of this gap and a striving for the ideal.

6. *Ambiguity:* movement ideology becomes vague and ambiguous when the movement presses beyond existing ideals to new goals that are unclear to others. (Gerlach and Hine admitted that Pentecostalism ideology includes widely accepted Christian ideals, but concretizes them in clear terms.)

7. *A dichotomous world view:* participants in a movement have a we/they dichotomy, or division of people. Either people are part of the in group, which is *pro,* or they are part of the out group, which is *con.* This black-and-white dichotomy leaves little room for any gray. It also provides for a clear definition of the opposition:

The essential ideological differences between a movement participant and a non-participant is the difference between one who is committed to radical personal or social change and one who holds to a gradualist concept of developmental change. This dichotomy is quite clear to committed participants. (Gerlach & Hine, 1970, pp. 174–175)

This dichotomy also provides the intellectual framework for maintaining a feeling of being opposed by the wider society—an important movement factor noted earlier.

8. *A conceptual filter or reinterpretation of data:* the movement participant ("fanatic") ideologically has the capacity of filtering out any negative feedback. In other words, all events, stimuli, and experiences—whether successes or failures—are interpreted as positive affirmations of his/her ideological position. For example, what an outsider would consider a failure, the participant reinterprets as either a sign of future success or a temporary test of devotion and courage.

> Immediately after the Baptism experience a newly "Spirit-filled" Pentecostal is almost invariably assailed with doubts concerning the validity of his experience. He is prapared for this, and it is told that these doubts indicate the increased activity of demonic forces as the believer comes into ever closer union with Christ. What supposedly more "realistic" and "rational" Christians might regard as debilitating doubt, which could even disapprove the experience, becomes, for a committed movement participant, clearer evidence of the opposing evil, increased assurance that he is on the right track, and an unmistakable sign of eventual victory. (Gerlach & Hine, 1970, p. 172)

These eight qualities of cognitive set are thought to be typical of glossolalics in Pentecostal and neo-Pentecostal groups.

Gerlach and Hine (1970) rejected Festinger, Riecken, and Schachter's (1956) motivational theory that cognitive dissonance would cause participants in a movement like Pentecostalism to proselytize or recruit new members. They argued that the motivation for recruitment comes rather from the nature of the commitment experience and from the ideological characteristic of reinterpreting data so that it is always positive. They also suggested that "the intellectual and emotional conflict and 'discomfort' that supposedly accompanied cognitive dissonance should be measurable in terms of anxiety scales (see Suinn, 1965)" (Gerlach & Hine, 1970, p. 96). They claimed that such anxiety has not been demonstrated for Pentecostals. However, as noted earlier, there is some good evidence that some Pentecostal samples do, indeed, experience anxiety at a nonpathological level.

Although we agree with Gerlach and Hine that cognitive dissonance does not seem to be a sufficiently powerful motivating force to cause Pentecostals to recruit new members, nevertheless, we do believe that the construct is helpful in understanding the cognitive restructuring or the ideological set that occurs for Pentecostals. The characteristic of using a conceptual filter, or reinterpreting negative feedback, could also be understood as a manifestation of cognitive dissonance. In fact, the doubt that occurs for the convert newly baptized by the Holy Spirit (as described earlier [Gerlach & Hine, 1970]) is exactly the same kind of doubt which Festinger (1957) described for the person who has made a decision (e.g., to buy a particular new car) and then has some doubts immediately after acting on his/her decision. It seems to us that Festinger's hypothesis that a person experiencing cognitive dissonance would avoid situations and information that might increase dissonance helps explain what Gerlach and Hine (1970) have called a cognitive filter, or a reinterpreting of negative feedback.

Of particular interest to linguists studying glossolalia is the cognitive set (ideological belief) of many Pentecostals that glossolalia can on occasion be xenoglossia (i.e., speaking in foreign languages).

As noted earlier, practically all classical Pentecostals hold to this belief. Probably more than 50% of the neo-Pentecostals hold to it, and probably less than 50% of the Catholic charismatics hold to it.

Linguists (Goodman, 1972c; Motley, 1967; Nida, 1964; Samarin, 1972c; Wolfram, 1966) have repeatedly demonstrated that samples of glossolalia that have been recorded in modern times are not interpretable as known human languages. Nevertheless, many glossolalics find it hard to accept this finding from linguists. Pattison (1968) evidently was the first one to suggest that this could be understood in terms of cognitive dissonance:

> There is no direct research on this aspect of glossolalia so far as I am aware. However, the now classical work on perceptual process by men like Solomon Asch and Leon Festinger indicate the crucial influence which social expectation and the need for cognitive coherence play in the ordering and interpretation of our perceptions. Thus, we can at least suggest that the reports of audience observers "verifying" the foreign language of glossolaists is not an indication of either malingering or pretense, but an honest report of *subjective* auditory perception, which of course may be quite different from the objective linguistic patterns spoken. (pp. 74–75)

Goodman (1972c) also discussed the belief of xenoglossia in terms of cognitive dissonance. She suggested that the belief is widely held for three reasons. First, glossolalia does have linguistic qualities that are shared with human speech, that is, speech sounds (consonants and vowels), accent, pauses, final contours, intonation. Second, the belief is reinforced by social needs. Third, she suggested that there are also a number of psychological factors that might account for the prevalence of the belief. In particular, she summarized a research study that illustrated that people have difficulty coping with incongruities or with anomalous data:

> In a psychological experiment carried out in 1949, J. S. Bruner and Leo Postman asked experimental subjects to identify on short and controlled exposure a series of playing cards. Many of the cards were normal, but some were anomalous, that is, a red six of spades and a black four of hearts. Soon all subjects identified all the cards correctly, except that the anomalous cards were almost always, without apparent hesitation or puzzlement, identified as normal.

> Listeners to tongue-speaking go through a similar process: they fit the audio-signal into a previously prepared category, namely language. (Goodman, 1972c, p. 151)

Although Samarin has not used the theory of cognitive dissonance in his work, nevertheless, some of his research findings can be interpreted in terms of cognitive dissonance. In a study of neo-Pentecostals, he asked: "If someone can show that tongues are not like the human language, what would [a glossolalist] have to consider them to be?" (1970, p. 278):

> Fifty per cent of the respondents (i.e. 42) said that tongues would have to be considered heavenly, spiritual, or angelic languages. Seven indicated that they had no idea, 15 gave no answer or gave an answer that was irrelevant, 7 said that they would have to be considered gibberish or some such thing, and 6 rejected the question altogether. (p. 273).

In other words, 50% of the respondents had a clear alternative explanation for glossolalia if it were shown that tongues were not like human language. Samarin was impressed that there was far less dogmatism about the nature of glossolalia than he had expected. We can see, however, that 50% of the respondents reinterpreted the alleged negative finding about glossolalia into positive terms, which is a way of reducing cognitive dissonance. The other 50% of the respondents were essentially avoiding the question altogether, which is another way of reducing cognitive dissonance.

As Pattison (1968) has intimated, this is a fertile field for research. Although, Festinger's (1957) theory of cognitive dissonance has been widely used in cognitive psychology, in social psychology, and in theories of motivation, it has not been used as much in exploring belief systems. Recently, Russell and Jones (1980) investigated belief in the paranormal and how that affects selective learning and rejection of new information. They concluded that "paranormal beliefs may persist among believers because contradictory evidence arouses sufficient dissonance to prevent the learning of such information. Thus, the persistence of paranormal beliefs is not a function of ignorance on the part of believers, but perhaps due to the high levels of dissonance aroused by challenges to important beliefs for the individual" (p. 87). Their type of research could well be used with glossolalic believers to confirm or disconfirm whether cognitive dissonance actually functions among glossolalics.

12

Behavioral Changes

This chapter will consider changes in behavior resulting from speaking in tongues. De Vol (1974), a graduate student in psychology, summarized in the *Journal of Religion and Health,* the effects on his behavior of using glossolalia in his daily one-hour period of meditation:

> Some of the more prominent changes included: a) an increase in study effectiveness, i.e., greater motivation, less reactive inhibition, increased ability to concentrate; b) decreased preoccupation with body appetites, e.g., eating just for the sake of eating; c) greater sensitivity and tolerance in relationships with others; d) less defensiveness and reticence; e) greater openness and spontaneity; f) increased interest in religion and "the things of God"; and g) stronger desire to share the "things of God" with others in the hope that they would come to have the same experience and personal relationship with God. (p. 288)

Although he included changes that we would not usually characterize as changes in external behavior, nevertheless, he observed some significant inner differences resulting from glossolalia, that is, less preoccupation with food, and an increased ability to concentrate on his studies, and an improvement in his interpersonal relationships. These are representative of the changes that we will note in this chapter. Three areas to be reviewed are addictive behaviors, homosexuality, and social action. Rather than rely on individual testimonies (as interesting as they may be), most of this research is based on surveys.

ADDICTIVE BEHAVIOR

Undoubtedly, David Wilkerson's autobiographical account of his ministry to drug addicts in New York City *The Cross and the Switchblade* (Wilkerson, Sherrill, & Sherrill, 1963), first brought to general attention the claim that the baptism of the Holy Spirit accompanied by glossolalia could break drug addiction. A third-generation Pentecostal, Wilkerson left a small Assembly of God Church in the mountains of Pennsylvania to go into the slums of New York to minister to teenage gangs hardened to drugs and to crime. He started his first center in Brooklyn, New York, in 1958. In ten years, there were twenty-two Teen Challenge Centers in various cities across the country creating what might be called a Teen Challenge movement. Wilkerson reported testimonies of ex-drug addicts in *Twelve Angels from Hell* (1969) and told the plight of the children of drug addicts in *The Little People* (1966).

Roman Catholic theologian Kilian McDonnell (1968d) spent two weeks at the Brooklyn Teen Challenge center conducting a field-study evaluation of the program. He reported it was basically a religious program of prayer, study, and counseling in which the addicts broke their drug habits cold turkey without the benefit of any mental health professionals, such as social workers, clinical psychologists, or psychiatrists. The program had two stages: six weeks at the center in town, then seven or eight months at a farm in the country where work was added to the religious program. McDonnell noted that these classical Pentecostals resisted the temptation to pray for the baptism of the Holy Spirit in the first stage of the program and waited until the second stage to lead these young people into the baptism. The Teen Challenge staff claimed a success rate of 80% for those who completed the program. However, McDonnell estimated that a more accurate assessment of the success rate of the program was probably about 50%.

Several other studies have been undertaken on the Teen Challenge program. Cato (1968/1970) conducted a comparative study to discover any differences between drug addicts in Teen Challenge and drug addicts in three secular rehabilitation programs in New York City (i.e., Anchor House, Addicts Rehabilitation Center, and Reality House). He assessed personal religious beliefs, treatment program preference, and interpersonal dependency needs. Although he found that, on average, the total group of addicts did not differ significantly from the normal adult male population, nevertheless, the addicts in the Teen Challenge program evidenced greater interpersonal dependency needs, greater religious beliefs, and a higher preference for a structured treatment program than those in secular programs.

Subsequently, Ridgway (1972) undertook a longitudinal study to test the hypothesis that Christian conversion and nurture were significant factors in the treatment program at Teen Challenge. A treatment group ($N = 21$) was assessed within three weeks of entry into the program and four-and-one-half months later. They were compared with a dropout group ($N = 20$) who left after the first three weeks. He also assessed 12 interested addicts at the four-and-one-half-month period and 8 addicts who had graduated from the total treatment program. Religiosity was treated as multidimensional.

Dropouts tended to score higher on psychopathology variables and lower on the religious conversion and commitment scales. Subjects demonstrated a movement toward rehabilitation over time as they rejected the deviant drug culture, as their anxiety lessened, as they reported the discovery of new goals and purpose in life, and as they demonstrated an improvement in their adaptive defenses. They also demonstrated a significant movement over time toward more self-acceptance, more acceptance of others, and an increasing belief in an accepting God. The importance of the religious aspect of the program was demonstrated by the increasing sense of commitment, conversion, forgiveness, and belief in an accepting God that was found over time. Correlations among religiosity, attitude, and personality variables tended consistently to support Ridgway's hypothesis. He concluded that an addict could be successfully rehabilitated from narcotic addiction by the Teen Challenge program to the degree that he was able to accept the validity of Christian conversion. Of particular interest in our present review of the literature was his conclusion that there was the lack of evidence found to support the hypothesis that the tongues experience was a significant factor in these changes. In other words, it was the religious experience as modeled and interpreted in the therapeutic community, that is, the religious milieu therapy, that was the significant factor for rehabilitation of the addicts rather than the use of glossolalia or a tongues experience itself.

Based on this and other research, Langrod, Joseph, and Valdes gave evidence for the validity of the Teen Challenge religious-treatment program in an article entitled, "The Role of Religion in the Treatment of Opiate Addiction" (1972).

In 1973, the staff of Teen Challenge requested the National Institute on Drug Abuse (NIDA) to fund a study of the effectiveness of their program.

In describing the Teen Challenge program, the NIDA report (Hess and Reynolds, 1977) noted two stages, that is, the initial phase at an induction center for detoxification cold turkey and a longer phase of eight months to one year at a training center, which provided a residential therapeutic community that emphasized spiritual support, vocational and educational assistance and strict supervision. The researchers interviewed and analyzed urine samples from participants and dropouts.

The final sample size of the participants in each group was: (1) introduction center dropouts, seventy; (2) introduction center graduates who later dropped out of the training center, fifty-two; and (3) graduates of the training center, sixty-four.

No statistical analyses were done with this data. However, the NIDA (1977) report did comment on the findings:

> At time of interview Teen Challenge graduates appear to be functioning more effectively than dropouts in terms of changes in arrest and educational status as well as employment. In addition, graduates report making less use of alcohol and tobacco and are more optimistic regarding their state of health. Both Training Center dropouts and graduates have greatly decreased their heroin use as indeed have induction center dropouts—although the later group less strikingly. [Interview] data for all three groups accorded closely with urinalysis findings. It should be noted that graduates exceed both dropout groups in numbers admitted to other treatment programs prior to entry

into Teen Challenge, and have correspondingly lower rates of entry into treatment programs post-Teen Challenge. Also, it is of interest that all groups report rather high rates of nervous/emotional difficulty at time of interview. (p. 8)

More recently, Peters (1980) completed a doctoral dissertation project at New York University that was a follow-up study of graduates from the Teen Challenge program in New York. She investigated the role of religious experience and commitment as a therapeutic measure in the program. She studied persons who had been graduated at least five years from the program.

She was able to locate twenty-two subjects from the research population of ninety-eight people. Of these twenty-two subjects, twelve became a positive treatment outcome group and ten became a negative treatment outcome group. Peters assessed patterns of drug usage, response to treatment, occurrence of relapse, and any significant growth and development in the direction of responsible adulthood.

She concluded from her case studies that "there is value in regarding religious experience and commitment as a positive therapeutic factor in the treatment and rehabilitation of drug addicts" (Peters, 1980, p. 282). She found a clear correlation between a sustained religious commitment and effective rehabilitation.

She discussed her findings as follows:

The twelve positive cases all expressed a verbal commitment to Christian beliefs as taught by Teen Challenge personnel. Nine of these maintained regular practices of prayer and Bible study, either individual or group. The other three continued these practices, but not regularly. Eight of the twelve were also employed by a religious organization. Whether this employment indicated a deep religious commitment, or an inability to function in a more threatening environment, is not shown conclusively by this study. However, it does indicate that these subjects are contributing positively to their respective societies.

The negative sample produced six subjects who reverted to drug abuse when they discontinued exercise of their commitment of faith, but were again able to function without drugs when they re-entered a therapeutic community which represented values similar to those of Teen Challenge, or Teen Challenge itself. Two of the three subjects who sustained no religious commitment at the time of the interview, have repeated programs in Teen Challenge related organizations and are currently drug-free. One subject maintains a religious commitment, but smokes marijuana. [Two are alcoholic.] (pp. 281–282)

In summary, the research on the Teen Challenge rehabilitation program for drug addicts resulted in a number of consistent findings. In this program, which was born out of the classical Pentecostal heritage through the work of David Wilkerson, the emphasis on Christian conversion and nurture is central and significant therapeutically. Those addicts who were able to subscribe to the religious beliefs and practices of the Teen

Challenge staff and who continued to maintain or nurture that belief system benefited significantly from the rehabilitation program. Those who left the therapeutic community prematurely, that is, dropped out before completing the entire program, did not benefit as much as the graduates. The completion rate of clients in the Teen Challenge program was comparable to the completion rate in secular therapeutic community programs for drug addicts. Graduates of the program made a dramatic change in breaking their addiction to heroin and alcohol. Dropouts were also able to make a dramatic change in heroin use but not in alcohol abuse. There is no research evidence to support the view that initial or sustained use of glossolalia is a significant part of the treatment program at Teen Challenge. The practice of glossolalia in this setting is only part of the total milieu therapy, rather than being a significant variable in and of itself for the rehabilitation of drug addicts. Although there does seem to be a religious effect, the unique effect of speaking in tongues is impossible to guess. However, it is reasonable to suggest that its effect was significant because glossolalia was an expected part of the religious ritual of this group.

Another movement that encourages the use of speaking in tongues and that has reported dramatic changes for drug and alcohol users is the Jesus Movement, which developed in the 1960s and 1970s in the western United States. Typically, these were adolescents and young adults who had opted out of the drug culture and became devout, fundamentalist Christians who experienced a personal conversion to Christ and frequently engaged in the use of glossolalia. They often lived in communes. Sociologists Adams and Fox (1972) engaged in a field study of the Jesus Movement in southern California (specifically Orange County) by visiting Gethsemane Chapel (a pseudonym), several communes, interviewing the ministers, and using a formal questionnaire to assess eighty-nine participants. In comparing the Jesus Movement to the drug culture, they found that "members of the Jesus Movement have a high incidence of past drug use, with 62 percent of those over 18 and 44 percent of those under 18 having used dope" (p. 53). Presumably, their current usage was insignificant or nil.

Harder, Richardson, and Simmonds (1972) also surveyed a Jesus Movement commune in the early 1970s. They interviewed eighty-eight members of Christ Commune (a pseudonym). They estimated that "ninety to ninety-five per cent of members of the group studied practiced glossolalia, although it was used only in private devotional times" (Simmonds, Richardson, & Harder, 1972, p. 27 fn. 6). From interview data, these researchers reached the following conclusions about drug, alcohol, and tobacco usage in the commune:

> Although 85 percent of the members formerly had used alcohol and 67 percent had used tobacco, only two reported that they continued to use tobacco, and only one said that he used alcohol. None reported using drugs, although 90 percent said they had had previous experience with drugs. Among the

former drug users, 45 percent had taken drugs for some time. We coded a person according to the hardest drug he or she admitted using. Twenty-one of the 79 users said they had taken opiates or cocaine; 43 others said they had used hallucinogens. Only seven reported that they had used only marijuana. Drugs played an important part in the former lives of 51 members, and 65 said that most of their friends on the outside were drug users. (Harder et al., 1972, pp. 50, 110).

The dramatic changes of these young people from a drug culture to a Jesus culture were interpreted in terms of Lifton's (1957, 1963) model of thought reform, which he used to explain the brainwashing done by the Chinese Communists on Chinese intellectuals and Western prisoners (Richardson et al., 1972). Lifton's (1957) model had three stages: (1) the great togetherness: group identification, (2) the closing in of the milieu: the period of emotional conflict, and (3) submission and rebirth. Here, also, as with the Teen Challenge rehabilitation program, the significant variable producing the dramatic change away from drugs does not seem to be so much the practice of glossolalia per se, but rather the milieu (or the group effect of membership) either in a church or more effectively in a commune.

More recently Womack (1980/1981) completed an anthropological study of a classical Pentecostal church. The Global Pentecostal Church (a pseudonym) had broken away from the United Pentecostal Church in 1977 in order to become completely autonomous. Her field research extended for three-and-one-half years from June 1976 until the fall of 1979. She used participant observation and interviews to gather her data. She did an intensive investigation of a subpopulation of converts to the congregation who had been alcohol and drug abusers before their conversion.

Womack (1980/1981) perceived the experience of "having the Holy Ghost" both as an initial conversion experience at the altar call and as a later manifestation of an ecstatic or trance experience, that is, an altered state of consciousness (ASC) following Goodman (1972c). Utilizing this assumption, she maintained that drug abuse and the experience of these converts to classical Pentecostalism were generically related because they were both ASC. She observed that both ASCs result in similar psychophysiological states of excitement, euphoria, and sometimes analgesia.

Womack (1980/1981) had two basic hypotheses in her dissertation:

The central hypothesis of this study is that [classical Pentecostal] religion is effective because it satisfies a triad of social, psychophysiological, and psychological needs. It is assumed that drug and alcohol abusers who join the church are able to make a relatively easy transition from drugs to ecstatic religion because the same social, psychophysiological, and psychological needs that are now being filled by the church had at an earlier time driven them to drug abuse.

A corollary hypothesis emphasizes the importance of continuing to satisfy certain psychophysiological needs that had been present in drug abuse through religious trance. In other words, the drug and alcohol abusers who joined the church are now achieving psychophysiological gratifications through ecstatic trance. This dissertation hypothesizes that the psychophysiological aspect of ecstatic religion creates a biochemical base of comparability between religion and drugs. The ease of transition from drugs to religion, as well as the enormous attraction ecstatic religion holds for *all* its adherents, both abusers and non-abusers, is possible because religious trance is as psychophysiologically addictive as drug and alcohol use. (pp. 1–2)

Although she offered no quantitative data to support her thesis, she claimed, "There must be a connector between drugs and religion in order to explain why trance can substitute for drugs as well as one drug can substitute for another" (p. 29).

Whether Womack's (1980/1981) hypothesis about a biochemical substrate for ecstatic Pentecostal experiences and drug addicts is correct or not, her emphasis on the psychological and social dimensions is similar to that of Ridgway (1972) on the Teen Challenge, and Richardson et al. (1972) on the Jesus Movement—that is, that the total milieu of these classical Pentecostal groups can be therapeutic or rehabilitative for substance abusers. Womack's (1980/1981) research indicates that the milieu does not have to be residential. However, her research does indicate that the milieu does need to be frequent and intensive for it to be rehabilitative for addicts. These studies indicate that a Christian conversion and a structured Christian community, according to classical Pentecostal beliefs and practices, can provide a therapeutic milieu that is at least as successful in rehabilitating drug and alcohol abusers as any secular treatment program.

These studies do not substantiate that glossolalia in and of itself is significant in breaking addictive behaviors. But the baptism of the Holy Spirit with glossolalia and the practice of glossolalia are part of classical Pentecostal ritual and milieu to which these authors allude.

HOMOSEXUALITY

There is much confusion and controversy in the medical and behavioral science disciplines as to the diagnosis, etiology, and treatment of homosexuality. Most professional opinion no longer thinks that homosexuality and heterosexuality are dichotomous dimensions, but rather that sexuality should be conceptualized as existing on a continuum. Kinsey, Pomeroy, and Martin (1948) developed a point scale, from 0 to 6, to measure sexual orientation from heterosexual (0) through bisexual (3) to homosexual (6). However, there is no consensus as to etiology. Some professionals think the causes of homosexuality are primarily genetic, that is, biochemical in nature. Others think the causes are primarily environmental, that is, owing to trauma and fixation at some psychosexual stage of development. Without any consensus as to etiology, there is also no consensus as to treatment. Recommendations range from accepting a homosexual orientation as a given that cannot be altered to attempting to alter the orientation to heterosexual orientation. There is consensus, however, that the probabilities of completely changing an orientation is quite small by using the currently available treatment modalities of the medical and behavioral science disciplines.

There are a few autobiographical accounts of individuals who have achieved a change of sexual orientation by means of religious conversion and nurture (Aaron, 1972; anonymous, 1975; Philpott, 1975). Agnes Sanford reportedly said that praying for a homosexual orientation to change was rather easy, although she never put that opinion into print (see Payne, 1981, pp. 52–54, for a secondhand report of how she prayed for homosexuals).

The psychiatrist E. Mansell Pattison and his wife, Myrna Loy Pattison, have published a recent longitudinal study on homosexuals who changed their sexual orientation in the context of the beliefs and practices of a Pentecostal Church environment. They state that "to our knowledge, this report is the first documented study (excluding single anecdotes) of profound behavioral and intrapsychic change in sexual orientation from exclusive homosexuality to exclusive heterosexuality without long-term psychotherapy" (Pattison & Pattison, 1980, p. 1559). Not only was their study a first, but it was also highly provocative in its implications. Their research population came from a classical Pentecostal Church that had a religious hot line program that offered crisis intervention services to homosexuals.

From the crisis program records of three hundred cases over a five-year period, the Pattisons found thirty cases in which individuals claimed to have changed from exclusive homosexuality to exclusive heterosexuality. From these thirty cases, they were able to obtain the cooperation of eleven men who were willing to be interviewed. They not only conducted structured interviews with these men, but also obtained corollary data from the crisis-program staff and from the wives of those clients who were married (six out of the eleven).

The Pattisons described the "treatment program":

> When our subjects came in contact with the church's crisis service for homosexuals, they found a welcome reception as homosexuals. No attempt was made to make them change their homosexuality. Rather, they were presented with the invitation to commit their life to Christ and the church. All subjects had an explicit Christian conversion or rededication. They were then invited into small church fellowship groups where they studied the Bible and learned expected Biblical patterns of mature lifestyles. This included an expectation to engage in loving, nonerotic relationships with both men and women in the fellowship groups. (p. 1558)

Thus, the homosexual was accepted primarily as a child of God not primarily as a homosexual. The congregation believed "that homosexuality is only a behavior and not the identity of the person" (p. 1561).

Within the church's ideology was the explicit assumption that homosexuality was a maturational deficit that resulted in an inability to engage in mature nonerotic love with both men and women. As a result of maturing in appropriate interpersonal relations, a man was expected to develop an erotic attraction to a woman as a mature love object. Sexual experience then would follow appropriately within the marriage. (p. 1556)

The Pattisons identified this process as a "folk therapy" that was not spontaneous, but rather involved the subject in a total sociocultural milieu:

The model of change proposed here involves ideological commitment; cognitive structuring of beliefs, values, and expectations; behavioral interactions over time between subjects and their social reference groups; and a sequence of mutually expected behavioral changes. (p. 1560)

Prior attempts by these subjects to change their homosexual behavior had been unsuccessful.

The Pattisons continue:

All of our subjects had come from some type of religious background and most had unsuccessfully attempted to pray or use religious activities to change their homosexuality. However, they did not reveal their homosexuality to their religious groups because as homosexuals they had experienced hostility before from religious groups. (p. 1558)

. . . all the subjects made a decision to change to heterosexuality after their religious conversion because of their commitment to the religion's ideology, which defined heterosexuality as a necessary component of a mature member of the church. (p. 1558)

The results of the data gathering are presented in Table 12.1. On the basis of the Kinsey rating scale, all eleven subjects showed a dramatic shift in sexual orientation. The Pattisons (1980) were also interested in intrapsychic evidence of homosexual tendencies.

Despite the fact that our subjects were currently living a heterosexual lifestyle and had a commitment to heterosexuality, we were particularly interested in whether they still experienced intrapsychic homosexual proclivities. Thus, we asked them to elucidate a history of their homosexual dreams, fantasies and impulses during the time of this claimed heterosexuality. None of our subjects reported a dramatic or immediate cessation of intrapsychic homosexual proclivity. Rather, they described the gradual diminution of their homosexual drives as they proceeded in a heterosexual life. (p. 1555)

On the basis of their intrapsychic findings, the Pattisons note: "Our data do not suggest some magical change or massive denial or repression, but rather they suggest the gradual development of a rejection of the homosexual object choice as an increased cathexis of the heterosexual object is developed" (p. 1555).

In discussing some of the limitations of their methodology, the Pattisons acknowledged that they had to rely primarily on retrospective data

Table 12.1 Characteristics of eleven homosexual men who changed to heterosexuality after religious participation

Subject	Age (years)	Age when homosexuality identified (years)	Age when changed to heterosexuality (years)	Years as heterosexual	Age at marriage (years)	Years married
1[b]	24	10	19	5	17	7
2	24	12	22	2	20	4
3[b]	28	15	24	4	25	3
4	21	13	20	1		
5	34	8	27	7		
6	23	14	22	1		
7[c]	26	10	22	4	24	2
8[b]	28	11	22	6	22	6
9	26	11	22	4		
10[c]	35	10	29	6		
11[c]	32	14	28	4	29	3

Subject	Intrapsychic evidence of current homosexuality			Kinsey ratings[a]	
	Dreams	Fantasies	Impulses	Before change	After change
1[b]	No	Yes	No	6	0
2	No	No	Yes	6	0
3[b]	No	No	No	6	0
4	No	No	No	6	1
5	No	Yes	No	6	1
6	No	No	Yes	6	1
7[c]	No	No	Yes	6	2
8[b]	Yes	No	No	6	0
9	No	No	No	6	0
10[c]	No	Yes	Yes	5	2
11[c]	No	No	Yes	4	2

[a] Kinsey scale: a rating of 0 is heterosexual, 3 is bisexual and 6 is homosexual.
[b] Subject at one time considered himself bisexual.
[c] Homosexual impulses were still source of neurotic conflict for subject.
From Pattison & Pattison (1980), p. 1555.

from the subject's memory during interview. Nevertheless, they had corollary data from the crisis center staff who had known the subjects well during their time of change, and the Pattisons themselves had known two of the subjects well over a five-year period.

In discussing their findings in relation to other research studies of homosexuals (especially see Bell & Weinberg, 1978; Kinsey et al., 1948; Masters & Johnson, 1979; Saghir & Robins, 1973), the Pattisons ackowledged that the age range of their sample was the optimal age range for change in sexual orientation. However, the motivation of their sample for changing sexual orientation was different from the motivation of other research samples because it was the result of a basic Christian conversion and for Christian ideological reasons. The motivation for marriage was also different, in that the Pentecostal sample did not marry as a screen or cover for their homosexuality. In fact, unlike other research samples, 100% of the Pentecostal sample told their wives before their marriage that they had been practicing homosexuals in the past.

In interpreting their results, the Pattisons wrote:

> The data provided a substantial body of evidence for the plausibility of change from exclusive homosexuality to exclusive heterosexuality, which is in accordance with the Kinsey statistical probabilities for such change, the Masters and Johnson data, and the clinical or observational anecdotes of such change. Our data demonstrate that such change has occurred through significant longitudinal experiences in "folk therapy" provided within a supernatural framework and utilizing generic methods of change common to folk therapy. Our data suggest the importance of ideology, expectation, and behavioral experience in producing change. The evidence suggests that cognitive change occurs first, followed by behavioral change, and finally intrapsychic resolution. Finally, the data suggest the importance of our concepts of homosexuality. When homosexuality is defined as an immutable and fixed condition that must be accepted, the potential for change seems slim. In our study, however, when homosexuality was defined as a changeable condition, it appears that change was possible. (p. 1562)

To summarize then, autobiographical and a few research accounts testify to the fact that homosexuality can be changed to heterosexuality by the intervention of Christian conversion and nurture. Also, the Pattisons have provided an empirical research of a longitudinal design that has documented bona fide changes from exclusive homosexuality to exclusive heterosexuality for subjects who were converted to Pentecostal beliefs and practices and were active in the Pentecostal community. As noted above for drug addicts, the significant feature of this folk therapy is the total therapeutic milieu: social, psychological, and spiritual. No one variable has been isolated from the therapeutic milieu that might be considered the most powerful or the most significant factor. But again, it should be noted that the baptism of the Holy Spirit with glossolalia and the practice of glossolalia are part of this classical Pentecostal milieu.

SOCIAL ACTION

It has usually been assumed that becoming Pentecostal, that is, glosso-lalic, tends to make a person withdraw from social action. This tendency is noted repeatedly in research with classical Pentecostals and is generally assumed to be true for neo-Pentecostals and Catholic charismatics as well. In his historical study of classical Pentecostals, Anderson (1979) wrote:

> One looks in vain for any glimmer of Pentecostal social activism beyond indi-vidual acts of charity at the congregational level before the second world war. (p. 200)

In summarizing the activities of classical Pentecostals in more recent years, he wrote:

> Since World War II, their preachers, editorialists and church authorities with few exceptions have endorsed the most conservative political, social and economic policies. . . . The Pentecostals have been decidedly negative on union militancy and strikes, mass demonstrations, the anti-war movement, anti-racist activism, student protest, movements to end sex discrimination and countercultural life styles. (p. 239)

In their sociological study of the more recent phenomenon of the Jesus Movement, Adams and Fox (1972) also noted the shift of converts toward a more conservative political orientation:

> The Jesus trip represents an almost violent ideological swing from far left to far right, a type of "reaction formation." A shift toward a conservative position in solving world problems is reported by 76 percent of those inter-viewed. . . . The focus here is still typically on the individual rather than on system change.
>
> . . . World problems, they now believe, "can only be solved through finding Christ"; "We can't have peace on the outside if we don't on the inside"; "If everyone was a Christian there wouldn't be any world problems." (pp. 53–54)

Similarly, the sociological team of Harder et al. (1972) interviewed eighty-eight members of a Jesus Movement commune in California and found a shift in political orientation:

> Before they joined the group, 42 of the members we interviewed in 1971 said they were radicals or liberals (although only two had led political demonstra-tions). Another 14 claimed to be moderates or conservatives. Only 27 said they had no interest in politics when they lived on the outside. When we asked them to categorize themselves at the time of the interview only four claimed to be liberals or radicals, and 71 said "nothing" or that they had lost all interest in politics.
>
> We asked them how one could change society if he took no part in politics, and they gave us replies consistent with religious fundamentalism. "The only way to change society is to change men's hearts," said one. "Politics is man's way not God's way, and it (politics) has failed," said another. We often heard

references to the Second Coming of Christ, which most members believe to be imminent, making energy spent on politics a waste of time. Our second visit to the group was during the hotly contested 1972 California primary, but not a single member mentioned this crucial contest. No one was interested. (p. 110)

In his sociological assessment of neo-Pentecostalism, that is, the Full Gospel Businessmen's Fellowship International (FGBMFI) in western Virginia, Bradfield (1979) found a similar attitude about social action:

It follows the ideology of Pentecostalism in all of its forms that change should not and probably cannot be brought about by planned social action. This explains part of their general disenchantment with religious social action programs [in their host churches]. The cause of social problems in American society is perceived to be individual sin rather than collective sin. Ultimately, following this perspective, all problems are spiritual or religious and the solution, therefore, must be the spiritual transformation of individuals. (p. 40)

However, in surveys of classical Pentecostal youth in southern California (Ramsey & Malony, 1971; Zwaanstra & Malony, 1970), it was found that there was a tendency for persons who were more frequently glossolalic to be more likely to be participants in mission projects in Mexico. Although, their evidence would seem to run contrary to the presumption that glossolalics were not socially active, it should be noted that visits to orphanages in Mexico where constructive help is given is a common youth activity in this area of the country and that such visits often are combined with evangelistic witnessing. Although the results imply a concern for others, they should not be easily identified with sociopolitical activity.

No widespread data exist regarding the general social concern of classical Pentecostals or of neo-Pentecostals. Anecdotal reports of South American Pentecostals indicate a strong concern with political activism. This may be confounded with the lower-social-class status of these groups and a culturally pervasive concern among many for social justice. However, in South America this is combined with a self-help philosophy that has made Pentecostals a middle-class phenomenon in many areas.

Researching the Catholic charismatic movement, Fichter (1975) noted that "several of the founding fathers of the movement who had been activists in socially progressive movements and crusades appear to have lost interest in them since receiving the charismatic gifts (p. 84). Commenting on this shift, Fichter quoted Nouwen's (1971) analogy of Pentecostal philosophy to Yogi philosophy.

It is not surprising, therefore, to find that the Pentecostal, like the Yogi, has often been accused of being aloof and indifferent to the great social problems of war, poverty, pollution, segregation, social injustice, and crime, and of having escaped into a personal garden where he can concentrate on his own soul, experience the stirrings of the Spirit, and make his own conversion the criterion for the solutions of the problems of this world. (pp. 78–79).

Fichter (1975) summarized his own understanding of the Catholic Pentecostal philosophy about social action as follows:

> The pentecostals are not satisfied with the world as it is, but they have no intention of trying to change it through organized collective action. Their basic conviction is that reform starts at home, in one's heart, and somehow spills over into other homes and other hearts until all of society is reformed. (p. 81)
>
> . . . Structures and systems of both Church and society really do not matter, that somehow "God will take care of them!" (p. 92)

Of interest was Fichter's finding that Catholic Pentecostals came from a much broader spectrum of political orientation than classical Pentecostal or neo-Pentecostal groups. As noted earlier, however, Fichter found that contrary to the conservative orientation of other Pentecostals, "the great majority of lay Catholic Charismatics express approval to 'liberal' programs like medicare [89%], open housing [74%], and higher minimum wages [77%]" (p. 77). These sociopolitical orientations did not change when Catholics became Pentecostal: "The comparative data prove conclusively that social attitudes may be retained even after the Pentecostal experience and that attachment to the charismatic renewal need not neutralize strongly held social attitudes" (p. 87).

Greeley (1974) conducted a comparative study of 216 Catholics, only 65% of whom "claimed to have received the gift of tongues" (p. 329). Her samples included religious professionals as well as lay persons. She found Catholic charismatics to be significantly more culturally isolated than Catholic noncharismatics. Of particular interest was her comparison of the two groups on what she called "horizontal involvement" (or social action). She used five measures that Davidson (1972) had used when questioning Protestant groups as to whether members had:

1. Joined any civic or community organizations to help other people in [their] city or community.
2. Participated in any sort of public demonstration against some social issue because [they] thought it was morally wrong.
3. Encouraged [their] parish priest to become involved in social issues in the community.
4. Publicly helped to bring about the desegregation of schools, churches or other institutions.
5. Written a letter to a newspaper, a local official, or a government employee about some issue. (Greeley, 1974, p. 325)

She summarized her findings thus:

> First, neither of the populations are characterized by frenzied sociopolitical activity; secondly, the populations are about equally active . . . neither of the populations see themselves as working much for desegregation. . . .
>
> Charismatics do not actually perceive the prayer group, however, as an organization for social change. (pp. 325–326)

In summarizing his research findings about social action in Catholic charismatic prayer groups, Fichter (1975) stated:

> The goal of the renewal movement is personal spiritual reform, not organized social reform, but this does not imply the absence of social concern. The movement's basic conviction is that a better society can emerge only when people have become better, yet it would be completely erroneous to interpret this as an individualistic and self-centered attitude. (p. 144)

This general conclusion would seem to be applicable to all types of Pentecostals.

13

Value Changes

This chapter will consider changes in values as a function of becoming glossolalic.

Most researchers have broadened the concept of value beyond mere moral values. R. M. Williams (1970) gives a helpful definition:

> . . . We here define values as those *conceptions of desirable states of affairs* that are utilized in selective conduct as *criteria* for preference or choice or as *justifications* for proposed or actual behavior. Values are closely related, conceptually and empirically, to social norms; but norms are the more specific, concrete, situation-bound specifications: values are the criteria by which norms themselves may be and are judged. (p. 442)

There are two aspects about value change of interest to the study of glossolalia. One is value change within the individual glossolalic; the second is the value change within the Pentecostal group to which an individual may belong.

Two theorists, Weber and Troeltsch, have been formative in attempts to understand the values expressed by glossolalic groups. Weber (1904–1905/1958) maintained that Protestantism—more specifically Calvinism, Pietism, Methodism, and the Baptist sects—had a "worldly asceticism" (pp. 95–154).

Of particular interest for understanding the later Holiness Pentecostal belief and practice is a quotation from Wesley that Weber used as an especially cogent illustration of this Protestant asceticism:

> I fear, wherever riches have increased, the essence of religion has decreased in the same proportion. Therefore I do not see how it is possible, in the nature of things, for any revival of true religion to continue long. For religion must necessarily produce both industry and frugality, and these cannot but produce riches. But as riches increase, so will pride, anger, and love of the world in all its branches. (1904–1905/1958, p. 175)

Troeltsch's most significant work is *The Social Teaching of the Christian Churches* first published in German in 1911 and then translated into English in 1931. Although the concept of sect had been used before by

Weber and others, Troeltsch developed a church-sect-mysticism typology
that traced these theoretical sociological categories down through Christian history until the eighteenth century. At the end of his long work,
Troeltsch briefly defined the three ideal types of his model:

> From the very beginning there appeared the three main types of the socio-
> logical development of Christian thought: the Church, the sect, and mysticism.
>
> The Church is an institution which has been endowed with grace and salva-
> tion as the result of the work of Redemption; it is able to receive the masses,
> and *to adjust itself to the world.*
>
> The sect is a voluntary society, composed of strict and definite Christian be-
> lievers bound to each other by the fact that all have experienced "the new
> birth." *These "believers" live apart from the world.*
>
> Mysticism means that the world of ideas which had hardened into formal
> worship and doctrine is transformed into a purely personal and inward ex-
> perience: this leads to the formation of groups on a purely personal basis,
> with no permanent form, which also tend to weaken the significance of forms
> of worship, doctrine, and the historical element. (p. 993; emphasis added)

In his provocative book, *The Social Sources of Denominationalism*
(1929), Niebuhr ignored the mysticism dimension of Troeltsch's typology.
He reaffirmed Wesley's hypothesis that an ascetic sectarian group only remains a sect for one generation and that the second generation of the sect
does, indeed, become a church. Thus, he changed the static concept of a
sect into a more dynamic or developmental concept:

> The most sociological character of sectarianism, however, is almost always
> modified in the course of time by the natural processes of birth and death,
> and on this change in structure changes in doctrine and ethics inevitably fol-
> low. By its very nature the sectarian type of organization is valid only for
> one generation. The children born to the voluntary members of the first
> generation begin to make the sect a church long before they have arrived at
> the years of discretion. For with their coming the sect must take on the char-
> acter of an educational and disciplinary institution, with the purpose of bring-
> ing the new generation into conformity with ideals and customs which have
> become traditional. Rarely does a second generation hold the convictions it
> has inherited with a fervor equal to that of its fathers. . . . *So the sect be-*
> *comes a church.* (pp. 19–20; emphasis added)

Niebuhr cited the historical examples of the Mennonites, Baptists, Methodists, and Quakers as evidence to support his hypothesis.

We will review some of the changes in values for Pentecostals. In particular, do glossolalics accept the values of their culture? Do they reject
the values of the dominant society? Or are they just indifferent? Sociologists of religion have repeatedly used classical pentecostals as an example
par excellence of Troeltsch's sect type. Researchers have investigated this
question of whether classical Pentecostals accept or reject the values of
society. It is more difficult to know how to classify the neo-Pentecostal
and Catholic charismatic according to Troeltsch's model. Again, the ques-

tion is what change of values may occur for these two later sociological manifestations of glossolalias.

The church historian Elmer T. Clark (1937/1949) conducted the first thorough historical study of sects in America. He used the dichotomy of church versus sect from Weber and Troeltsch as interpreted by Niebuhr. Clark developed seven categories of sects on the basis of their theological doctrines: (1) the pessimistic or adventist sects, (2) the perfectionist or subjectivist sects, (3) the charismatic or Pentecostal sects, (4) the communistic sects, (5) the legalistic or objectivist sects, (6) the egocentric or new-thought sects, and (7) the esoteric or mystic sects.

As far as a value orientation toward other religious groups and to the wider culture is concerned, Clark stated: "A deep-seated suspicion of all others save themselves is a characteristic of many sects" (p. 233). Clark recognized that this counterculture orientation produced a "conservatism which resists change of every sort" (p. 233). Boisen (1939) was particularly impressed by the fact that these Holy Rollers (or classical Pentecostals) had a different value orientation about race or color than other church people of their same socioeconomic and racial background.

He commented about the change of values that occurred in a black Pentecostal mission congregation he visited:

> It is worth noting at this point that the tendency of a vital religious faith to bring about a thorough-going change of social attitudes is strikingly exemplified in Mr. T. and in his House of Prayer. Where conventional negro churches in that city were much occupied with the problem of white superiority and were endeavoring to meet it by imitating the whites, the House of Prayer and other groups of its kind were so firmly convinced that they had found the fellowship supremely worthwhile, that other white persons besides Mr. T. were joining their circle. And white Pentecostal groups frequently welcomed negroes. The new basis of fellowship which they had found gives them a new set of social values which transcend and disregard the lines of color and class. (Boisen, 1939, p. 191)

Boisen (1955) also noted that, "occasionally one hears derogatory reference to education and educated people" (p. 76). Boisen also noted that these Holiness Pentecostal people improved their economic and social status. The fact that their value systems improved their economic and social status, as would have been predicted by Weber (1904–1905/1976) and Neibuhr (1929), is a separate issue we discussed earlier.

In an early formative article, Holt (1940) postulated that migrants who come from a rural situation and settle in an urban situation experience a culture shock that is

> characterized by a loosening of mores from strict social control, a liberation of the individual from his group, an impersonalism as against the personal character of the rural environment, an increasing mobility as contrasted with the old stability and isolation, and on top of these changes, a blasting disruption of personal and occupational habits and status. (p. 744)

As evidence of this culture shock, Holt cited demographic data on the phenomenal growth of the Holiness and Pentecostal sects in the southeastern states. The value orientation of these sects was definitely a counterculture orientation in their new setting. Holt reported:

> The adjustment of the Holiness and Pentecostal groups represents the defense of the old standards and modes of behavior rather than a reconstruction of attitudes and behavior to fit the altered situation or a revolution against both the old and the new, which would merely postpone the necessary reconstruction. (p. 746)

Holt acknowledged that his supportive data was quite inadequate to validate his hypothesis, and he called for further research to help explain the growth of the Holiness and Pentecostal sects in the southeastern states.

Subsequently, Liston Pope (1942) surveyed thirteen denominations of which two (Church of God and Pentecostal Holiness) were classical Pentecostal denominations that were composed primarily of mill workers. These classical Pentecostals did, indeed, begin as a counterculture, but they gradually made an accommodation to the culture of Gastonia and Gastonia County, North Carolina. Pope utilized Troeltsch's (1911/1931) distinction of church type and sect type. He investigated the thesis of Niebuhr (1929) that sects become churches over time and he developed twenty-one indices of this change. Pope discovered an interesting fact: although the sect as a religious organization may change over time into a church, nevertheless, the members themselves do not change their socioeconomic class. He suggested the following process:

> A sect, as it gains adherents and the promise of success, begins to reach out toward greater influence in society. . . . In the process it accommodates gradually to the culture it is attempting to conquer, and thereby loses influence over those relatively estranged from that culture. . . . Though at any given moment of transition the rising sect is associated especially with one economic group, it does not necessarily carry that group as it moves on. There is no indication that classes rise as classes but there is proof that denominations do. (p. 119)

The counterculture value system of sects helps account for the development of their own subculture. Pope described the counterculture posture:

> As over against segregation from the community, the newer sects affirm separation from the world; in the face of exclusion on educational, economic, and religious grounds, they affirm exclusion from their own fellowship of those who engage in mixed bathing, dancing, card playing, bobbing the hair, gambling, baseball, county fairs, drinking, and using tobacco. Because they have no jewelry to wear, they make refusal to wear jewelry, including wedding rings, a religious requirement. They transmute poverty into a symptom of Grace. Having no money, they redeem their economic status by rigid tithing of the small income they do possess, and thus far surpass members of churches of any other type or denomination in per capita contributions, despite the fact that they stand at the bottom of the economic scale. (p. 137)

Goldschmidt (1944) found the same process at work in a rural agricultural community in the San Joaquin Valley of California. An Assembly of God Church (Pentecostal), which originally appealed to those on the periphery of the society, had "grown in size and wealth, and in restraint, with the result that an avowedly Pentecostal group has split off" (p. 353). The schismatic Pentecostal group was made up entirely of laborers with 82% unskilled. The Assembly of God Church, on the other hand, had only 60% laborers with 20% unskilled. As the Assembly of God Church adopted more middle-class values, those individuals who were on the periphery of the society established a newer Pentecostal sect.

Young (1960) examined the adaptation process of the Pentecostal Church of God in America as it moved from sect to "established sect" in an urban strip along the California coast. He summarized his findings about this sect's counterculture value orientation:

> Finally, Pentecostals express a general antipathy toward the dominant pursuits of the rest of the community. Dancing, smoking, movies, drinking, and other secular activities, whether business, politics, or sometimes even food, are tainted. When a Pentecostal testifies that he once led a life of sin, he may mean only that he smoked and took an occasional drink. (Young, 1960, pp. 145–146)

With the acquisition of wealth both personally and corporately, the members of the Highland Church, one particular congregation of the sect, began to change their values into a more adaptive orientation to the dominant culture, but they still remained oppositional in their basic value orientation.

Two Roman Catholic sociologists, Poblete and O'Dea (1960) first challenged the assumption that classical Pentecostals were necessarily counterculture in their values. They understood the development of classical Pentecostal sects as a response to anomie:

> In short, it may be said that the sect represents a response of the restructuralization of religious attitudes and orientations in a condition of what Durkheim has called anomie. For Durkheim [1897/1951] anomie was characterized by two interrelated elements. First of all there is a breakdown of those social structures in which the individual found the psychological support and nurture requisite to personal and psychological security. Secondly, there is a loss of consensus or general agreement upon the standards and norms that previously provided the normative orientations and existential definitions in terms of which individual and group life was meaningful. (p. 25)

Poblete and O'Dea studied the formation of classical Pentecostal sect congregations by Puerto Rican migrants to a section of the southern Bronx in New York City. Within the confines of St. Athanasius Roman Catholic Parish, they located ten storefront churches and two larger congregations. They observed worship services of the "Asambleas de Dios" and were able to interview (in Spanish) twenty-eight persons.

They did not find these Pentecostals to have a counterculture orienta-

tion. Rather, they concluded that these Spanish-speaking U.S. citizens—
who had migrated to the mainland—formed these sectarian Pentecostal
sects as a way out of anomie and as a quest for community.

> The interviews strongly suggest that isolation is one of the things from which
> such people are saved by the salvation experience of conversion. . . . It is
> important to note that the group solidarity appears to the converted not as a
> loss of individuality but rather as a chance to develop his own personality—to
> experience a worthwhile fulfillment. (1960, pp. 32–33)

Poblete and O'Dea also noted that there was a large Protestant Pentecostal Church in the same neighborhood that had had a membership of
eight hundred persons. Founded in 1935, it had grown so that it had had
to purchase a reconditioned theatre with a seating capacity of eighteen
hundred and it required two full-time paid ministers on its staff. Poblete
and O'Dea felt that this large "established sect" had all the same characteristics of the smaller storefront congregations. They did not consider
the large Pentecostal church to have become a denomination or a Church
type.

Benton Johnson (1961) also challenged the usual assumption that traditional Pentecostals had counterculture values. In an article entitled,
"Do Holiness Sects Socialize in Dominant Values?" he examined the
question in a theoretical treatment of the subject. This theoretical article
was prompted by an earlier unpublished dissertation (1953) that compared the values of Holiness Pentecostals ($N = 10$) to the values of evan-
gelicals ($N = 10$) from the same socioeconomic level in both rural and
urban populations in North Carolina. Johnson continued in the tradition of Weber by emphasizing that, "It is the ascetic norms and not the
experiencing of a state of spiritual exaltation that are the substance of
the day-to-day religious code of the Holiness believer" (1961, p. 314).
Specifying these ascetic norms more concretely, Johnson listed the following:

> Members of Holiness sects are forbidden to consume alcoholic beverages, to
> dance, to gamble or to play cards, to "smoke, dip or chew" tobacco. They may
> not attend places of "worldly amusement" such as plays, movies, fairs, ball
> games, or poolrooms. They may not engage in mixed bathing; women may
> not use makeup or wear short skirts, short sleeves, short hair or ornamental
> jewelry. Profanity is forbidden, and strict Sabbath observance is enjoined.
> Obligations, including debts, must be faithfully discharged. There are a few
> other specific commandments varying from denomination to denomination
> and from congregation to congregation, but the above list is the hard core of
> those categorical behavioral injunctions, chiefly of a prohibitive nature, to
> which most Holiness sects subscribe. (1961, p. 313)

In other words, it was not glossolalia or a religious experience that was
important in understanding these Pentecostal people, but rather the behavioral norms that came from their Holiness beliefs of sanctification
and perfection. Although these behavioral norms seemed on the surface

to reject the values of society, Johnson argued that these classcical Pente-costals essentially accepted the more fundamental values of American society.

Johnson (1961) argued "that the specifically religious values of the Holiness groups converge with several features of the secular value sys-tem" (p. 310). In particular, he argued that, "The positive emphasis on self-application, consistency, and achievement, are the principal Holiness themes that directly converge with dominant American values" (p. 316). The following quote summarizes his argument:

> . . . the Holiness groups encourage an orientation toward the world that con-strains their members to adopt both motivationally and behaviorally an out-look similar in many respects to that of higher, more privileged social strata. Upward mobility may be an important long-term consequence of this orienta-tion, but more fundamental is the possession of the orientation itself, which governs the believer's behavior toward the secular world. (p. 310)

Right after Glock first proposed his typology of deprivation (noted earlier) in 1964, Elinson suggested the phrase "compound deprivation" to describe the followers of the classical Pentecostal evangelist A. A. Allen. "In addition to the economic and social deprivation shared by most members, some individuals are burdened with "organismic deprivations" in the form of serious physical and psychological ailments" (Elinson, 1965, p. 408).

Elinson did find, however, that the basic value orientation of these classical Pentecostals was counterculture. Elinson did not agree with the thesis of Johnson (1961). He stated:

> Despite the sobriety of the moral standards and the support given financial success as a goal, we cannot agree without major qualifications to Benton Johnson's assertion that Holiness religion "socializes in dominant values." (Elinson, 1965, p. 408n)

Elinson examined the implications of A. A. Allen's Pentecostal reli-gious teachings for three areas of secular life: intellectualism, politics, and race relations. Allen's religious teachings were basically anti-intellec-tual. "However, we ought not forget that for many of Allen's followers this is probably not a new anti-intellectualism, but an articulation of their long-standing ignorance and distrust of things of the mind" (Elin-son, 1965, p. 410). With the Bible used as the primary authority and interpreted according to strict fundamentalism, Allen totally rejected liter-ature, social science, psychiatry, and philosophy. He consigned the bio-logical and physical sciences to relatively insignificant roles in human affairs. Medical science was either totally denigrated or accepted only for its diagnostic purposes. Allen's religious teachings encouraged a with-drawal from political activities. Yet Allen's religious teachings eradicated racial prejudice in his religious setting. But his religious teachings seemed to have no effect on race relations beyond the religious setting:

The pronouncements on race relations are purely religious. They make no mention of secular struggles for civil rights. There is no hint of either support or disapproval of civil rights organizations, government activity in the area of race relations, or political action to advance integration. On race relations as on other issues Allen proves to be unconcerned with worldly solutions. (Elinson, 1965, p. 415)

Two sociologists, Nelsen and Whitt, published an article in 1972 in response to Holt's (1940) earlier call for more research on migrants. Their hypothesis was "that rural migrants, rather than succumbing to culture shock and alienation, undergo a process of gradual resocialization to the urban setting. If this process is indeed occurring, the religious life of rural to urban migrants should be intermediate between the urban and rural pattern" (Nelsen & Whitt, 1972, p. 381). Holt (1940) had only used demographic data to support his thesis.

Nelsen and Whitt (1972) did a secondary analysis of the raw data from the General Household Survey of the Southern Appalachian studies (Lenski, 1958) and the Lenski Detroit area study (Lenski, 1963). The religious pattern of the respondents was determined by such criteria as sectarianism in belief, sectarianism in membership changes, religious service attendance, and Bible reading. The rural-to-urban-migrants in both Appalachia and Detroit were compared to the residents at their places of origin. The findings indicated that migrants tended to fall midway between the rural and urban religious patterns. There was no evidence of an increase in sectarianism in either belief or membership for the rural-to-urban-migrants in either Appalachia or Detroit. Thus, the researchers found no empirical confirmation for Holt's (1940) cultural shock thesis. Their empirical findings, instead, confirmed their own hypothesis that rural-to-urban-migrants experience a gradual resocialization process.

It should be noted that Nelsen and Whitt (1972) did not really focus on Pentecostal sects as Holt (1940) had done, rather, they focused on rural-to-urban-migrants in general. In fact, from their published data, there is no way of obtaining any information about Pentecostals as such. However, the study suggests that classical Pentecostals who migrate from rural to urban settings do not have a counterculture value orientation, but rather that they may possibly have an accommodating orientation to the dominant culture where they have moved.

Dearman (1972/1973, 1974) undertook an empirical study of classical Pentecostals, that is, the United Pentecostal Church. His research was designed specifically to assess the thesis of Johnson (1961) that Holiness (and Pentecostal) sects actually socialize their members into the dominant values of American society. Dearman followed Johnson in utilizing the value-belief clusterings of the American society from Robin M. Williams (1951). But Dearman used an expanded list of value orientations that Williams had developed in 1967:

We have distinguished some fifteen major value-belief clusterings that are salient in American culture as follows: (1) activity and work; (2) achievement and success; (3) moral orientation; (4) humanitarianism; (5) efficiency and practicality; (6) science and secular rationality; (7) material comfort; (8) progress; (9) equality; (10) freedom; (11) democracy; (12) external conformity; (13) nationalism and patriotism; (14) individual personality; (15) racism and related group superiority. (R. M. Williams, 1967, p. 33)

Dearman concluded that this Holiness sect did socialize its members in the fundamental values of the dominant society. Although the sect had a negative attitude toward secular education and officially held a pacifist position, nevertheless, the subjects held values that were much the same as those of the dominant society. On the basis of the content of his interviews, Dearman made the following conclusions: "I believe my data convincingly demonstrate that these pentecostals, these "holiness people," do not assume an attitude of rejection of society; rather the word to be used should be *reformation* (1974, p. 452).

Dearman (1974) also examined what special features, beliefs, or practices of these Holiness Pentecostal people seemed to be effective in socializing members to these dominant values. He examined several socialization mechanisms, that is, frequent church attendance, the use of leisure time for religiously approved activities, the high frequency of friends within the sect, the lack of friends from employment settings. Two mechanisms of socialization seemed particularly important to Dearman:

Apparently, and somewhat ironically, one of the most effective mechanisms for the socialization in dominant values seem to be the pentecostals' definitions of the components of a Christlike life. A Christian should live "like Him," in a Christlike manner, at home, at work, and even in privacy. This has several behavioral consequences: cleanliness, moderation, temperance (in appearance and actions), honesty, reliability, obedience and other similar traits considered to be Christlike. (1974, p. 451)

In other words, it is the very holiness or sanctification tradition that Weber (1904–1905/1976) would have called a "worldly asceticism" that socializes this type of glossolalist into the dominant social values that are professed in America. Glossolalia itself is only important in the socialization process because it is part of the conversion experience for these classical Pentecostals.

In their follow-up sociological study of Gastonia, North Carolina, three decades later, Earle, Knudsen, and Shriver (1976) found that many of the earlier hypotheses of Pope (1942) were confirmed. Pentecostal sects had, indeed, taken on denominational qualities, and new sects continued to form to meet the needs of those on the periphery of society:

The number of sect groups increased from about 40 in 1939, or about 25% of all religious organizations, to perhaps 120 congregations and about 40% of the total in 1969. (Earle et al., 1976, p. 102)

There is little doubt that sectarian groups in Gastonia experience serious challenges to their continuity and persistence: nearly half of the 84 identifiable sectarian organizations that were begun between 1940 and 1965 had been dissolved by 1969. Those that have persisted in one location have frequently altered their names to coincide with a new insight or a new loyalty. (p. 103)

The career of Thomas Dixon, an Assembly of God pastor, is perhaps the best illustration in this follow-up study of Gastonia of the acculturation process that occurs for the established Pentecostal sect. Far from showing a counterculture orientation, Pastor Dixon "moves conceptually, with hardly a blink, from the language of the spirit to the language of psychology and social analysis" (p. 127). "He encourages his congregation to go to the polls; he helps them get jobs by writing employment recommendations for them; and he thinks it appropriate on occasion to inform a congregation about which side of the fence a given political candidate may be on" (p. 129).

This longitudinal sociological study of Gastonia provides invaluable empirical data showing that classical Pentecostal sectarian groups, which began with a counterculture orientation for those on the periphery of society, either died organizationally or socialized in the dominant values of the culture and became established sects or denominations. Those individuals who remained on the periphery of society formed new sectarian groups, which then repeated the same developmental process.

Robert Mapes Anderson wrote the most thorough historical study of classical Pentecostalism to date in his book, *Vision of the Disinherited* (1979). Like Clark, Anderson assessed the value orientation of the early Pentecostals as a counterculture orientation. In fact, Anderson states that their counterculture orientation was at first an essentially revolutionary one:

> Their wholesale condemnation of the world and all its works and their longing for the fulfillment of its imminent destruction constituted a radical criticism of society. The Pentecostals were asocial in practice, but antisocial and therefore potentially revolutionary in impulse. (p. 202)

Unlike Clark, however, Anderson places much more emphasis on the gradual shift from the counterculture orientation to an accommodating orientation:

> In the earliest years the Pentecostal movement did indeed evidence the revolutionary potential of all millenarian movements, but conservative elements eventually triumphed over revolutionary and progressive ones. The most remarkable manifestation of Pentecostal progressivism was its interracial, multi-ethnic composition. This was in itself a radical criticism of prevailing race relations and a radical departure from them. But, as we have seen, in time Pentecostals succumbed to segregation. (pp. 195–196)

Summarizing his historical research, which focused on the formative phase of classical Pentecostalism from the late nineteenth century to the early 1930s, Anderson ended his book with these statements:

> Even the presumed "radical" or "extremist" practices of tongues, exorcism, and healing are conservative in effect, because they have kept the Pente-

Table 13.1 Research on classical Pentecostals investigating their value orientation

Researcher	Type	Value orientation	Research population	Geographic area
T. E. Clark (1987/1949)	Theoretical	Counterculture	Lower socioeconomic	n/a
Boisen (1939, 1955)	Empirical	Counterculture	Lower socioeconomic	Southeastern states
Holt (1940)	Theoretical	Counterculture	Rural-to-urban-immigrants	Southeastern states
Pope (1942)	Empirical	Counterculture (accommo-dating over time)	Textile mill workers	Gastonia, North Carolina
Goldschmidt (1944)	Empirical	Counterculture (accommo-dating over time)	Agricultural workers	Rural California
Young (1960)	Empirical	Counterculture	Lower socioeconomic	Urban California coast
Poblete & O'Dea (1960)	Empirical	Tolerant of culture	Puerto Rican migrants	New York City
Johnson (1961)	Theoretical	Socialize in dominant values	Lower socioeconomic	Rural and urban, North Carolina
Elinson (1965)	Empirical	Counterculture	Lower socioeconomic	South and southwestern states
Nelsen & Whitt (1972)	Empirical	Socialize in dominant values	Rural-to-urban-migrants	Southeastern states and Detroit
Dearman (1972/1973, 1974)	Empirical	Socialize in dominant values	Lower middle class	Rural and urban Oregon
Earle, Knudsen, & Shriver (1976)	Empirical	Socialize in dominant values	Textile mill workers	Gastonia, North Carolina
Anderson (1979)	Theoretical	Counterculture (accommo-dating over time)	Lower socioeconomic	n/a

costals busily engaged in activities which have no impact whatever on the fundamental political economy or social relations of American society, and because they serve to reconcile the Pentecostals to things as they are. Because these practices are so "different" they have appeared to challenge the status quo, but they have been mere rituals of rebellion, cathartic mechanisms which in fact stabilize the social order.

The radical social impulse inherent in the vision of the disinherited was transformed into social passivity, ecstatic escape, and, finally, a most conservative conformity. (pp. 239–240)

In summary, the sociological studies of classical Pentecostals reviewed in this section are summarized in Table 13.1.

From a discussion of classical Pentecostal value changes, we turn next to neo-Pentecostal value changes.

Neo-Pentecostals do not belong to sects, established sects, or denominational classical Pentecostal churches. Instead, they have remained within their respective mainline Protestant churches after they have experienced the baptism of the Spirit and speaking in tongues. By comparison to classical Pentecostals, there has been less research about neo-Pentecostals. This is partly a methodological problem because neo-Pentecostals tend to remain hidden or unidentified in their own mainline churches. But it also may be due in part to the fact that neo-Pentecostals do not fit the usual typologies that have been made about classical Pentecostals.

Martin W. Marty, University of Chicago, a non-Pentecostal historian, wrote an article in 1975 for a book edited by Vinson Synan, a classical Pentecostal historian; then, he revised his article as a chapter for a book of his own in 1976. Marty compared and contrasted classical Pentecostalism and the newer charismatic movements as two separate aspects of Pentecostalism. It was not then apparent that the Catholic charismatic renewal should be considered separately from neo-Pentecostalism within the mianline Protestant churches. Using Troeltsch's (1911/1931) ideal types of sect and church, Marty (1976) commented: "That old-line Pentecostalism had always been in the process of moving from being sectarian to being churchly, while newer Charismatic movements were always in the process of moving from being churchly toward becoming sectarian" (p. 111).

Marty (1975) emphasized that speaking in tongues is the distinctive feature of the classical Pentecostal as well as the newer charismatic. But he also noted that there are two types of newer charismatics: (1) the "hard" charismatic who sees speaking in tongues as "an absolute necessity or as integral to the experience of the Baptism of the Holy Spirit" (p. 215) following the tradition of the classical Pentecostal and (2) the "soft" charismatic who does not take this hard line as to the absolute necessity of speaking in tongues:

A distinction might be made between "soft" and "hard" Charismatics. The soft one is basically a Christian renewalist responsive to the language about and the experience of the Holy Spirit. He or she follows the prescriptions and patterns of the movement, but is gentle with non-Pentecostal Christians, more or less hoping and praying that they will seek the gift, but not looking on them as second-class Christians. The hard Charismatic makes the second Baptism or the blessing in the Spirit into a sign of qualitative difference and cannot help but rule that those who do not have it and seek it are truly unfinished Christian products, more or less "half safe." The former have the problem of being assimilated back into more nondescript renewal styles. The latter risk dividing the church and in almost every case they cause conflict and tension—which, to many of them, are signs of the validity of their witness. (1976, p. 123)

"Hard" charismatics, thus, are more sectarian than "soft" charismatics who emphasize renewal. This distinction made by Marty foreshadowed the need to identify as a separate subcultural group the Catholic charismatic renewal, which has usually taken the "soft" position rather than the "hard" line. Neo-Pentecostals tend to have a more equal mix of "soft" and "hard" positions.

Richard Quebedeaux (1976) compared and contrasted the old classical Pentecostal and the new neo-Pentecostal of the mainline Protestant churches and of the Catholic Church. Like Marty, he wrote from the perspective of a modern church historian, but with much more emphasis on theological issues. Quebedeaux also adopted the ideal types of sect and church from Troeltsch (1911/1931), especially as expanded by B. R. Wilson (1967), to characterize the differences between classical Pentecostalism and the neo-Pentecostal. The differences in value orientations which Quebedeaux enumerated in his historical treatment are summarized in Table 13.2.

Cecil Bradfield (1975, 1979) was the first sociologist to conduct empirical research on a pure neo-Pentecostal sample. He studied a chapter of the Full Gospel Businessmen's Fellowship International (FGBMFI) in western Virginia. The FGBMFI draws its membership from middle-class Pentecostals who belong to mainline churches and who have remained in their respective churches. Bradfield mentions a number of value orientations that differ from those of classical Pentecostals.

Table 13.2 Different value orientations of classical Pentecostalism and neo-Pentecostalism according to Quebedeaux (1976)

Value orientation	Classical Pentecostalism	Neo-Pentecostalism
Ecclesiastical	Sectarian	Ecumenism
Intellectual	Anti-intellectual	Prointellectual
Cultural	Counterculture	Affirmative of culture
Social action	Social unconcern	Social conscience
Liturgical	Spirit of confusion	The quiet spirit
Theological	Fundamentalism	Progressive evangelicalism

First of all, these neo-Pentecostals have not organized as sectarian counter culture movements:

> The major reason that the respondents give for staying in their respective churches was that they should stay to witness about their Baptism experience to others. A secondary reason given for not leaving was so they would not be the cause of schisms. (1979, p. 17)

Initially, this witnessing caused some conflict between the Pentecostal and the non-Pentecostal in the same church. But gradually the level of conflict subsided and an accommodation was worked out:

> In many churches the charismatics are permitted to have their meetings under the auspices of the churches and in turn they "agree" not to interfere with the ongoing progress of the churches. This means that the charismatics may meet in the church building on Wednesday night and "speak in tongues," etc., but they would not be permitted to do this at the Sunday morning worship service. (p. 18)

This accommodation also had another dimension for the neo-Pentecostal who stayed within his/her denomination but was active in the FGBMFI:

> Thus, the neo-Pentecostal has been confronted in the past with a basic dilemma as to whether he should stay in a religious group with which he has a basic dissatisfaction. Many neo-Pentecostals have dealt with this dilemma by establishing their primary religious group affiliation with other charismatics while continuing a kind of secondary group affiliation with their mainline religious group. (p. 18)

In essence, then, these neo-Pentecostals are not as countercultural as classical Pentecostals, but rather accommodate to the cultural demands of their respective churches.

Second, neo-Pentecostals have a different attitude and place a different value on wealth as compared to the classical Pentecostal:

> Only about one-fifth of the respondents to the questionnaire indicated the belief that wealth "almost always leads Christians away from the things of God." The other four-fifths believed that wealth, in fact, may bring a person closer to God rather than to separate him from God. It was always regarded as important that the individual be "Spirit directed" rather than "self-directed" in the accumulation and use of his wealth. (p. 21)

In addition, three fourths of the respondents believed that they had been helped financially as a direct result of the baptism in the Holy Spirit. These middle-class neo-Pentecostals placed a higher value on wealth than classical Pentecostals who usually came from a lower economic level:

> They [the neo-Pentecostals] have integrated wealth into their belief system by attributing it to God rather than to themselves. If they have wealth, it is usually taken as an unmistakable sign that God favors it. Therefore, they are relieved of the conflict between financial success and their religious values. (p. 23)

Third, these neo-Pentecostals placed a higher value on education than classical Pentecostals, who tended to be suspicious of education. Nevertheless, the neo-Pentecostal respondents were divided as to whether education was a hindrance to receiving the baptism in the Spirit or not, that is, half said yes, half said no:

> As compared to classic Pentecostals, neo-Pentecostals have a more positive attitude toward education. At the same time, however, they view it as a potential hindrance to initially receiving the "baptism in the Holy Spirit." However, once the educated person overcomes this initial hindrance, he is given a special status among neo-Pentecostals attesting to the middle class value placed on educational achievement. (p. 50)

Bradfield (1979) summarized his findings about these values:

> In classic Pentecostalism the making of money, educational achievement, and occupational pursuits were considered "worldly" or in sociological terms "secular." These have been redefined by neo-Pentecostals as "sacred" in the sense that they are attributed to God. This is an indication of the extent to which neo-Pentecostals have "sacralized" the whole of life. This procedure provides them with a means of avoiding the conflicts that emerge within a competitive, bureaucratic social system. (p. 60)

In a sense, then, the changes Bradfield found had more to do with a new self-concept or a new identity, that is, a cognitive restructuring, rather than with new cultural values. Bradfield several times noted the need for longitudinal research to help identify genuine changes. To evaluate Bradfield's research in the perspective of our present study, it needs to be pointed out that the research population of FGBMFI is a transitional group from classical Pentecostalism to neo-Pentecostalism.

Douglas B. McGaw (1980) undertook a sociological survey for the Hartford Seminary Foundation of a neo-Pentecostal congregation whose members were "soft" charismatics according to Marty's distinction. The congregation studied, however, was entirely charismatic, which is not the usual ecclesiastical situation for neo-Pentecostals. McGaw (1980) described this unique congregation:

> The Charismatic Congregation, or "CC," is located in an upper-middle class surburban-rural area about fifteen miles from Hartford, Connecticut. It was founded in 1959 and has adopted neo-pentecostalism since 1964. It is affiliated with the United Presbyterian Church in the U.S.A., although this affiliation is of minor concern to many of the members. Most of the family heads in the CC work in Hartford and are classifiable as upper-middle class both in terms of lifestyle and income (68 percent earned $15,000 or more in 1974). For the most part, the members cannot be described as either socioeconomically or psychologically deprived, as pentecostals have been described so often in the past. (p. 285)

McGaw (1979) compared this neo-Pentecostal congregation to another Presbyterian congregation of the same socioeconomic status (SES) and the same region. To understand the various mechanisms of commitment, he compared six measures of meaning (i.e., the belief system) and five measures of belonging (i.e., actual behavior). He found the neo-Pentecostal congregation significantly higher on almost all measures. He concluded that "the charismatic congregation has stronger commitment and that it does so because it is more effective at providing meaning and belonging to its members through stronger closure, strictness, consensus on authority, and cohesion" (p. 146). Although McGaw does not address the question of value changes in this comparison study, it is evident in his ethnographic sketch of the neo-Pentecostal congregation that it adopted more of a separatist stance toward both the dominant culture and the denominational affiliation than did the noncharismatic Presbyterian congregation. But the neo-Pentecostal group also had a concern to help "revitalize" other churches.

Recently, Rarick (1982) compared classical Pentecostal and neo-Pentecostal college and seminary students. He compared a voluntary sample of 212 neo-Pentecostal with 663 traditional college and seminary students from an earlier survey (Rarick & Malony, 1981). He used a questionnaire that included several measurements: (1) the Extrinsic-Intrinsic Religious Orientation scale of Allport, (2) the Committed and Consensual scales of Spilka, (3) an opinion question as to whether the church should be involved in social action; (4) a self-report as to whether the student actually had participated in a social action project, (5) two questions assessing the importance of religion (hours spent in church-related activities and ratings of the importance of religion) from the Salience of Religion scale (Bahr, Bartel & Chadwick, 1971), and (6) several questions concerning the practice of religious glossolalia.

Rarick expected neo-Pentecostals to be less sectarian than the classical Pentecostals. On this assumption, he predicted that:

1. Classical Pentecostals would be more concerned with status needs and group expectation than neo-Pentecostals, that its, score higher on the intrinsic and committed scales, and score lower on the extrinsic and consensual scales, than neo-Pentecostals.
2. Classical Pentecostals would score higher than neo-Pentecostals on measures of the importance of religion.
3. Classical Pentecostals would use glossolalia more often than neo-Pentecostals and would use glossolalia more in large settings (i.e., church), whereas neo-Pentecostals would use glossolalia in a small group setting (i.e., prayer groups).
4. Classical Pentecostals would not rate social action as important as neo-Pentecostals.
5. Classical Pentecostals would come from a lower socioeconomic class generally than neo-Pentecostals.

His results confirmed that neo-Pentecostals do, indeed, come from significantly higher socioeconomic classes. He also found that classical Pentecostals used large groups significantly more than the neo-Pentecostals. In addition he noted that the neo-Pentecostals used glossolalia alone significantly more than the classical Pentecostals.

There was no significant difference in the number of hours that the two groups spend in church-related activities.

Surprisingly, all the other hypotheses were not only not confirmed, but evidenced significant differences in the *opposite* direction. The neo-Pentecostals were more intrinsic and committed and less extrinsic and consensual in their religious orientations than the classical Pentecostals ($p < .001$). The neo-Pentecostals rated the importance of religion higher than the classical Pentecostals ($p < .005$) and used glossolalia more frequently than the classical Pentecostals ($p < .001$).

Rarick concluded that his results indicated that the church-sect typology Wilson (1967) had described does not accurately describe the neo-Pentecostals and the traditional Pentecostals he sampled. In fact, Rarick (1982) stated: "The results of the current study suggest that Neo-Pentecostals who are participants in mainline Protestant denominations may be *more* sectarian than members of classical Pentecostal churches, in spite of income differences" (p. 18).

This would support the tendency noted earlier by Marty (1976) for classical Pentecostals to become more churchlike, whereas neo-Pentecostals became more sectarian.

Theoretical confusion regarding the church-sect typology has probably contributed to the lack of sociological research on neo-Pentecostals as they do not seem to fit into any of the preexisting typologies. In fact, it has only been gradually that the sociologists of religion have even acknowledged the existence of the neo-Pentecostals. When they have recognized the existence of a neo-Pentecostal movement—as opposed to the classical Pentecostal movement—they usually include the Catholic Pentecostal movement as well; then, they focus on the Catholic expression more than on the expression within the mainline Protestant denominations.

In conclusion, then, for neo-Pentecostals who remain in the mainline Protestant denominations there is little research concerning change of values, especially with respect to their orientation toward the dominant culture, both secular and religious. Marty (1975, 1976) and Quebedeaux (1976) as historians have emphasized the distinction between the neo-Pentecostal movement and the classical Pentecostal movement, and they have offered some insights that are helpful for behavioral scientists. Bradfield (1975, 1979) researched the FGBMFI, which is an early transitional group from classical Pentecostalism to neo-Pentecostalism. McGaw (1979, 1980) researched a mainline Protestant congregation that was entirely neo-Pentecostal, which again is not typical for most neo-Pentecostals. The samples of Bradfield and McGaw represent two ends of the range for neo-Pentecostals, most of whom remain as loyal members of their respective denominations in a minority status. Perhaps Rarick's (1982) neo-Pentecostal sample represented this middle range, but this is unclear. We can speculate that neo-Pentecostals probably do not have as great a counter-culture orientation as classical Pentecostals or they would not have remained within their original denominations, but more research is obviously needed.

The history of the Catholic charismatic renewal, which began in 1967 at Duquesne University, Pittsburgh, Pennsylvania, and quickly spread to the University of Notre Dame, South Bend, Indiana, to Michigan State University, East Lansing, and to the University of Michigan, Ann Arbor, has been covered by early participants (O'Connor, 1971; Ranaghan & Ranaghan, 1969). A nonparticipant Catholic theologian, Kilian McDonnell, had worked for four years with the anthropological research team of Luther Gerlach at the University of Minnesota and had published on the subject of classical Pentecostalism in 1966 before the beginning of the Catholic movement. Subsequently, McDonnell (1968a, 1968b, 1968c, 1968d, 1970, 1975, 1978, 1979, 1980) published extensively evaluating and interpreting Catholic Pentecostalism primarily within a theological frame of reference. It was McDonnell (1970, p. 35; 1980, vol. I, p. xiv) who coined the phrase "classical Pentecostal" in order to distinguish the original subculture of Pentecostalism from neo-Pentecostalism and Catholic Pentecostalism. René Laurentin (1974/1977), a French theologian and historian, has written a journalistic account of Catholic Pentecostalism that is comparable in style to the earlier book by journalist John Sherrill (1964), which popularized the neo-Pentecostal movement. Some have continued to interpret Pentecostalism within the Catholic Church with the same concepts of psychological stress and maladaption as had been used previously (e.g., Nouwen, 1969). However, the phrase, "Catholic Pentecostalism" seemed almost a contradiction in terms sociologically. As Fichter (1975) noted:

> What is probably the most fascinating and challenging aspect of Catholic pentecostalism is that it came as a surprise to sociologists of religion. We had studied the so-called religious revival as a statistical phenomenon of church membership during and after the Second World War, while at the same time witnessing a long-term trend toward secularization. It may well be that the lower-class Protestant denominations, conservative and pentecostal, represented a counter-trend to materialism and secularism, but no one expected an elaborately liturgical, sacramental, and hierarchical religion like Catholicism to imitate them. (p. 6)

In other words, the basic reason for this surprise was the fact that sociologists of religion had considered glossolalia and other charismatic gifts as correlates of sectarianism according to the sect-church typology of Troeltsch (1911/1931). Yet here was glossolalia or Pentecostalism within the most churchly of the church types.

Although they do not provide specific information as to time and location, Gerlach and Hine (1970) engaged in the first sociological analysis of this new subculture of Pentecostalism. They did not fully recognize the Catholic manifestation of Pentecostalism as being a new subculture, and they included it as part of the neo-Pentecostal movement. Nevertheless, their early findings are important and probably should be listed first in the chronology of data gathering for Catholic Pentecostalism. This University of Minnesota anthropological team did their field work in seven locations. One of these fieldwork locations was a prayer group at an unnamed Catholic university in the United States. They described the prayer group (Notre Dame University?) as follows:

> A sixth group represents a special phenomenon in the Pentecostal Movement—the outbreak of a revival and the outpouring of the Spirit on college campuses. At the time [unspecified] of our field work, the group consisted of students—graduate and undergraduate—and three members of the faculty at a large Catholic university. . . . In addition to the usual occurrences of glossolalia and other charisms, there was a great deal of emphasis upon the use and meaning of traditional Catholic ritual; the importance of such ritual seems to be heightened by the Pentecostal experience under these conditions. (Gerlach & Hine, 1970, p. 11)

The researchers further noted that a year after their fieldwork study of the campus prayer group, this Catholic Pentecostal movement had moved beyond college campuses:

> Catholic Pentecostals are no longer predominantly students. The University [Notre Dame?] now holds annual meetings of "Spirit-filled" Catholics from all over the United States, during which new converts are made, new crosslinks formed, and old faith renewed. . . . although there is no official opposition from the higher levels of Catholic organization, there is apparently sufficient informal opposition at the local level from non-participating Catholics to create a type of subtle conflict. (pp. 11–12)

Gerlach and Hine focused on the issues of movement growth and social transformation for Pentecostalism in general and also on the Black Power movement. However, they did make some general observations about the sect-church continuum that are important for our current discussion. They defined the sect-to-church development in terms of organizational development, which includes the "routinization process" Weber (1922/1963) had described. Writing about this continuum, they observed:

> It is among the newly forming charismatic groups and the "tongues movements" within the main-line denominations that one finds the fervor, the near absence of formal organization, the spontaneity, the exponential growth rates, and the emphasis on religious experience usually associated with sects. Toward the middle of the continuum, the independent bodies of somewhat longer tenure have more formalized structure, more permanent leadership, and more bureaucratic routine. Finally, it is the so-called sects which are approaching a "steady state," developing the most rigid structure and hierarchical organization, and placing relatively less emphasis on spontaneous "leadings of the Spirit" and other charismata. In short, they approach the status of regular churches. (pp. 4–5)

According to Gerlach and Hine, therefore, the classical Pentecostal de-nominations are more churchlike, whereas the newer neo-Pentecostal movements, both Protestant and Catholic, are more sectlike, a proposi-tion with which other writers previously noted would agree.

Max Heirich, professor of sociology at the University of Michigan, Ann Arbor, quickly realized that the Catholic Pentecostal movement de-veloping at his university represented a unique sociological opportunity and encouraged several of his graduate students to do research on this new religious movement (e.g., M. I. Harrison and R. C. Keane). With the assistance of a student-participant, Phillip Thibideau and others, Heirich designed a questionnaire that was administered to the Ann Arbor prayer group in 1968 in what was evidently the first pilot study on Catholic Pentecostalism as a separate research sample.

Although the movement seemed to resemble counterculture move-ments, like the Jesus Movement, nevertheless, this new movement did not show the same attraction for individuals who had experimented with psy-chedelic drugs. In fact, Harrison (1974b) reporting on this pilot study stated that "there is no evidence that drug use per se predisposes indi-viduals toward Catholic Pentecostalism" (p. 53). In the pilot study, only 26% ($N = 42$) of the participants said that they had ever smoked mari-juana. The issue of drug use seemed so inconsequential that questions relating to it were dropped in the next revision of the questionnaire. The Catholic Pentecostal movement was certainly not countercultural to the extent that it either fostered drug use or appealed primarily to those who came out of a drug culture.

In 1969, Harrison administered a second questionnaire of thirty-one pages length. This was an extensive revision of the earlier version adminis-tered to all regular participants of the same prayer group at Ann Arbor (65% return; $N = 231$) as well as participants of prayer groups in East Lansing (88% return; $N = 30$), and Flint, Michigan (67% return, $N = 16$). Harrison was also a participant observer of the weekly prayer meetings at Ann Arbor for eight months, when their attendance averaged over two hundred per meeting, and he interviewed prominent members of all three prayer groups.

Harrison also administered a shorter form of the same questionnaire to a probability sample from a file of Catholic students (over 5,000) at-tending the University of Michigan at Ann Arbor and whose names were listed at the Newman Center (72% return; $N = 158$). This second sample provided a comparison group to the students in the Ann Arbor prayer group. He published several articles reporting the results of this first in-depth sociological study of Catholic Pentecostalism (1974a, 1974b, 1975). Although he did not designate it as such, Harrison, (1971/1972) essen-tially wrote the initial ethnographic study of Catholic Pentecostalism, which focused on the Ann Arbor prayer group—the prototype for most subsequent prayer groups and the center for future national leadership of the movement. His ethnographic description occurred before Stephen

B. Clark, one of the core leadership of the prayer group, had designed and published his "Life in the Spirit Seminars" (1971, 1972a, 1972b, 1973), a catechetical instruction for the baptism of the Spirit.

Writing about the commitment experience, Harrison (1974a) also made a distinction between the terms "conversion" and "renewal." Thus, the basic value orientation of Catholic Pentecostalism is one of renewal, and not a sectarian counterculture orientation. "Catholic Pentecostalism appears to reaffirm the value of piety and loyalty to the Church" (1974b, p. 52). Harrison (1975) noted, however, that within the Catholic charismatic movement "a sectarian core has emerged" (p. 150), by which he meant the leadership of the prayer group, "which is capable of carrying its intense spirituality and insuring its effective organizational functioning" (p. 151). In defining the adjective "sectarian," Harrison (1971/1972) referred to the ten attributes that B. R. Wilson (1959, p. 4) had suggested early in his writings: a voluntary association; some claim to personal merit; exclusiveness (including expulsion); an "elect" self-conception; personal perfection; the priesthood of all believers; a high level of lay participation; spontaneous expression of commitment; hostility or indifference to the secular society and to the state. Parenthetically, we notice that Wilson here seems to be relying much more on Weber's (1904–1905/1976) emphasis on the sect as a voluntary association than on Troeltsch's (1911/1931) emphasis on the sect as a counterculture movement. Harrison (1971, 1972) saw these qualities of sectarianism, as defined by Wilson (1959), developing within the core leadership rather than within the general membership. "In their radical piety, their rejection of 'middle-class values,' and in their efforts to build a Christian community" (Harrison, 1971/1972, p. 166), the elite core leadership showed sectarian tendencies, but Harrison acknowledged that even this core was "willing to seek such personal and social transformations within the context of the Roman Church" (p. 166).

Another early researcher in the beginning years of the Catholic Pentecostal movement was Charles L. Harper who interviewed some twenty-five persons in his participant observation of the movement between 1970 and 1972. Initially, C. L. Harper (1974) hypothesized:

> The movement would appeal especially to those Catholic academics and students who had come from very traditional and religiously orthodox homes. Thus the tensions giving rise to pentecostal participation were viewed as the product of a dramatic disjuncture between primary socialization (traditionalistic) and secondary socialization (secular/"modernistic"), and further that becoming a spirit-filled Catholic represented a rejection of a highly secularized and rationalistic world view encountered in a university setting. (pp. 317–318)

In other words, in the early years of the movement, when the Catholic Pentecostal movement was largely confined to university campuses, C. L. Harper saw its members' value orientation as a rejection of the values of American society in general. However, as he continued to gather case histories, C. L. Harper realized that participants were no longer confined to academic settings. In fact, he found that "Catholics who became pentecostals were such a heterogenous [sic] group that it was almost impossible to describe them in common social, economic, cultural, or demographic categories" (p. 318). He wrote:

> Indeed, the only two common "background" features of the subjects of this study seem to be (1) strong early religious socialization, and (2) some kind of alienating experience with regard to the church. Thus, unfashionable and sociologically incomplete as it may be, these factors restrict the analysis to the religious frame of reference. (p. 318)

Recognizing that his data were limited, C. L. Harper tentatively proposed an individual "process model," which he derived from his case histories. The "process model" individuals seemed to go through included five sequential steps: (1) early socialization (in religion), (2) growing ambivalence toward a system of orientation (the Catholic Church), (3) search for options, (4) the turning point (i.e., conversion to the movement), and, finally, (5) continuing commitment (to the movement).

Of importance to our current discussion of changes in value orientations, we note that C. L. Harper (1974) made the following observation near the end of his article reporting his research:

> Thus, it seems that the movement is in the process of converting instrumental energies directed at structural changes into expressive energies which little threaten the existing status quo. Thus while there will continue to be some tensions between the movement and institutionalized Church (especially over the issues of ecumenism and the genuineness of "personalized" religious experiences), it is suggested that the contextual effects of the movement are supportive of the church. (p. 323)

In other words, C. L. Harper considered the Catholic Pentecostal movement to have only a low level of tension with the Catholic Church. Thus, he would probably not classify the movement as having a sectarian orientation, but rather as having a renewal or revitalizing orientation.

In a study of 155 prayer groups, Fichter (1975) asked each contact person or prayer-group leader to give the questionnaire to three laymen and three laywomen in their respective prayer groups. He sampled only adult Catholic laity and excluded priests, religious, students, seminarians, and non-Catholics in order to have a research sample of some homogeneity and to rule out as much as possible extraneous variables that might contaminate the results. Fichter acknowledged that his sample was not a random sample, that is, a true cross-section of the movement, because there were unquestionably more women than men in the prayer groups, and he had asked for three questionnaires from each sex in each prayer group.

Fichter (1975) categorized the value orientation of the movement as a "spiritual counter-culture" orientation.

One of the frequent expressions of the movement's leadership is "We've got to build a new society within the shell of the old." This is an effort not to Christianize the socio-cultural system, but to set up a cultural environment within, along side of, and essentially counter to the secular culture. (p. 6)

Second, he reported that the majority of Catholic charismatics were not anticlerical or against the authority of the church hierarchy:

there is no clear and wide manifestation of anti-clericalism among the charismatics, nor is there any tendency to separate themselves from the Catholic clergy and hierarchy. Eight out of ten (78%) affirm that Pope Paul VI is the infallible Vicar of Christ. Three-quarters of them are of the opinion that the charismatic movement could not continue in existence without the presence and aid of priests. More than half (55%) report that they have had the parish priest in their home during the past year. The same proportion would obey their bishop if he were to prohibit charismatic prayer meetings in his diocese. (p. 29)

In agreement with C. L. Harper (1974), Fichter (1975) considered Catholic charismatics to constitute an "expressive movement." The prayer groups have less tension with the Church and society than the "covenant communities," which have withdrawn into much more tight-knit exclusive residential communities.

In sociological terms (because the movement is not sectarian), Fichter categorized the Catholic Pentecostal movement as a cult. In fact, he titles his book (1975), *The Catholic Cult of the Paraclete.*

Fichter's definition of cult relied heavily on that of Becker (1932) which emphasized the goal "of purely personal ecstatic experience, salvation, comfort, and mental or physical healing" (p. 627). Fichter also quotes a description of mysticism from Troeltsch (1911/1931, p. 730). In a 1970 lecture, Fichter (1974b) had argued that "the large-scale American religious bodies fit generally into Troeltsch's *ecclesia* category, and also that each of these large religious bodies contains elements, or segments, or strata, or subdivisions, that are denominational, sectarian and cultic (mystical)" (pp. 90–91). Fichter was here defining cult as primarily mystical, and he also categorized the early stages of the Catholic Pentecostal movement as essentially mystical: "If one thinks of mysticism as a set of esoteric rituals performed within a small group he might refer to modern examples of speaking with tongues, or of so-called pentecostal emotionalism, or of experimental and informal eucharistic liturgies" (p. 94).

One of Fichter's major research interests was the sociopolitical orientation toward the world and the presence or absence of social action among Catholic charismatics. He was interested in the question of whether there was a change either in orientation or in social action among Catholics who became pentecostals. Fichter (1974a) concluded that "the social attitudes of the members, whether liberal, moderate or conservative, appear to be neither effect nor cause of adherence to the Pentecostal movement" (p. 310). Evidently, these attitudes or orientations did not change significantly after conversion to Pentecostalism:

The findings of our survey demonstrate that despite their spiritual unity, the members have not abandoned their diverse political and social convictions. In their religious convictions they are basically of one-mind-in-the-spirit, but in social matters they still range along the whole continuum from very liberal to very conservative. (Fichter, 1975, p. 93)

In the matter of social action, however, Fichter (1975) concluded that "the charismatic renewal movement tends to withdraw its members from the struggle for social justice and to blunt their zeal for social reform" (p. 92). To substantiate his conclusion, he analyzed three levels of social action: corporate action by the prayer groups, individual action in "outside" groups, and individual acts of charity (or what have been called "corporal works of mercy" in traditional Catholic morality). At the first level, he concluded that "It would be a rare and probably very small prayer group that could get its members to agree on a specific, organized, social action program" (p. 93). At the second level, he found that "fewer than one out of five of all our respondents have been or are now involved in voter registration campaigns, peace demonstrations, grape or lettuce boycotts, the interracial movement or the National Conference of Christian and Jews" (p. 90). At the third level, he found that "most of the members report an increase in their performance of the corporal works of mercy since they joined the charismatic renewal" (p. 96).

There was a difference, however, between how the conventional Catholic parish did these corporal works of mercy and how the charismatics did them. Whereas most parishioners provided their charity impersonally through welfare organizations, the charismatic would get personally or individually involved in meeting human needs: "Working with alcoholics and drug addicts, preparing meals for shut-ins, visiting the sick and lonely in hospitals and nursing homes, sitting with the elderly, and providing food, clothing, and money to needy families" (p. 96). Fichter's findings on social action could be summarized by his statement: "The pentecostals are not satisfied with the world as it is, but they have no intention of trying to change it through organized collective action. Their basic conviction is that reform starts at home, in one's heart, and somehow spills over into other homes and other hearts until all of society is reformed" (p. 81).

However, when Fichter (1975) examined the sociopolitical orientation toward the world of newcomers and old timers in these groups, he found that there was little change: "The great majority of lay Catholic charismatics express approval of 'liberal' programs like medicare, open housing, and higher minimum wages, and there is practically no difference here between the attitudes of old-timers and newcomers" (p. 77). Examining the specific issue of orientation toward race relations, he also found that there was little change: "Three-quarters of both old-timers and newcomers approve the civil-rights movement, and an even higher proportion of both (86%) say that they favor racially integrated schools" (p. 77). Examining attitudes as to whether the clergy or the Church as an institution should become active in sociopolitical issues, he found:

There is a small percentage difference that consistently shows the old-timers to be more conservative than the newcomers. In response to the statement that "priests have a place on the picket lines," more of the newcomers (63%) than the old-timers (57%) are in agreement. Again, more of the newcomers (60%) than of the veterans (50%) think that "the Church should lead in social protest movements." Only a minority (29%) of all respondents holds that the Church should support women's liberation, but more of the new-comers (33%) than of the old-timers (28%) hold this position. (p. 78)

Examining personal involvement in social action, however, Fichter found that the old-timers were more active than the newcomers.

There is a marked difference in response, however, when we ask about their personal involvement in interracial movements, with the old-timers twice as likely (32%) as the newcomers (16%) to report that they are now, or have been, participants. . . . The old-timers are also more likely (25%) than the newcomers (15%) to say that they give active support to Caesar Chavez's grape and lettuce boycotts. (p. 77)

Interestingly, Fichter interpreted these differences in sociopolitical orientation and in social action *not* as changes over time but rather as changes in the constitution of new recruits to the movement. A higher percentage (35%) of working-class people were in the newcomers group than in the old-timers group (20%). A lower percentage (65%) of college graduates were in the newcomers group than in the old-timers (75%); but of even more importance a lower percentage (38%) had attended Catholic colleges in the newcomers group than in the old-timers (50%). Newcomers also seemed to have been much less active in renewal movements in the church than the old-timers. Without groups matched on these variables of class, education (Catholic and non-Catholic), and prior religious ac-tivity, there really is no way of determining whether these differences in sociopolitical orientation and in social action between the old-timers and the newcomers are changes over time or whether they reflect new recruit-ment patterns of the renewal movement.

Richard J. Bord and Joseph E. Faulkner (1975), two sociologists at Pennsylvania State University, undertook a subsequent empirical study that confirmed some of the more descriptive findings of Fichter, although they did not refer to his national survey. Like Fichter, they used the *Directory of Catholic Charismatic Prayer Groups,* which was published annually. They selected fifteen prayer groups on the basis of size, that is, five from each of three groups: large (over 200 members), medium (100–199 members), and small (lass than 100 members). These fifteen prayer groups were located geographically in Indiana, Louisiana, Maryland, Michigan, New Jersey, New York, Pennsylvania, and Wisconsin. Bord and Faulkner visited eleven of the prayer groups themselves for partici-pant observation. But their primary data were from a questionnaire dis-tributed to these prayer groups ($N = 987$, with an approximate 50% re-turn rate). Their primary research interest was to establish that in religious groups sociopolitical attitudes (or value orientations toward the world) are determined not so much by religious factors as they are by socio-personal background characteristics and by attitudinal-motivational states.

When Board and Faulkner (1975) calculated the means and standard deviations for the three religious factors, that is, the personal-motivational states, the social activism attitudes, and the attitudes toward science, they had a number of interesting descriptive findings about the Catholic Pentecostal movement:

> As expected, the sample was highly orthodox (p. 263) . . . Interesting enough, our respondents were quite highly involved in both the institutional church and the movement. This supports the movement leaders' continued emphasis that this is a movement within, and for the renewal of, the Church. There was fairly high agreement that life is a struggle between opposing forces, that man alone is powerless, and that evil forces abound. Attitudes toward protest are in a slightly liberal direction. Finally, there was high agreement that science is limited as a tool for solving our most important problems. (p. 264)

To compare and contrast these findings with the earlier findings of Fichter (1975), we observe that both studies found that the majority of Catholic Pentecostals had a liberal sociopolitical attitude (orientation) toward the world but that there was a broad range of sociopolitical attitudes that were not changed when the respondents became charismatic or when they became more involved in the movement over time. Both studies found that the participant's orientation toward the world was determined much more by other variables (i.e., level of education, Church or secular education, socioeconomic status) than by becoming charismatic or participating in the Catholic Pentecostal movement. Both studies also found that movement participants became increasingly obedient to Church authority as they remained in the movement over time so that their orientation to the Church became increasingly less sectarian.

The next researcher, Meredith B. McGuire, sociologist in the field of religion at Montclair State College, began researching Catholic Pentecostal prayer groups almost by accident. Originally, she was conducting longitudinal research on sixteen "underground church" groups in Northern New Jersey from 1969 to 1973. She had even published a sociological interpretation of the "underground church" movement in 1972. Then, she found that two of these groups became Pentecostal:

> As these sixteen underground church groups continued to develop, the two least action-oriented became pentecostals, while the others became progressively more activist and more communalist.
>
> The major changes in these groups' behavior between 1969 and 1973 were the introduction of glossolalia and an increasing exclusivism. The members, however, interpreted their pentecostal experience as both a major turning point for the group and a major personal conversion. (1974, p. 59)

Her first article on Catholic Pentecostalism in 1974 compared and contrasted it with the Underground Church movement, her original research population:

> On the surface, much of the data about these two developments show them to be parallel: their memberships are recruited from middle-class, educated, active Catholics; their liturgies are innovative and lively; they have certain ecumenical leanings, and the members' religious convictions are central to their every-day lives and actions. . . . The points of similarly between the underground church and the Catholic pentecostals should not obscure the radical differences between the two movements. The underground Catholic groups are "liberal" in their theologies and they tend to be strong social activists. By contrast, the pentecostal groups more generally reflect the conservatism and biblical literalism of their Protestant counterparts, and they emphasize interior spiritual concerns rather than social action. (pp. 57–58)

Table 13.3 summarizes McGuire's findings about the different value orientations or attitudes of the two movements.

According to McGuire (1975), the heavy emphasis on community in both movements can be understood as their attempt to reduce cognitive dissonance. "The support of such cognitive dissonance requires the close-knit group of fellow believers" (p. 102). McGuire also used this attribute, "the close-knit group of fellow believers," as the definition of the sect (1972, p. 45; 1975, p. 102) in writing about both movements.

Writing about Catholic Pentecostals, specifically as a cognitive minority, McGuire (1975) gave the following description of their attitudes or value orientation toward the Catholic Church:

> Members of the groups studied can certainly be considered a cognitive minority, even though they did not consider themselves to be dissenters. Most Pentecostal Catholics studied were highly critical of the religion prac-

Table 13.3 A comparison of values for Pentecostal and underground church movements according to McQuire (1974)

Value/attitudes	Pentecostal	Underground church
Social/Action	Conservative with little activism	Liberal, with much more activism
Authority	Respectfully critical, with obedience dominant	Protestingly critical, with disobedience dominant
Doctrine	Traditional	Progressive
Liturgy	Mass at parish church plus other devotional practices encouraged	Mass at own meetings without other devotional practices encouraged
Ecumenism	Some affiliation with intercommunion discouraged	Some affiliation with intercommunion encouraged
Structure	No communes developed	Communes developed

ticed by most Catholics and of the lack of leadership by church authorities. Specifically, they criticized the uncertainty and lack of authoritative direction of the church, the inability of the liturgy (as reconstructed) to reflect experiential religion, and the failure of the church to focus on scripture and community. Pentecostal Catholics interviewed indicated that the American Catholic Church was in a state of "crisis of faith," and the charismatic renewal was God's answer to the crisis. (p. 100)

Writing about Catholic Pentecostals specifically as a cognitive minority, McGuide (1975) gave the following description of their attitudes or value orientation toward American society:

Pentecostal Catholics can be considered a cognitive minority relative to the rest of American society in general because of their insistence on a religion which overarches all spheres of everyday life. With the rest of society, however, the Pentecostal Catholics tend to accept most of the prevailing social and political system but interpret it within their religious framework. Nevertheless, the Pentecostal belief-system with its emphasis upon interior spiritual concerns has an inherent bias toward accepting the status quo in "worldly" affairs. (p. 101)

Benedict J. Mawn did the next empirical study, which followed soon after Fichter's (1975) national survey. In a dissertation project done at Boston University Graduate School, Mawn (1975) surveyed Catholic charismatics in the Boston area and in five national regions.

Replicating what Fichter (1975) had found, Mawn also found that a high percentage of Catholic charismatics had attended Catholic schools exclusively at the elementary level (53%), secondary level (45%), and college level (31%) and that Catholic charismatics "reflect the moderately liberal central tendency found in the political profile of the general Catholic population" (Mawn, 1975, p. 79).

Mawn also examined his data to see whether he could find evidence that the deprivation model of Glock (1973) applied for Catholic Pentecostals. He found no evidence to substantiate an economic, social, organismic, or ethical deprivation. However, there was a substantial minority (38%) in the sample who indicated a felt psychic deprivation in response to three questions. He claimed that the psychic deprivation could best be understood as a "transcendency deprivation of an affective or experiential, rather than of a cognitive nature" (p. 139).

Mawn defined his construct of a transcendency deprivation as "a felt absence of a personal, direct relationship with a Being of supreme existence, who is the inmost principle, the ground and the goal of the individual human creature" (p. 146); in another place he defined it as "the absence of a personal, existential, experienced-based relationship with the *realissimum*" (p. 268).

Of particular interest in our current discussion of changes over time of value orientations is the next section of Mawn's discussion. Mawn quoted Hood (1973) who had found that the intrinsically oriented religious type "report significant personal experiences codifiable as experiences of transcendence" (Hood, 1973, p. 447). Therefore, Mawn reasoned that these Catholic Pentecostals must have been deprived in this area of transcendent religious experience before they became Catholic Pentecostals.

Further, he found that there were some changes, even some dramatic changes over time in orientation of Catholic Pentecostals (1) towards religious beliefs in the existence of God, (2) towards the source of their religious beliefs, (3) in attitudes about religious practices, and (4) towards religious experiences. There was a dramatic increase in those who believed without any doubts in the existence of God. There was a dramatic decrease of those who relied on early socialization (i.e., early religious training) for their source of belief, and there was a dramatic increase of those who relied on later socialization (i.e., the presence of the Holy Spirit manifested in the love shown by Christians) for their source of belief. Finally, there was a dramatic decrease of those who reported a punitive type of religious experience as well as a dramatic increase of those who had salvific, ecstatic, and revelational types of religious experiences.

The third method of data collection that Mawn used provides us with his most interesting empirical data, which (as far as we know) had not been obtained before and has not been replicated since. Mawn sent a brief questionnaire to the chancellors of the archdioceses in the continental United States to obtain the hierarchy's perception of the Catholic Pentecostal movement. He received twenty-one responses which was a 72% response rate. To complement this, in his questionnaire to the prayer groups he also had two questions about the relationship of the movement toward the institutional Church and vice versa. These data may not seem related to our discussion of changes in value orientations, but they are related in an indirect way. The question is what changes in value orientation occur for Catholic charismatics in their attitude and relationship toward the institutional Church. Do they become sectarian in the sense of seceding from the institution or not? Of course, such an orientation does not develop in a vacuum, but depends a great deal on the institution's attitude toward the movement.

Mawn first noted historically two documents produced by the hierarchy. An episcopal committee on doctrine made its report to a meeting of the National Conference of Catholic Bishops on November 14, 1969 (McDonnell, 1980, vol 1, pp. 209–210). It was a short (650 words) document, intending to take a Gamaliel (Acts 5:38–39) attitude of wait-and-see neutrality. But it was interpreted by many as a positive document because, unlike previous official denominational statements with regard to classical Pentecostalism and neo-Pentecostalism, the Catholic bishops did not take a condemning attitude. Then in 1975, the Committee on Pastoral Research and Practices of the National Conference of Catholic Bishops issued a report that was both cautionary and positive in its attitude toward the Catholic Pentecostal movement (McDonnell, 1980, vol 2, pp. 105–114). It was in this historical setting that Mawn conducted his survey.

The sociological model Mawn used to understand the relationship between the movement and the institutional Church was an *ecclesiola in ecclesia* (a little church *within* the Church). Although it is difficult, if not impossible, to determine historically who first applied this sociological model to the Catholic Pentecostal movement, there is no question that Mawn has provided the most, if not the best, empirical data to substantiate the use of this model for Catholic Pentecostalism. He referred to Werner Stark's (1967) discussion of the devotional circles of the German Lutheran Pietists, the "societies" of the English Methodists, and the movement of the Russian Stundists. Stark classified them all as *ecclesiolae in ecclesia*, as reform movements within established national churches hoping to renew the institutional Church.

However, Stark noted that there was a sectarian tendency in these "little churches" that ultimately led to schism when the nation-states (not the established churches) forced the issue by taking a legalistic attitude toward the "little churches" (Stark, 1967, vol. 2, pp. 82–83). Mawn (1975) concluded that "at present the Catholic Pentecostal movement would have to be described as an *ecclesiola in ecclesia*, a little church renewing the larger, Mother-church from within" (p. 279).

Almost as a postscript, Mawn included some questions that assessed the orientation of the Catholic Pentecostals toward the sociopolitical world around them. His results confirmed Fichter's (1975) earlier findings that Catholic Pentecostals tended to have a liberal sociopolitical orientation. Mawn (1975) also asked some questions about actual involvement of prayer groups in the "social apostolate" (i.e., social action) as well as questions about opinion concerning such involvement. Of the respondents, 55%, said that their prayer groups were involved in the "social apostolate." In response to an open-ended question, that is, "If yes, please state the nature of this apostolate" (p. 308), 21 (4.6%) responded with "work for poor," 19 (4.2%) responded with "work for prison reform," 15 (3.3%) responded with "work for sick and/or elderly," 3 (0.7%) responded with "work for race relations," one (0.2%) responded with "work with alcoholics and addicts," and 162 (35.6%) had "various social apostolates" (unspecified by Mawn). In other words, 16% (74) of the respondents reported that some specific social apostolate existed in their prayer group and 36% (162) reported that various unspecified social apostolates existed in their prayer groups. These findings are radically different from Fichter's (1975) who found almost no social action among Catholic Pentecostal prayer groups.

It may well be that Mawn's (1975) results are of questionable validity because his respondents may not have understood the phrase "social apostolate" to be "social action" and may have understood it to mean something else. Mawn recognized this because he commented that "interviews, however, showed that, in many cases, the 'social apostolate' amounted to evangelizing among the groups listed" (p. 210). Mawn took issue with Fichter's (1973) conclusion that Catholic Pentecostals were more interested in spiritual comfort than they were in social awareness:

> On the contrary, the Catholic Pentecostals observed and those interviewed (especially the young and the middle-aged) manifested a keen awareness of social evils and their obligation to respond corporatively. The prevailing attitude, however, is that *for the present* priority of attention must be given to personal renewal. (Mawn, 1975, p. 213)

In sum, then, with respect to changes in value orientations, Mawn found that, in religious belief and experience, the Catholic Pentecostals changed to a more mystical orientation than before their Pentecostal experience, perhaps thus resolving a "transcendency deprivation." Mawn also found, in the relationship between the movement and the institution, that Catholic Pentecostals overtly expressed nearly unanimous loyalty but that covertly there was a mild degree of tension. This tension was not enough to justify labelling this movement as sectarian. Instead, Mawn used the sociological category of *ecclesiola in ecclesia* to describe the movement. Finally, in relation to the sociopolitical culture, Mawn found the Catholic charismatics to be liberal in orientation and interested, but probably not really active, in social action.

The final study to be considered is that of Max Heirich (1977). He utilized the comparison group of the University of Michigan Catholic students ($N = 158$) as a "control" group for "converts" to the Catholic Pentecostal movement ($N = 152$). He used as "converts" only those Catholics in the new movement who reported receiving the Baptism of the Holy Spirit. Heirich focused his research analysis on psychological stress, previous socialization, and various forms of direct social influence as separate and combined causes for conversion. At first looking at the data without the control group, he found support for these classical social science causes of religious conversion. But then looking at the data with the control group by means of several sophisticated statistical analyses (i.e., Somers's "D"; Multiple Classification Analysis including an Automatic Interaction Detection), he found that the evidence to support these classical social science causes of religious conversion was not confirmed. The most prominent finding of these analyses was that those Catholics who received the Baptism of the Spirit—the "converts"—"differed strikingly from the controls in reported religious practice (Mass attendance and personal piety)" (p. 664). In fact, one analysis showed that "Mass attendance is almost twice as powerful an influence as are all the others combined [stress, socialization, and social influence]" (p. 670). Thus Heirich concluded that at the time his data were collected (early in the rise of the movement) that for the majority of the converts conversion "involved both a fairly radical *reorientation* of religious understanding and a *continuing religious quest*" (p. 661). In his theoretical discussion of his findings, Heirich argued strongly that social scientists pay more attention to the *content* of any new vision. "To be convincing, any causal argument should have to show links between content and experience. Mere correlational data would not in itself be convincing" (p. 675). For the purposes of our present discussion, we note that Heirich's further statistical analyses of the same data that Harrison collected in 1969 also substantiated the conclusion that the value orientation for this new religious movement is basically one of "a continuing religious quest," a renewal movement within its religious context rather than a sectarian or counterculture movement.

Table 13.4 summarizes the investigations we have surveyed in this discussion. As can be seen, the dominant theme has been personal rather than institutional or social renewal.

Thus, overall it could be said that these investigations conclude that the charismatic experience becomes a matter of profound personal importance but has relatively little impact on attitudes toward issues of social justice.

Table 13.4 Research on Catholic characteristics investigating their value orientations

Researcher(s)	Date(s)	Research sample	Value orientation	Sociological model
Gerlach & Hine	1970	1 prayer group	Counterculture	Sectarian
Harrison	1974a, 1974b, 1975	1 prayer group	Renewal	Sectarian tendencies
Harper	1974	25 case histories	Renewal	Process model
Fichter	1974a, 1974b, 1975	155 prayer groups	Counterculture	Cult
Bord & Faulkner	1975	15 prayer groups	Renewal	None
McGuire	1972, 1974, 1975	7 prayer groups	Counterculture	Cognitive minority
Mawn	1975	6 prayer groups, 19 archdioceses	Renewal	Ecclesiola in ecclesia
Heirich	1977	1 prayer group	Renewal	Religious quest; encapsulation

Conclusions

14

Integrated Interpretation

C. S. Lewis, the well-known British writer, preached a sermon in the Mansfield College Chapel of Oxford University one Pentecost Sunday that provides a useful model for a considered understanding of the phenomenon of speaking in tongues.

He began by saying that glossolalia had often been an embarrassment and stumbling block to him, just as it had been for St. Paul, who had urged the first-century Christian church to turn its attention to more edifying gifts of the Holy Spirit. Yet, Lewis continued, one had to admit that even St. Paul boasted that he could speak in tongues better than anyone else. Lewis also noted that speaking in tongues had remained an *occasional* variety of religious experience throughout Christian history.

He further observed that approaching the phenomenon from one direction, a person could see it as an involuntary or even hysteric discharge of nervous excitement, but that, on the other hand, one should recognize that Jesus called on his disciples to expect Pentecost and, thus, such an experience was at the core of the birth-story of the Christian church. Lewis concluded: "It looks, therefore, as if we shall have to say that the very same phenomena which is sometimes not only natural but even pathological is at other times (or at least at one other time) the organ of the Holy Ghost" (1949, p. 17).

This double sidedness is not unique to glossolalia, or even to religious experience. Lewis mentioned love and lust, justice and revenge, aesthetic enjoyment and anxiety as other examples. In none of these pairs can a clear distinction be made either on behavioral or on physiological grounds. Love and lust end in the same act, that is, intercourse. The same is true of justice and revenge, that is, punishment. Only the experiencer can tell us whether she/he is anxious or thrilled during a given event. The body reacts in an identical manner to enjoyment and to fear.

Lewis concluded, quite correctly from our point of view, that the life of the emotions is "higher" than the life of the sensations. It is richer and more subtle. The sensations can mean many things. There is no simple one-to-one correspondence between emotions and sensations. As

Lewis states, "If the richer system is to be represented in the poorer at all, this can only be by giving each element in the poorer system more than one meaning" (p. 21).

He illustrated this by noting that if one translates from a language with a large vocabulary into one with a small vocabulary, then some words in the latter language must carry more than one meaning. Similarly, if one writes piano reductions of orchestral compositions, then the same piano notes will have to represent flutes at one time and violins at another!

Lewis's point here is critical to an understanding of the interrelationship of natural and supernatural interpretations of such an event as glossolalia. He suggested that "in each case what is happening in the lower medium can be understood only if we know the higher medium" (p. 22). Thus, for example, the piano arrangement of the symphony is one thing to the person who knows that it was originally written for and played by an orchestra and another thing to the person who hears it for the first time as a piano piece. The way in which we perceive a drawing provides another vivid example. We can understand pictures that are on a two-dimensional surface because we inhabit a three-dimensional world. The former, that is, drawings, are understood because of our prior knowledge of the latter, that is, three dimensional reality. Lewis noted that a creature who perceived only two dimensions might have difficulty in understanding what was meant by saying that a given drawing was a "house" or a "road." The creature might say, "But that is the same shape which you said earlier was a triangle or a straight line." And we might answer, "But that was then and this is now." The creature would not understand, however, because it would have had no acquaintance with anything above two dimensions.

Lewis suggested that just this dilemma in reasoning had characterized the dialogue about speaking in tongues. Glossolalics speak of deeper and richer meaning to the sounds they make, yet those who have not experienced such reality interpret them in terms of a lower model. As with the two dimensional creatures, there is an inability to perceive what is being said. The problem is somewhat circular. On the one hand, only as the higher is known can the lower be reinterpreted or understood in a new manner. Yet there is a dimension of truth to what those who have never experienced such a reality as glossolalia say about it. For them, speaking in tongues is speech that occurs in a world that is not constantly intruded upon by transempirical realities.

Thus, although what is apparent may have deeper meaning to some, there is still warrant for talking about its more mundane meaning from a less informed perspective.

In defense of the validity of an enriched perspective, such as that reported by glossolalics, Lewis coined the term "transposition." According to him, transposition occurs "whenever the higher reproduces itself in the lower" (p. 24). This is illustrated by the mind-body relationship. If one assumed a one-to-one correspondence between every mental event and a parallel brain event, an almost unbelievable complexity to the brain would be required. It is preferable to suggest that the brain responds in an adequate and, indeed, exquisite manner to the almost infiinite variety of self consciousness without there having to be a physical modification for each change in thought or emotion.

It should be noted that this implies an existence for the mind independent of the brain, just as it would imply an existence for God independent from the speech of the glossolalic. There is no way for the sceptic to see in behavior anything more than the limited elements of physical existence and, in fact, transposition does not imply the addition of any physiological element to the situation. It does imply, however, that the elements of a natural event embody meaning beyond themselves and incorporate a reality that is not apparent. It should be added that science would not disagree with this to the extent that research always involves seeking the reality beneath appearance.

Lewis further distinguished transposition from "symbolic," "sacramental," and "developmental" understandings of the interaction between the natural and the spiritual. The relationship between speech and writing is symbolic, in that there is no factual correspondence between the two. The relationship between the sun in a picture and the real sun is sacramental, in that one could not see the painted sun apart from the light of the real sun. Further, the developmental model implies that one thing turns into the other with the passage of time. In this regard, the natural act of eating would be assumed to blossom into the Lord's Supper simply as a function of a developmental process. Lewis contended that transposition was different from any of these. It implies a willingness to consider the possibility that a natural, or lower, form of existence has been taken over by a spiritual, or higher, mode and that the lower now embodies and expresses this in a true manner.

From one point of view, if Lewis should be taken seriously, there would be no need for a volume such as this in which a study of glossolalia by the social/behavior sciences is detailed. These sciences limit themselves to natural explanations and self-consciously bracket or exclude both their personal experience and the use of transempirical influences to explain events. According to Lewis's discussion of these matters, social/behavioral scientists should be thought of as those who approach such phenomena from a "lower" perspective and who would thus, *prima facie,* be unable to perceive events save through these less informed understandings. They cannot put the situation into a new or higher perspective.

Yet perhaps a more cautious evaluation of Lewis's ideas should be made. Lewis is a persuasive writer. Before we accept totally his contention that only those who have experienced a "higher" dimension can perceive its presence in a "lower" dimension, for example, God speaking through human voices, we should, however, recognize that Lewis's argument resembles the romantic protests that have been lodged against scientific endeavors for almost two hundred years. Those protests, it should be noted, have not always been in the name of religion! They have also come from humanists of every stripe who insisted that "the whole is more than the sum of its parts" and that there is an authenticity to subjective reports of everyday experience. William Wordsworth spoke for these persons in his poem "The Tables Turned":

> One impulse from a vernal wood
> May teach you more of man,
> Of moral evil and of good
> Than all the sages can.
> Sweet is the lore which Nature brings;
> Our meddling intellect
> Mis-shapes the beauteous forms of things;
> —We murder to dissect.

In fact, this protest is part of a centuries-long contest between religion and science. It did not originate with the Romantics of the early nineteenth century who were appalled at the advance of technology and the application of the physical sciences to human experience.

Galileo thought he had solved the problem with his two roads to truth, science and revelation. However, he merely complicated the issue and posed the agenda for succeeding generations by suggesting that individual experience could not be trusted and that science had to be based on controlled observation: personal experiences of beauty, love, awe, and so on, were secondary and irrelevant for understanding what was *really* happening. Of course, what happened long before the present event, that is, first causes, and what would happen in the future, that is final causes, could only be comprehended by revelation—not science. In these matters, personal assurance of salvation was legitimate.

However, intellectual history shows that Galileo's two roads to truth became one. Science, with its emphasis on immediate causation, has preempted other forms of knowledge. Lewis might well call this development "giving knowledge over to a lower medium." Many scientists would respond by referring to the law of parsimony and suggest that as long as events can be explained in terms of their scientific laws, there is no need to refer matters to a "higher" mode of understanding. They would not see this as arbitrary or deceptive. Glossolalia would be a natural event happening in the here and now. There would be no inherent requirement for a transcendent explanation unless its form or its effect was obviously outside the bounds of the scientific approach. They would agree with Laplace, the eighteenth century scientist who, when asked by Napoleon what part God had played in his theory of planetary motion, responded "I had no need of that hypothesis" (Barbour, 1966, p. 42).

Thus, for example, the fact that the speech of glossolalics cannot be demonstrated to be a language is proof enough for many researchers to insist that it is gibberish. They would suggest that if the believers continue to insist that the words have meaning, they should attempt to divine that meaning in a manner with which everyone would agree and to find an extant language that is similar to the words being spoken.

This is quite a convincing argument. It does not totally discount the glossolalics' claim, and it remains open to the possibility that a proof can be found. It should be noted, however, that this approach inadvertently tends to limit us to a single road to truth, that is, the scientific. If glossolalics attempt to find such proof, it is tantamount to saying that someday speaking in tongues will meet scientific standards of validation. Those who suggest that all the world's languages have not yet been studied and that some time in the future a language will be found to match the tongues are accommodating their claims to this scientific model. Even those who insist that glossolalia is God's language and does not follow human rules are subtly conforming to this paradigm.

Lewis would decry this accommodation. He would propose that validating glossolalia as a known language or even a language similar in structure to known grammar would not prove "transposition," that is, a lower structure being penetrated with higher meaning. We are inclined to agree at the same time that we as social/behavioral scientists accord legitimacy to the endeavor to understand these phenomena in an empirical way. Nevertheless, we acknowledge the limitations imposed by our methods and assumptions, and we accord a "transposed" dimension of meaning that comes only through personal experience. In fact, we confess to a knowledge of glossolalia from this subjective perspective also. Thus, our integrated understanding of glossolalia includes a willingness to accept individual reports about the meaning and purpose of the experience even though we emphasize the objective conclusions of scientific theorizing and research.

With these considerations in mind, we shall now summarize our conclusions and propose a paradigm for viewing glossolalia within Troeltsch's (1911/1931) rubric of "mysticism."

As will be recalled, this book adopted the model proposed by Hutch (1980) in suggesting that glossolalia could be considered to be *anomalous, aberrant,* or *extraordinary* behavior. The investigation of glossolalia from these three points of view by social/behavioral scientists provided the basis for a major portion of the book.

Hutch (1980) defined *anomalous* behavior as that which is significantly different in degree and kind from usual behavior. So, in this case, the "language" of glossolalics has been studied in an effort to assess whether or how it differs from ordinary speech. Further, *aberrant* behavior was defined as behavior that reflects personality differences at least or emotional disturbance at most. So, glossolalics have been studied in an effort to assess how they differ from other persons. Finally, *extraordinary* behavior was defined as that which was unusual or atypical for the individual or for the culture. So, in this case, glossolalics have been studied in an effort to assess whether their behavior was determined by the setting, the mind set, or the subculture of which they were a part.

In regard to the first perspective, that is, glossolalia as *anomalous* behavior, initial attempts systematically to study glossolalic speech were not investigations of persons who were religious. These were psychical and psychiatric studies, such as those of Flournoy (1900/1963) and Jung (1902/1970). Both of these authors noted similarities of glossolalic speech to known languages (Sanskrit and French, respectively) and concluded that the verbiage was determined, in part, by the linguistic background of the speakers. During the same period Richet (1905) reported a case of a person who, while in trance, was able to write long sentences in Greek—a language she had never studied. Richet coined the term "xenoglossia" for this phenomenon, although a more correct term would be "xenographia" as the material was written, not spoken.

These studies of the "language" of glossolalia provoked several attempts at taxonomies, the most inclusive of which was that of May (1956). Here, as in the studies noted earlier, the conclusions were not based on religious glossolalics but on the speech of shamans in non-Western cultures. May ranked glossolalic speech along a continuum and placed xenoglossia and ermeneglossia (the interpretation of tongues) at the top of the list.

Although this taxonomy applied to glossolalic-type speech in both secular and religious settings, it provided a basis for more focused linguistic investigations of Christian tongue speaking, such as that conducted by Samarin (1972c) and others. Two specific questions have been addressed by these researchers: (1) "Is glossolalia a *known* language?" and (2) "Is glossolalia a language from any point of view?"

Although many persons from the time of the New Testament to the present have claimed to hear *known* languages when people spoke in tongues, up to now these claims have not been independently verified. It may well be that linguists who have analyzed these speeches are not acquainted with all of the over three thousand languages in the world, as some apologists have argued, but experienced judges—in such studies as those of Goodman (1972c) and Anderson (1979)—have found evidence for no more than an occasional word in any known language. The only exception to this has been the unexplained, but verified, ability of an American housewife to converse in Swedish while in trance (Stevenson, 1974)—a phenomenon quite different from the claims of some religious glossolalics who have insisted that the ability was given them in order that they could spread the gospel! Thus, xenoglossia has not, as yet, been validated by social/behavioral scientists.

The question of whether glossolalia has the characteristics of "language" is a related, but somewhat different, question. Even those who do not claim xenoglossia insist they are speaking a language—even if it is

God's language. They assert that the interpretations others give are of speech that has form and meaning. Although glossolalics seem to adopt a pattern that is individually unique, there does not seem to be a vocabulary that can be identified, nor are interpretations of such speech word-for-word translations as Wolfram (1966) has clearly demonstrated. Samarin (1972c) concluded that, overall, glossolalia does not meet the criteria for language, in that it does not have a systematic syntax and it cannot be used to communicate about communication. Nevertheless, in another study Samarin (1972c) found that, although no cognitive content was communicated, a definite sense of emotional meaning was understood.

Turning next to glossolalia as *aberrant* behavior, the first issue that was addressed concerned the psychological meaning of the experience. Some of the themes were suggested early by such authors as James (1902/1958) and Flournoy (1900/1963), who concluded that the phenomenon reflected automatic behavior under the control of overdeveloped subliminal regions of the mind to which the tongue speaker had regressed because of unsettled memories of the past. In contrast to this somewhat negative point of view, Lombard (1907) opined that glossolalia could have positive value, in that it broke down previous personality structures and allowed for superior reorganization. Both points of view found support in later investigations.

Pfister (1912), a compatriot of Freud, agreed with his mentor that the speaking in tongues (which he observed in a patient) was evidence of a psychic complex to be treated. A contemporary psychoanalyst, Julius Laffal (Laffal, Monahan, & Richman, 1974) agreed with Pfister and concluded that glossolalic speech was meaningful, in that it expressed inhibited impulses and thoughts. Other analytic thinkers, such as Pruyser (1978), have interpreted the experience more benignly but, even they perceived glossolalia as evidence of narcissistic self-preoccupation.

Jungian theorists have tended to take the more positive point of view. Kelsey (1964) noted that Jung saw glossolalia as preparation for personality integration, in that the experience put one into contact with the collective unconscious in which the religious impulse was as basic as any other. Vivier (1968) took this one step further by asserting that speaking in tongues was a preeminent means by which one could awaken this religious dynamism. Later, Lovekin (1977), suggested the experience was deepening rather than regressive.

Ego psychologists have equivocated between the two standpoints. Alland (1961) concluded that the experience, although regressive, could be "in the service of the ego," provided it had an intellectual, as opposed to a totally emotional, component to it. Others, such as Lapsley and Simpson (1964b), have interpreted the experience as indicative of deep conflict that was being resolved in a dissociative manner. Pattison (1968) offered a combined viewpoint by suggesting that the cultural context was as important as the psychological state. He further distinguished between

"playful" (conflict free) and "serious" (conflictual) glossolalia and concluded that the differences between the positive and negative functions
of the experience could be understood by means of this model.

Most recently, Brende and Rinsley (1979) have contended that glossolalia only occurs in borderline personalities with weak egoes who are
attempting to regain control of themselves through the experience. In a
sense, speaking in tongues is a healthy sign, in that it gives power in the
personality over to the good part (God) and indicates healing has begun.
However, because this theory was based on research among mentally ill
adolescents, there is some question as to the applicability of the model to
more "normal," nonhospitalized glossolalics who may not have such ego
weakness. Pattison's (1968) advice that the cultural context be considered
is important to keep in mind.

This leads us to a more detailed summary of the findings about individual differences among those who do and who do not become glossolalic.
Although Cutten (1927) postulated that glossolalics were characterized by hyperexcitability, inferior intelligence, and illiteracy, these findings have been supported only partially by the research. Smith (1977), in
one of the more recent investigations of these issues, concluded that
tongue speakers were less intelligent and less educated than nontongue
speakers and that they were higher on the tendency toward "energy discharge," yet showed no greater tendency toward "susceptibility to emotional upheaval." In contrast, Bradfield (1979) found glossolalics to be
better educated than the general population. Thus, Cutten's (1927) contentions have yet to be proven unequivocably.

In regard to the life situation of those who speak in tongues, there
seems to be solid evidence that they are in the midst of a crisis at the time
the experience first occurs. Although Stanley, Bartlett, and Moyle's (1978)
research in Australia lent no support to this thesis, the great bulk of
previous studies (Bradfield, 1979; Hoffman, 1975/1976; Kildahl, 1972;
Mawn, 1975; Vivier, 1960) reported that personal stress was a precursor
of glossolalia.

Family background has been a focus of some studies. Although glossolalia occurs more often among those whose parents were glossolalic, the
frequency of the practice seems to be related more to personal religiosity
than to parental example (Malony, Zwaanstra, and Ramsey, 1972). However, the more serious type of glossolalia (according to Pattison's, 1968,
model) has not been found to be associated with speaking in tongues
among those who were going against parental example (Pavelsky, Hart &
Malony, 1975) as might be expected.

Comparisons of the personality traits of glossolalics with those of nonglossolalics have yielded somewhat confusing results. Vivier (1960) found
glossolalics to be more neurotic, self-effacing, and impulsive but less suggestible. However, Kildahl (1972) suggested that although glossolalics
were not lower in general mental health, they were more dependent, submissive, and suggestible. Rarick and Malony (1981) found support for

these conclusions among classical Pentecostals. In a study of a commune population, Richardson (1973) found tongue speakers to be lower on defensiveness, self-confidence, self-control, dominance, endurance, and order than the average person. Thus, over a variety of glossolalic groups, it appears that they are more suggestible, extroverted, and intrinsically religiously oriented, although they are not less mentally healthy than nonglossolalics.

This finding of absence of psychopathology among glossolalics is characteristic of a number of studies, although the presence of mental disturbance before or during the experience had been hypothesized by numerous theorists (Cutten, 1927; Mackie, 1921; I. J. Martin, 1960). The research to date has found none of the glossolalic groups more abnormal or hysteric and, in some cases, glossolalics have been found to be *more* mentally healthy than the general population (Alland, 1961; Gerrard, Gerrard, & Tellegen, 1966; Kildahl, 1972; Lovekin & Malony, 1977).

The third perspective suggested by Hutch (1980) for studying glossolalia was that it was *extraordinary* behavior. Issues discussed under this heading included the state of mind, the socioeconomic situation, and the immediate environment of those who spoke in tongues.

Efforts to speak in tongues have been variously interpreted as desires to participate in rites of initiation (Ranaghan, 1974), a token of group acceptance (Lapsley & Simpson, 1964a), a rite of passage (Hutch, 1980), and an act of commitment (Hine, 1970). The most useful paradigm for understanding the stance of the glossolalic is that of Holm (1978) who described the experience as "structured role enactment." Using the theories of his fellow countryman, Helmut Sundén, he depicted glossolalia as similar to all religious experience in which a person adopts a role out of his/her religious tradition and assumes that God will reciprocate as in the past. Therefore, the individual plays the role of one who is possessed by the Holy Spirit and is confirmed in this presumption.

The environmental setting of glossolalia has also been studied. Numerous studies have confirmed the conclusion that the experience typically occurs when one has been brought by friends and they are present (Gerlach & Hine, 1970; Harrison, 1972; Samarin, 1972c). Although reports of becoming glossolalic by oneself are not uncommon, group settings in which there is encouragement and suggestion are more typical. Even teaching and practice are fairly common (S. B. Clark, 1973; Samarin, 1972c). The guidance is often quite specific and direct. Frequently, this results in very stylized, ritualized, and expected speaking in tongues. This has led Samarin (1969b/1972c), among others, to conclude that glossolalia is, above all, a learned phenomenon. Nevertheless, it should be noted that although the group experience is transformative, conformity is never total as the Lovekin and Malony (1977) study vividly illustrated. In that study, almost a third of those attending a seminar for receiving the experience failed to receive it.

In an analysis of the factors that provoked persons to remain in groups where glossolalia was practiced, Gerlach and Hine (1968) delineated five factors that included a nontraditional organizational structure, an ideology of participation and power, and a perception that the group was under attack from the outside. These were over and above the experience of glossolalia itself. Environmental factors such as these provoke intense commitment and involvement.

It was noted that possession by God was a universal perception among glossolalics but that they differed considerably in regard to whether they claimed or admitted to being in an altered state of consciousness or trance. Goodman (1972c), along with several other scholars, asserted that glossolalia always involved trance and sought to validate her claim by analysis of the phonetic structure of glossolalic speeches. Attempts to validate physiologically such changes of consciousness (e.g., Palmer, 1966; Pavelsky, Hart, & Malony, 1975; Spanos & Hewitt, 1979) have not been successful, however. Samarin (1972b) has taken the position that Goodman (1969b) was wrong and has proposed a sociolinguistic rather than a neurophysiological explanation for the phenomenon. His chief contention has been that glossolalia is learned behavior and that it is not necessarily accompanied by any altered mental state. There is warrant, however, in spite of the lack of firm evidence to date, to agree with Goodman that the experience does involve some change in consciousness because tongue speakers typically claim they are not in total control and because susceptibility to change in mental status may be a perfectly natural ability that is distributed normally in the population. Swanson (1978) offered a model of trance in everyday life that supports this point of view.

Turning next to the socioeconomic situation out of which glossolalics come, the deprivation hypothesis has dominated the research to date. It is at this point that the frequently noted distinctions among classical Pentecostals and neo-Pentecostals should be recalled. Although the Holiness movements of the late nineteenth century, which culminated in the establishment of Pentecostal churches in the twentieth century, probably appealed predominantly to those of the lower social classes, the neo-Pentecostals of mainline and Catholic churches, which have appeared since the 1950s, did not. Nor is it true today that current members of the older Pentecostal churches are necessarily from the lower strata of society. Currently, there seems to be a social and economic mix of persons who are glossolalic, and the contention that the experience was provoked primarily as a compensation for lack of achievement in society is not valid today, though it may well have been true for classical Pentecostalism at the turn of the century (Anderson's *Vision of the Disinherited*, 1979).

Glock's (1973) taxonomy of types of deprivation provided a helpful means by which to distinguish the sect-type Pentecostal movements of the early 1900s from recent neo-Pentecostal movements in which participants remained within their Protestant and Catholic churches. The differences between the two can be understood in terms of economic deprivation among the former and psychic/meaning deprivation in the latter. Bradfield's (1979) research on the motives for glossolalia among the Full Gospel Businessmen's Fellowship International (FGBMFI) validated this distinction. Here participants tended to remain within their former churches and expressed feelings of loss of meaning rather than economic difficulties.

McGuire (1975) and others have reported a tendency for glossolalics to feel culturally isolated. This is less a sign of economic deprivation (discussed earlier) than a sense of the breakdown of the structures that hold society together. This crisis mentality seems to be characteristic of both older and younger glossolalics. It reflects, according to Reidy and Richardson (1978), order deprivation, in which persons are anxious about the state of their world. Speaking in tongues is one form of redefinition of the reality in which one lives. It is interesting to note in this regard, however, that such uneasiness with society has not typically resulted in greater social action after becoming glossolalic, as Reidy and Richardson (1978) have noted. In fact, Hine (1970) has suggested that this concern for social order may be more a result than a cause of the experience because in her studies very few persons reported such dissatisfaction before they became glossolalic.

This leads to a consideration of other perceptual set variables that have been thought to provoke glossolalia. Neo-Pentecostals have found their religious experiences in their churches to be shallow and devoid of enthusiasm. This is a similar feeling to that expressed by classical Pentecostals earlier in this century. However, neo-Pentecostals have tended to seek this new depth in their experience through fellowship groups outside their churches and have attempted to reform and revitalize their denominations without leaving them.

Mawn (1975) in his study of Catholic Pentecostals termed this a sense of "transcendency deprivation." Although Pruyser (1978) concluded this was a sign of immature self-preoccupation, Haglof (1971) suggested it was but an indication of maturation in which persons were developing in the spiritual dimension of their lives.

It is from this perspective of the search for more immediate religious experience, that is, transcendency deprivation, that we feel glossolalia is best understood. In our opinion, this sense of need is grounded in a basic human propensity (cf. Luckman, 1967) that breaks through social structures again and again throughout human history. It is expressed in a variety of ways, including glossolalia, and a variety of settings, including the Christian church. In essence, these expressions are examples of Troeltsch's (1911/1931) third religious type—mysticism. It is our contention, along with Thompson (1977), that glossolalia is more appropriately considered in these terms than under the rubric of sect as has been the case with much past theorizing.

GLOSSOLALIA AS MYSTICISM

Although this is not widely recognized, Ernst Troeltsch in *The Social Teachings of the Christian Churches* (1911/1931) suggested a threefold, not a twofold, model for understanding religious groups. In addition to the well-known typology of church-sect, he proposed mysticism—a type based on inward, immediate experience of the transcendent that functioned to legitimize participation in religious institutions. Troeltsch placed glossolalia under this rubric:

> It is to this Mysticism that the so-called "Enthusiasm" of the Primitive Christian Church, a large part of the "spiritual gifts," the speaking with tongues, the power of exorcism, the whole of spiritual activity, belongs; this phenomenon recurs again and again, in the Christian sect-movement, down to the present day, bringing home with great power the redemptive energy of the Gospel to the individual soul. (1911/1931, p. 732)

Taking his cue from Troeltsch, Thompson (1977) concluded that Catholic charismatics exemplified this type of religious expression. We are convinced that this model is comprehensive enough to encompass most, if not all, contemporary expressions of glossolalia among classical Pentecostal and neo-Pentecostal groups. We feel it is a much better category than sect for understanding these phenomena, even though historically certain groupings of glossolalics have taken on sect-type qualities.

In a subsequent article, Thompson (1980, pp. 31–38) constructed an outline of Troeltsch's (1911/1931) typology, which we reproduce here in part in Table 14.1 because of its clarity in depicting some of the issues among the types.

Other categories on which Thompson (1980) compares these types are: New Testament foundations, attitudes toward ascetism, moral theory, doctrines of salvation, and attitudes toward group participation.

Of course, pure types never exist in reality, but there is ample warrant for suggesting that glossolalics most nearly fit the mysticism type in their experience and in their structure. In fact, Pattison & Casey (1969), who make no reference to Troeltsch, boldly entitled their essay "Glossolalia: A Contemporary *mystical* Experience" (emphasis added). Although, they have at times been pushed to form new organizations, most often glossolalics have been motivated to revitalize the groups of which they were members and have been content to reinstate experience as a prime form of worship.

This "wider form of mysticism," as Troeltsch was wont to call it, has traditionally used the religious structure in which it found itself and has sought renewal rather than revolution. As such, it expresses what we believe to be an innate human need to find meaning and vitality through contact with the divine. Although glossolalics have not been known to emphasize theological innovations or to initiate novel social action, they have reinstituted "experience" as the heart of religion. Troeltsch (1911/1931) stated it best when he said:

Table 14.1 Outline of church, sect, and mysticism typology

Types	Features		
	Membership	Participants	Self-conception
Church	Ascribed	All members of society	Objective holiness in institution as repository of grace
	Infant baptism	Clerical-laity division	Universal and inclusive
			Hierarchical
Sect	Achieved	Lower classes	Subjective holiness in perfection of members
	Voluntary commitment based on conversion	Lay	Exclusive, "the elect"
	Adult baptism		Democratic
Mysticism	Voluntary based on inner experience	Middle classes	Ad hoc groups of loosely knit individuals "invisible church" of all who have experienced a "new birth"
		Lay	Noninclusive and nonexclusive
			Democratic

Based on **Troeltsch, 1911/1931.**

The vitality of the religious sense, however, when it is faced with objectified religion, easily and often develops mystical characteristics. It expresses itself in ecstasy and frenzy, in visions and in hallucinations, in subjective religious experience and "inwardness," in concentration upon the purely interior and emotional side of religious experience. Certainly these visions are rarely creative in the sense of imparting fresh knowledge; they are almost always expansions and interpretations of the common faith, as was the case with the spiritual gifts of the early Christians, and with the innumerable visions and prophecies of mediaeval recluses and saints, an experience which has been repeated all through the centuries, down to the present day. (p. 731)

We feel that such an interpretation satisfies both the concerns of C. S. Lewis, with which this chapter began, and the canons of the social/behavior sciences, which have been our major concern in this volume. Although such a "mystical" model does not settle, by any means, the issues that such sciences have addressed, it does place glossolalia in a context that takes the experience seriously and treats the phenomenon as a valid object of study by the human sciences. We agree with Garrett (1974) that such an approach avoids the errors of reductionism and functionalism in which glossolalia would be presumed to be explainable in purely natural terms or understood as simply a cultural expression of psychological dynamics. We affirm the stance of "phenomenological numenalism" (Garrett, 1974, pp. 173–176) whereby human needs, transcendent reality, and religious experience are all assumed to be substantively real and worthy of serious study. We also opine that this approach explains why glossolalia is an essential feature of the social groups in which the personality, value, and behavioral changes we have reported occur. Although it has been impossible to isolate the unique contribution that glossolalia makes to the group impact of these experiences, we yet feel that whereas the group may be the necessary, speaking in tongues is the sufficient, cause of these changes. This we say in spite of our inability to isolate a glossolalia effect in our research (Lovekin & Malony, 1977).

A final word: compilations such as this volume should always be considered state-of-the-art reports. Even as we publish, we acknowledge that the field has moved beyond us. This is as it should be. If we have contributed in part to this development by bringing these materials together, we shall be satisfied. We hope to be a part of that future which, we hope, will see an even more enlightened understanding of these phenomena.

References

Aaron, W. *Straight: A heterosexual talks about his homosexual past*. New York: Doubleday, 1972.

Aberle, D. F. A note on relative deprivation theory as applied to millenarian and other cult movements. In W. A. Lessa & E. Z. Vogt (Eds.), *Reader in Comparative Religion*. New York: Harper, 1965.

Adams, R. L., & Fox, R. J. "Mainlining Jesus: The new trip." *Society*, 1972, *9*(4), 50–56.

Aita, M. J., & Nye, J. *Catholic Pentecostals: An example of "over-conforming" deviants*. Paper presented at the meeting of the Society for the Scientific Study of Religion and the Religious Research Association, Chicago, October 28–30, 1977.

Alland, A. "Possession in a revivalist Negro church." *Journal for the Scientific Study of Religion*, 1962, *1*, 204–213.

Anderson, R. M. *Vision of the disinherited: The making of American Pentecostalism*. New York: Oxford University Press, 1979.

Anonymous. *Gay liberation*. Tustin, Calif.: PTL Publications, 1975.

Bach, M. *The inner ecstasy: The power and the glory of speaking in tongues*. Nashville: Abingdon, 1969.

Bahr, H. M., Bartel, L. F., & Chadwick, B. A. "Orthodoxy, activism and the salience of religion." *Journal for the Scientific Study of Religion*, 1971, *10*, 69–75.

Barbour, I. G. *Issues in Science and Religion*. New York: Harper & Row, 1966.

Basham, D. *Face Up with a Miracle*. Monroeville, Pa.: Whitaker Books, 1971.

Beck, S. J., Beck, A. G., Levitt, E. E., & Melish, H. B. *Rorschach's Test: I. Basic Processes (3rd Edition)*. New York: Grune and Stratton, 1961.

Becker, H. *Systematic sociology*. New York: Wiley, 1932.

Beckman, D. M. "Trance: from Africa to Pentecostalism." *Concordia Theological Monthly*, January 1974, *45*, 11–26.

Bell, A. P., & Weinberg, M. S. *Homosexualities*. New York: Simon & Schuster, 1978.

Bennett, D. J. *Nine o'clock in the morning*. Plainfield, N.J.: Logos International, 1970.

Berger, P. L. *The Social Reality of Religion*. London: Faber and Faber, 1969.

Blank, G., & Blank, R. *Ego Psychology: Theory and Practice*. New York: Columbia University Press, 1974.

Bobon, J. "Contribution à l'étude des phénomènes régressifs en psychopathologie: Les pseudo-glossolalies ludiques et magiques." *Journal Belge de Neurologie et de Psychiatrie,* 1947, *47,* 327–395.

Boisen, A. T. *Religion in crises and custom: A sociological and psychological study.* New York: Harper, 1955.

Boisen, A. T. "Economic distress and religious experience: A study of the Holy Rollers." *Psychiatry,* 1939, *2,* 185–194.

Bord, R. J., & Faulkner, J. E. "Religiosity and secular attitudes: The case of Catholic Pentecostals." *Journal for the Scientific Study of Religion,* 1975, *14,* 257–270.

Bourguignon, E. The self, the behavioral environment, and the theory of spirit possession. In M. E. Spiro (Ed.), *Context and meaning in cultural anthropology.* New York: Free Press, 1965.

Brackbill, Y., and Little, K. B. "Guessing the meaning of foreign words." *Journal of Abnormal and Social Psychology.* 1957, *54,* 312–319.

Bradfield, C. D. *Neo-Pentecostalism: A sociological assessment.* Washington: University Press of America, 1979.

Bradfield, C. D. An investigation of neo-Pentecostalism (Doctoral dissertation, American University, 1975). *Dissertation Abstracts International,* 1975, *36,* 4031A–4032A. (University Microfilms No. 75–28,932.)

Brende, J. O. Speaking in tongues: A psychological study. In C. L. Rousey (Ed.), *Psychiatric assessment by speech and hearing behavior.* Springfield, Ill.: Charles C. Thomas, 1974.

Brende, J. O., & Rinsley, D. B. "Borderline disorder, altered states of consciousness, and glossolalia." *Journal of the American Academy of Psychoanalysis,* 1979, *7,* 165–188.

Brooks, J. P. *The Divine Church.* El Dorado Springs, Mo.: Witt, 1891, 1960.

Bryant, E. T., & O'Connell, D. "A phonemic analysis of nine samples of glossolalic speech." *Psychonomic Science,* 1971, *22,* 81–83.

Cato, J. D. The aftercare preferences of drug users and the relationship of these preferences to religious orientation and to a manifest personality need (Doctoral dissertation, New York University, 1968). *Dissertation Abstracts International,* 1970, *30,* 2869A–2870A. (University Microfilms No. 70–724.)

Christenson, L. *A message to the charismatic movement.* Minneapolis: Dimension Books, 1972.

Clark, E. T. *The small sects in America* (rev. ed.). New York: Abingdon-Cokesbury Press, 1949. (Originally published, 1937.)

Clark, S. B. *The Life in the Spirit Seminars: Team Manual (3rd Edition).* South Bend, Ind.: Charismatic Renewal Services, 1973.

Clark, S. B. *Finding new life in the Spirit: A guidebook for the life in the Spirit seminars* (2nd ed.). Notre Dame, Ind.: Charismatic Renewal Services, 1972a.

Clark, S. B. (Ed.). *Team manual for the life in the Spirit seminars* (2nd ed.). Notre Dame, Ind.: Charismatic Renewal Services, 1972b.

Clark, S. B. *Team manual for the life in the Spirit seminars* (1st ed.). Notre Dame, Ind.: Charismatic Renewal Services, 1971.

Clark, W. H., Malony, H. N., Daane, J., & Tippett, A. *Religious Experience: Its nature and function in the human psyche.* Springfield, Ill.: Charles C. Thomas, 1973.

Clow, H. K. Ritual, belief, and the social context: An analysis of a southern Pentecostal sect (Doctoral dissertation, Duke University, 1976). *Dissertation Abstracts International,* 1977, *37,* 4449A. (University Microfilms No. 77–1059.)

Coulson, J. E., & Johnson, R. W. "Glossolalia and internal-external locus of control." *Journal of Psychology and Theology*, 1977, *5*, 312–317.

Cutten, G. B. *Speaking with tongues: Historically and psychologically considered.* New Haven, Conn.: Yale University, 1927.

Davidson, J. D. "Religious belief as an independent variable." *Journal for the Scientific Study of Religion*, 1972, *11*, 65–75.

Dearman, M. V. "Christ and conformity: A study of Pentecostal values." *Journal for the Scientific Study of Religion*, 1974, *13*, 437–453.

Dearman, M. V. Do holiness sects socialize in dominant values?: An empirical inquiry (Doctoral dissertation, University of Oregon, 1972). *Dissertation Abstracts International*, 1973, *33*, 5296A–5297A. (University Microfilms No. 73–7879.)

Deikman, A. J. "De-automatization and the mystic experience." *Psychiatry*, 1966a, *29*, 324–338.

Deikman, A. J. "Implications of experimentally induced contemplative meditation." *Journal of Nervous and Mental Disease*, 1966b, *142*, 101–116.

De Vol, T. I. "Ecstatic Pentecostal prayer and meditation." *Journal of Religion and Health*, 1974, *13*, 285–288.

Directory of Catholic Charismatic Prayer Groups. South Bend, Ind.: Charismatic Communication Center, University of Notre Dame, annual.

Du Plessis, D. J. *The Spirit bade me go: The astounding move of God in the denominational churches (Rev. Ed.).* Plainfield, N.J.: Logos International, 1970. (Originally published, 1961.)

Durkheim, E. *Suicide: A study in sociology* (J. A. Spoulding and G. Simpson, Trans.). New York: Free Press, 1951. (Originally published, 1897.)

Earle, J. R., Knudsen, D. D., & Shriver, D. W. *Spindles and spires: A re-study of religion and social change in Gastonia.* Atlanta: John Knox Press, 1976.

Eliade, M. *Shamanism: Archaic techniques of ecstasy.* Princeton, N.J.: Princeton University Press, 1964. (Originally published, 1951.)

Elinson, H. "The implications of Pentecostal religion for intellectualism, politics, and race relations." *American Journal of Sociology*, 1965, *70*, 403–415.

English, H. B., & English, A. C. *A Comprehensive Dictionary of Psychological and Psychoanalytical Terms—A Guide to Usage.* New York: David McKay, 1958.

Episcopal Church, Diocese of California, Division of Pastoral Services, Study Commission on Glossolalia, Preliminary Report, 1963. Reprinted in F. McDonnell (Ed.), *Presence, Power, Praise: Documents on the Charismatic Renewal, Vol. 2.* Collegeville, Minn.: Liturgical Press, 1980, 71–95.

Festinger, L. *A Theory of Cognitive Dissonance.* Evanston, Ill.: Row, Peterson, 1957.

Festinger, L., Riecken, H. W., & Schachter, S. *When prophecy fails.* Minneapolis: University of Minnesota Press, 1956.

Fichter, J. H. "The trend to spiritual narcissism." *Commonweal*, March 17, 1978, 169–173.

Fichter, J. H. *The Catholic cult of the Paraclete.* New York: Sheed & Ward, 1975.

Fichter, J. H. "Liberal and conservative Catholic Pentecostals." *Social Compass*, 1974a, *21*, 303–310.

Fichter, J. H. *Organization man in the church.* Cambridge, Mass.: Schenkman, 1974b.

Fichter, J. H. "Pentecostals: Comfort vs. awareness." *America*, September 1, 1973, 114–116.

Finch, J. G. "God-inspired or self-induced?" *Christian Herald,* 1964, *87,* 12–13, 17–19.

Flournoy, T. *From India to the Planet Mars: A Study of a Case of Somnambulism with Glossolalia.* New Hyde Park: New York University, 1963. (Originally published, 1900.)

Ford, J. M. *Which way for Catholic Pentecostals?* New York: Harper & Row, 1976.

Frank, J. D. *Persuasion and Healing.* Baltimore: Johns Hopkins Press, 1961.

Freud, S. *Psychoanalysis and faith: The letters of Sigmund Freud and Oscar Pfister* (H. Meng & E. L. Freud, Eds.; E. Mosbacher, Trans.). New York: Basic Books, 1963. (Originally published, 1910.)

Garrett, W. R. "Troublesome transcendence: The supernatural in the scientific study of religion." *Sociological Analysis,* 1974, *35,* 167–180.

Gerlach, L. P. Pentecostalism: Revolution or counter-revolution. In I. I. Zaretsky & M. P. Leone (Eds.), *Religious movements in contemporary America.* Princeton, N.J.: Princeton University Press, 1974.

Gerlach, L. P., & Hine, V. H. *People, power, change: Movements of social transformation.* Indianapolis: Bobbs-Merrill, 1970.

Gerlach, L. P., & Hine, V. H. "Five factors crucial to the growth and spread of a modern religious movement." *Journal for the Scientific Study of Religion,* 1968, *7,* 23–40.

Gerrard, N. L. Churches of the stationary poor in southern Appalachia. In J. D. Photiadis & H. K. Schwarzweller (Eds.), *Change in rural Appalachia: Implications for action programs.* Philadelphia: University of Pennsylvania Press, 1970.

Gerrard, N. L., Gerrard, L. B., & Tellegen, A. *Scrabble Creek folks: Part II mental health.* Unpublished manuscript. Morris Harvey College, Charleston, W.V., 1966.

Gibbons, D., & De Jarnette, J. "Hypnotic susceptibility and religious experience." *Journal for the Scientific Study of Religion,* 1972, *11,* 152–156.

Gilbert, E. J. Some personality correlates of certain religious beliefs, attitudes, practices, and experiences in students attending a fundamentalist Pentecostal church college. (Doctoral dissertation, University of Tennessee, 1972). *Dissertation Abstracts International,* 1972, *33,* 1817A. (University Microfilms No. 72–27,466.)

Gill, M. M., & Brenman, M. *Hypnosis and related states: Psychoanalytic studies in regression.* New York: International Universities Press, 1959.

Gilmore, S. K. "Personality differences between high and low dogmatism groups of Pentecostal believers." *Journal for the Scientific Study of Religion,* 1968, *8,* 161–164.

Glock, C. Y. On the origin and evolution of religious groups. In C. Y. Glock (Ed.), *Religion in sociological perspective: Essays in the empirical study of religion.* Belmont, Calif.: Wadsworth, 1973.

Glock, C. Y. The role of deprivation in the origin and evolution of religious groups. In R. Lee & M. Marty (Eds.), *Religion and social conflict.* New York: Oxford University Press, 1964.

Goldman-Eisler, F. "Speech analysis and mental processes." *Language and Speech,* 1958, *1,* 59–75.

Goldschmidt, W. R. Class denominationalism in rural churches." *American Journal of Sociology,* 1944, *49,* 348–355.

Gonsalvez, H. E. The theology and psychology of glossolalia (Doctoral dissertation, Northwestern University, 1978). *Dissertation Abstracts International*, 1979, *39*, 6178A–6179A. (University Microfilms No. 79–07,879.)

Goodman, F. D. "Triggering of altered states of consciousness as group event: A new case from Yucatan." *Confinia Psychiatrica* (Basel), 1980, *23*(1), 26–34.

Goodman, F. D. Prognosis: A new religion? In I. I. Karetsky & M. P. Leone (Eds.), *Religious Movements in Contemporary America*. Princeton, N.J.: Princeton University Press, 1977a.

Goodman, F. D. Disturbances in the Apostolic Church: A trance-based upheaval in Yucatan. In F. D. Goodman, J. Henney, & E. J. Pressel (Eds.), *Trance, Healing and Hallucination: Three Field Studies in Religious Experience*. New York: Wiley, 1974b.

Goodman, F. D. Glossolalia and hallucination in Pentecostal congregations." *Psychiatria Clinica* (Basel), 1973, *6*(2), 97–103.

Goodman, F. D. "Altered mental state vs. 'style of discourse.' Reply to Samarin." *Journal for the Scientific Study of Religion*, 1972a, *11*, 297–299.

Goodman, F. D. "Speaking in tongues." *New Society*, 1972b, *22*(531), 565–566.

Goodman, F. D. *Speaking in tongues: A cross-cultural study of glossolalia*. Chicago: University of Chicago Press, 1972c.

Goodman, F. D. "The acquisition of glossolalia behavior." *Semiotica*, 1971a, *3*, 77–82.

Goodman, F. D. "Glossolalia and single-limb trances: Some parallels." *Psychotherapy and Psychosomatics*, 1971b, *19*, 92–103.

Goodman, F. D. "Glossolalia: Speaking in tongues in four cultural settings." *Confinia Psychiatrica* (Basel), Switzerland, 1969a, *12*(2), 113–129.

Goodman, F. D. "Phonetic analysis of glossolalia in four cultural settings." *Journal for the Scientific Study of Religion*, 1969b, *8*, 227–239.

Greeley, M. E. "Charismatics and noncharismatics, a comparison." *Review for Religious*, 1974, *33*, 315–335.

Haglof, A. "Psychology and the Pentecostal experience." *Spiritual Life*, 1971, *17*, 198–211.

Hamilton, M. P. *The Charismatic Movement*. Grand Rapids, Mich.: Eerdmans, 1975.

Harder, M. W., Richardson, J. T., & Simmonds, R. B. "Jesus people." *Psychology Today*, 1972, *6*(7), 45–50, 110–113.

Harner, M. J. "Jivaro souls." *American Anthropologist*, 1962, 158–272.

Harper, C. L. "Spirit-filled Catholics: Some biographical comparisons." *Social Compass*, 1974, *21*, 311–324.

Harper, M. *As at the Beginning: The twentieth century Pentecostal revival*. Plainfield, N.J.: Logos International, 1965.

Harrison, M. I. "The maintenance of enthusiasm: Involvement in a new religious movement." *Sociological Analysis*, 1975, *36*, 150–160.

Harrison, M. I. "Preparation for life in the spirit." *Urban Life and Culture*, 1974a, *2*, 387–414.

Harrison, M. I. "Sources of recruitment to Catholic Pentecostalism." *Journal for the Scientific Study of Religion*, 1974b, *13*, 49–64.

Harrison, M. I. The organization of commitment in the Catholic Pentecostal movement (Doctoral dissertation, University of Michigan, 1971). *Dissertation Abstracts International*, 1972, *33*, 2513A–2514A. (University Microfilms No. 72–29, 080.)

Harrison, M. I. *The adjustment of a social movement to its organizational en-*

vironment. Paper presented at the meeting of the American Sociological Association, 1971.

Hartmann, H. *Ego Psychology and the Problem of Adaptation.* New York: International Universities Press, 1958. (Originally published, 1939.)

Hartmann, H. *Essays in Ego Psychology.* New York: International Universities Press, 1964.

Havens, J. (Ed.). *Psychology and religion: A contemporary dialogue.* Princeton, N.J.: D. Van Nostrand, 1968.

Hayes, D. A. *The Gift of Tongues.* New York: Eaton and Main, 1913.

Heirich, M. "Change of heart: A test of some widely held theories about religious conversion." *American Journal of Sociology, 1977, 83, 653*–680.

Hess, C. B., & Reynolds, D. E. *An evaluation of the Teen Challenge treatment program* (DHHS Publication No. ADM 81–425). Rockville, Md.: Alcohol, Drug Abuse, and Mental Health Administration, 1977.

Hilgard, J. *Personality and Hypnosis: A Study of Imaginative Involvement.* Chicago: University of Chicago Press, 1970.

Hine, V. H. The deprivation and disorganization theories of social movements. In I. I. Zaretsky & M. P. Leone (Eds.), *Religious Movements in Contemporary America.* Princeton, N.J.: Princeton University Press, 1974.

Hine, V. H. "Pentecostal glossolalia: Toward a functional interpretation." *Journal for the Scientific Study of Religion, 1969, 8, 211*–226.

Hockett, C. F. The problem of universals in language. In J. H. Greenberg (Ed.), *Universals in Language.* London: Cambridge University Press, 1963.

Hofman, C. A. A psychological study of conversion experiences in the Catholic charismatic movement (Doctoral dissertation, California School of Professional Psychology, San Francisco, 1975). *Dissertation Abstracts International, 1976, 36, 4159B.* (University Microfilms No. 76–2068.)

Hofstadter, R. *Anti-intellectualism in American life.* New York: Alfred A. Knopf, 1963.

Hollenweger, W. J. *The Pentecostals: The Charismatic movement in the churches.* Minneapolis: Augsburg, 1972.

Holm, N. G. "Functions of glossolalia in the Pentecostal movement." In Thorvald Källstad (Ed.), *Psychological Studies of Religious Man.* Uppsala: Acta Universitatis Upsaliensis, *Psychologia Religionum 7, 1978, 141*–158.

Holt, J. "Holiness religion: Cultural shock and social reorganization." *American Sociological Review, 1940, 5, 740*–747.

Hood, R. W. "Religious orientation and the experience of transcendence." *Journal for the Scientific Study of Religion, 1973, 12, 441*–448.

Hutch, R. A. "The personal ritual of glossolalia." *Journal for the Scientific Study of Religion, 1980, 19, 255*–266.

James, W. *The varieties of religious experience.* New York: New American Library (Mentor), 1958. (Originally published, 1902.)

Janet, P. *L'etat mental des hysteriques (the major symptoms of hysteria),* 2nd edition. New York: Macmillan, 1924. (Originally published, 1907.)

Jaquith, J. R. "Toward a typology of formal communicative behaviors: Glossolalia." *Anthropological Linguistics, 1967, 9*(8), 1–8.

Javillonar, G. V. Toward a social psychological model of sectarianism. (Doctoral dissertation, University of Nebraska, 1971). *Dissertation Abstracts International, 1971, 35, 2808A.* (University Microfilms No. 71–28,622.)

Jeanrenaud, S. *Non-pathological glossolalic joy.* Unpublished manuscript. Fuller Theological Seminary, 1972.

Jennings, G. J. "An ethnological study of glossolalia." *Journal of the American Scientific Affiliation*, 1968, *20*, 5–16.

Johnson, B. "Do Holiness sects socialize in dominant values?" *Social Forces*, 1961, *39*, 309–316.

Johnson, B. A framework for the analysis of religious action with special reference to Holiness and non-Holiness groups. Doctoral dissertation, Harvard University, 1953.

Journal of the General Conference of the Methodist Episcopal Church. Nashville, 1894.

Jung, C. G. On the psychology and pathology of so-called occult phenomena. In C. G. Jung, *Psychiatric Studies* (2nd ed.). Princeton, N.J.: Princeton University Press (Bollingen Series XX), 1970. (Originally published, 1902.)

Jung, C. G. A psychological approach to the Trinity. In C. G. Jung, *Psychology and Religion: West and East.* New York: Pantheon Books (Bollingen Series XX), 1958. (Originally published, 1948.)

Jung, C. G. Transformation symbolism in the mass. In C. G. Jung, *Psychology and Religion: West and East.* New York: Pantheon Books (Bollingen Series XX), 1958. (Originally published, 1940.)

Kelley, D. M. *Why Conservative Churches Are Growing: A Study in the Sociology of Religion.* New York: Harper & Row, 1972.

Kelsey, M. T. *Healing and Christianity.* New York: Harper & Row, 1973.

Kelsey, M. T. *Tongue speaking: An experiment in spiritual experience.* Garden City, N.Y.: Doubleday, 1964.

Kernberg, O. F. *Borderline conditions and pathological narcissism.* New York: Jason Aronson, 1975.

Kernberg, O. F. "Early ego integration and object relations." *New York Academy of Sciences,* 1972, *193*, 233–247.

Kiev, A. The psychotherapeutic value of spirit-possession in Haiti. In R. Prince (Ed.), *Trance and possession states.* Proceedings of the Second Annual Conference of the R. M. Bucke Memorial Society, Montreal, 1966.

Kiev, A. *Magic, faith, and healing: Studies in Primitive Psychiatry today.* New York: Free Press, 1964a.

Kiev, A. "Psychotherapeutic aspects of Pentacostal sects among West Indian immigrants to England." *British Journal of Sociology,* 1964b, *15*, 129–138.

Kiev, A. "Beliefs and delusions of West Indian immigrants to London." *British Journal of Psychiatry,* 1963, *109*, 356–363.

Kildahl, J. P. *The psychology of speaking in tongues.* New York: Harper & Row, 1972.

Kildahl, J. P., & Qualben, P. A. *Final progress report: Glossolalia and mental health,* MH–10514–01, Washington: National Institute of Mental Health, 1971.

Kimura, D. "The asymmetry of the human brain." *Scientific American,* 1973, *228*, 70–78.

Kinsey, A., Pomeroy, W., & Martin, C. *Sexual behavior in the human male.* Philadelphia. W. B. Saunders, 1948.

Knox, R. A. *Enthusiasm: A chapter in the history of religion with special reference to the XVII and XVIII centuries.* New York: Oxford University Press, 1950.

Kris, E. (Ed.). *Psychoanalytic explorations in art.* London: Allen & Unwin, 1953.

Kris, E. The psychology of caricature. In E. Kris (Ed.), *Psychoanalytic explorations in art.* London: Allen & Unwin, 1953. (Originally published, 1934.)

Kris, E. On preconscious mental processes. In D. Rapaport (Ed.), *Organization and pathology of thought*. New York: Columbia University Press, 1951. (Originally published, 1950.)

Kris, E., & Kaplan, A. Aesthetic ambiguity. In E. Kris (Ed.), *Psychoanalytic explorations in art*. London: Allen & Unwin, 1953. (Originally published, 1948.)

Kroll-Smith, J. S. "The testimony as performance: The relationship of an expressive event to the belief system of a Holiness sect." *Journal for the Scientific Study of Religion*, 1980, *19*, 16–25.

Kuhlman, K. *Nothing is impossible with God*. Englewood Cliffs, N.J.: Prentice-Hall, 1974.

Kuhlman, K. *God can do it again*. Englewood Cliffs, N.J.: Prentice-Hall, 1969.

Kuhlman, K. *I believe in miracles*. Englewood Cliffs, N.J.: Prentice-Hall, 1962.

La Barre, W. *They shall take up serpents: Psychology of the Southern snake-handling cult*. Minneapolis: University of Minnesota Press, 1962.

Laffal, J., Monahan, J., & Richman, P. "Communication of meaning in glossolalia." *Journal of Social Psychology*, 1974, *92*(2), 277–291.

Laffal, J. "Language, consciousness, and experience." *Psychoanalytic Quarterly*, 1967, *36*, 61–66.

Laffal, J. *Pathological and normal language*. New York: Atherton Press, 1965.

Langrod, J., Joseph, H., & Valdes, K. The role of religion in the treatment of opiate addition. In L. Brill & L. Lieberman (Eds.), *Major modalities in the treatment of drug abuse*. New York: Behavioral Publications, 1972.

Lapsley, J. N. & Simpson, J. H. "Speaking in tongues: Token of group acceptance and divine approval." *Pastoral Psychology*, 1964a, *15*(144), 48–55.

Lapsley, J. N., & Simpson, J. H. "Speaking in tongues: Infantile babble or song of the self? Part II." *Pastoral Psychology*, 1964b, *15*(146), 16–24.

Laurentin, R. *Catholic Pentecostalism* (M. J. O'Connell, Trans.). Garden City, N.Y.: Doubleday, 1977. (Originally published, 1974.)

Le Baron, A. "A case of psychic automatism, including 'speaking with tongues.' " *Proceedings of the Society for Psychical Research*, 1896–1897, *12*, 277–297.

Le Bon, G. *Psychologie des foules*. Paris: F. Olean, 1896. (Translated as *The Crowd*, London: T. Fisher Unwim, 1896.)

Lenski, G. Codebook: a study of religious participation, Project 849 (unpublished manuscript). Ann Arbor, Mich.: University of Michigan, 1958.

Lenski, G. *The Religious Factor (Rev. Ed.)*. New York: Doubleday, 1963.

Lewis, C. S. *The Weight of Glory: Transposition and Other Addresses*. New York: Macmillan, 1949.

Lifton, R. J. *Thought reform and the psychology of totalism*. New York: W. W. Norton, 1963.

Lifton, R. J. "Thought reform of Chinese intellectuals: A psychiatric evolution." *Journal of Social Issues*, 1957, *13*(3), 5–20.

Lofland, J., & Stark, R. "Becoming a world saver: a theory of conversion to a deviant perspective." *American Sociological Review*, 1965, *30*, 862–875.

Lombard, E. *De le glossalalie: Chez les premiers Chrétiens et des phénomènes similaires: Études d'exégèse et de psychologie*. Lausanne, Switz.: Bridel, 1910.

Lombard, M. E. Essai d'une classification des phénomènes de glossolalie. *Archives de Psychologie*, 1907, *7*, 1–51.

Lovekin, A. A. Religious glossolalia: A longitudinal study of personality changes (Doctoral dissertation, Fuller Theological Seminary, School of Psychology,

1975). *Dissertation Abstracts International,* 1977, *38,* 3404B–3405B. (University Microfilms No. 77–30, 008.)

Lovekin, A. A. *Glossolalia: A critical study of alleged origins, the New Testament and the early church.* Unpublished master's thesis, University of the South, 1962.

Lovekin, A. A., & Malony, H. N. "Religious glossolalia: A longitudinal study of personality changes." *Journal for the Scientific Study of Religion,* 1977, *16,* 383–393.

Luckman, T. *The Invisible Religion: The Problem of Religion in Modern Society.* New York: MacMillan, 1967.

Ludwig, A. M. "The trance." *Comprehensive Psychiatry,* 1967, *8*(1), 7–15.

Ludwig, A. M. "Altered states of consciousness." *Archives of General Psychiatry,* 1966, *15,* 225–234.

Mackie, A. *The Gift of Tongues: A Study in Pathological Aspects of Christianity.* New York: George H. Doran, 1921.

MacNutt, F. *Healing.* Notre Dame, Ind.: Ave Maria, 1974.

Maeder, A. "La langue d'une aliéné: Analyse d'un cas de glossolalie." *Archives de Psychologie,* 1910, *9,* 208–216.

Malony, H. N. "Debunking some of the myths about glossolalia." *Journal of the American Scientific Affiliation,* 1982, *34,* 144–148.

Malony, H. N. *The concomitants of glossolalia: A summary of a program of research.* Unpublished manuscript. Fuller Theological Seminary, Pasadena, Calif., 1980.

Malony, H. N. "When God says your child is healed: A case study in revelation (or psychopathology)." *Bulletin of the Christian Association for Psychological Studies,* 1979, *5*(2), 23–26.

Malony, H. N. *Understanding Your Faith.* Nashville: Abingdon, 1978.

Malony, H. N., Zwaanstra, N., & Ramsey, J. W. *Personal and situational determinants of glossolalia: A literature review and report of ongoing research.* Paper presented at the International Congress of Religious Studies, Los Angeles, September 1–5, 1972.

Martin, I. J. *Glossolalia in the Apostolic Church: A survey study of tongue-speech.* Berea, Ky.: Berea College Press, 1960.

Marty, M. E. *A nation of behavers.* Chicago: University of Chicago Press, 1976.

Marty, M. E. Pentecostalism in the context of American piety and practice. In V. Synan (Ed.), *Aspects of Pentecostal-charismatic origins.* Plainfield, N.J.: Logos International, 1975.

Masters, W. H., & Johnson, V. E. *Homosexuality in perspective.* Boston: Little, Brown, 1979.

Mawn, B. J. Testing the spirits: An empirical search for the socio-cultural situational roots of the Catholic Pentecostal religious experience (Doctoral dissertation, Boston University Graduate School, 1975). *Dissertation Abstracts International,* 1975, *36,* 1972B–1973B. (University Microfilms No. 75–21, 005.)

May, H. G., & Metzger, B. M. (Eds.). *The Oxford Annotated Bible: Revised Standard Version.* New York: Oxford University Press, 1962.

May, L. C. "A survey of glossolalia and related phenomena in non-Christian religions." *American Anthropologist,* 1956, *58,* 75–96.

McDonnell, K. (Ed.). *Presence, power, praise: Documents on the charismatic renewal* (3 vols.). Collegeville, Minn.: Liturgical Press, 1980.

McDonnell, K. The experience of the Holy Spirit in the Catholic charismatic renewal. In H. Kung & J. Moltmann (Eds.), *Conflicts about the Holy Spirit.* New York: Seabury Press, 1979.

McDonnell, K. *The charismatic renewal and ecumenism.* New York: Paulist Press, 1978.

McDonnell, K. *Charismatic renewal and the churches.* New York: Seabury Press, 1976.

McDonnell, K. (Ed.). *The Holy Spirit and power: The Catholic charismatic renewal.* Garden City, N.Y.: Doubleday, 1975.

McDonnell, K. "Catholic Pentecostalism: Problems in evaluation." *Dialog,* 1970, *9,* 35–54.

McDonnell, K. "Holy Spirit and Pentecostalism." *Commonweal,* 1968a, *39,* 198–204.

McDonnell, K. "The ideology of Pentecostal conversion." *Journal of Ecumenical Studies,* 1968b, *5*(1), 105–125.

McDonnell, K. *Pentecostalism: Charism or hysteria? From classical Pentecostalism to Catholic Pentecostalism.* Unpublished manuscript, 1968c.

McDonnell, K. "The Pentecostals and drug addiction." *America,* 1968d, *118,* 402–406.

McDonnell, K. "The ecumenical significance of the Pentecostal movement." *Worship,* 1966, *40,* 608–629.

McGaw, D. B. "Meaning and belonging in a charismatic congregation—an investigation into sources of neo-Pentecostal success." *Review of Religious Research,* 1980, *21,* 284–301.

McGaw, D. B. "Commitment and religious community: A comparison of a charismatic and a mainline congregation." *Journal for the Scientific Study of religion,* 1979, *18,* 146–163.

McGuire, M. B. *Pentecostal Catholics: Power, charisma, and order in a religious movement.* Philadelphia: Temple University Press, 1982.

McGuire, M. B. *Religion: The social context.* Belmont, Calif.: Wadsworth, 1981.

McGuire, M. B. "The social context of prophecy—word gifts of Spirit among Catholic Pentecostals." *Review of Religious Research,* 1977, *18,* 134–147.

McGuire, M. B. "Toward a sociological interpretation of the Catholic Pentecostal movement." *Review of Religious Research,* 1975, *16,* 94–104.

McGuire, M. B. "An interpretive comparison of elements of Pentecostal and underground church movements in American Catholicism." *Sociological Analysis,* 1974, *35,* 57–65.

McGuire, M. B. "Toward a sociological interpretation of the 'Underground church' movement." *Review of Religious Research,* 1972, *12,* 41–47.

Merton, R. K. *Social Theory and Social Structure.* Glencoe, Ill.: The Free Press, 1957.

Mills, W. E. "Ecstaticism as a background for glossolalia." *Journal of the American Scientific Affiliation,* 1975, *27,* 165–171.

Morentz, P. *Lecture on glossolalia.* Unpublished manuscript. University of California, Berkeley, 1966.

Mosiman, E. *Das Zungenreden, geschichtlich und psychologisch untersucht.* Tübingen: Mohr, 1911.

Moss, T., & Johnson, K. L. "What about Kirlian photography?" *Psychic,* July 1972, 9–12.

Motley, M. T. *Glossolalia: Analyses of selected aspects of phonology and morphology.* Unpublished master's thesis, University of Texas, 1967.

Myers, I. B. *Gifts Differing.* Palo Alto, Calif.: Consulting Psychologists Press, 1980.

National Institute on Drug Abuse. *Statistical Series: Quarterly Report: January–March, 1976* (Series 4, No. 1). NIDA, Division of Scientific and Program Information, 1976.

Needleman, J., & Baker, G. (Eds.). *Understanding the New Religions.* New York: Seabury Press, 1978.

Nelsen, H. M., & Whitt, H. P. "Religion and the migrant in the city: A test of Holt's culture shock thesis." *Social Forces,* 1972, *50,* 379–384.

Ness, R. C., & Wintrob, R. M. The emotional impact of fundamentalist religious participation: An empirical study of intra-group variation." *American Journal of Orthopsychiatry,* 1980, *50,* 302–315.

Nida, E. A. Preliminary report on glossolalia: A case of pseudo-linguistic structure. Paper presented at the thirty-ninth meeting of the Linguistic Society of America, New York, 1964.

Niebuhr, H. R. *The social sources of denominationalism.* New York: Henry Holt, 1929.

Niesz, N. L. Rorschach data from neo-Pentecostal and charismatic subjects. Paper presented at the meeting of the Society of the Scientific Study of Religion, Chicago, October 28–30, 1977.

Niesz, N. L., & Kronenberger, E. J. "Self-actualization in glossolalic and non-glossolalic Pentecostals." *Sociological Analysis,* 1978, *39,* 250–256.

Nouwen, H. J. M. *Creative Ministry.* Garden City, N.Y.: Doubleday, 1971.

Nouwen, H. J. *Intimacy.* Notre Dame, Ind.: Fides Press, 1969.

O'Connell, D. C., & Bryant, E. T. "Some psychological reflections on glossolalia." *Review for Religious,* 1973, *31,* 974–977.

O'Connor, E. D. *The Pentecostal movement in the Catholic Church.* Notre Dame, Ind.: Ave Maria, 1971.

Oden, T. *The Intensive Group Experience: The New Pietism.* Philadelphia: Westminster Press, 1972.

Oesterreich, T. K. *Possession: Demonical and Other.* Secaucus, N.J.: Lyle Stuart, 1966. (Originally published, 1921.)

Oman, J. B. "On 'speaking in tongues': A psychological analysis." *Pastoral psychology,* 1963, *14*(139), 48–51.

Palmer, G. *Trance and dissociation: A cross-cultural study in psychophysiology.* Unpublished master's thesis, University of Minnesota, 1966.

Parham, S. E. *The Life of Charles F. Parham: Founder of the Apostolic Faith Movement.* Birmingham, Ala.: Commercial Printing Co., 1930.

Pattison, E. M. Ideological support for the marginal middle class: Faith healing and glossolalia. In I. I. Zaretsky & M. P. Leone (Eds.), *Contemporary religious movements in America.* Princeton, N.J.: Princeton University Press, 1974.

Pattison, E. M. "Behavioral science research on the nature of glossolalia." *Journal of American Scientific Affiliation,* 1968, *20,* 73–86.

Pattison, E. M., & Casey, R. L. "Glossolalia: A contemporary mystical experience." *International Psychiatry Clinics,* 1969, *5*(4), 133–148.

Pattison, E. M., Kahan, J., & Hurd, G. S. Trance and possession states. In B. B. Wolman & M. Uilman (Eds.), *Handbook of altered states of consciousness.* New York: Van Nostrand Reinhold, in press.

Pattison, E. M., Lapine, N. A., & Doerr, H. A. "Faith healing: A study of personality and function." *Journal of Nervous and Mental Disease,* 1973, *157,* 397–409.

Pattison, E. M., & Pattison, M. L., " 'Ex-Gays: Religiously mediated change in homosexuals." *American Journal of Psychiatry*, 1980, *137*, 1553–1562.

Pavelsky, R. L., Hart, A., & Malony, H. N. *Toward a definition of act and process glossolalia: Social, physiological, and personality determinants.* Unpublished manuscript. Graduate School of Psychology, Fuller Theological Seminary, 1975.

Payne, L. *The Broken Image: Restoring Personal Wholeness through Healing Prayer.* Westchester, Ill.: Cornerstone Press, 1981.

Penfield, W., & Rasmussen, T. *The Cerebral Cortex of Man.* New York: Macmillan, 1950.

Peters, T. K. An investigation into the role of religious experience and commitment as a therapeutic factor in the treatment and rehabilitation of selected drug addicts from Teen Challenge: A follow-up study (Doctoral dissertation, New York University, 1980). *Dissertation Abstracts International*, 1980, *41*, 704A. (University Microfilms No. 8017521.)

Pfister, O. "Die psychologische Enträtselung der religiösen Glossolalie und der automatischen Kryptographie." *Jahrbuch für Psychoanalytische und Psychopathologische Forschungen*, 1912, *3*, 427–468.

Philpott, K. *The third sex?* Plainfield, N.J.: Logos International, 1975.

Pike, J. A. "Pastoral letter on glossolalia." *Living Church*, 1963, *146*(20), 11–12. Reprinted in *Pastoral Psychology*, 1964, *15*(144), 56–61; and in K. McDonnell (Ed.), *Presence, Power, and Praise: Documents on the Charismatic Renewal*, vol. 1. Collegeville, Minn.: Liturgical Press, 1980.

Plog, S. C., & Pitcher, S. Summary of group questionnaires on the Blessed Trinity Society meetings, Los Angeles Christian Advances, and St. Luke's Church, Seattle. Unpublished paper. University of California, Los Angeles, 1965.

Poblete, R., & O'Dea, T. F. "Anomie and the 'quest for community': The formation of sects among the Puerto Ricans of New York." *American Catholic Sociological Review*, 1960, *21*(1), 18–36.

Poloma, M. M. *The charismatic movement: Is there a new Pentecost?* Boston, Mass.: Twayne, 1982.

Pope, L. *Millhands and preachers: A study of Gastonia.* New Haven, Conn.: Yale University Press, 1942.

Poythress, V. S. "The nature of Corinthian glossolalia: Possible options." *Westminster Theological Journal*, 1977, *40*(1), 130–135.

Pruyser, P. W. *The Psychological Examination: A Guide for Clinicians.* New York: International Universities Press, 1979.

Pruyser, P. W. "Narcissism in contemporary religion." *Journal of Pastoral Care*, 1978, *32*, 219–231.

Pruyser, P. W. *A dynamic psychology of religion.* New York: Harper & Row, 1968.

Quebedeaux, R. *The new charismatics: Origins, development, and significance of neo-Pentecostalism.* Garden City, N.Y.: Doubleday, 1976.

Ramsey, J. W., & Malony, H. N. *Differences in glossolalia, religious belief, and religious orientations among involved and uninvolved Assembly of God youth.* Unpublished manuscript. Graduate School of Psychology, Fuller Theological Seminary, 1971.

Ranaghan, K. M. Rites of initiation in representative Pentecostal churches in the United States, 1901–1972. (Doctoral dissertation, University of Notre Dame, 1974). *Dissertation Abstracts International*, 1974, *38*, 1216A. (University Microfilms No. 74–19,055.)

Ranaghan, K. M., & Ranaghan, D. (Eds.). *As the Spirit leads us.* Paramus, N.J.: Paulist Press, 1971.

Ranaghan, K. M., & Ranaghan, D. *Catholic Pentecostals.* Paramus, N.J.: Paulist Press, 1969.

Rarick, W. J. The socio-cultural context of glossolalia: A comparison of Pentecostal and neo-Pentecostal religious attitudes and behavior (Doctoral dissertation, Fuller Theological Seminary, Gradaute School of Psychology, 1982). *Dissertation Abstracts International,* 1982, *43,* 916B. (University Microfilms No. DA82–18, 611.)

Rarick, W. J., & Malony, H. N. Glossolalic expressions among Pentecostal college and seminary students. Paper presented at the meeting of the Society for the Scientific Study of Religion, Baltimore, November 26–29, 1981.

Reidy, M. T. V., & Richardson, J. T. Roman Catholic neo-Pentecostalism: The New Zealand experience. *Australian and New Zealand Journal of Sociology,* 1978, *14,* 222–230.

Remez, R. E., Rubin, P. E., Pisoni, D. B., & Carreil, T. D. "Speech perception without traditional speech cues." *Science,* May 22, 1981, *212,* 947–949.

Richardson, J. T. "Psychological interpretations of glossolalia: A reexamination of research." *Journal for the Scientific Study of Religion,* 1973, *12,* 199–207.

Richardson, J. T., Harder, M., & Simmonds, R. B. "Thought reform and the Jesus Movement." *Youth and Society,* 1972, *4,* 185–202.

Richet, C. "Xenoglossie: L'écriture automatique en langues étrangers." *Proceedings of the Society for Psychical Research,* 1905, *19,* 162–194.

Ridgway, J. M. B. Some attitudinal and motivational changes among heroin addicts involved in a religiously oriented program of rehabilitation (Doctoral dissertation, Drew University, 1972). *Dissertation Abstracts International,* 1972, *33,* 2330B. (University Microfilms No. 72–29, 417.)

Riggs, R. M. *The Spirit Himself.* Springfield, Mo.: Gospel Publishing House, 1949.

Roberts, O. *Oral Roberts' Life Story.* Garden City, N.Y.: Country Life Press, 1952.

Roberts, O. *The Call: An Autobiography.* Old Tappan, N.J.: Spire Books, 1971.

Rokeach, M. *The open and closed mind.* New York: Basic Books, 1960.

Rolin, F. C. "Pentecôtisme et société au Brésil." *Social Compass,* 1979, *26,* 345–372.

Russell, D., & Jones, W. H. "When superstition fails: Reactions to disconfirmation of paranormal beliefs." *Personality and Social Psychology Bulletin,* 1980, *6,* 83–88.

Sadler, A. W. "Glossolalia and possession: An appeal to the Episcopal Study Commission." *Journal for the Scientific Study of Religion,* 1964, *4,* 84–90.

Saghir, M. T., & Robins, E. *Male and Female Homosexuality.* Baltimore: Williams & Wilkins, 1973.

Salzman, L. "The psychology of religion and ideological conversion." *Psychiatry,* 1953, *16,* 177–187.

Samarin, W. J. [Review of *Speaking in tongues: A cross-cultural study of glossolalia* by F. D. Goodman.] *Language,* 1974, *50,* 207–212.

Samarin, W. J. "Glossolalia as regressive speech." *Language and Speech,* 1973a, *16*(1), 77–89.

Samarin, W. J. "Religious motives in religious movements." *International Yearbook for the Sociology of Religion,* F. Middelhauve (Ed.), Opladen, Germany: Westdeutscher Verlag, 1973b, 163–174.

Samarin, W. J. "Variation and variables in religious glossolalia." *Language in Society,* 1972a, *1*(1), 121–130.

Samarin, W. J. "Sociolinguistics vs. neurophysiological explanations for glossolalia: Comment on Goodman's paper." *Journal for the Scientific Study of Religion,* 1972b, *11,* 293–296.

Samarin, W. J. *Tongues of men and angels: The religious language of Pentecostalism.* New York: Macmillan, 1972c.

Samarin, W. J. "Evolution in glossolalic private language." *Anthropological Linguistics,* 1971a, *13*(2), 55–67.

Samarin, W. J. Salient and substantive pidginization. In D. Hymes, *Pidginization and creolozation of language.* New York: Cambridge University Press, 1971b.

Samarin, W. J. "Language in resocialization." *Practical Anthropology,* 1970, *17,* 269–279.

Samarin, W. J. "Forms and functions of nonsense language." *Linquistics,* 1969a, *50,* 70–74.

Samarin, W. J. "Glossolalia as learned behavior." *Canadian Journal of Theology,* 1969b, *15,* 60–64.

Samarin, W. J. The linguisticality of glossolalia. *Hartford Quarterly,* 1968, *8*(4), 49–75.

Sanford, A. *Sealed orders.* Plainfield, N.J.: Logos International, 1972.

Sanford, A. *The healing power of the Bible.* Philadelphia: J. B. Lippincott, 1969.

Sanford, A. *The healing gifts of the Spirit.* Philadelphia. J. B. Lippincott Company, 1966.

Sargant, W. *Battle for the mind: A physiology of conversion and brainwashing.* New York: Harper & Row, 1971. (Originally published, 1957.)

Sargant, W. "Some cultural group abreactive techniques and their relation to modern treatments." *Proceedings of the Royal Society of Medicine.* 1949, *42,* 367–374.

Schjelderup, H. K. Psychologische Analyse eines Falles von Zungenreden. *Zeitschrift fur Psychologie,* 1931, *122,* 1–27.

Schwarz, B. "Ordeal by serpents, fire and strychnine." *Psychiatric Quarterly,* 1960, *34,* 405–429.

Sherrill, J. L. *They speak with other tongues.* New York: McGraw-Hill, 1964.

Shulka, V. R., & Pattison, E. M. *Organically induced glossolalia.* Unpublished manuscript. Medical College of Georgia, Augusta, Georgia, 1983.

Shumway, C. W. *A critical history of glossolalia.* Doctoral dissertation, Boston University, 1919.

Simmonds, R. B., Richardson, J. T., & Harder, M. W. "Organizational aspects of a Jesus movement community." *Social Compass,* 1974, *21,* 269–281.

Simmonds, R. B., Richardson, J. T., & Harder, M. W. *The Jesus movement: An adjective check list assessment of members of a fundamentalist religious community.* Paper presented at the meeting of the Western Psychological Association, Portland, Ore., April 26–29, 1972.

Smith, D. S. Glossolalia: The personality correlates of conventional and unconventional subgroups (Doctoral dissertation, Rosemead Graduate School of Psychology, 1977). *Dissertation Abstracts International,* 1977, *38,* 1962B. (University Microfilms No. 77–21, 537.)

Southard, S. "Sectarianism and the psychoses." *Religion in Life,* 1955, *5 & 6,* 580–590.

Spanos, N. P., & Hewitt, E. C. "Glossolalia: Test of the trance and psychopathology hypotheses." *Journal of Abnormal Psychology,* 1979, *88,* 427–434.

Spoerri, T. Ekstatische Rede und Glossolalie. *Bibliotheca Psychiatrica et Neuro-logica*. Basel: S. Karger, 1967, *134*, 137–152.

Stanley, G., Bartlett, W. K., & Moyle, T. "Some characteristics of charismatic experience: Glossolalia in Australia." *Journal for the Scientific Study of Religion*, 1978, *17*, 269–278.

Stark, W. *The Sociology of Religion: A Study of Christendom, Vol. 2, Sectarian Religion*. New York: Fordham University Press, 1967.

Stevenson, I. *Xenoglossy: A review and report of a case*. Charlottesville: University Press of Virginia, 1974. (Also published as vol. 31 of *Proceedings of the American Society for Psychical Research*.)

Stevenson, I. [Review of *Tongue speaking: An experiment in spiritual experience* by M. T. Kelsey]. *Journal of the American Society for Psychical Research*, 1966, *60*, 300–303.

Stewart, C. *Adolescent Religion: A Developmental Study of Religion and Youth*. Nashville: Abingdon, 1967.

Strickland, B. R., & Shaffer, S. "I-E, E-I, and F." *Journal for the Scientific Study of Religion*, 1971, *10*, 366–369.

Strom, A. J., & Malony, H. N. *The use of Kirlian photography to assess altered states of consciousness and group differences between glossolalics and non-glossolalics*. Paper presented at the meeting of the Society for the Scientific Study of Religion, San Antonio, Texas, October 26–28, 1979.

Suinn, R. "Anxiety and cognitive dissonance." *Journal of General Psychology*, 1965, *73*(1), 113–116.

Sunden, H. *Religionpsykologi*. Stockholm: Med Bidrag as Gustav Stahlberg, 1974.

Swanson, G. E. "Trance and possession: Studies of charismatic influence." *Review of Religious Research*, 1978, *19*, 253–278.

Synan, V. (Ed.). *Aspects of Pentecostal-charismatic origins*. Plainfield, N.J.: Logos International, 1975.

Synan, V. *The Holiness-Pentecostal movement in the United States*. Grand Rapids, Mich.: Eerdmans, 1971.

Tappeiner, D. A. "The function of tongue-speaking for the individual: a psycho-theological model." *Journal of the American Scientific Affiliation*, 1974, *26*(1), 29–32.

Tellegen, A., Gerrard, N. L., Gerrard, L. E., & Butcher, J. N. Personality characteristics of members of a serpent-handling religious cult. In J. N. Butcher (Ed.), *MMPI Research Developments and Clinical Applications*. New York: McGraw-Hill, 1969.

Thompson, J. R. *Mysticism and social structure: Neglected sociological factors and implications in Troeltsch's typology*. Paper presented at the meeting of the Canadian Society for the Study of Religion, Montreal, May 2–4, 1980.

Thompson, J. R. Social processes related to revivifying religious forms within an institutional context: A case study of charismatic renewal among Roman Catholics in southern California (Doctoral dissertation, University of California, Santa Barbara, 1977).

Tinney, J. S. "Black origins of the Pentecostal movement." *Christianity Today*, 1971, *16*(1), 4–6.

Troeltsch, E. *The social teachings of the Christian churches* (O. Wyon, Trans.). New York: Macmillan, 1931. (Originally published, 1911.)

Van Gennep, A. *The Rites of Passage*. Chicago: University of Chicago Press, 1960.

Vivier, L. M. The glossolalic and his personality. In T. Spoerri (Ed.), *Beitrage zurekstase. Bibliotheca Psychiatrica et Neurologica,* no. 134, Basel: S. Karger, 1968, *134,* 153–175.

Vivier, L. M., V. E. *Glossolalia.* Doctoral Dissertation, University of Witwatersrand, South Africa, 1960. (Microfilm, University of Chicago Library.)

Wallace, A. F. C. "Revitalization movements." *American Anthropologist,* 1956, *58,* 264–281.

Weber, M. *The Protestant ethic and the spirit of capitalism* (T. Parsons, Trans.). New York: Scribners, 1958. (Originally published, 1904–1905.)

Wilkerson, D. *Twelve angels from hell.* Old Tappan, N.J.: Fleming H. Revell, 1969.

Wilkerson, D., & Murphy, P. *The little people.* Fleming H. Revell: Old Tappan, N.J., 1966.

Wilkerson, D., Sherrill, J., & Sherrill, E. *The cross and the switchblade.* Old Tappan, N.J.: Fleming H. Revell, 1963.

Williams, C. G. *Tongues of the Spirit: A study of Pentecostal glossolalia and related phenomena.* Cardiff: University of Wales Press, 1981.

Williams, J. R. "The coming of the holy spirit." *Theology, News and Notes,* March, 1974, 14–16.

Williams, R. M. *American society: A sociological interpretation* (3rd ed.) New York: Alfred A. Knopf, 1970.

Williams, R. M. "Individual and group values." *Annals of the American Academy of political and social science,* 1967, *371,* 20–37.

Williams, R. M. *American Society: A Sociological Interpretation.* New York: Knopf, 1951.

Wilson, B. R. *Magic and the millennium: A sociological study of religious movements of protest among tribal and third-world peoples.* London: Heinemann Educational Books, 1973.

Wilson, B. R. *Religious sects: A sociological study.* New York: McGraw-Hill, 1970.

Wilson, B. R. (Ed.). *Patterns of Sectarianism.* London: Heinemann Educational Books, 1967.

Wilson, B. R. *Sects and society: A sociological study of the Elim Tabernacle, Christian Science, and Christadelphians.* Berkeley: University of California Press, 1961.

Wilson, B. R. An analysis of sect development. *American Sociological Review,* 1959, *24*(1), 3–15.

Wolcott, R. H. "Schizophrenese: A private language." *Journal of Health and Social Behavior,* 1970, *11,* 126–134.

Wolfram, W. A. *The sociolinguistics of glossolalia.* Master's thesis, Hartford Seminary, 1966.

Womack, S. A. *Therapeutic aspects of a Pentecostal Church on alcohol and drug abusers* (Doctoral dissertation, University of Texas at Austin, 1980). *Dissertation Abstracts International,* 1981, *41,* 3172A. (University Microfilms No. 8100984.)

Wood, W. W. *Culture and personality aspects of the Pentecostal Holiness religion.* Paris: Moulton, 1965.

Wood, W. W. Culture and the personality aspects of the Pentecostal Holiness religion (Doctoral dissertation, University of North Carolina, 1961). *Dissertation Abstracts International,* 1962, *23,* 333 (University Microfilms No. 62–3157.)

Yinger, J. M. *Religion, Society and the Individual.* New York: Macmillan, 1957.

Young, F. W. "Adaptation and pattern integration of a California sect." *Review of Religious Research,* 1960, *1,* 137–150.

Zwaanstra, N., & Malony, H. N. Correlates of glossolalia among Assembly of God youth. Unpublished manuscript, Graduate School of Psychology, Fuller Theological Seminary, 1970.

Subject Index

Author Index